40,001 best Baby names

40,001 best Baby names

Diane Stafford

SOURCEBOOKS, INC.®
NAPERVILLE, ILLINOIS

Published by Sourcebooks, Inc.
P.O. Box 4410, Naperville, Illinois 60567-4410
(630) 961-3900
FAX: (630) 961-2168
www.sourcebooks.com

Library of Congress Cataloging-in-Publication Data

Stafford, Diane.
40,001 best baby names / by Diane Stafford.
p. cm.
Includes bibliographical references (p.   ).
ISBN 1-4022-0103-6 (alk. paper)
1. Names, Personal—Dictionaries. I. Title: Forty thousand and one best baby names. II. Title.
CS2377.S57 2003
929.4'4'03—dc21
2003007137

Printed and bound in the United States of America
VHG   10 9 8 7 6

For precious Ben, with all my love

Acknowledgments

Sincere thanks to: Ed Knappman of New England Publishing Associates, for giving me the opportunity to write this book—and to Elizabeth Frost Knappman, literary agent and friend, who has made my dreams come true.

Hillel Black of Sourcebooks, for his patience, support, direction, and kindness. Amy Baxter of Sourcebooks for her hard work on *40,001 Best Baby Names*.

Dana Chandler, Slavek Rotkiewicz, Camilla Pierce, Gabriela Baeza Ventura, and Jennifer Shoquist San Luis, for their help with this book.

And special thanks to my wonderful family and friends, whose names will always be tops on my list of favorites:

Jennifer, Benjamin, Robert, Clinton, Belle, Allen, Christina, Austin, Xanthe, Richard, Camilla, Britt, Gina, Curtis, Lindsay, Cameron, Josh, Jake, David, Amber, Dan, Fletcher, Russ, Martin, Dinah, Chris, Donna, Annie, Angela, Jami, Lucy, Tessie, Bob, Lily, Carolyn, Beth, Dot, Laurens, Cynthia, Laura, Jeffrey, Dana, Clarence, Eddi, Jay, Jim, Martha, Carrie, Natasha, Kathleen, Rachel, Renee, Wendy, Kristina, Jennifer, Liz, Elizabeth, Christy, Shannon, John, Shari, JoAnn, Alice, Gary, C.D., Bernice, Karla, Karen, Doug, Michael, Tom, Joanne, Mark, Fred, Spiker, Scott, Dominique, Russell, Evin, Dennis, Patrick, Cari.

Table of Contents

Introduction

Your name. Those two words should make you smile.

Nothing is more personal. Whether one-of-a-kind (Shawnikwaronda) or most-popular-of-the-century (Jennifer), your name gives you an identity that sets you apart from the twenty other kids in kindergarten and labels you the first day of a new job. If your name is memorable or a perfect fit, people say it more often. But if yours is hard to pronounce or difficult to remember, chances are good that you will go through life rarely hearing your "Daphinola" at all.

Indeed, a name can affect the ebb and flow of your entire existence. That's exactly why parents-to-be often give the baby-naming process numerous hours of list-perusing, head-scratching, and poll-taking.

For a kid who feels "stuck" with an albatross name, life can be long and bumpy. While people with better names seem to glide through social encounters effortlessly, the name-challenged types are more likely to stumble and bungle their way through the jungle.

If you have any doubt, note the baby-naming efforts of a person who grew up as Nyleen or Hortense, Huelett or Drakeston, and you'll probably find that this individual will have offspring named John or Ann. Just having a sibling with a tough moniker will nudge us in the direction of plain when it comes to naming a tiny, innocent baby.

What's the significance of all of this for you, the parent-in-waiting? You are dead-on right in thinking that finding the "right" name constitutes a major responsibility. This occasion is momentous enough to merit lots of discussion and lots of thumbing through the baby-naming book until you finally hit on it—The Right Name.

Whether or not you want to admit it, you really and truly want your child to like his name. No wonder you feel awed by the job! Most parents fret and falter, marvel and malinger, worry and wonder—sometimes for the entire nine months of pregnancy.

And that's because authors and songwriters immortalize names. People in love grow misty-eyed just thinking of them. Names are glorified and mocked, loved and loathed.

You're looking for a name that resonates, one that's memorable and perfect—but not *frighteningly* memorable or overly perfect. You're out to locate a name that is absolutely sure, 100 percent guaranteed, to have a positive effect on your little tyke's life. For that reason alone, you're willing to give the baby-naming gig quite a few hours of over-analysis.

We all want great names. We all struggle with the thousands of contenders.

Couldn't that little embryo give us a hint as to what name he would prefer? Is it better to be one of ten Davids in your class at school, or is it more of a challenge to try to pull off a quirky Ringo?

Maybe you're already submitting name-nominees to the acid tests: Is it too cute? Overly hip? Brutally boring? And, what's wrong with just going with your gut? This is your baby, after all. So why not tag that little biscuit with the way-cool name you've had squirreled away since your Barbie-and-Ken days!

Have fun with the name game. Approach it with wackiness, high spirits, and good insider information. Stay on message, and don't let yourself get sidetracked by relative-schmoozing or movie-star-mimicking. Carefully assess the pros and cons of your finalists, and you're bound to come up with a winner.

And while you're at it, do weigh the fact that a name can shape personality, career, and self-esteem. (How could a girl named Buzzie be anything other than a cheerleader?) And just as clearly, a person's name can be a lifelong drawback, as in the guy whose parents reversed the letters of their surname, and came up with an unpronounceable humdinger that made kids laugh at the boy all the way through school. So what happens to this kind of nuisance-name? When the man turns twenty-one, he goes to the courthouse and banishes that kookiness forever. What used to be "Enord" becomes the benign letter "E."

Also, consider any nasty connotations. Erica took on a whole new and scary feel after thirty years of being kicked around by the malevolent Erica Kane on the soap *All My Children.* And, by a different, somewhat slatternly yardstick, who could in good conscience name an innocent baby girl Monica in the post–Bill Clinton era?

At the same time, names can be an asset, a source of pride and distinction. Who would bet on anything other than a promising future for a Theodore or a Saul, a Grace or a Claire?

Some parents get so confused that they throw up their hands and pick a generic name. That way, the child can make what he wants of it. (Think how many times you've met Anne, Patricia, Carol, Michael, Richard, David, and Mark.)

Everyone knows what his own name did for him growing up (and what it didn't do). Maybe your parents envisioned a man being sworn in for President and chose Adlai,

John, Roosevelt, or George. Or, perhaps, your mother had warm, fuzzy feelings about a good old boy she knew growing up, so you were christened Billy Bob, certainly well suited for country-western singing (or for tattooing Angelina Jolie). Or your aunt loved the "artist formerly known as Prince" and made sure your birth certificate registered the eccentric "Purple Rain."

Boggled by mega-input, many parents toss around names for the entire nine months. And adding to the confusion is the steady stream of names offered by well-meaning grandparents, aunts, uncles, cousins, coworkers, employees, repairmen, and friends.

Baby-naming can even become so daunting that perplexed parents-to-be waffle daily. And then after they have identified a few winners, a couple faces the key issue that often comes into play—finding a name they can agree on. Usually, the result is a rush to judgment on delivery day, when Mom and Dad are finally forced to choose a name in the maternity ward.

Basic attitudes toward baby-naming can range from frivolous and cavalier to serious and tradition-laden. One Houston mother with the surname Palms named her African-American son White so that each time he introduced himself, "I'm White Palms," he was greeted with a grin or a look of disbelief. The same goes for a Texan named King Solomon, whose name is so memorable that this author was introduced to him at age fifteen, and decades later can still remember the shock of meeting a very confident kid who actually managed to pull off that spectacular name. (Some children can make a traffic-stopping name a big asset. But, some can't.) A friend of mine named Jeffrey wore her boy-name like a badge of honor, growing up to be both funny and popular. But, another girl whose parents chose a masculine name (Christopher) struggled with the name lifelong, forced to live with kids' ridicule.

That brings up a major trend going strong currently, the meshing of names to come up with something brand new. The U.S. Social Security Administration shows growing numbers of "creations" such as Tamikas and Rayshons, but don't mistake the proliferation for anything resembling approval by the kids so named. Most children don't appreciate their parents' inventiveness because teachers either mispronounce or avoid made-up names (as they have through the ages), and classmates make a hobby of terrorizing kids with odd names.

Some folks consider the practice of giving an old name a new spelling—Genefur for Jennifer, for example—a very cool way to go, while others scoff at this as downright laughable. By the same token, plenty of parents contend that giving new spellings to old names lends a fresh and splashy feel.

In some ethnic groups, a baby's name reflects the mother's pregnancy impressions. One book titled *Narco* tells of a Spanish mother who had a complicated process for naming seven sons. Each long name was a three-pronged affair consisting of a number for the birth order, a word that represented the mother's main obsession during the nine months, and the name of a famous writer. Cuatro Conrad Confabulation was the fourth son—Cuatro, meaning fourth son; Conrad, for the writer Joseph Conrad; and Confabulation, indicating that she spent her pregnancy gossiping with other pregnant women. Cinco Cervantes Cirrus, by the same token, was the fifth child, named for the writer Miguel Cervantes, and Cirrus, a cloud name that represents the mother's daydreaming pregnancy.

On the other end of the spectrum from those parents who dream up bizarre, fanciful names are the families who view baby-naming as a holy act, right up there with baptism. Some societies believe that names hold spiritual and prophetic significance, and that a child's name is sure to have an enormous impact on his future. The people of Ghana, for instance, think that a name is a mark of religious identification that carries honor and respect. A good name is highly treasured in Ghanaian society, and each baby is honored with a naming ceremony.

Obviously, no science has ever been devised to pinpoint the whys and hows of choosing a name. But, in this book, we give you 40,001 names, tips on the selection process, and, most importantly, clues as to how our names affect us. Be sure to read Part II, which features anecdotes from people who reflect on their names and how they were shaped (or weren't) by their names.

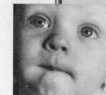

part one

Tips for Naming Your Baby

What do most people do? Some of the baby-naming approaches frequently used include the following:

- Mesh two names together to form a new one.
- Pick a name you've always loved.
- Find a name that bodes well for a promising career.
- Go with a name that connotes a trait—honesty, friendliness, *savoir faire*.
- Use the mother's maiden name for the first name.
- Honor a beloved relative by using his name.
- Stick with something time-honored and safe.
- Make up a name, a practice that some people consider *tres gauche*, and others rate high on the creativity scale.

And while you are dabbling in the name game, be sure to remember these naming taboos:

- Avoid a name that's carrying baggage equivalent to Amtrak, as in Cher, Michael Jackson, Richard Simmons, Billy Joel, or Sting.
- Don't let family members talk you into a "junior" unless you don't mind your child being called "Little John" or "Junior" lifelong. Listen to all the suggestions relatives fling your way, but you make the call.
- Don't be too bothered by existing connotations that you associate with a name ("I knew a Margaret in school, and she was the meanest person in our class," "I sat next to a Stone in college, and he had a million moles," or "I dated a Morgan, and she was the most boring girl I've ever known"). The reason you shouldn't let old associations trip you up is that once you name your child Tasha or Truman, there isn't another person in the world with that name who matters. *Trust me on this.*

Ten Great Tips for Successful Baby-Naming

A "set of rules" can ratchet up your confidence. If you don't really need a framework, just read the following tips as a fun diversion.

Here are ten steps for naming your baby:

1. Consider the sound—does it work with your last name?

When the full name is said aloud, you want something that has a nice ring, not a tongue-twister or a rhyme. You may find that a long last name jibes best with a short first name; by the same token, put a long first name with a short last name, and you may have a winner.

The union of a first name ending in a vowel paired with a last name that starts with a vowel is not the greatest choice. For example: Ava Amazon. It's just hard to say. Puns aren't good omens for a happy life, either. Look at the infamous Ima Hogg name of a Houston philanthropist. If the poor woman wasn't burdened enough, she also had to deal with life-long rumors of a sister named Ura.

2. Know exactly what happens when you give your baby a crowd-pleaser name.

Give your kid a common name, and she'll probably end up Sarah B. in a classroom with six Sarahs. She may be comfortable with the anonymity that a plain-Jane name lends her—considering it far better than being the class Brunhilda, who gets ridiculed daily. Or, she may ask you every other day of her childhood why you weren't more original in naming her: "Why did you give me the same name fifty million other kids have? Why couldn't you have come up with something better? Why didn't you take more time?"

3. Think seriously about the repercussions of choosing a name that's over-the-top in uniqueness.

You are definitely sticking your neck out by giving your child the name Rusty if your last name is Nail. Sure, he may muster up enough swagger to pull it off, but what if he does-n't? Lots of people with unusual or hard-to-spell last names will purposely opt for a simple first name for their child, just to ease the load of having two names to spell over and over. Some research suggests that kids with odd names get more taunting from peers and are less well socialized. You can be sure that junior-high kids will make fun of a boy named Stone, but later, as an adult, he may enjoy having an unusual name.

Just make sure you don't choose a "fun" name simply because you like the idea of having people praise your creativity—instead, ask yourself how your child will feel about being a Bark or a Lake.

4. Ponder the wisdom of carrying on that family name.
Aunt Priscilla did fine with her name, but how will your tiny tot feel in a classroom full of Ambers and Britneys? Extremely old-fashioned names sometimes make their way back into circulation and do just fine, but sometimes they don't. (Will we really ever see the name Durwood soar again?)

5. Consider the confusion that is spawned by a namesake.
A kid named after a parent won't like being "Junior" or "Little Al." Ask anyone who has been in that position about the amount of confusion it generates in regard to credit cards and other personal I.D. information. You'll spend half your life unraveling the mix-ups. Psychiatrists (many of them juniors themselves) will tell you that giving a child his very own name is a much better jumpstart than making him a spin-off or a mini-me.

At the same time, we have all run across someone who absolutely loves being Trey or a III because the name represents tradition and history.

6. Make your family/background name an understudy (the middle name).
Let's say you want your baby's name to reflect his heritage or religion, but you strongly prefer more mainstream names. You can fill both bills by using the ancestry name as a middle name.

7. Ponder whether the name's meaning matters to you.
For some people, knowing a name's meaning is extremely important, often much more so than its Greek or German origin. And your child could turn out to be the type who loves investigating such things. So what happens when that offspring of yours finds out that her name Delilah means "whimpering harlot guttersnipe"? She may wish you had taken a longer look at the name's baggage.

8. Look at shortened versions of a name and check out initials.
Don't think your child's schoolmates will fail to notice that his initials spell out S.C.U.M. And, you can be sure that Harrison will become "Harry" or, occasionally, "Hairy." View the teasing as being as much a given as school backpacks, and think twice about whether you want to give your child's peer group something they can really grab onto. Tread lightly. Naming always starts with good intentions, but you can do your kid a favor by considering each name-candidate's bullying potential.

9. After you've narrowed your list, try out each name and see how it feels.
Say, "Barnabus Higgins, get yourself over here!" Or, "Harrison Higgins, have you done your homework?" Or, "Hannibal Higgins, would you like some fava beans?"

10. Once you and your mate have decided on a name, don't broadcast it.
You may want to keep your name choice a secret, otherwise relatives and friends are likely to share all of their issues with the name and a long string of other, "better" options. Another possibility is that people will start calling the unborn baby that name, which will be unfortunate if you happen to find one you like better.

Bottom line: take the Name Game seriously, but don't be afraid to go with the one that just *feels right*. That precious infant who will change your life dramatically is sure to be the best thing that has ever happened to you—give him or her a name that you will love singing and saying every single day, a million times over.

Baby Ben (Jen), I'm so glad you're mine.

part two

How Names Shape Our Lives

Here, twenty-one people share their thoughts on their names:

Camilla Shirley Pierce, homemaker and mother, Houston: "Although I was named for a beloved great aunt, I always felt that carrying around such an unusual name was not great. When I was a child, no one could pronounce it or spell it. It was a source of embarrassment and aggravation. Now, at age sixty-two, when people read my name they still mispronounce it, and I always feel like saying, 'How hard can it be? I could pronounce it at age three!' "

David Nordin, proposal writer: "I always liked my name because it had more character than other names. David has Biblical history, and it's more elegant and regal than your average name. On the flip side, my odd middle name caused me years of embarrassment. Teachers would call out that name during roll call, and people would laugh and make fun of me...As soon as I was grown, I had it legally changed. Parents should never name their kids anything that could make them objects of ridicule."

Clarence Raymond Chandler, President of Marshall & Winston, Inc., in Midland, Texas: "I was named after my dad's favorite brother, who was a great guy I admired. I was raised in south Texas (Benavides), where my friends were named Roberto, Jose, Ricardo, Jesus, and Francisco, so being a George, Bill, Jerry, Charles, or Roger never really came up on my 'wish list.' I was content! Today, technology has caused the minor inconvenience of not being able to find enough room on forms to print out my long name, much less my signature." Chandler adds: "I had it easy compared to my dad, who was born in an era when children were named after famous people; he got incessant ribbing, not to mention playground fights, when he was growing up, because his challenge was answering to Napoleon Bonaparte Chandler, which is right up there with the ranks of Johnny Cash's 'how do you do, my name is Sue.' In school, it was common knowledge that you only picked on him once, or you had a real dogfight on your hands. To avoid 'you gotta be kidding' comments, he adopted the name 'Nap' Chandler. He was a great dad, patriot, WWII veteran, ethical businessman, champion for the little guy, and a loving and tough SOB—he was my hero!"

Jennifer Wright, a psychiatrist in Atlanta, Georgia: "I've always liked my name. Some of my best friends have been named Jennifer also, and I think it suits our personalities. The benefit of having a 'common' name is that I never have difficulty finding personalized items. Plus, I like the nicknames 'Jen' and 'Jenny.' "

Kristina Kaczmarek Holt, a graphic artist in Canada: "I have always liked my name because it was unique. I had never come across a Kristina with a 'K' until I was a teenager, and then it was usually a Kristy or Kristine. I liked the sound of my first and last name together (the two Ks)—that seemed to work. My name was a heck of a thing to learn to spell in kindergarten, but it was all mine. They used to tape your name to those thick green pencils you learned to write with, and I was always sharpening my pencil down into my name. It wasn't until I recently had a child of my own (Noah) that my dad told me where he got my name. I assumed he picked it because it was a Polish name, and his family was half-Polish. But instead, he named me after a woman who was especially nice to him when he was young, who must have made a strong impression because the name stuck with him until I was born."

Homemaker Dana Huggins Chandler: "I like to be just a little different from everyone else around me, so I always loved my name. There are now many people named Dana, but most don't have the same pronunciation. My name rhymes with Anna and Lana. I always tell people I was named after my dad—Dan—which isn't true, but it does help people remember how to pronounce my name."

Houston TV anchor Dominique Sachse: "Considering you can't pick your name at birth, I'm quite pleased with the one my parents chose for me. I think it has a level of sophistication, and it's unique and European, which I am. I've never considered changing it, shortening it, or going by a nickname. It's a name I feel I've had to live up to."

Cari LaGrange, Internet business owner: "I liked my name growing up, but like most kids, I went through a phase when I wished I could change it, the way girls with straight hair want curly hair and vice versa. Thankfully, my name and its spelling were unique in the town where I grew up, so there was no other girl by my name to compare my identity to."

Jane Vitrano, homemaker in Midland, Texas: "My mother named my sister Linda and me Jane because she hated her own name, Lula Mae, and said she would never want her daughters to have anything but plain names—and no middle names."

Donna Pate, technical writer: "I was neutral about my name. It was okay but not too exciting or interesting. At least it didn't lend itself to juvenile humor. There was the chance of being labeled 'Prima Donna,' but that was beyond the vocabulary of most kids. I liked my name better after I learned what it meant, but that wasn't until I was an adult."

Natasha Graf, acquisitions editor for Wiley Publishing, New York: "My name is pretty special because I was named after a very important woman in my father's life. When I was young and wanted to be like every other girl with an American name, I didn't always like my name because it was unusual at the time, being Russian and all. However, when my father shared with me who I was named after, I came to love it because I feel like I am connected to her somehow. She was a professor at my father's college, and she spoke seven languages—a brilliant woman who had emigrated from Russia. She was his mentor—the first really intellectual person he met during college, and they stayed friends after he went to medical school. It was not an affair—more a meeting of the minds. They wrote to each other. He saved every letter she wrote, and he let me read them. It was so interesting to see my father as a young person through these letters. She died before I was born, before my father was married. I wish I could have met her; I wonder what she would have thought of me. As you can tell, I wouldn't want my name to be anything else."

JoAnn Roberson, fifth-grade teacher in Edna, Texas: "I didn't like my name because it reminded me of a boy's name—Joe. My dad said they were going to name me Jacquelyn, but an uncle said that was too long a name for a little baby, and I would never learn to spell it. I always wished that was my name."

Trey Speegle, art director for *US Weekly*, New York City: "I've always appreciated my name, although when I was very young and wanted to fit in, I wished I had a more normal name, like Chris, or a cool name like Skip. My great-grandmother named me; I was born on her birthday, April 13, and I was her thirteenth great-grandson. Her son (my grandfather) was John Hugh Speegle Sr., and my father is John Hugh Speegle Jr., so she named me Trey John—'the third' John."

Angela Theresa Clark, co-owner of Court Record Research, Inc.: "My mother named me Angela Theresa after two of her favorite Carmelite nuns. I was known as Theresa until sixth grade, when I tired of telling teachers that I didn't go by Angela and just surrendered to being called that. I thought it was stupid to be named something so close to the word 'angel.' Angels are imaginary, soft, and I saw them as easy prey. I was also afraid people might think I was angelic. I thought I had to be tough in my family, with five brothers and two big (mean) older sisters (ha!). I was tomboyish, and Theresa just fit better. Some family members still call me Theresa, although it doesn't fit me anymore because now I'm softer and much more vulnerable. I love my name."

Spiker Davis, dentist, Houston, Texas: "I really liked my name because people always remembered it, and there's no one to get confused with. Also, with a last name like Davis (seventh most common name in the U.S.), you need something to separate you from the crowd."

Cristy Ann Hayes, journalist and mother of two: "My name became a primary focus when I was young and searching for a sense of self, like other preteens. I was disappointed when people would ask what Cristy was short for, and I had to reply 'nothing.' I would wish my mom had taken more time to give me a name as substantial as Christina or Christian. My name also worked well as a taunt for my brother, who insisted I was the only one of the three siblings whose name didn't start with W, so I was not part of the family. Will and Wendy could be rascals that way. My mom thought it was clever to give my name an unconventional spelling, so I have, my entire life, had to take special care in spelling my name, and often people will add an *h*. My driver's license is incorrect because of this, and many of my in-laws still spell it wrong. But after years of frustration regarding the spelling, I now appreciate the measuring tool it has become for me, showing how attuned someone is to me. I hold in high regard those who actually take the time to recognize the unique spelling and write it correctly. I believe it says something about one's character and approach to life when you take care to get a name right!"

Frank Vitrano, retired petroleum engineer in Midland, Texas: "I was born in Waco, Texas, of a Sicilian father, and I was named for my grandfather, Frank Anthony, which is the Italian custom for the first-born son. You get your grandfather's name."

Jennifer Colwell, commercial property management, Midland, Texas: "Since I'm in my fifties, there were not very many Jennifers when I was growing up, and I always loved my name. I thought it was pretty and considered it an asset."

Christopher (Chris) Fleming, female computer consultant, Houston, Texas: "Growing up, I hated my name, Christopher Anne. I was called Christopher Columbus, was sent a draft notice, and was labeled 'effeminate' on an aptitude test in high school. I finally told my mother how much I had hated my name, and she was surprised. In my opinion, parents should choose a name that indicates the child's sex (not one that's androgynous), and that's easy to spell. I don't think it's good to give a baby a name that's bizarre or made up from several words."

Wendy Schnakenberg Corson, EMT: "I have always hated my name. There were never any other Wendys, and if there were, they certainly weren't popular. My parents said they also liked the name Robin, which is a name I love; I told them how mad I was that they chose such a terrible name for me. Also, my middle name, Anne, is just boring. I was never teased about my name, so I suppose that is a positive. But, of course, kids had my last name—Schnakenberg—to tease me with!"

Carey Layne Davis, male landscape architect: "I have always liked my name and never wanted to be called anything else. It was somewhat unique, and I was never teased."

part three

Changing Your Name

Typically, U.S. hospital officials require parents to name their child before leaving the hospital. Other places, such as Canada, give a couple ten days to make their decision.

If you want to change your name, you can hire a lawyer to give you all of the specifics and forms, or you can go to LawGuru.com on the Internet. The latter route gives you, for a fee, the legal forms your state requires.

For your money, you get a name-change package that has forms and instructions for circulating your name-change to government agencies and other groups such as employers, the Social Security Administration, post offices, banks, clubs, the driver's license bureau, insurance companies, the IRS, and the state tax commission, as well as forms for changing your legal documents, including your will.

part four

75 Fun Lists

Boy names that give you a leg up in life

Barrett
Benjamin
Blake
Burke
Daniel
David
Ethan
Graham
Gus
Julian
Kyle
Lance
Logan
Mason
Matt
Max
Michael
Nathaniel
Patrick
Ralph
Samuel
Tyler
Will

Girl names that give you a leg up in life

Anna
Ashley
Bella
Caroline
Celeste
Claire
Danielle
Dominique
Elizabeth
Emma
Grace
Isabella
Jennifer
Julia
Kim
Margaret
Marion
Merit
Michelle
Natalie
Nicole
Rose/Rosa
Sadie
Sidney
Sophie

Patriotic names

America
Amerigo
Asia
Blue
Cherokee
Cheyenne
Columbus
Eagle
Flag
Free
Liberty
Librada
Lincoln
Loyalty
Nation
Pacifika
Patriot
Peace
Red
Sailor
Salute
Spirit
Starr
Utopia
Victory

Burdensome boy names

- Ambrose
- Ankoma
- Archibald
- Bartholomew
- Boaz
- Bouvier
- Cord
- Dakarai
- Durwood
- Gershom
- Godfrey
- Hercules
- Humphrey
- Ignatius
- Kalunga
- Lafayette
- Lazarus
- Marmaduke
- Mortimer
- Percy
- Reginald
- Thelonius
- Vladimar
- Wolfgang
- Zacharias

Burdensome girl names

- Alfre
- Antigone
- Bathsheba
- Chastity
- Clotilde
- Columbine
- Cornelia
- Cricket
- Edna
- Elspeth
- Flannery
- Henrietta
- Indiana
- Keturah
- Majidah
- Millicent
- Minerva
- Muriel
- Priscilla
- Prudence
- Purity
- Thomasina
- Ursula
- Zona
- Zuwena

Boy names for children of lesbians and gays

- Alex
- Anson
- Avery
- Bevan
- Brett
- Caleb
- Carson
- Casey
- Clay
- Derek
- Ethan
- Forrest
- Jake
- Kyle
- Logan
- Marco
- Matt
- Noel
- Owen
- Ray
- Silas
- Spencer
- Yale
- Zack
- Zeke

Girl names for children of lesbians and gays

Amber
Annabelle
April
Bianca
Brianna
Candace
Celeste
Chloe
Daisy
Darcy
Feo
Gloria
Hilary
Ingrid
Jessica
Kirsten
Lara
Lola
Maura
Mia
Molly
Noele
Pia
Ramona
Sharon

Famous mob names

Angelo "Docile Don" Bruno
Aniello Dellecroce
Antonio "Tony Bananas" Caponigro
Dominick "Little Dom" Curra
Frank "Frankie Fap" Fappiano
James J. "Whitey" Bulger
John "Jackie Nose" D'Amico
John Gotti
Joseph "Skinny Joey" Merlino
Louis "Big Louie" Vallario
Lucky Luciano
Michael "Mikey Scars" DiLeonardo
Nicky "The Little Guy" Corozzo
Paul Castellano
Paulie Cimino
Peter "The Crumb" Caprio
Ralph Natale
Salvatore "Sammy the Bull" Gravano
Sonny Visconti
Stephen "The Rifleman" Flemmi
Vincent "The Chin" Gigante
Vincent Palermo

Over-the-top boy names to avoid

Achilles
Adonis
Amadeus
Aristotle
Attila
Bark
Beauregard
Brando
Caesar
Eagle
Goliath
Hamlet
Jock
Lancelot
Laramie
Lobo
Lord
Lothario
Rambo
Rip
Rocco
Rod
Stormy
Sylvester
Titan

Over-the-top girl names to avoid

Aphrodite
Asp
Bijou
Birdie
Blaze
Bless
Blossom
Blush
Butter
Chantilly
Chastity
Cher
Cleopatra
Desire
Fantasia
Fashion
Fawn
Fluffy
Honesty
Jezebel
Loyalty
Ophelia
Psyche
Purity
Tempest

Androgynous names

Andy/Andi
Bailey
Cameron
Carol, Carroll
Chris
Corey
Dakota
Dale, Dell
Darcy
Darryl
Dylan
Gail/Gale
Jamie
Jean, Gene
Jordan
Kat
Kelly
Kerry/Carrie
Lane
Lee
Leslie
Morgan
Pat
Shawn, Sean
Terry

Names that make you smile

Angel
Bambi
Bitsie
Boots
Buffalo
Buffy
Bunny
Champagne
Cheer
Cherry-Sue
Cookie
Corky
Dusty
Fluffy
Galaxy
Harmony
Honey
Peach
Poppy
Ritz
Snooks
Sundancer
Sunny
Tweetie

Soap opera names for boys

Blake
Carson
Cyrano
Dag
Dante
Dario
Dax
Dean
Deone
Destin
Diego
Dom
Duke
Fabio
Harley
Keller
Maximilian
Rico
Rip
Romeo
Ryan
Sebastian
Shiloh
Thor
Wells

Soap opera names for girls

Allura
Amanda
Amber
Bianca
Brandy
Brisa
Candy
Carmen
Charmaine
Cocoa
Dakota
Desiree
Fawn
Madonna
Monica
Renee
Salome
Samantha
Sasha
Simone
Tatiana
Tawny
Tish
Treece
Yolie

Made-up names for boys

- Bryton
- Damarcus
- Dantrell
- Daquan
- Dashawn
- Derlin
- Devonte
- Donyell
- Jabari
- Jaquawn
- Jashon
- Javaris
- Juwon
- Keshon
- Kyan
- Leeron
- Markell
- Quintavius
- Raekwon
- Roshaun
- Shaquille
- Shawnell
- Tevin
- Tre
- Tyree

Made-up names for girls

- Alexakai
- Amberkalay
- Bryelle
- Dalondra
- Danelle
- Darlonna
- Darshell
- Dashawn
- Dashika
- Dasmine
- Davelyn
- Dawntelle
- Jaleesa
- Jameka
- Kaneesha
- Keoshawn
- Latasha
- Noemi
- Quanisha
- Shalonda
- Shanique
- Shawanna
- Tamika
- Tamyrah
- Teagan

Alternative spellings for boy names you can't pronounce

- Adolfus (Adolphus)
- Amadayus (Amadeus)
- Booveeay (Bouvier)
- Breeahno (Briano)
- Byorn (Bjorn)
- Dalanee (Delaney)
- Dameetree (Dmitri)
- Dolf (Dolph)
- Eve (Yves)
- Flavean (Flavian)
- Gweedo (Guido)
- Jordahno (Giordano)
- Keyohtee (Quixote)
- Klev (Cleve)
- Loocho (Lucho)
- Lukah (Luca)
- Makale (Mikhail)
- Malla-Ki (Malachi)
- Odisius (Odysseus)
- Playtoh (Plato)
- Preemoh (Primo)
- Shawn (Sean)
- Sonteeahgo (Santiago)
- Ulissus (Ulysses)

Alternative spellings for girl names you can't pronounce

Afrodytee (Aphrodite)
Alaygrah (Allegra)
Alaytheea (Aleithea)
Anewk (Anouk)
Dafnee (Daphne)
Dayna (Dana)
Duhnell (Danelle)
Egzanth (Xanthe)
Elkie (Elke)
Felisha (Felicia)
Hiah (Heija)
Kamela (Camilla)
Katelyn (Kaitlin)
Margo (Margot)
Mazie (Maisie)
Maxeeme (Maxime)
Moneek (Monique)
Q-malee (Cumale)
Sade (Sharday)
Salowmee (Salome)
Shanade (Sinead)
Sheelyah (Shelia)
Shivan (Siobhan)
Skyler (Schulyer)
Tateeahna (Tatianna)

Biblical and saintly names for boys

Abel
Adam
Benjamin
Daniel
David
Elijah
Ezekial
Isaac
Isaiah
Jacob
Jesus
Job
John
Jonah
Joseph
Joshua
Judas
Lazarus
Luke
Mark
Matthew
Moses
Noah
Paul
Peter
Samuel
Solomon

Biblical and saintly names for girls

Anna
Bathsheba
Deborah
Delilah
Dinah
Esther
Eve
Joanna
Judith
Julia
Leah
Magdalene
Martha
Mary
Miriam
Naamah
Naomi
Phoebe
Rachel
Rebekah
Ruth
Salome
Sarah
Tamar
Zipporah

Names for future architects (boys)

Aaron
Alan
Alexander
Art
Ed
Jack
Jay
Lawrence
Liam
Paul
Rafael
Robert
Ron
Royce
Sage
Sam
Sebastian
Seth
Shaw
Smith
Sterling
Taylor
Theo
Victor
Walt

Names for future architects (girls)

Adrianna
Alana
Annie
Beata
Candace
Deandra
Diana
Ernestine
Fawn
Fortune
Grace
Hannah
Janna
Joann
Justine
Katy
Kelly
Landa
Marianne
Olga
Penelope
Queen
Stella
Susannah
Treece

Good names for race-car drivers

A.J. (Foyt)
Al (Unser)
Alex (Tagiliani)
Arie (Luyendyk)
Bruno (Junqueira)
Buddy (Lazier)
Danny (Sullivan)
Dario (Resta)
Eddie (Cheever, Jr.)
Helio (Castroneves)
Jacques (Villeneuve)
Johnny (Rutherford)
Juan (Montoya)
Jules (Goux)
Kenny (Brack)
Leo (Kinnunen)
Mario (Andretti,
     Dominguez)
Mauri (Rose)
Oriol (Servia)
Rick (Mears)
Sam (Hanks)

Boy celebrity names

Antonio
Ashton
Ben
Booker
Brad
Burt
Casey
Casper
Damon
Denzel
Fabrice
Fernando
Goran
Griffin
Hudson
Keenan
Kiefer
Liam
Marc
Matthew
Mel
Patrick
Russell
Ryan
Tom

Girl celebrity names

Charlize
Demi
Drea
Drew
Fiona
Halle
Isabella
Jennifer
Jessica
Julia
Kate
Lara
Liv
Natasha
Oprah
Portia
Reese
Renee
Rosanna
Sela
Selma
Sheena
Simone
Thora
Tuesday
Uma

Names celebrities give their baby boys

Aaron (Robert De Niro and Toukie Smith)
Bailey (Anthony Edwards and Jeannine Lobell)
Blanket (Michael Jackson)
Boston (Kurt Russell and Season Hubley)
Chance (Larry King and Shawn Southwick)
Chester (Tom Hanks and Rita Wilson)
Connor (Tom Cruise and Nicole Kidman)
Elijah Blue (Cher and Gregg Allman)
Giacomo (Sting and Trudie Styler)
Gib (Connie Selleca and Gil Gerard)
Griffin (Brendan Fraser and Afton Smith)
Hughie (Marg Helgenberger and Alan Rosenberg)
Jett (John Travolta and Kelly Preston)

Joaquin (Kelly Ripa and
    Mark Consuelos)
Miles (Eddie and Nicole
    Murphy)
Pedro (Frances
    McDormand and Joel
    Coen)
Prince Michael (Michael
    Jackson)
Rafferty (Jude Law and
    Sadie Frost)
Roman Caruso (Dee Dee
    and Dan Cortese)
Satchel (Woody Allen
    and Mia Farrow)
Theo (Kate Capshaw and
    Steven Spielberg)
Zachary (Robin Williams
    and Valerie Velardi)

Names celebrities give their baby girls

Beige Dawn (Don
    Adams)
Bria (Eddie and Nicole
    Murphy)
Brielle Nicole (Desiree
    and Blair Underwood)
Carys Zeta (Catherine
    Zeta Jones and
    Michael Douglas)
Cassidy (Kathy Lee and
    Frank Gifford)
Ella Bleu (John Travolta
    and Kelly Preston)
Eulala (Marcia Gay
    Harden and Thaddeus
    Scheel)
Giovanna (Vanna White
    and George Santo
    Pietro)
Gracie (Faith Hill and Tim
    McGraw)
Greta (Phoebe Cates and
    Kevin Kline)
Ireland (Kim Basinger
    and Alec Baldwin)
Kenya (Natassja Kinski
    and Quincy Jones)

Maggie (Faith Hill and
    Tim McGraw)
Mary Willa (Meryl Streep
    and Donald Gummer)
Paris (Michael Jackson)
Prima (Connie Sellecca
    and John Tesh)
Rumer Glenn (Demi
    Moore and Bruce
    Willis)
Sailor (Christie Brinkley
    and Peter Cook)
Scarlett (Mick Jagger
    and Jerry Hall)
Scout LaRue (Demi
    Moore and Bruce
    Willis)
Shayne (Eddie and
    Nicole Murphy)
Starlite Melody (Marisa
    Berenson)
Wylie Quinn (Richard
    Dean Anderson and
    Apryl Prose)
Zola (Eddie and Nicole
    Murphy)

Cool names for athletes

Akeem (Olajuwon)
Althea (Gibson)
Arnold (Palmer)
Babe (Ruth, Dedrikson)
Ben (Hogan)
Bill (Russell)
Billie Jean (King)
Bo (Jackson)
Bonnie (Blair)
Carl (Lewis)
Craig (Biggio)
Cy (Young)
Deion (Sanders)
Evander (Holyfield)
Gale (Sayers)
George (Foreman)
Gordie (Howe)
Greg (Louganis)
Hank (Aaron)
Jack (Nicklaus)
Jackie (Robinson, Joyner-
    Kersee)
Jeff (Bagwell)
Jerry (Rice)
Jesse (Owens)
Jim (Brown, Thorpe)
Joe (DiMaggio, Louis,
    Montana, Namath)

Johnny (Unitas)
Julius (Erving)
Kareem (Abdul-Jabbar)
Lance (Armstrong)
Larry (Bird)
Lou (Gehrig)
Magic (Johnson)
Mark (Spitz)
Martina (Navratilova)
Michael (Jordan)
Mickey (Mantle)
Muhammad (Ali)
Picabo (Street)
Red (Grange)
Sandy (Koufax)
Serena (Williams)
Stan (Musial)
Sugar Ray (Robinson)
Ted (Williams)
Tiger (Woods)
Ty (Cobb)
Venus (Williams)
Walter (Payton)
Wayne (Gretzky)
Willie (Mays)
Wilma (Rudolph)
Wilt (Chamberlain)

Old-fashioned boy names that are cute again

Atticus
Barney
Casper
Charlie
Chester
Clem
Curtis
Dexter
Duane
Duke
Elmer
Gill
Harvey
Homer
Luke
Mitchell
Monty
Mort
Myron
Ned
Norm
Oscar
Stanley
Wilbur
Wyatt

Old-fashioned girl names that are cute again

Abby
Alma
Annette
Arden
Arlene
Ava
Belle
Betsy
Beulah
Corinna
Ethel
Flo
Hazel
Inez
Irene
Isabel
Kay
Kyra
Laverne
Loretta
Lorraine
Lydia
Mabel
Polly
Trudy

Names for future doctors (boys)

Bryant
Charles
Dimitri
Frazier
George
Herbert
James
John
Judd
Lister
Mark
Martin
Mason
Murray
Newell
Nick
Niles
Peter
Philip
Ralph
Randall
Reagan
Rell
Russell
Sabin

Names for future doctors (girls)

Ann
Athena
Brenda
Bryce
Catrice
Claire
Dana
Donna
Elaine
Elizabeth
Freda
Greta
Jane
Jennifer
Linda
Lydia
Lynn
Marianne
Mary
Maureen
Miriam
Sarah
Suzanne
Tina
Victoria

Names for future artists (boys)

Ballard
Blaze
Ceron
Eduardo
Francesco
Francoise
Frederic
Gansta
Graham
Hector
Jean-Claude
Jean-Pierre
Jose
Laurent
Lionel
Maximilian
Michael
Octavio
Oscar
Paulo
Pash
Pedro
Ronnie
Sancho
Sebastian
Stephan

Names for future artists (girls)

Alexis
Ashantia
Azure
Caramia
Chantal
DeeDee
Emelle
Eve
Janice
Jenna
Kavita
Lace
Lanee
Lavonne
Margina
Mary-Catherine
Michaele
Mona
Regine
Sisteene
Skyler
Tallulah
Zora

Names for future lawyers (boys)

Atticus
Bryan
Caleb
Carlson
Dick
Gary
Jack
Jacob
John
Josh
Lawrence
Noble
Preston
Price
Quinn
Reese
Roark
Robert
Rush
Rusty
Ryder
Samuel
Sander
Sandford
Tom

Names for future lawyers (girls)

Ann
Brianna
Campbell
Carlisle
Charlotte
Dana
Emily
Haley
Joanna
Kate
Kendra
Lane
Madison
Mariel
Mason
Meg
Parker
Rachel
Sally
Sarah
Serena
Sloan
Taylor
Tekla
Terese

Good names for mechanics

Brewster
Carl
Chubby
Ernie
Fred
Gary
Hal
Hank
Harry
Jake
Joey
Leon
Max
Merle
Moey
Ralph
Red
Rusty
Sonny
Spanky
Terry
Toby
Zeke

Names from mythology and astrology

Ajax
Alala
Argus
Aries
Bacchus
Bran
Cadmus
Cressida
Evander
Galatea
Gawain
Gemini
Kalliope
Lake
Lancelot
Merlin
Nestor
Ocean
Penelope
Phoenix
Tane
Terra
Thor
Venus
Zeus

Scary/creepy boy names

Bigram
Brick
Bruno
Butcher
Delete
Dweezil
Elmo
Graven
Gruver
Horatio
Izzy
Modred
Nada
Napoleon
Narcissus
Nellie
Neptune
Nero
Percival
Pontius
Seymour
Sindbad
Sisyphus
Socrates
Zero

Scary/creepy girl names

Adelaide
Agnes
Arlette
Beatrix
Crispy
Denz
Earlene
Edna
Hortense
Lakeesha
Nunu
Nyleen
Peta
Phyllida
Quinceanos
Randelle
Scylla
Sharama
Swoosie
Tashanee
Uzbek
Winnie
Wyetta
Zeb
Zulemita

World's strangest names

Adjanys
Bego
Blue
Bucko
Bukola
Car
Dix
Dweezil
Edju
Idarah
Kermit
Kiwa
Lovella
Moon Unit
Nimrod
Oak
Obey
Pity
Rudow
Swell
Tiago
Tilla
Zap
Zip
Zone

Unforgettable names

Allegra
Aura
Bai
Cocoa
Hyacinth
Jumbe
King
Lake
Leelee
Lindberg
Madonna
Momo
Montague
Pink
Prince
Rivers
Santeene
Schmoopie
Spirit
Sting
Symphony
Talent
Tame
Trocky
Wyclef

Boy names teachers can't pronounce

Artemus
Declan
Dionysus
Flody
Gyth
Hamif
Hermes
Hieronymos
Honorato
Iago
Ignatius
Ioannis
Isidro
Jetal
Jovan
Larrmyne
Mihow
Mischa
Moey
Raoul
Revin
Seth
Sladkey
Slavek
Takeya

Girl names teachers can't pronounce

Aisha
Aleithea
Camilla
Carenleigh
Chesskwana
Deighan
Falesyia
Gisbelle
Gresia
Madchen
Maromisa
Mayghaen
Meyka
Naeemah
Nissie
Nunibelle
Rhonwen
Ruthemma
Sade
Shaleina
Sharrona
Shawneequa
Tanyav
Tierah
Twyla

Names for Mister Perfect

Alex
Anthony
Ben
Blake
Brent
Christian
Christopher
Clint
Fletcher
Giancarlo
Harrison
Hunter
James
Joaquin
Justin
Kirk
Kyle
Monty
Reese
Riley
Robert
Rory
Ryan
Wells
Zack

Names for Miss Perfect

Alexandra
Allison
Bailey
Brittney
Celeste
Christiane
Courtney
Danielle
Elizabeth
Hollyn
Jennifer
Jill
Leah
Lexi
Marissa
Meredith
Merit
Mia
Miranda
Natalie
Nia
Riley
Shara
Sloan

Names that will help make your baby boy popular

Britt
Cam
Cody
Dylan
Ethan
Evan
Fletch
Gino
Gus
Heath
Hunter
Ian
Jake
Jason
Jeremy
Jerod
Joshua
Julian
Justin
Kyle
London
Max
Morgan
Nick
Tyler

Names that will help make your baby girl popular	Comfy names that boys like having	Comfy names that girls like having
Ava	Allen	Allison
Britney	Ben	Amber
Clancy	Brent	Annie
Coby	Casey	Ashley
Coco	Chad	Becca
Emma	Daniel	Callie
Gina	Dave	Carrie
Lauren	Ethan	Danielle
Lexi	Gavin	Diane
Lily	Jack	Emily
Lindsay	Jake	Hailey
Lola	Jason	Heather
London	Jesse	Isabel
Lyla	Josh	Jessica
Mackenzie	Justin	Jordan
Madison	Logan	Justine
Morgan	Matt	Kim
Nicole	Max	Lauren
Piper	Mike	Liz
Reese	Nicholas	Maggie
Samantha	Rob	Nicole
Skye	Sam	Rachel
Sophie	Tyler	Samantha
Tara		Selena
Taylor		

Names for boys that sound presidential

Abraham
Adam
Adlai
Andrew
Benjamin
Blake
Calvin
Charles
Daniel
Dwight
Earnest
George
Hamilton
Hampton
Harrison
Henry
Hudson
James
John
Reagan
Robert
Roger
Ronald
Winston
Zachary

Names for girls that sound presidential

Andrea
Ann
Carolyn
Claire
Elizabeth
Ella
Emily
Emma
Evan
Helen
Hilary
Isabel
Julia
Kay
Kelly
Kyle
Lauren
Madison
Mia
Miriam
Parker
Rachel
Rose
Stella
Taylor

Season/weather names

Autumn
Cloudy
Dusky
Easter
Fog
Frosty
Holly
Misty
Noel
Rain
Rainbow
Season
Sky
Snow
Soleil
Spring
Storm
Summer
Sunny
Sunshine
Typhoon
Windy
Winter

Exotic names for your baby boy	Exotic names for your baby girl	Names of rich Americans
Desiderio	Cherokee	Abigail (Johnson)
Destin	Cheyenne	Amy (Brinkley)
Diego	Chiara	Andre (Agassi)
Enrique	Kia	Ann (Moore), Anne
Enzo	Kimone	(Mulcahy)
Esme	Lakesha	Betsy (Holden, Bernard)
Francesco	Lani	Bobby (Kotick)
Franco	Laurent	Brad (Pitt)
Frederic	Pax	Colleen (Barrett)
Gabriel	Pepita	Dan (Snyder)
Gaston	Phaedra	David (Filo, Hitz)
Genaro	Philomena	Elon (Musk)
Giancarlo	Phyllida	Halsey (Minor)
Hamlet	Quanda	Jeff/Jeffrey (Skoll, Bezos,
Hansel	Rania	Citron, Mallett, Zients)
Hawke	Rasheeda	Jerry (Yang, Greenberg)
Heinz	Rhiannon	Joe (Liemandt)
Helio	Saffron	Judy (McGrath, Lewent)
Hermes	Santana	Julia (Roberts)
Honorato	Sasha	Karen (Katen)
Jacques	Sequoia	Lois (Juliber)
Janus	Sheba	Marc (Andreessen,
Javier	Shoshana	Ewing)
Jean-Paul	Simone	Michael (Dell, Jordan,
Johann	Solange	Robertson)
		Oprah (Winfrey)
		Pat (Woertz, Russo)
		Paul (Gauthier)

Percy (Miller)
Raul (Fernandez)
Scott (Blum)
Sean (Combs)—P. Diddy
Shaquille (O'Neal)
Sherry (Lansing)
Stacey (Snider)
Ted (Waitt)
Tiger (Woods)
Vinny (Smith)
Will (Smith)

Nerd/dork/wallflower names

Barney
Bruce
Cheryl
Chester
Dabney
Dudley
Durwood
Edgar
Edward
Elwood
Emory
Engelbert
Estes
Ethelbert
Eugene
Eustace
Ewan
Fagan
Fairfax
Gomer
Pembroke
Percy
Priscilla
Ted
Warren

Names that make boys feel weird

Bloo
Butler
Car
Delete
Elmo
Elmore
Ervin
Excell
Fabio
Fable
Fergus
Fife
Forester
Geronimo
Gomer
Maverick
Oswald
Paris
Prince
Rebel
Stone
Stormy
Welcome
Ziggy

Names that make girls feel weird

Breezy
Charm
Chastity
Cherish
Delite
Fashion
Glory
Harmony
Lake
Leaf
Liberty
Michelin
Misty
Oceana
Panther
Peace
Pity
Precious
Promise
Purity
Rain
Sweetpea
Tree
True
Vixen

Names for eccentrics

Antigone
Balfour
Bark
Beetle
Bird
Chantilly
Cloudy
Echo
Ecstasy
Flirt
Free
Fudge
Galatea
Gawain
Goliath
Lady
LaRue
Lazarus
Obedience
Orson
Oz
Rambo
Stoli
Webb
Zeus

Names for boys who are handsome

Allen
Austin
Benjamin
Cal
Cameron
Chad
Cooper
Dax
Dylan
Ethan
Fletcher
Gus
Hudson
Ian
Jan-Erik
Jude
Julian
Kyle
Logan
Owen
Riley
Ryan
Sebastian
Shiloh
Will

Names for girls who are beautiful

Addison
Anabelle
Annie
Ashley
Ava
Belle
Catrice
Dominique
Eden
Gina
Jade
Jennifer
Jessica
Jinx
Jolie
Jordan
Liz
Marisol
Miranda
Natasha
Petra
Rachel
Renee
Sheyn
Trista

Jewish/Hebrew names for boys

Aaron
Abe
Barry
Benjamin
Daniel
David
Eli
Esau
Ethan
Gabriel
Harrison
Ira
Isaac
Jake
Jay
Joshua
Levi
Marvin
Milton
Nathan
Sam
Saul
Sheldon
Solomon
Stanley

Jewish/Hebrew names for girls

Anne
Claire
Esther
Golda
Hannah
Ilana
Jenny
Johanna
Judith
Leah
Lena
Lillian
Linda
Mary
Miriam
Naomi
Rachel
Rebekah
Ruth
Sadie
Sarah
Shara
Sophie
Sylvia
Tovah

Arabic/Islamic names for boys

Abdul-Jabbar
Ahmad, Ahmed
Ali
Amir
Dawud
Fariol
Ghassan
Habib
Hakim, Hakeem
Hamid
Hasan
Ibrahim
Jabir, Jabbar
Jamal
Kamal, Kamil
Kareem
Khalid
Mahmud
Muhammad,
    Mohammad
Nuri
Rafi
Rashid
Salim
Sharif
Yasir

Arabic/Islamic names for girls

Aisha
Almira
Asma
Bathsira
Cala
Dhelal
Fatima
Habibah
Hadil
Hajar, Hagir
Hayfa
Ihab
Jamila
Kalila
Karima
Laila
Leila
Malak
Nada
Nima
Rashidah
Rida
Sabah
Salima

Scandinavian names for boys

Aksel
Anders
Anton
Bjorn
Christian
Claus
Dirk
Erik
Gustav
Hendrik
Ingmar
Isak
Johannes
Karl
Knut
Krister
Lars
Matts
Mikael
Niels
Niklas
Oskar
Per
Rudolf
Stellan

Scandinavian names for girls

Astrid
Birgit
Bonnevie
Dufvenius
Elsa
Erika
Fia
Frida
Gudrun
Gunilla
Inge
Ingrid
Janna
Johanna
Kristina
Liv
Lotta
Mini
Sabina
Sanna
Sigrid
Sofia
Sonya
Ursula
Wilhelmina

Italian names for boys

Aldo
Alessandro
Angelo
Arturo
Carlo
Carmine
Ciro
Cosmo
Dante
Emilio
Enrico
Franco
Gianni
Gino
Giorgio
Guido
Leonardo
Lorenzo
Luciano
Marco
Mario
Salvatore
Tomasso
Vincenzo
Vito

Italian names for girls

Annamaria
Bella
Cara
Caramia
Carissa
Carlotta
Chiara
Elda
Elena
Eliana
Elisa
Elletra
Faustina
Fidelia
Gina
Isabella
Maria
Melania
Paulina
Pia
Rosa
Rosamaria
Sophia

French names for boys

Alain
Charles
Claude
Francois
Frederic
Gaston
Gerard
Germain
Gregoire
Guy
Henri
Isidore
Jacques
Jean
Jean-Claude
Jean-Michel
Jean-Paul
Laurent
Louis
Luc
Marcel
Maxime
Phillipe
Robert
Yves

French names for girls

Aimee
Amelie
Anais
Angelique
Antoinette
Arianne
Chantal
Claire
Colette
Daniele
Desiree
Dominique
Eliane
Elisabeth
Emmanuelle
Esmee
Gabrielle
Genevieve
Giselle
Maria
Michele
Monique
Simone
Yvette
Yvonne

German names for boys

Claus, Klaus
Erik
Folker
Freiderich
Garrick
Gerhard
Gunther
Gustaf
Heinrich
Helmut
Hendrik
Karl
Konrad
Kurt
Leopold
Max
Norbert
Oswald
Otto
Ralph
Roger
Rudy
Stefan
Wilhelm
Wolfgang

German names for girls

Ada
Anke
Anneliese
Annemarie
Beata
Clotilda
Constanze
Cordula
Ebba
Elisabeth
Elsa
Emma
Felicie
Gudrun
Heidi
Hilda
Juliana
Karoline
Katharina
Kristina
Margarite
Maria
Martina
Rosa
Ursula

Polish names for boys

Aleksander
Andrzej
Aniol
Anzelm
Bogdan
Boleslaw
Czeslaw
Dobromir
Helmut
Jacek
Jozef
Karol
Kazimierz
Krzysztof
Marek
Pawel
Ryszard
Slawomir
Waclaw
Walenty
Witold
Wladymir
Wladyslaw
Wojtek
Zbigniew

Polish names for girls

Anna
Barbara
Cecilia
Celestyna
Gabriela
Gizela
Grazyna
Hanna
Honorata
Iwona
Jadwiga
Kamilia
Karolina
Krysta
Krystyna
Lucja
Maria
Marusya
Matylda
Mirka
Monika
Otylia
Roksana
Waleria
Wiktoria

Russian names for boys

Adya
Alek
Aleksei
Denis
Dmitri
Grigori
Igor
Ivan
Karl
Maksimilian
Mikhail
Misha
Nikita
Nikolai
Oleg
Pavel
Sasha
Sergei
Sidor
Stanislav
Valentin
Valeri
Vlad
Vladimir
Vladja

Russian names for girls

Anastasiya
Anninka
Dariya
Dasha
Duscha
Elena
Evelina
Inessa
Irene/Irina
Ivanna
Kira
Lara
Lia
Masha
Nadya
Natalia
Natasha
Oksana
Olga
Polina
Sasha
Sofya
Sonya
Svetlana
Tatiana

Irish names for boys

Aidan
Art
Bran
Brendan
Brian
Colin
Curran
Devin
Farris
Fergus
Finn
Ian
James
Jamie
John
Kevin
Kieran, Keiran
Killian
Liam
Lochlain
Owen
Patrick
Rowan
Sean
Shay

Irish names for girls

Aileen
Amanda
Annie
Brenda
Briana
Catherine
Cathleen
Ciara
Deirdre
Dorren
Eavan
Eliza
Emma
Ethnea
Karen
Kate
Kathy
Maggie
Molly
Nancy
Nessa
Polly
Riona
Sally
Sinead

Scottish names for boys

Ainsley
Alan
Angus
Bean
Bennett
Cally
Cameron
Charles
Clement
Conall
Donald
Fergus
Gregor
Harry
Iagan
Ian
James
Jock
Jon
Kenneth
Peader
Roddy
Scott
Stewart
Walter

Scottish names for girls

Alexandra
Alison
Annella
Christy
Dina
Fiona
Heather
Jeanie
Jenny
Lexine
Lexy
Lindsay
Lucy
Maidie
Maisie
Margaret
Nan
Netta
Nora
Peigi
Robina
Rona
Rowena
Sandy
Tory

English names for boys	English names for girls	African names for boys
Arthur	Agnes	Addae
Charles	Alexandra	Adio
Clinton	Althea	Ayo
Clive	Amanda	Bakari
Colin	Andie	Bomani
Earl	Angie	Dalila
Edward	Anna/Anne	Dumisani
George	Becky	Hamidi
Harry	Betty	Harun
Henry	Carla	Hasani
Jay	Connie	Hondo
Jeff	Cynthia	Jaja
Max	Elizabeth	Kamal
Michael	Esther	Kamau
Nicholas	Georgina	Muhhamad
Nigel	Hayley	Rudo
Norman	Ida	Runako
Peter	Jennifer	Saeed
Philip	Jill	Salehe
Roger	Katherine	Salim
Roland	Margaret	Sekani
Ronald	Moira	Themba
Toby	Pippa	Umi
William	Rhonda	Zikomo
Winston	Wendy	Zuberi

African names for girls

Aamori
Abayomi
Adia
Aisha
Asabi
Bayo
Eshe
Fatima
Femi
Habiba
Hasina
Jumoke
Kibibi
Kissa
Lateefa
Maudisa
Nailah
Nomble
Omorose
Oni
Rufaro
Salama
Taliba
Tisa
Zahra

Spanish names for boys

Adonis
Alejandro
Alfonso
Angel
Benito
Carlos
Damaso
Diego
Emilio
Enrique
Esteban
Fiero
Francisco
Hector
Isidoro
Javier
Jorge
Jose
Juan
Julio
Miguel
Mundo
Raoul
Roberto
Tomas

Spanish names for girls

Angela
Beila
Beilarosa
Bonita
Caliopa
Carlotta
Carmen
Clementina
Consuelo
Delicia
Delfina
Destina
Elena
Flora
Graciela
Guadalupe
Honoria
Juanita
Maria
Mariposa
Odelita
Paloma
Primalia
Soledad

Greek names for boys

Alexandros
Andreas
Ari
Basil
Cletus
Demetri
Demetrios
Demos
Flavian
Hilarion
Jason
Lucas
Markos
Nikos
Paul
Sander
Seth
Socrates
Stephanos
Theo
Theodoros
Theophilos
Tito
Verniamin
Zeno

Greek names for girls

Aggie
Andrianna
Ariane
Athena
Calista
Calla
Chloe
Damalla
Delos
Diona
Filia
Gillian
Helena
Iona
Isadora
Kali
Kalidas
Kori
Kynthia
Leandra
Nia
Phyllis
Pia
Theodora
Zoe

Asian names for boys

An (Chinese)
Chang (Chinese)
Dong (Chinese)
Hiro (Japanese)
Huang (Chinese)
Ibu (Japanese)
Ji (Chinese)
Jin (Chinese)
Jing (Chinese)
Ju-Long (Chinese)
Kang (Korean)
Li (Chinese)
Liang (Chinese)
Pin (Vietnamese)
Quon (Chinese)
Shen (Chinese)
Sheng (Chinese)
Shuu (Japanese)
So (Vietnamese)
Tan (Japanese)
Tung (Chinese,
    Vietnamese)
Yen (Chinese)
Yu (Chinese)
Yuan (Chinese)
Zhong (Chinese)

Asian names for girls

Bao (Chinese)
Bay (Vietnamese)
Cai (Chinese)
Connie-Kim (Vietnamese)
De (Chinese)
Fang (Chinese)
Ha (Vietnamese)
Lei (Chinese)
Li (Chinese)
Lian (Chinese)
Ling (Chinese)
Mai (Japanese)
Min (Chinese)
Ming (Chinese)
Niu (Chinese)
Nu (Vietnamese)
Pang (Chinese)
Tam (Japanese)
Thim (Thai)
Veata (Cambodian)
Yu (Chinese)
Zan (Chinese)
Zhi (Chinese)
Zhong (Chinese)
Zi (Chinese)

Boy names that get shortened

Alexander
Augustus
Barnabus
Bradford
Christopher
Cornelius
Donovan
Emmanuel
Enrique
Franklin
Frederic
Gregory
Jonathon
Nathaniel
Nicholas
Randolph
Roberto
Roderick
Roosevelt
Salvador
Samuel
Solomon
Timothy
Wilfredo
Woodrow

Girl names that get shortened

Alexandra
Anastasia
Angelina
Cassandra
Charmaine
Constance
Deborah
Elizabeth
Evangeline
Gabrielle
Guadalupe
Gwendolyn
Jacqueline
Jennifer
Josephine
Kimberly
Lucretia
Magdalena
Nanette
Penelope
Rebecca
Rosalinda
Roxanna
Susannah

Boy names that spawn nasty nicknames

Adolf
Aldred
Alec, Alek
Alfonso
Apple
Ash
Asher
Ashley
Ashton
Babe
Boris
Bucky
Butler
Byrd
Clement
Dominic
Farley
Farnham
Farr
Ferdinand
Harry
Haywood
Jericho
Titus

Girl names that spawn nasty nicknames

Christopher
Cocoa
Dusky-Dream
Earlene
Feather
Fortune
Gay
Harriet
Haute
Hedy
Hermione
Hodge
Hortense
Lesbia
Monica
Rainey
Romona
Ruta
Scarlett
Sesame
Sigrun
Sweetpea
Taffy
Teddi
Winifred

Hippie-sounding names

Apple
Breezy
Cloud
Dune
Free
Gypsy
Happy
Maverick
Oceana
Peace
Peaches
Rain
Rainbow
River
Sea
Serenity
Sierra
Spring
Star
Summer
Sunny
Tree
True
Willow
Winner

Names for smart boys

Adam
Allen
Barry
Benjamin
Brent
Byron
Chet
Clarence
Curtis
David
Eric
Gray
Guy
Hillel
Jack
Kent
Laurens
Martin
Maximilian
Peter
Philip
Richard
Rob
Russell
Scott
Trevor
William

Names for smart girls

Allene
Beth
Carolyn
Carrie
Colby
Dana
Dominique
Donna
Elizabeth
Jamie
Jennifer
Karen
Kathleen
Kristina
Leticia
Maude
Micheline
Natasha
Page
Shannon
Shari
Shaune
Suzanne
Tessie
Zoann

Names for playful personalities

Babe
Bebe
Bliss
Bunny
Buzzie
Chica
Dusky
Fluffy
Happy
Jandy
Jinx
Lily
Merrilee
Miranda
Pal
Pixie
Poppy
Precious
Queenie
Rabbit
Schmoopie
Skip
Sunny
Trixie
Viveca

Place names (boys)

Aberdeen
Albany
Aleppo
Alps
America
Beaumont
Bexley
Billings
Bradford
Carson
Cuba
Cyprus
Dodge
Elam
Gobi
Gwent
Hollywood
Hull
Logan
Macon
Orlando
Rainier
Sydney
Texas
Yukon

Place names (girls)

Asia
Bali
Bonn
Cairo
Cambay
Capri
China
Dallas
Dayton
Easter
Egypt
Flanders
Georgia
India
Indiana
Ireland
Jordan
Kansas
Kentucky
Kenya
Lansing
Odessa
Persia
Savannah
Venice

Boy names derived from literature

Ahab
Ali Baba
Boswell
Cervantes
Chaucer
Cummings
Cyrano
Dickens
Don Quixote
Dryden
Emerson
Foster
Grimm
Hunter
Keats
Lowell
Milton
Norman
Pope
Rhett
Sherman
Spenser
Swift
Wordsworth
Yeats

Girl names derived from literature

Alice
Austen
Bronte
Browning
Cale
Charlotte
Colette
Daisy
Godiva
Grisham
Harper
Jane
Kipling
Lara
McMurtry
Meg
Melanie
Millay
Patricia
Sadie
Scarlett
Scout
Simone
Stella
Whitman
Whittier

Bad-to-the-bone, death-row names for boys

Adolph (Hernandez)
Clydell (Coleman)
David (Hammer, Long)
Excell (White)
Henry Lee (Lucas)
Jeffrey (Dahmer, Lundgren)
Jemarr (Arnold)
Jessie (Patrick)
John (Baltazar, Martinez)
John Wayne (Gacy)
Leonard (Rojas)
Mack (Hill)
Markum (Duff-Smith)
Napoleon (Beazley)
Randy (Knese)
Reginald (Reeves)
Richard (Ramirez, Speck, Kutzner, Dinkins)
Ricky (McGinn)
Robert (Atworth)
Rodolfo (Hernandez)
Stanley (Baker)
Ted (Bundy)
Timothy (McVeigh)
Toronto (Patterson)
Windell (Broussard)

Bad-to-the-bone, death-row names for girls

Aileen Carol (Wuomos)
Ana (Cardona)
Andrea (Jackson)
Antoinette (Frank)
Betty (Beets)
Blanche (Moore)
Caroline (Young)
Christa Gail (Pike)
Darlie Lynn Routier
Debra (Milke)
Delores (Rivers)
Faye (Copeland)
Frances (Newton)
Gail Kirsey (Owens)
Jaqueline (Williams)
Karla Faye (Tucker)
Kerry (Dalton)
Latasha (Pulliam)
Maria (del Rosio Alfaro)
Marilyn (Plantz)
Mary Ellen (Samuels)
Maureen (McDermott)
Nadine (Smith)
Pamela (Perillo)
Vernice (Ballenger)

Country-western singer names (boys)	Country-western singer names (girls)	Wimpy names
Alan (Jackson)	Allison (Krauss)	Babe
Billy Ray (Cyrus)	Anne (Murray)	Barney
Brad (Paisley)	Barbara (Mandrell)	Bobo
Buck (Owens)	Brenda (Lee)	Brownie
Cash (Moline)	Carlene (Carter)	Brucie
Chance (Martin)	Cristy (Lane)	Byrd
Charley (Pride)	Dolly (Parton)	Chubby
Chet (Atkins)	Emily (Robison)	Clydell
Clay (Walker)	Faith (Hill)	Corky
Clint (Black)	Jo Dee (Messina)	Denny
Conway (Twitty)	Kitty (Wells)	Dewey
Dwight (Yoakum)	LeAnn (Rimes)	Dudley
Garth (Brooks)	Lee Ann (Womack)	Dusty
George (Strait)	Loretta (Lynn)	Dwight
Hank (Williams)	Martie (Maguire)	Feo
Kenny (Rogers)	Martina (McBride)	Fergie
Lyle (Lovett)	Maybelle (Carter)	Fuddy
Merle (Haggard)	Natalie (Maines)	Perry
Tex (Ritter)	Pam (Tillis)	Skeeter
Tim (McGraw)	Patsy (Cline)	Skippy
Toby (Keith)	Reba (McIntire)	Spanky
Travis (Tritt)	Shania (Twain)	Terry
Vince (Gill)	Tamara (Walker)	Timmy
Waylon (Jennings)	Trisha (Yearwood)	Tippy
Willie (Nelson)	Wynonna (Judd)	Wendell

Girlie-girl names

- Bebe
- Bubbles
- Buffy
- Bunny
- Cherry
- Cinderella
- Cinnamon
- Cookie
- Darlie
- Debbie-Jean
- Deedee
- Dolly
- Fluffy
- Melrose
- Poppy
- Posy
- Precious
- Primrose
- Princess
- Prissy
- Sissy
- Sugar
- Sweetpea
- Tippie
- Trixiebelle

Boy names that are so over

- Al
- Bob
- Dennis
- Donald
- Douglas
- Ernie
- Frank
- Garland
- Gary
- Glanville
- Harold
- Harvey
- Jaden
- Jason
- Jerry
- Juwon
- Ken
- Leon
- Marvin
- Morey
- Oscar
- Ottis
- Randy
- Rick
- Todd

Girl names that are so over

- Bertie
- Betty
- Carla
- Delores
- Edith
- Faye
- Frances
- Gail
- Hilary
- Judy
- Loretta
- Louise
- Marilyn
- Maureen
- Minnie
- Myrna
- Nancy
- Nina
- Priscilla
- Stacy
- Tiffany
- Tracy
- Veronica
- Wanda
- Winona

Overpowering boy names

- Abbott
- Axelrod
- Baldridge
- Balthazar
- Domenico
- Don Quixote
- Dontrell
- Esmond
- Gabbana
- Galbraith
- Huntley
- Hyde
- Kensington
- Lothario
- Montague
- Napoleon
- Ottway
- Pluto
- Quintavius
- Reginald
- Rochester
- Ronford
- Roosevelt
- Thor
- Wyclef

Overpowering girl names

- Antoinette
- Aunjanue
- Bjork
- Calista
- Colemand
- Deja-Marie
- Gwyneth
- Illeana
- Ione
- Jowannah
- Kallioppe
- Karalenae
- Madonna
- Mariangela
- Oprah
- Perabo
- Penelope
- Philomena
- Russo
- Sahara
- Siphronia
- Stockard
- Teah
- Thora
- Winifred

Macho names

- Bucko
- Butch
- Buzz
- Cal
- Cash
- Duke
- Esteban
- Evander
- Hud
- Hugo
- Jock
- Judd
- Mack
- Ram
- Rebel
- Reem
- Rip
- Rocco
- Sam
- Santiago
- Spike
- Stone
- Trocky
- Waylon
- Zoom

Sweetie-pie names

Alicia
Angie
Annabelle
Bay
Brook
Darcy
Dolce
Dove
Faith
Goldie
Honey
Jenny
Julianna
Kate
Laurel
Lisa
Marina
Robin
Rosa
Roseanne
Sarah-Jessica
Tammy
Wylie
Yolie

Powerful boy names

Andrew
Angus
Anthony
Charles
Cole
Colin
Easton
Ford
Grant
Harrison
Heath
Jacob
James
Jon
Justice
Lamar
Louis
Michael
Nash
Nolan
Quentin
Reagan
Solomon
Thomas
William

Powerful girl names

Anna
Blake
Campbell
Candace
Elizabeth
Evan
Grace
Greta
Harper
Honor
Hope
Jessica
Julia
Lauren
Madison
Margaret
Olivia
Pace
Parker
Pilar
Quinn
Reeve
Rhea
Sarah
Wylie

Most popular names of the 1990s (boys)

1. Michael
2. Christopher
3. Matthew
4. Joshua
5. Jacob
6. Andrew
7. Daniel
8. Nicholas
9. Tyler
10. Joseph
11. David
12. Brandon
13. James
14. John
15. Ryan
16. Zachary
17. Justin
18. Anthony
19. William
20. Robert
21. Jonathan
22. Kyle
23. Austin
24. Alexander
25. Kevin
26. Cody
27. Thomas
28. Jordan
29. Eric
30. Benjamin
31. Aaron
32. Jose
33. Christian
34. Steven
35. Samuel
36. Brian
37. Dylan
38. Timothy
39. Adam
40. Nathan
41. Richard
42. Sean
43. Charles
44. Patrick
45. Jason
46. Luis
47. Jeremy
48. Stephen
49. Mark
50. Jesse

part four

Most popular names of the 1990s (girls)

1. Ashley
2. Jessica
3. Emily
4. Sarah
5. Samantha
6. Brittany
7. Amanda
8. Elizabeth
9. Taylor
10. Megan
11. Stephanie
12. Kayla
13. Lauren
14. Jennifer
15. Rachel
16. Hannah
17. Nicole
18. Amber
19. Alexis
20. Courtney
21. Victoria
22. Danielle
23. Alyssa
24. Rebecca
25. Jasmine
26. Katherine
27. Melissa
28. Alexandra
29. Brianna
30. Chelsea
31. Michelle
32. Morgan
33. Kelsey
34. Tiffany
35. Kimberly
36. Christina
37. Madison
38. Heather
39. Shelby
40. Anna
41. Mary
42. Maria
43. Allison
44. Sara
45. Laura
46. Andrea
47. Olivia
48. Erin
49. Haley
50. Abigail

Most popular names of the 1980s (boys)

1. Michael
2. Christopher
3. Matthew
4. Joshua
5. David
6. Daniel
7. James
8. Robert
9. John
10. Joseph
11. Jason
12. Justin
13. Andrew
14. Ryan
15. William
16. Brian
17. Jonathan
18. Brandon
19. Nicholas
20. Anthony
21. Eric
22. Adam
23. Kevin
24. Steven
25. Thomas
26. Timothy
27. Richard
28. Jeremy
29. Kyle
30. Jeffrey
31. Benjamin
32. Aaron
33. Mark
34. Charles
35. Jacob
36. Stephen
37. Jose
38. Patrick
39. Scott
40. Paul
41. Nathan
42. Sean
43. Zachary
44. Travis
45. Dustin
46. Gregory
47. Kenneth
48. Alexander
49. Jesse
50. Tyler

Most popular names of the 1980s (girls)

1. Jessica
2. Jennifer
3. Amanda
4. Ashley
5. Sarah
6. Stephanie
7. Melissa
8. Nicole
9. Elizabeth
10. Heather
11. Tiffany
12. Michelle
13. Amber
14. Megan
15. Rachel
16. Amy
17. Lauren
18. Kimberly
19. Christina
20. Brittany
21. Crystal
22. Rebecca
23. Laura
24. Emily
25. Danielle
26. Samantha
27. Angela
28. Erin
29. Kelly
30. Sara
31. Lisa
32. Katherine
33. Andrea
34. Mary
35. Jamie
36. Erica
37. Courtney
38. Kristen
39. Shannon
40. April
41. Maria
42. Kristin
43. Katie
44. Lindsey
45. Alicia
46. Vanessa
47. Lindsay
48. Christine
49. Allison
50. Kathryn

Most popular names of the 1970s (boys)

1. Michael
2. Christopher
3. Jason
4. David
5. James
6. John
7. Robert
8. Brian
9. William
10. Matthew
11. Daniel
12. Joseph
13. Kevin
14. Eric
15. Jeffrey
16. Richard
17. Scott
18. Mark
19. Steven
20. Timothy
21. Thomas
22. Anthony
23. Charles
24. Jeremy
25. Joshua
26. Ryan
27. Paul
28. Andrew
29. Gregory
30. Chad
31. Kenneth
32. Stephen
33. Jonathan
34. Shawn
35. Jose
36. Aaron
37. Patrick
38. Adam
39. Justin
40. Edward
41. Sean
42. Benjamin
43. Todd
44. Donald
45. Ronald
46. Keith
47. Bryan
48. Gary
49. George
50. Nathan

Most popular names of the 1970s (girls)

1. Jennifer
2. Amy
3. Melissa
4. Michelle
5. Kimberly
6. Lisa
7. Angela
8. Heather
9. Stephanie
10. Jessica
11. Elizabeth
12. Nicole
13. Rebecca
14. Kelly
15. Mary
16. Christina
17. Amanda
18. Sarah
19. Laura
20. Julie
21. Shannon
22. Christine
23. Tammy
24. Karen
25. Tracy
26. Maria
27. Dawn
28. Susan
29. Andrea
30. Tina
31. Cynthia
32. Patricia
33. Rachel
34. April
35. Lori
36. Crystal
37. Wendy
38. Stacy
39. Sandra
40. Jamie
41. Erin
42. Carrie
43. Tara
44. Tiffany
45. Monica
46. Danielle
47. Stacey
48. Teresa
49. Pamela
50. Sara

Most popular names of the 1960s (boys)

1. Michael
2. David
3. John
4. James
5. Robert
6. Mark
7. William
8. Richard
9. Thomas
10. Jeffrey
11. Steven
12. Joseph
13. Timothy
14. Kevin
15. Scott
16. Brian
17. Charles
18. Daniel
19. Paul
20. Christopher
21. Kenneth
22. Anthony
23. Gregory
24. Ronald
25. Donald
26. Gary
27. Eric
28. Stephen
29. Edward
30. Douglas
31. Todd
32. Patrick
33. George
34. Keith
35. Larry
36. Matthew
37. Terry
38. Andrew
39. Randy
40. Dennis
41. Jerry
42. Peter
43. Jose
44. Frank
45. Craig
46. Raymond
47. Jeffrey
48. Bruce
49. Mike
50. Tony

Most popular names of the 1960s (girls)

1. Lisa
2. Mary
3. Karen
4. Susan
5. Kimberly
6. Patricia
7. Linda
8. Donna
9. Michelle
10. Cynthia
11. Sandra
12. Deborah
13. Pamela
14. Tammy
15. Laura
16. Lori
17. Elizabeth
18. Julie
19. Jennifer
20. Brenda
21. Angela
22. Barbara
23. Debra
24. Sharon
25. Teresa
26. Nancy
27. Christine
28. Cheryl
29. Denise
30. Tina
31. Kelly
32. Maria
33. Kathleen
34. Melissa
35. Amy
36. Robin
37. Dawn
38. Carol
39. Diane
40. Rebecca
41. Tracy
42. Kathy
43. Theresa
44. Kim
45. Stephanie
46. Rhonda
47. Wendy
48. Cindy
49. Janet
50. Michele

Most popular names of the 1950s (boys)

1. Michael
2. James
3. Robert
4. John
5. David
6. William
7. Richard
8. Thomas
9. Mark
10. Charles
11. Steven
12. Gary
13. Joseph
14. Donald
15. Ronald
16. Kenneth
17. Paul
18. Larry
19. Daniel
20. Stephen
21. Dennis
22. Timothy
23. Edward
24. Jeffrey
25. George
26. Gregory
27. Kevin
28. Douglas
29. Terry
30. Anthony
31. Jerry
32. Bruce
33. Randy
34. Frank
35. Brian
36. Scott
37. Raymond
38. Roger
39. Peter
40. Patrick
41. Lawrence
42. Keith
43. Wayne
44. Danny
45. Alan
46. Gerald
47. Jose
48. Carl
49. Christopher
50. Ricky

Most popular names of the 1950s (girls)

1. Mary
2. Linda
3. Patricia
4. Susan
5. Deborah
6. Barbara
7. Debra
8. Karen
9. Nancy
10. Donna
11. Cynthia
12. Sandra
13. Pamela
14. Sharon
15. Kathleen
16. Carol
17. Diane
18. Brenda
19. Cheryl
20. Elizabeth
21. Janet
22. Kathy
23. Margaret
24. Janice
25. Carolyn
26. Denise
27. Judy
28. Teresa
29. Rebecca
30. Christine
31. Joyce
32. Shirley
33. Judith
34. Catherine
35. Betty
36. Maria
37. Beverly
38. Lisa
39. Laura
40. Gloria
41. Theresa
42. Connie
43. Gail
44. Julie
45. Ann
46. Martha
47. Joan
48. Paula
49. Robin
50. Bonnie

Most popular names in 2001 (boys)

(Social Security Administration Statistics)

1. Jacob
2. Michael
3. Matthew
4. Joshua
5. Christopher
6. Nicholas
7. Andrew
8. Joseph
9. Daniel
10. William

Most popular names in 2001 (girls)

(Social Security Administration Statistics)

1. Emily
2. Madison
3. Hannah
4. Ashley
5. Alexis
6. Samantha
7. Sarah
8. Abigail
9. Elizabeth
10. Jessica

Boys

Aaron
(Hebrew) revered; sharer
Aarone, Ahren, Ahron, Arin, Aron, Arron

Abacus
(Word as name) device for doing calcalutions; clever
Abacas, Abakus, Abba

Abbas
(Arabic) harsh
Ab, Abba

Abbey, Abby
(Hebrew) spiritual
Abbie, Abie

Abbott
(Hebrew) father; leader
Abbitt, Abott, Abotte

Abdiel
(Arabic) serving Allah

Abdul
(Arabic) servant of Allah
Ab, Abdel, Abul

Abdul-Jabbar
(Arabic) comforting

Abdullah
(Arabic) Allah's servant
Abdallah, Abdulah, Abdulla

Abe
(Hebrew) short for Abraham; father of many
Abey, Abie

Abel
(Hebrew) vital
Abe, Abele, Abell, Abey, Abie, Able

Abelard
(German) firm
Abbey, Abby, Abe, Abel, Abelerd

Abelino
(Spanish) from Biblical Abel, son of Adam and Eve; naive
Abel, Able

Aberdeen
(Place name) serene
Aber, Dean, Deen

Abilene
(Place name) town in Texas; good-old-boy
Abalene, Abileen

Abir
(Hebrew) strong
Abeer

Abner
(Hebrew) cheerful leader
Abnir, Abnor

Abraham
(Hebrew) fathering multitudes
Abe, Abrahim, Abrahm, Abram, Bram

Abram
(Hebrew) short for Abraham
Abe, Bram

Abraxas
(Spanish) bright
Aba

Abs
(Hebrew) short for Absalom; muscular
Abe

Absalom
(Hebrew) peaceful; handsome
Abe, Abs

Abundio
(Spanish) living in abundance
Abun, Abund

Ace
(Latin) one; unity
Acey

Achilles
(Greek) hero of *The Iliad*
Achille, Ackill, Akilles

Acker
(American)
Aker

Acton
   (English) sturdy; oaks
   *Acten, Actin, Actohn,
   Actone*
Adair
   (Scottish) negotiator
   Adaire, Adare, Ade
Adalberto
   (Spanish) bright;
   dignified
   Adal, Berto
Adam
   (Hebrew) first man;
   original
   *Ad, Adahm, Adamo,
   Addam, Addams, Addie,
   Addy, Adem*
Adamson
   (Hebrew) Adam's son
   Adamsen, Adamsson
Adan
   (Irish) bold spirit
   *Aden, Adin, Adyn, Aidan,
   Aiden*
Addae
   (African) the sun
Addis
   (English) short for
   Addison; masculine
   *Addace, Addice, Addy,
   Adis*
Addison
   (English) Adam's son
   Ad, Adison, Adisson

Addy
   (German) awesome;
   outgoing
   Addi, Addie, Adi
Adel
   (German) royal
   *Adal, Addey, Addie,
   Addy*
Adelard
   (German) brave
   Addy, Adelarde
Adeone
   (Welsh) royal
   Addy, Adeon
Adio
   (African) devout
Adlai
   (Hebrew) ornamented
   *Ad, Addy, Adlay, Adley,
   Adlie*
Adler
   (German) eagle-eyed
   Adlar
Adnee
   (English) loner
   Adni, Adny
Ado
   (American) respected
   Ad, Addy
Adolf
   (German) sly wolf
   Adolfe, Adolph

Adolfus
   (German) form of
   Adolphus
Adonis
   (Greek) gorgeous
   (Aphrodite's love in
   mythology)
   *Addonis, Adones,
   Adonys, Andonice*
Adrian
   (Latin) wealthy; dark-
   skinned
   *Ade, Addie, Adreeyan,
   Adriann, Adrien, Adrion,
   Adryan, Aydrien,
   Aydrienne*
Adriano
   (Italian) wealthy
   Adriannho, Adrianno
Adriel
   (Hebrew) God's follower
   Adrial, Adryel
Adrien
   (French) form of Adrian
   Ade, Adriene, Adrienn
Adya
   (Russian) man from
   Adria
Adyn
   (Irish) manly
   *Adann, Ade, Aden,
   Aidan, Ayden*

Aeneas
(Greek) worthy of praise
*Aineas, Aineias, Eneas,
Eneis*

Afton
(English) dignified
Affton, Aftawn, Aften

Agamemnon
(Greek) slow but sure
Agamem

Agustin
(Latin) dignified
*Aguste, Auggie,
Augustin*

Ahab
(Hebrew) father's
brother; sea captain in
Moby Dick

Ahmad, Ahmed
(Arabic) praised man
Achmed, Amad, Amed

Aidan
(Irish) fiery spirit
*Adan, Adin, Aiden,
Aydan*

Aiken
(English) hardy;
oakhewn
Aikin, Ayken, Aykin

Ainsley
(Scottish) in a meadow
*Ansley, Ainslee, Ainsli,
Aynsley, Aynslie*

Ajax
(Greek) daring
Ajacks

Ajay
(American) spontaneous
A.J., Aj, Ajah

Akeem
(Arab) form of Hakeem;
skilled; introspective
*Ackeem, Ackim, Akieme,
Akim, Hakeem, Hakim*

Aki
(Scandinavian)

Akilles
(Greek) form of Achilles;
heroic

Aksel
(Scandinavian) calm

Al
(Irish) short for
Alexander and Alan;
attractive

Aladdin
(Arabic) believer
Al, Aladdein, Aladen

Alain
(French) form of Alan
and Allen
Allain, Alun

Alair
(Gaelic) happy
Alaire

Alan
(Irish) handsome boy
*Al, Aland, Alen, Allan,
Allen, Alley, Allie, Allin,
Allyn, Alon, Alun*

Alando
(Spanish) form of Alan;
attractive
*Al, Alaindo, Alan , Aland,
Alano, Allen, Allie, Alun,
Alundo, Alyn*

Alasdair
(Scottish) form of
Alistair; highbrow
*Al, Alasdaire, Alasdare,
Alisdair*

Alastair
(Scottish) strong leader
*Alastere, Alastaire,
Allastair, Alystair*

Alaster
(American) form of
Alastair; staunch
advocate
Alaste, Alester, Allaster

Alban
(Latin) white man (from
Alba's white hill)
*Abion, Albee, Alben,
Albi, Albie, Albin, Alby*

Albanse
(Invented) from the place name Albany, New York; white
Alban, Albance, Albanee, Albany, Albie, Alby

Albany
(Place name) restless
Albanee, Albanie

Albert
(German) distinguished
Al, Alberto, Albie, Alby, Ally

Alberto
(Italian) distinguished
Al, Albert, Bertie

Albie
(German) short for Albert; smart
Albee, Albi, Alby

Albion
(Greek) old-fashioned
Albionne, Albyon

Alcordia
(American) in accord with others
Alcord, Alkie, Alky

Alden
(English) wise
Al, Aldan, Aldon

Aldo
(Italian) older one; jovial
Aldoh

Aldorse
(American) form of Aldo; old
Al, Aldo, Aldorce, Aldors

Aldred
(English) advisor; judgmental
Al, Aldrid, Aldy, Alldred

Aldren
(English) old friend
Al, Aldran, Aldie, Aldrun, Aldy, Aldryn

Aldrich
(English) wise advisor
Aldie, Aldrick, Aldrish, Alldrich

Alec
(Greek) high-minded
Al, Aleck, Alic

Alejandro
(Spanish) defender; bold and brave
Alejandra

Alek
(Russian) short for Aleksei; brilliant
Aleks

Aleksander
(Greek and Polish) defender
Alek, Sander

Aleksei
(Russian) defender; brilliant
Alek, Alik, Alexi

Aleppo
(Place name) easygoing
Alepo

Alessandro
(Italian) helpful; defender
Allessandro

Alex
(Greek) short for Alexander; leader
Alecs, Alix, Allex

Alexander
(Greek) great leader; helpful
Al, Alec, Alex, Alexandor, Alexsander

Alexandros
(Greek) form of Alexander; helpful
Alesandros, Alexandras

Alexis
(Greek) short for Alexander
Alexace, Alexes, Alexi, Alexy, Lex

Alfeus
(Hebrew) follower
Alpheus

Alfie
(English) short for Alfred; friendly
Alf, Alfi, Alfy

Alfonso
(Spanish) bright;
prepared
*Alf, Alfie, Alfons,
Alfonsin, Alfonso,
Alfonz, Alphonsus, Fons,
Fonzie, Fonzy*

Alfred
(English) counselor
*Al, Alf, Alfie, Alfrede,
Alfryd*

Alfredo
(Italian and Spanish)
advisor
*Alf, Alfie, Alfreedo,
Alfrido*

Alfredrick
(American) combo of
Alfred and Fredrick;
pretentious
*Al, Alf, Alfred, Freddy,
Fredrik*

Alger
(German) hardworking
Algar

Algernon
(English) man with facial
hair
Al, Alger, Algie, Algy

Algia
(German) prepared; kind
Alge, Algie

Ali
(Arabic) greatest
Alee, Aly

Ali-Baba
(Literature) *A Thousand
and One Nights*

Alisander
(Greek) form of
Alexander
Alissander, Alsandare

Allan
(Irish) form of Alan
Allane

Allard
(English) brave man
Alard

Allegheny
(Place name) mountains
of the Appalachian
system; grand
*Al, Alleg, Alleganie,
Alleghenie*

Allen
(Irish) handsome
*Al, Alen, Allie, Allin,
Allyn, Alon*

Almar
(German) form of
Almarine; strong
Al, Almarr, Almer

Almere
(American) director
Almer

Alonzo
(Spanish) enthusiastic
*Alonso, Alonze, Elonzo,
Lon*

Aloysius
(German) famed
Aloisius

Alphonse
(German) distinguished
*Alf, Alfonse, Alphonso,
Fonsi, Fonsie, Fonz,
Fonzie*

Alps
(Place name) climber
Alp

Alquince
(American) old and fifth
*Al, Alquense, Alquin,
Alquins, Alquinse,
Alqwence*

Alrick
(German) leader
Alrec, Alric

Alroy
(American) combo of Al
and Roy; sedate
Al, Alroi

Alston
(English) serious;
nobleman
Allston, Alsten, Alstin

Altarius
(African-American) from
Greek Altair; shining star
*Altare, Altair, Altareus,
Alterius, Alltair, Al*

Alter
(Hebrew) old; will live to
be old

Alto
(Place name) town in
Texas; alto voice;
easygoing
Al

Alton
(English) excellent; kind
*Allton, Altawn, Alten,
Altyn*

Altus
(Latin) form of Alta; high
Al, Alta

Alva
(Hebrew) intelligent;
beloved friend
Alvah

Alvarado
(Spanish) peacemaker
*Alvaradoh, Alvaro, Alvie,
Alvy*

Alvaro
(Spanish) just
*Alvaroh, Alvarro, Alvey,
Alvie, Alvy*

Alvern
(English) old friend
Al, Alverne, Alvurn

Alvin
(Latin) light-haired;
loved
Alv, Alven, Alvie

Alvincent
(American) combo of
Alvin and Vincent; giving
friend
*Alvin, Alvince, Vin,
Vince, Vincent, Vinse*

Alvis
(American) form of Elvis;
old friend
Al, Alviss, Alvy

Amadayus
(Invented) form of
Amadeus
Amadayes

Amadeo
(Italian) blessed by God;
artistic

Amadeus
(Latin) god-loving
Amad, Amadayus

Amado
(Spanish) loved
*Amadee, Amadeo,
Amadi, Amadis, Amadus,
Amando*

Amadour
(French) loved
Amador, Amadore

Amal
(Hebrew) hardworking;
optimistic
Amahl, Amhall

Amar
(Arabic) making a home
Ammar

Amarillo
(Place name) in Spanish,
it means yellow;
renegade
Amarille, Amarilo

Amato
(Italian) loving
Amahto, Amatoh

Ambrose
(German) everlasting
*Amba, Ambie, Ambroce,
Amby*

America
(Place name) patriotic

Americo
(Spanish) patriotic
*Ame, America, Americus,
Ameriko*

Amerigo
(Italian) ruler (name of
Italian explorer)
Amer, Americo, Ameriko

Ames
(French) friendly
Aims

Amiel
(Hebrew) my people's
God
Ameal, Amheel, Ammiel

Amin
(Arabic) honorable;
dependable
Aman, Ameen

Amir
(Arabic) royal; ruler
Ameer, Amire

Amiti
(Japanese) endless friend

Amor
(Latin) love
Amerie, Amoree, Amori, Amorie

Amory
(German) home ruler
Amor

Amos
(Hebrew) strong
Amus

Ampy
(American) fast
Amp, Ampee, Ampey, Amps

Amyas
(Latin) lovable
Aimeus, Ameus, Amias, Amyes

An
(Chinese) peaceful; safe

Anan
(Irish) outdoorsy
An, Annan

Anastasius
(Greek) reborn
Anastase, Anastasio, Anasticius

Anatole
(French) exotic
Anatol, Anatoly, Anitolle

Ancel
(French) creative
Ance, Ancell, Anse, Ansel, Ansell

Andel
(Scandinavian) honored

Ander
(English) form of Andrew; masculine

Anders
(Swedish) masculine
Ander, Andirs, Andries, Andy

Andras
(French) form of Andrew; masculine
Andrae, Andres, Andrus, Ondrae, Ondras

André
(French) masculine
Andre, Andree

Andreas
(Greek) masculine
Andrieas, Adryus, Andy

Andres
(Spanish) macho
Andrez, Andy

Andretti
(Italian) speedy
Andrette, Andy

Andrew
(Greek) manly and brave
Aindrew, Anders, Andi, Andie, Andreas, Andres, Andru, Andrue, Andy

Andros
(Polish) masculine
Andrus

Andru
(Greek) form of Andrew; masculine
Andrue

Andrzej
(Polish) manly

Andy
(Greek) short for Andrew; masculine
Andee, Andie

Anferny
(American) variation of Anthony
Andee, Anfernee, Anferney, Anferni, Anfernie, Anfurny

Angel
(Greek) angelic messenger
Ange, Angele

Angelberto
(Spanish) shining angel
Angel, Angelbert, Bert, Berto

Angelo
(Italian) angelic
Ange, Angeloh, Anjelo

Angle
(Invented) word as name; spin-doctor
Ange, Angul

Anglin
(Greek) angelic
Anglen, Anglinn, Anglun

Angus
(Scottish) standout; important
Ange, Angos

Anibal
(Spanish) brave noble

Aniello
(Italian) risk-taker

Aniol
(Polish) angel
Ahnjol, Ahnyolle

Ankoma
(African) last-born child

Annatto
(Botanical) tree; tough
Annatta

Anolus
(Greek) masculine
Ano, Anol

Anrue
(American) masculine
Anrae, Anroo

Ansel
(French) creative
Ancell, Anse, Ansell

Anselm
(German) protective
Anse, Ansehlm, Ansellm

Anselmo
(Spanish) protected by God
Ancel, Ancelmo, Anse, Ansel, Anselm, Anzelmo, Selmo

Anson
(German) divine male
Anse, Ansonn, Ansun

Anthony
(Latin) outstanding
Anth, Anthoney, Anthonie, Anton, Tony

Antoine
(French) worthy of praise
Antone, Antwan, Antwon, Antwone

Anton
(Latin) outstanding
Antan, Antawn

Antonce
(African-American) form of Anthony; valued
Antawnce

Antonio
(Spanish) superb
Antone, Antonioh, Antonyo, Antonyia, Tony

Antony
(Latin) good
Antawny, Antonah, Antone, Antoney, Antonie, Tone, Tony

Antrinell
(African-American) valued
Antrie, Antrinel, Antry

Antroy
(African-American) form of Anthony; prized
Antroe, Antroye

Antwan
(American) form of Antoine; achiever

Antwone
(American) variant of Antoine; achiever
Antwonn

Anwar
(Arabic) shining
Anwhour

Anzelm
(Polish) protective
Ahnzelm

Apolinar
(Spanish) manly and wise
Apollo

Apollo
(Greek) masculine (a god in mythology)
Apolloh, Apolo, Apoloniah, Applonian

Apostle
(Greek) follower; disciple
Apos

Apostolos
(Greek) disciple
Apos

Apple
(American) favorite;
wholesome
Apel

Aquila
(Spanish) eagle-eyed
Aquile, Aquilla

Aquileo
(Spanish) warrior
Akweleo, Aquilo

Aramis
(French) clever
*Arames, Aramyse,
Arhames*

Arbet
(Last name as first
name) high
Arb, Arby

Arceneaux
(French) friendly;
heavenly
Arce, Arcen, Arceno

Arch
(English) short for Archie
and Archibald; athletic
Arche

Archer
(English) athletic;
bowman
Arch, Archie

Archibald
(German) bold leader
Arch, Archibold, Archie

Archie
(English) short for
Archibald; bold
Arch, Archi, Archy

Ardee
(American) ardent
Ard, Ardie, Ardy

Ardell
(Latin) go-getter
Ardel

Arden, Ardon
(Latin) ball-of-fire
*Ard, Arda, Ardie, Ardin,
Ardon, Arrden*

Ardmohr
(Latin) more ardent than
others
Ard, Ardmoor, Ardmore

Arenda
(Spanish)

Aristeo
(Spanish) best
Aris, Aristio, Aristo, Ary

Argan
(American) leader
*Argee, Argen, Argey,
Argi, Argie, Argun*

Argento
(Spanish) silver
Arge, Argey, Argi, Argy

Argus
(Greek) careful; bright
Arjus

Ari
(Greek) best
Ahree, Arie, Arih, Arri

Aric
(English) leader
Arec

Ariel
(Hebrew) God's spirited
lion
*Ari, Arie, Ariele, Arielle,
Arriel*

Aries
(Greek) god of war
(mythology)
Arees

Arion
(Greek) enchanted man
Ari, Arrian, Arie, Ariohn

Aristides
(Greek) son of the
outstanding
Ari, Aris

Aristotle
(Greek) best man
*Ari, Aris, Aristie,
Aristottle*

Arkyn
(Scandinavian) royal
offspring
Ark, Arken, Arkin

Arle
(Irish) sworn
Arlee, Arley, Arly

Arledge
(English) lives by a lake
Arleedj, Arles, Arlidge

Arleigh
(Irish) sworn
Arly

Arlen
(Irish) dedicated
Arl, Arlan, Arle, Arlin

Arlis
(Hebrew) dedicated; in charge
Arlas, Arles, Arless, Arly

Arlo
(German) strong
Arloh

Arlonn
(Irish) sworn; cheerful
Arlan, Arlann, Arlen, Arlon

Arlys
(Hebrew) pledged
Arlis

Arm
(English) arm
Arma, Arman, Arme

Armand
(German) strong soldier
Armando, Arme, Ormand

Armando
(Spanish) entertainer
Armand, Arme, Armondo

Armani
(Italian) army; disciplined talent
Amani, Arman, Armanie, Armon, Armoni

Armen
(Spanish) from the name Armenta
Arme, Arment, Armenta

Armitage
(Last name as first name) safe haven
Armi, Armita, Army

Armon
(Hebrew) strong as a fortress
Arman, Arme, Armen, Armin

Armstrong
(English) strong-armed
Arme, Army

Arnaud
(French) strong
Arnaldo, Arnauld

Arnborn
(Scandinavian) eagle-bear; animal instincts
Arn, Arne, Arnborne, Arnbourne

Arndt
(German) strong
Arne, Arnee, Arney, Arni, Arnie

Arne
(German) short for Arnold; ruler
Arn

Arnie
(German) short for Arnold; ruler
Arne, Arney, Arni, Arny

Arnithan
(African-American) form of Arnie and Jonathan; eagle-eyed
Arnee, Arnie, Nithan

Arno
(German) far-sighted
Arn, Arne, Arnoh

Arnold
(German) ruler; strong
Arnald, Arne, Arnie, Arny

Arnome
(Invented) powerful
Arnom

Arnst
(Scandinavian) eagle-eyed (arn means eagle)
Arn

Arnulfo
(Spanish) strong
Arne, Arnie, Arny

Aron
(Hebrew) generous
Aaron, Arron, Erinn

Arsenio
(Greek) macho; virile
Arne, Arsinio, Arsonio

Art
(English) bear-like;
wealthy
Arte, Artie

Artemus
(Greek) gifted
*Art, Artemis, Artie,
Artimus*

Arthisus
(Origin unknown) stuffy
Arth, Arthi, Arthy

Arthur
(English) distinguished
*Art, Arther, Arthor, Artie,
Artur, Arty, Aurthur*

Artie
(English) short for
Arthur; wealthy
Art, Artee, Arty

Arturo
(Italian) talented
Art, Arture, Arturro

Arun
(Hindi) the color of the
sky before dawn

Arvin
(German) friendly
Arv, Arven, Arvy

Arwen
(German) friend
*Arwee, Arwene, Arwhen,
Arwy*

Ary
(Hebrew) lionine; fierce
Ari, Arye

Asa
(Hebrew) healer
Ase, Aza

Ash
(Botanical) tree; bold
Ashe

Ashbel
(Hebrew) fiery god

Ashby
(Scandinavian) brash
*Ashbee, Ashbey, Ashie,
Ashy*

Asher
(Hebrew) joyful
Ash, Ashur

Ashford
(English) spunky
Ash, Ashferd

Ashley
(English) smooth
Ash, Ashie, Ashlee, Ashly

Ashton
(English) handsome
Ashteen, Ashtin

Atam
(American) form of
Adam; tough
Atame, Atom, Atym

Atanacio
(Spanish) everlasting
Atan, Atanasio

Atkins
(Last name as first
name) linked; known
Atkin

Atlas
(Greek) courier of
greatness
Atlass

Atticus
(Greek) ethical
Aticus, Attikus

Attila
(Gothic) powerful
Atila, Atlya, Att

Atwell
(English) place name;
the well; full of gusto

Atwood
(English) place name;
the woods; outdoorsy

Auberon
(German) like a bear;
highborn
Aube

Aubert
(German) leader
Auber, Aubey

Aubin
(French) ruler; elfin
Auben

Aubrey
(English) ruler
*Aube, Aubree, Aubry,
Bree*

Auburn
(Latin) brown with red
cast; tenacious
Aubern, Aubie, Auburne

Auden
(English) old friend
Aude, Audie

Audencio
(Spanish)
Auden

Audie
(German) strong man
Aude, Audee

Augie
(Latin) short for
Augustus
Aug, Auggie , Augy

August
(Latin) determined
Auge, Augie

Augustine
(Latin) serious and
revered
*Aug, Augie, August,
Augustene, Augustin*

Augusto, Augustin
(Spanish) respected;
serious
*Agusto, Augey, Auggie,
Austeo*

Augustus
(Latin) highly esteemed
*Aug, Auge, Augie,
August*

Aulie
(English) form of Audley
Awlie

Aurelius
(Latin) golden son
Aurel, Aurie, Aury

Austin
(Latin); capital of Texas;
ingenious;
Southwestern
*Aust, Austen, Auston,
Austyn*

Auther
(American) form of
Arthur; brave and smart
Authar, Authur

Averill
(French) April-born child
Ave, Averil, Avryl, Avrylle

Avery
(English) softspoken
Avary, Ave, Averie, Avry

Avion
(French) flyer
Aveonn, Avyon, Avyun

Axel
(German) peaceful;
contemporary
Aksel, Ax, Axe, Axil

Ayo
(African) happy

Ayson
(Origin unknown) lucky
Aison

Azael
(Spanish) God-loved
Azzael

Babe
(American) athlete

Babu
(Hindi) fierce

Bacchus
(Greek) reveler; jaded
Baakus, Bakkus, Bakus

Bach
(Last name as first
name) talented
Bok

Bacon
(English) literary;
outspoken
Baco, Bake, Bakon

Badger
(Last name as first
name) difficult
*Badge, Badgeant, Bage,
Bagent*

Bailey
(French) attentive
Baile, Baily, Baley, Baylie

Bainbridge
(Irish) bridge; negotiator
*Bain, Banebridge,
Beebee*

Baines
(Last name as first name) pale
Baine, Baynes

Bainlon
(American) form of Bailey; pale
Bailey, Baily

Baird
(Irish) singer/poet; creative
Bard, Bayrde

Bakari
(African) promising

Baker
(English) baker
Baiker, Baykar

Baldemar
(Spanish) form of Balthasar; brave and wise
Baldy

Baldric
(German) leader
Baldrick, Baledric, Bauldric

Baldridge
(English) persuasive

Baldwin
(German) steadfast friend
Baldwinn, Baldwynn, Bally

Baley
(American) form of Bailey
Baleye

Balfour
(Scottish) landowner
Balf, Balfore

Balfre
(Spanish) brave

Ballance
(American) courageous
Balance, Ballans

Ballard
(German) brave
Ballerd

Balthasar
(Greek) God save the king
Bath, Bathazar

Balwin
(Last name as first name) friendly and brave
Ball, Winn

Bancroft
(English) bean field; gardener
Banc, Bankie, Bankroft

Bandy
(Origin unknown) gregarious
Bandee, Bandi

Banks
(Last name as first name) focused
Bank

Banning
(Irish) fair-haired
Bannie, Banny, Bannyng

Barclay
(Scottish) audacious man; birch tree meadow
Bar, Barclaye, Bark, Barklay, Barky

Bard
(Irish) singer
Bar, Barr

Barden
(English) peaceful; valley-dweller
Bardon

Bargo
(Last name as first name) outspoken
Barg

Bark
(English) short for Barker; outgoing
Birk

Barker
(English) handles bark; lumberjack
Bark, Barkker

Barlow
(English) hardy
Barloe, Barlowe

Barman
(Last name as first name) bright; blessed
Barr

Barn
(American) word as name; works in barns
Barnee, Barney, Barny

Barnabas
(Hebrew) seer; comforter
Barn, Barnaby, Barnebus, Barney, Barnie, Barny

Barnaby
(Hebrew) companionable
Barn, Barnabee, Barnabie, Barnie, Barny

Barner
(English) mercurial
Barn, Barnerr, Barney, Barny

Barnes
(English) powerful; bear

Barnett
(English) leader of men
Barn, Barnet, Barney

Barney
(English) short for Barnett
Barn, Barni, Barnie, Barny

Barnum
(German) safe; barn
Barnham, Barnhem, Barnie

Baron
(English) noble leader
Bare, Baren, Barren, Baryne

Barrett
(German) strong and bearlike
Bar, Baret, Barett, Barette, Barry

Barrington
(English) dignified
Bare, Baring, Berrington

Barry
(Irish) candid
Barre, Barrie, Bary

Bart
(Hebrew) persistent
Bartee, Bartie, Barty

Bartley
(Last name as first name) rural man
Bart, Bartle, Bartlee, Bartli, Bartly

Barth
(Hebrew) protective
Bart, Barthe, Barts

Bartholomew
(Hebrew) friendly; earthy
Bart, Barthlolmewe, Bartie

Barto
(Spanish) form of Bartholomew; upward
Bartelo, Bartol, Bartoli, Bartolo, Bartolomeo

Barton
(English) persistent man; Bart's town
Bart, Barty

Bartram
(English) intelligent
Bart, Barty

Baruch
(Hebrew) most blessed
Barry

Basford
(American) charming; low-profile
Bas, Basferd, Basfor

Bash
(American) party-loving
Bashi, Bashey, Bashy

Basil
(Greek) regal
Basel, Basey, Basile, Bazil

Bass
(Last name as first name) fish; charmer
Bassee, Bassey, Bassi, Bassy

Bassett
(English) small man
Baset, Basett, Basey, Basse

Bastian
(Greek) respected
Bastien, Bastyun

Basye
(American) home-based; centered
Base, Basey

Batch
(French) short for Bachelor; unmarried man
Bat, Bats, Batsh

Bates
(English) romantic
Bate

Baxley
(English) from the meadow; outdoorsy
Bax, Baxlee, Baxli

Baxter
(English) tenacious
Bax, Baxey, Baxie, Baxther

Bay
(English) hair of russet; vocal
Baye, Bayie

Bayard
(English) russet-haired
Bay, Baye, Bayerd

Baylon
(English) from the bay; outdoorsman

Bazzy
(American) loud
Bazzee, Bazzi, Bazzie

Bazooka
(American) fun-loving; unusual
Bazookah

Beach
(English) fun-loving
Bee, Beech

Beacher
(English) pale-skinned; beech tree
Beach, Beachie, Beachy, Beecher

Beale
(French) attractive
Beal, Beally

Beamer
(English) musician
Beam, Beamy, Beemer

Bean
(Scottish) lively
Beann

Beasley
(English) nurturing; pea field
Beas, Beasie, Beesly

Beate
(German) serious
Bay, Baye, Bayahtah, Beahta, Beahtae

Beau
(French) handsome man
Beaubeau, Bo, Boo, Bow

Beauford
(French) attractive
Beau, Beauf

Beaumont
(French) attractive and strong
Bo, Bomont, Bowmont, Beau

Beauregard
(French) a face much admired
Beau, Beauregarde, Beaurigard, Bobo

Beaver
(French) tenacious
Beav, Beever, Bevoh, The Beave

Bebe
(Spanish) baby
Be-Be

Becher
(Hebrew) firstborn
Bee

Beck
(English) stream; laid-back
Bec, Becc, Becke, Becker, Bek

Becker
(English) calm
Bekker

Beckett
(English) methodical
Beck, Beket, Bekette

Bede
(English) prayerful
Bea, Bead, Beda, Bedah

Bedro
(Spanish) form of Pedro;
surprising
Bed

Beebe
(English) tending bees;
tenacious
B.B., Bee-be, Beebee

Beeson
(Last name as first
name) son of
beekeeper; wary
Bees

Beggs
(Last name as first
name) admired
Begg, Begs

Beige
(American) calm
Bayge

Belden
(English) plain-spoken
*Beld, Beldene, Beldon,
Bell, Bellden, Belldon*

Bell
(French) handsome man

Bellamy
(French) beautiful friend
*Belamie, Bell, Bellamie,
Bellmee, Belmy*

Bellindo
(German) ferocious;
attractive
*Balindo, Belindo,
Belyndo*

Belmount
(French) gracious
*Belmon, Belmond,
Belmonde, Belmont,
Belmonta*

Belton
(English) from a lovely
town of bells
Beltan, Belten

Belvin
(American) form of
Melvin; attractive
Belven

Ben
(Hebrew) short for
Benjamin; wonderful
*Benjy, Bennie, Benno,
Benny*

Bence
(American) short for
Benson; good
Bens, Bense, Binse

Bend
(American) word as
name; lithe
Ben

Benedict
(Latin) blessed man
*Ben, Benedik, Benne,
Bennie, Benny*

Bender
(American) tweaker;
diplomatic
Ben, Bend

Bendo
(American) soothing
Ben, Bend

Beniah
(Hebrew) articulate
Benia, Benyah

Benicio
(Spanish) adventurous
Benecio, Benito

Benito
(Italian) blessed
Benedo, Beni, Beno

Benjamin
(Hebrew) son of right
hand; wonderful boy
*Behnjamin, Ben,
Benjamen, Benjamine,
Benjy, Benni, Bennie,
Benny, Benyamin*

Bennett
(French) blessed
*Ben, Benet, Benett,
Bennette, Benny*

Benno
(Italian) form of Ben;
wonderful; best
Beno

Benny
(Hebrew) short for
Benjamin
Benge, Benjy, Benni,
Bennie

Benoit
(French) growing and
flourishing
Ben, Benoyt

Bensey
(American) easygoing;
fine
Bence, Bens, Bensee

Benson
(Hebrew) son of Ben;
brave heart
Bensahn, Bensen

Bent
(English) short for
Benton
Bynt

Bentley
(English) clever
Bent, Bentlee, Leye

Benton
(English) formidable
Bentan, Bentawn,
Bentone

Benvenuto
(Italian) welcomed child
Ben

Benz
(German) from carmaker
Mercedes-Benz; upscale
Bens

Ber
(Hebrew) bear

Berfit
(Origin unknown)
farming; outdoorsman
Berf

Berg
(German) tall; mountain
Bergh, Berj, Burg, Burgh

Berger
(French) watchful;
shepherd
Bergher, Bergie

Bergin
(Swedish) loquacious;
lives on the hill
Bergan, Berge, Bergen,
Berger, Bergin, Birgin

Berkeley
(English) place name;
idolized
Berk, Berkeley, Berki,
Berkie, Berklee, Berkley,
Berklie, Berkly, Berky

Berko
(Hebrew) bear
Ber

Berks
(American) adored
Berk, Berke, Berkelee,
Berkey, Berkli, Berksie,
Berkslee, Berky, Birklee,
Birksey, Burks, Burksey

Berman
(German) steady
Bermahn, Bermen,
Bermin

Bernabe
(German) bold
Bernabee, Bernabey,
Bernaby, Bernby,
Bernebe, Berns, Bernus,
Burnby

Bernal
(German) bear-like
Bern

Bernard
(German) brave and
dependable
Bern, Bernarde, Bernee,
Bernerd, Bernie, Berny,
Burnard

Bernardo
(Spanish) brave; bear
Berna, Bernardo,
Barnardoh, Berny

Bernave
(American) form of
Bernard; smart
Bernav, Bernee,
Berneve, Berni

Bernd
(German) bear-like
Bern, Berne, Bernee,
Berney, Berny

Berne
(German) courageous
*Bern, Berni, Bernie,
Bernne, Berny*

Bernie
(German) brave boy
*Bern, Berni, Berny,
Birnie, Burney*

Bert
(English) shining
example
*Berti, Bertie, Berty, Birt,
Burt*

Berthold
(German) bold ruler
*Bert, Berthol, Berthuld,
Berty*

Berthrand
(German) form of
Bertram; strong; raven
*Bert, Berthran, Bertie,
Bertrand, Berty*

Bertin
(English) form of Burton;
dramatic
Berton, Burtun

Bertoldo
(Spanish) ruler
Bert

Berton
(American) form of
Burton; brave; dramatic
Bert, Bertan, Berty

Bertram
(German) outstanding
*Bert, Bertie, Bertrem,
Bertrom, Berty*

Bertrand
(German) bright
*Bert, Bertie,Bertran,
Bertrund, Birtryn*

Berty
(English) form of Bert;
shining
Bert, Bertie, Burty

Bervick
(American) upwardly
mobile; brave
Bervey

Berwyn
(English) loyal friend
*Berrie, Berwin, Berwynd,
Berwynne*

Besley
(Last name as first
name) calm
Bes, Bez

Best
(American) word as
name; quintessential
man
Beste

Bettis
(American) vocal
Bettes, Bettus, Betus

Beuford
(Last name as first
name) form of Buford;
country boy
Beuf, Bu, Bueford

Bevan
(Welsh) beguiling
*Bev, Bevahn, Beven,
Bevin*

Bever
(English) form of Bevis;
sophisticated

Bevil
(English) form of Bevis;
dignified

Bevis
(French) strong-willed
*Bev, Bevas, Beves,
Bevvis, Bevys, Bevyss*

Bexal
(American) studious
Bex, Bexlee, Bexly, Bexy

Bexley
(Place name)
distinguished

Biaggio
(Italian) stutters; unsure
Biage, Biagio

Biffy
(American) popular
Bibbee, Biff

Bigram
(Origin unknown)
handsome
Bigraham, Bygram

Bill
(German) short for William; strong; resolute
Billi, Billie, Billy

Billings
(Place name) sophisticated

Billy
(German) short for William; strong
Bilie, Bill, Billee, Billi, Billie, Bily

Billybob
(American) combo of Billy and Bob
B.B., Billibob, Billiebob, BillyBob, Billy Bob

Billy-Dale
(American) from William and Dale; countrified
Billidell, Billydale

Billyjoe
(American) combo of Billy and Joe
Billiejoe, Billijo, Billjo, BillyJoe

Billymack
(American) combo of Billy and Mack
Billiemac, Billimac, Billy, BillyMack, Mackie

Billyray
(American) combo of Billy and Ray
Billirae, Billy Ray

Bing
(German) outgoing
Beng

Bingo
(American) spunky
Bengo, Bingoh

Binkie
(English) energetic
Bink, Binki, Binky

Birch
(English) white and shining; birch
Berch, Bir, Burch

Bird
(American) soaring
Byrd

Biren
(American) form of Byron
Biran

Birkett
(English) living in birches; calming
Birk, Birket, Birkie, Birkitt, Burkett, Burkette, Burkitt

Birley
(English) outdoorsy; meadow
Berl, Birl, Birlee, Birly

Birney
(English) single-minded; island
Birne, Birni, Birny, Burney

Bish
(Hindi) universal

Bishop
(Greek) supervisor; serving the bishop
Bish, Bishie, Bishoppe

Bix
(American) hip
Bicks, Bixe

Bjorn
(Swedish) athletic
Bjarn, Bjarne, Bjonie, Bjorne, Bjorny

Black
(Scottish) dark
Blacke, Blackee, Blackie

Blade
(Spanish) prepared; knife
Bladie, Blayd

Blaine
(Irish) svelte
Blain, Blane, Blayne

Blair
(Irish) open
Blaire, Blare, Blayree

Blaise, Blaze
(French) audacious
Blasé, Blayse

Blake
(English) dark and handsome
Blaike, Blakey, Blakie

Blakeley
(English) outdoorsy; meadow
Blake, Blakelee, Blakely, Blakie

Blame
(American) sad
Blaim, Blaime

Blanchard
(Last name as first name) white
Blan

Blanco
(Spanish) light
Blancoh, Blonco, Blonko

Blank
(American) word as name; blank slate; open
Blanc

Blanket
(Invented) baby attached to a security blanket
Blank, Blankee, Blankett, Blankey, Blankie, Blanky

Blanton
(English) mild-mannered
Blanten, Blantun

Blasio
(Spanish) stutterer
Blaseo, Blasios, Blaze

Blaze
(English and American) daring
Blaase, Blaise, Blazey, Blazie

Bliss
(English) happy
Blice, Blyss

Blithe
(English) merry
Bly, Blye, Blythe

Blitzer
(German) adventurous
Blitz, Blitze

Blocker
(Last name as first name) block
Bloc, Block, Blok

Bloo
(American) zany

Blue
(Color name) hip
Bleu, Blu

Blye
(American) joyful
Blie

Bo
(Scandinavian) lively
Beau

Boat
(American) word as name; sealoving
Bo

Boaz
(Hebrew) strong; swift
Bo, Boase, Boaze, Boz

Bob
(English) short for Robert; bright; outstanding
Bobbi, Bobbie, Bobby

Bobby
(English) short for Robert; bright; outstanding
Bob, Bobbie, Bobi

Bobbydee
(American) combo of Bobby and Dee; country boy
Bobbidee, Bobby D, Bobby Dee, Bobby-Dee

Bobbymack
(American) combo of Bobby and Mack; jovial
Bobbimac, Bobbymac, Bobby-Mack

Bobby-Wayne
(American) combo of Bobby and Wayne; small-town boy
Bob, Bobbiwayne, Bobbi-Wayne, Bobby, Bobby Wayne, Bobbywayne, Wain, Wayne

Boden
(French) communicator
Bodin, Bodun, Bowden

Bodhi
(Buddhist) Bodhi-Dharma was founder of Ch'an Buddhism in China
Bodhee

Bogart
(German) bold, strong man
Bo, Bobo, Bogardte, Boge, Bogert, Bogey, Bogie

Bogdan
(Polish) God's gift

Bogdari
(Polish) gift from God
Bogdi

Boggle
(American) confusing
Bogg

Bojesse
(American) comical
Boje, Bojee, Bojeesie, Bojess

Bola
(American) careful; bold
Bolah, Boli

Bolden
(American) bold man
Boldun

Boleslaw
(Polish) in glory
Boleslav

Bolin
(Last name as first name) bold
Bolen

Bolivar
(Spanish) aggressive
Bolley, Bollivar, Bolly

Bolley
(American) strong
Bolly

Bomani
(African) fighter
Boman

Bon
(French) good
Bonne

Bonar
(French) gentle
Bonarr, Bonnar, Bonner

Bonaventura
(Spanish) good fortune
Bona, Bonavento, Buenaventura, Buenaventure, Ventura

Bonaventure
(Latin) humble
Bonaventura, Bonnaventura, Buenaventure

Bond
(English) farmer; renegade
Bondee, Bondie, Bondy

Bongo
(American) type of drum; musical
Bong, Bongy

Boni
(Latin) fortunate
Bonne

Bonifacio
(Spanish) benefactor
Bona, Boni, Boniface

Bono
(Spanish) good
Bonno

Booker
(English) lover of books
Book, Booki, Bookie, Booky

Boone
(French) blessed; good
Boon, Boonie, Boony

Booth
(German) protective
Boot, Boothe, Boothie, Bootsie

Boots
(American) cowboy
Bootsey, Bootsie, Bootz

Booveeay
(Invented) form of Bouvier
Boo

Bordan
(English) secretive; of the boar
Borde, Bordee, Borden, Bordi, Bordie, Bordy

Border
(American) word as name; fair-minded; aggressive
Bord

Borg
(Scandinavian) fortified; castle
Borge, Borgh

Boris
(Russian) combative
Boras, Bore, Bores

Bos
(English) woodsman
Boz

Boscoe
(English) woodsman

Bosley
(English) thriving; grove
Bos, Boslee, Boslie, Bosly

Bost
(Place name) from Boston, Massachusetts; audacious
Bostt

Boston
(Place name) distinctive
Boss, Bost

Boswell
(English) well near woods; dignified
Bos, Bosswell, Boz, Bozwell

Botolf
(English) wolf; standoffish
Botof

Bourbon
(Place name) jazzy
Borbon, Bourbonn, Bourbonne

Bourne
(French) planner; boundary
Bourn, Bourney, Bournie, Byrn, Byrne, Byrnie

Bouvier
(French) elegant; sturdy; ox
Bouveah, Bouveay, Bouviay

Bowen
(Welsh) shy
Bowie, Bowin

Bowie
(Irish) brash; western
Booie, Bowen

Boyce
(French) defender
Boice, Boy, Boyce

Boyd
(Scottish) fair-haired
Boide, Boydie

Bovo
(Last name as first name) macho
Bovoh

Bowing
(Last name as first name) blond and young
Beau, Bo, Bow, Bowen

Bowman
(Last name as first name) young; archer
Bow

Bowry
(Irish) form of Bowie; able; young
Bowy

Boy

(American) boy child of the family

Boydine

(French) from the woods

Boyse

Boyer

(French) woodsman

Brack

(English) from the plant bracken; fine

Bracke

Bracken

(English) plant name; debonair

Brack, Brackan, Brackin, Brackun

Brad

(English) short for Bradley; expansive

Braddie, Braddy

Bradan

(English) open-minded

Braden, Bradin, Brady, Bradyn, Braedyn, Braid

Bradford

(English) mediator

Brad, Brady

Bradley

(English) prosperous; expansive

Brad, Bradie, Bradlee, Bradlie, Bradly

Bradshaw

(English) broad-minded

Brad, Brad-Shaw, Bradshie

Brady

(Irish) high-spirited

Brade, Bradee, Bradey

Brain

(Invented) word as name; brilliant

Brane

Bram

(Hebrew) short for Abraham; great father

Brahm, Bramm

Bran

(Irish) raven; blessed

Brann

Branch

(Latin) growing

Bran, Branche

Branco

(Last name as first name)

Brank, Branko

Brand

(English) fiery

Brandd, Brande, Brandy, Brann

Brando

(American) talented

Brand

Brandon

(English) hill; high-spirited

Bradonn, Bran, Brandan, Brandin, Branny

Brandt

(English) dignified

Bran, Brandtt, Brant

Brandy

(English) firebrand; bold; brandy drink

Brand, Brandee, Brandey, Brandi, Brandie

Brannon

(Irish) bright-minded

Bran, Brann, Brannen, Branon

Branson

(English) persistent

Bran, Brans, Bransan, Bransen

Brant

(English) hothead

Brandt

Brashier

(French) brash

Brashear, Brasheer

Bratcher

(Last name as first name) aggressive

Bratch

Bravillo

(Spanish) brave

Braville

Bravo
(Italian) topnotch
Bravoh, Bravvo

Braxton
(English) worldly
Brack, Brackston, Brax,
Braxsten, Braxt

Bray
(English) vocal
Brae

Brayan
(Origin unknown)
Brayen

Braydon
(English) effective
Braedan, Braedon,
Brayden, Braydun

Breck
(Irish) fair and freckled
Breckie, Breckle, Brek

Breeahno
(Invented) form of
Briano

Breeon
(American) strong

Breeson
(American) strong
Breece, Breese, Bresen

Breeze, Breezy
(American) happy
Breese, Breez

Brendan
(Irish) armed
Brend, Brenden,
Brendie, Brendin,
Brendon

Brennan
(English) pensive
Bren, Brenn, Brennen,
Brennon, Brenny

Brenson
(Last name as first
name) disturbed;
masculine
Brens, Brenz

Brent
(English) prepared; on
the mountain
Bren, Brint

Brenton
(English) forward-
thinking
Brent, Brenten, Brintin

Brett
(Scottish) man from
Britain; innovative
Bret, Breton, Brette,
Bretton, Britt

Brettson
(American) manly man;
Briton
Brett

Brewster
(English) creative;
brewer
Brew, Brewer

Breyen
(Irish) strong; aggressive
Brey, Breyan

Brian
(Irish) strong man of
honor
Bri, Briann, Brien,
Brienn, Bry, Bryan

Brice
(Welsh) go-getter
Bryce

Brick
(English) alert; bridge
Bricke, Brik

Brickle
(American) surprising
Brick, Brickel, Brickell,
Bricken, Brickton,
Brickun, Brik

Brigdo
(American) leader
Brigg, Briggy

Brigham
(English) mediator
Brigg, Briggie, Briggs,
Brighum

Briley
(English) calm
Bri, Brilee, Brilie, Brily

Briscoe
(Last name as first
name) forceful
Brisco, Brisko, Briskoe

Britt
(English) humorous;
from Britain
Brit, Britts

Britton
(English) loyal; from
Britain

Brock
(English) forceful
*Broc, Brocke, Brockie,
Brocky, Brok*

Brockly
(English) place name;
aggressive
*Brocklee, Brockli,
Broklee, Broklie, Brokly*

Brockton
(English) badger; stuffy
Brock

Brod
(English) short for
Broderick
Broddie, Broddy

Broderick
(English) broad-minded;
brother
*Brod, Broddee, Broddie,
Broddy, Broderik,
Brodric, Brodrick*

Brodie
(Irish) builder
Brode, Brodee, Brody

Brogan
(Irish) sturdy shoe;
dependable
Brogann

Bromley
(English) meadow of the
shrubs; unpredictable
*Brom, Bromlee, Bromlie,
Bromly*

Bronc
(Spanish) wild; horse
Bronco, Bronk, Bronko

Bronco
(Spanish) wild; spirited
*Broncoh, Bronko,
Bronnco*

Brondo
(Last name as first
name) macho
Bron, Brond

Bronson
(English) Brown's son
*Bron, Brondson, Bronni,
Bronnie, Bronny,
Bronsan, Bronsen*

Bronto
(American) short for
brontosaurus;
thunderous
*Bront, Brontee, Brontey,
Bronti, Bronty*

Bronze
(Metal) alloy of tin and
copper; brown
Bronz

Brook
(English) easygoing
*Brooke, Brookee,
Brookie*

Brooks
(English) easygoing
Brookes, Brooky

Brow
(American) word as
name; highbrow; snob
Browy

Brown
(English) tan
*Browne, Brownie,
Browny*

Brownie
(American) brown-haired
Brown

Bruce
(French) complicated
(from a thicket of
brushwood)
Bru, Brucie, Brucy, Brue

Brumley
(French) smart;
scattered
Brum

Bruno
(German) brown-skinned
Brune, Brunne, Brunoh
Bruiser
(American) tough guy
Bruezer, Bruser, Bruzer
Bryan
(Irish) ethical; strong
Brye, Bryen
Bryant
(Irish) honest; strong
Bryan, Bryent
Bryce
(Welsh) spunky
Brice, Bry, Brye
Brydon
(American)
magnanimous
Bridon, Brydan, Bryden, Brydun
Bryson
(Welsh) Bryce's son; smart
Briceson, Bry, Bryse
Bryton
(Welsh) hill town
Bubba
(German) a regular guy
Bub, Buba, Bubb, Bubbah
Buck
(English) studly; buck deer
Buckey, Buckie, Bucko, Bucky

Buckley
(English) outdoorsy; a meadow for deer
Buckey, Buckie, Bucklee, Bucklie, Bucks, Bucky
Bucko
(American) macho
Bukko
Bucky
(American) warm-hearted
Buck, Buckey, Buckie
Bud
(English) courier
Budd, Buddie, Buddy, Budi, Budster
Buddy
(American) courier
Bud, Buddi, Buddie, Budi
Buell
(German) upward; hill
Bue
Buffalo
(American) tough-minded
Buff, Buffer, Buffy
Buford
(English) diligent
Bueford, Bufe, Buforde
Bulgara
(Slavic) hardworking
Bulgar, Bulgarah, Bulgaruh

Bulldog
(American) rough-and-tough
Bull, Dawg, Dog
Bullock
(Last name as first name) practical
Bumpus
(Last name as first name) humorous
Bump, Bumpey, Bumpy
Bunard
(English) good
Bunerd, Bunn
Bunyan
(English) good and burly
Bunyan, Bunyen
Buran
(American) complex
Burann, Burun
Burditt
(Last name as first name) shy
Burdett, Burdette, Burdey
Burge
(English) form of Burgess; middle-class
Burges, Burgis, Burr
Burgess
(English) businessman
Berge, Burge, Burges, Burgiss

Burke
(German) fortified
*Berk, Berke, Burk,
Burkie*

Burley
(English) nature-lover;
wooded meadow
*Burl, Burlea, Burlee,
Burli, Burly, Burr*

Burnis
(English) by the brook
*Burn, Burnes, Burney,
Burr*

Burr
(English) prickly;
brusque
Burry

Burrick
(English) townsman
Bur, Burr, Burry

Burney
(English) loner; island
*Burn, Burne, Burnie,
Burny*

Burris
(English) sophisticated;
living in the town
*Berris, Buris, Burr,
Burres*

Burt
(English) shining man
*Bert, Bertee, Burtie,
Burty*

Burton
(English) protective;
town that is well
fortified
Burt, Burty, Brutie

Busby
(Scottish) artist; village
*Busbee, Busbi, Buzbie,
Buzz, Buzzie*

Busher
(Last name as first
name) bold
Bush

Buster
(American) fun
Bustah

Butcher
(English) worker
Butch, Butchy

Butler
(English) directing the
house; handsome
*Butler, Butlir, Butlyr,
Buttler*

Buzz
(Scottish) popular
*Buzy, Buzzi, Buzzie,
Buzzy*

Byorn
(American) form of Bjorn

Byram
(English) stealthy; yard
that houses cattle
Bye, Byrem, Byrie, Byrim

Byrd
(English) birdlike
Bird

Byrne
(English) loner
*Birn, Birne, Byrn, Byrni,
Byrnie, Byrny*

Byrnett
(Last name as first
name) stable
*Burn, Burnett, Burney,
Burns, Byrne, Byrney*

Byron
(English) reclusive; small
cottage
*Biron, Biryn, Bye, Byren,
Byrom, Byrone, Byryn*

C

Cab
(American) word as name
Cabby, Kab

Cabrera
(Spanish) able
Cabrere

Cack
(American) laughing
Cackey, Cackie, Cacky, Cassy, Caz, Kass, Kassy, Khaki

Cactus
(Botanical) plant as name; prickly
Cack, Kactus

Cade
(English) stylish; bold; round
Cadye, Kade

Caden
(English) spirited
Cadan, Cade, Cadun, Caiden, Kaden, Kayden

Cadmus
(Greek) one who excels; prince
Cad, Cadmuss, Kadmus

Cady
(American) forthright
Cadee, Cadey, Cadie

Caesar
(Latin) focused leader
Caeser, Caez, Caezer, Cesaro, Cezar, Seezer

Cage
(American) dramatic
Cadge

Cailen
(American) gentle
Kail, Kailen, Kale

Cain
(Hebrew) aggressive
Caine, Cane, Kain, Kane

Cal
(Latin) short for Calvin; kind
Callie, Kal

Calbert
(American) cowboy
Cal, Calbart, Calberte, Calburt, Callie, Colbert

Calder
(English) stream; flowing
Cald, Kalder

Calderon
(Spanish) stream; flowing
Cald, Kald, Kalder, Kalderon

Caldwell
(English) refreshing; cold well

Cale
(Hebrew) slim; good heart
Kale

Caleb
(Hebrew) faithful; brave
Calab, Cale, Caley, Calie, Calub, Kaleb

Calek
(American) fighter; loyal
Calec, Kalec, Kalek

Calf
(American) cowboy
Kalf

Calhoun
(Irish) limited; from the narrow woods
Cal, Calhoon, Calhoune, Callie

Calixto
(Spanish) handsome
Calex, Calexto, Cali, Calisto, Calix, Callie, Cally, Kalixto

Callahan
(Irish) spiritual
Cal, Calahan, Calihan, Callie

Callie
(American) short for Calvin; kind
Cal, Calley, Calli, Cally

Callo
(American) attractive
Cal, Cally, Kallo

Cally
(Scottish) peacemaker

Calman
(Last name as first name) caring
Cal

Calum
(Irish, Scottish) peaceful
Cal, Callum, Calym, Calyme

Calvary
(American) word as name; herding all
Cal, Kal, Kalvary

Calvert
(English) respected; herding
Cal, Calber, Calbert, Calver, Kal, Kalvert

Calvin
(Latin) bold
Cal, Calvie, Kal

Cam
(Scottish) short for Cameron; loving
Camm, Cammey, Cammie, Cammy, Kam

Cambell
(American) form of Campbell; reliable (irregular mouth)
Cam, Cambel, Cammy, Kambell

Camberg
(Last name as first name) valley man
Cam

Camden
(Scottish) conflicted
Cam, Camdan, Camdon

Cameron
(Scottish) mischievous; crooked nose
Cam, Camaron, Camerohn, Cami, Cammy, Camren, Camron

Camilo
(Latin) helpful; (Italian) free
Cam, Camillo

Campbell
(Scottish) bountiful; crooked mouth
Cambell, Cammie, Camp, Campie, Campy

Camron
(Scottish) short for Cameron
Camren

Canaan
(Biblical) spiritual leanings
Cane, Kanaan, Kanan

Canal
(Word as name) waterway
Kanal

Candelario
(Spanish) bright and glowing
Cadelario

Cander, Candor
(American) candid
Can, Candy, Kan, Kander, Kandy

Candido
(Spanish) pure; candid
Can, Candi, Candide, Candy

Candle
(American) bright; hip name
Candell

Cannon
(French) courageous
Canney, Canni, Cannie, Canny, Canon, Canyn, Kannon, Kanon

Canute
(Scandinavian) great
Knut, Knute

Cappy
(French) breezy; lucky
Cappey, Cappi

Carad
(American) wily
Karad

Card
(English) short for
Carden; crafty
Kard

Cardan, Carden
(English) crafty; carder
Card, Cardon

Cardwell
(English) craftsman
Kardwell

Carey
(Welsh) masculine; by
the castle
Care, Cari, Cary, Karey

Cari
(English) masculine
Care, Carie, Cary

Carl
(Swedish) kingly
Karl

Carlfred
(American) combo of
Carl and Fred; dignified
Carl-Fred, Carlfree

Carlin
(Irish) winning
*Carlan, Carle, Carlen,
Carlie, Carly*

Carlisle
(English) strengthens
Carl, Carly, Carlyle

Carlo
(Italian) sensual; manly
Carl, Carloh

Carlon
(Irish) form of Carl;
winning
Karlon, Carlonn

Carlos
(Spanish) manly;
sensual
Carl, Carlo

Carlson
(English) son of manly
man
Carls, Carlsan, Carlsen

Carlton
(English) leader; town
of Carl
*Carltan, Carlten,
Carltown, Carltynne*

Carmel
(Hebrew) growing;
garden
Carmell, Karmel

Carmello
(Italian) flourishing
*Carm, Carmel, Carmelo,
Karmello*

Carmichael
(Scottish) bold;
Michael's follower
Car, Kar, Karmichael

Carmine
(Italian, Latin) dear song
*Carmane, Carmin,
Carmyne, Karmen,
Karmine*

Carmody
(French) manly; adult
Carmodee

Carnell
(Irish) victor
*Car, Carny, Kar, Karnell,
Karney*

Carney
(Irish) winner
Carn, Carnee, Carnie

Carr
(Scandinavian)
outdoorsy
Car, Kar

Carroll
(German) masculine;
winner
*Carall, Care, Carell,
Caroll, Carrol, Carrolle,
Carry, Caryl*

Carson
(English) confident
*Carr, Cars, Carsan,
Carsen*

Cart
(American) word as name; practical
Cartee, Cartey, Kart

Carter
(English) insightful
Cart, Cartah, Cartie

Cartrell
(English) practical
Car, Cartrelle, Cartrey, Cartrie, Cartrill, Kar, Kartrel, Kartrell

Cartwright
(English) creative
Cart, Cartright, Kart, Kartwright

Caruso
(Italian) musically inclined
Karuso

Carvell
(English) innovative
Carvel, Carvelle, Carver, Karvel

Carver
(English) carver
Carve, Carvey, Karver, Karvey

Cary
(English) place name; pretty brook; charming
Carey

Casdeen
(American) assertive; ingenious
Kassdeen

Case
(Irish) highly esteemed
Casey

Casey
(Irish) courageous
Case, Casey, Casi, Casie, Kacie, Kacy, Kase, Kaysie

Cash
(Latin) conceited
Casha, Cashe, Cazh

Cashmere
(American) smooth; softspoken
Cash, Cashmeer, Cashmyre, Kashmere

Cashone
(American) cash-loving
Casho

Casimir
(Polish) peace-loving
Casmer, Casmir

Casimiro
(Spanish) famous; aggressor
Casmiro, Kasimiro

Casper
(German) secretive
Caspar, Casper, Caspey, Caspi, Caspie, Cass

Cass
(Irish) short for Cassidy; funny
Kass

Cassidy
(Irish) humorous
Casidy, Cass, Cassadie, Cassidee, Cassidie, Kasidy, Kass, Kassidy

Cassie
(Irish) short for Cassidy; clever
Casi, Cass, Cassy

Cassius
(Latin) protective
Cass, Casseus, Casshus

Cast
(Greek) form of Castor; fiery star
Casta, Caste, Kast

Casto
(Mythology) from Castor, a Gemini twin
Cass, Kasto

Castor
(Greek) eager protector
Cass, Caster, Castie

Castulo
(Spanish) aggressor
Castu, Kastulo

Cato
(Latin) zany and bright
Catoe, Kato

Catarino
(Spanish) unflawed;
perfect
Catrino

Cavan
(Irish) attractive man
Cavahn, Caven, Cavin

Cavance
(Irish) handsome
*Caeven, Cavanse,
Kaeven, Kavance*

Cayce
(American) form of
Casey; brave
Cace, Case, Kayce

Caynce
(Invented) form of
Cayce; daring
Caincy, Cainse, Kaynse

Cazare
(Last name as first
name) daring
Cazares

Cecil
(Latin) unseeing;
hardheaded; blind
Cece, Cecel

Cedar
(Botanical) tree name;
sturdy
Ced, Sed, Sedar

Cedric
(English) leader
Ced, Ceda, Cedrick

Celso
(Italian) heavenly
*Celesteno, Celestino,
Celesto, Celestyno,
Celsus, Selso*

Celumiel
(Spanish) of the heavens
Celu

Centola
(Spanish) tenth child
Cento

Century
(Invented) remarkable
Cen, Cent

Cerone
(French) serene; creative
Serone

Cervantes
(Literature, Spanish)
original
Cervantez

Cesar
(Spanish) leader
Cesare, Cezar, Zarr

Chad
(English) firebrand
Chadd, Chaddy

Chadwick
(English) warrior
Chad, Chadwyck

Chaggy
(American) cocky
Chagg, Shagg, Shaggy

Chaim
(Hebrew) life
*Chai, Chayim, Haim, Hy,
Hyman, Hymie, Khaim,
Manny*

Chalmer
(Scottish) the lord's son
Chall, Chally, Chalmers

Chalmers
(French) chambers;
surrounded
Chalm

Chamblin
(American) easygoing
Cham

Chance
(English) good fortune;
happy
*Chancey, Chanci, Chancy,
Chanse, Chanz,
Chauncey*

Chancellor
(English) bookkeeper
Chance, Chancey

Chandell
(African-American)
innovator
*Chandelle, Chandey,
Chandie, Shandel,
Shandell*

Chandler
(English) ingenious;
(French) maker of candles
Chand, Chandey

Chaney
(French) strong
Chane, Chanie, Chayne, Chaynee

Chang
(Chinese) free; flowing

Channing
(English) brilliant
Chann, Channy

Chante
(French) singer
Chant, Chanta, Chantay, Chantie

Chapa
(Last name as first name) merchant; spirited
Chap, Chappy

Chaparro
(Spanish) from chaparral (southern landscape); cowboy
Chap, Chaps

Chapman
(English) businessman
Chap, Chappy

Charles
(German) manly; well-loved
Charl, Charli, Charlie, Charly, Chas, Chaz, Chazz

Charles-Wesley
(German) combo of Charles and Wesley; strong and sensitive
Charles Wes, Charles Wesley

Charlie
(German) manly
Charl, Charley, Charli, Charly

Charlton
(English) leader
Charles, Charley, Charlie, Charlt

Charome
(American) masculine
Char, Charoam, Charom, Charrone, Charry

Charro
(Spanish) wild-spirited cowboy
Charo, Charroh

Chase
(French) hunter
Chace, Chass

Chat
(American) happy
Chatt

Chaucer
(Literature, English) distinguished
Chauce, Chauser

Chauncey
(English) fair-minded
Chance, Chancey, Chanse, Chaunce

Chayne
(Scottish) swagger
Chane, Channe, Chay

Chaz
(German) short for Charles; manly
Chas, Chazz, Chazzie, Chazzy

Ché
(Spanish) short for José; aggressive
Chay, Shae, Shay

Chee
(American) high-energy
Che

Cheramy
(American) form of Jeremy; excitable
Cheramee, Charamie, Chermy

Chesley
(American) patient
Ches, Cheslee, Chez, Chezlee

Chester
(English) comfy-cozy
Ches, Chessie, Chessy

Chet
(English) creative
Chett

Chevalier
(French) gallant
Chev, Chevy

Chevalle
(French) dignified
Chev, Chevi, Chevy

Cheven
(Invented) playful
Chevy

Chevery
(French) from Chevy; elegant
Chev, Shevery

Cheves
(American) from liquor name Chivas; jaded
Chevez, Shevas

Chevy
(French) clever
Chev, Chevi, Chevie, Chevv

Chick
(English) short for Charles; friendly
Chic, Chickie, Chicky

Chico
(Spanish) boy
Chicoh, Chiko

Chili
(American) appetite for hot food

Chilton
(English) serene; farm
Chill, Chillton, Chilly, Chilt

Chip
(English) chip off the old block; like father, like son
Chipp, Chipper

Chris
(Greek) short for Christopher; close to Christ
Cris, Chrissy, Chrys

Chisholm
(Place name) Chisholm Trail; pioneer spirit
Chis, Chishom,Chiz

Christer
(Norwegian) religious
Krister

Christian
(Latin) follower of Christ
Chris, Christen, Christiane, Christyan, Cristian, Kris, Krist, Kristian

Christophe
(French) beloved of Christ
Cristoph, Kristophe

Christopher
(Greek) the bearer of Christ
Chris, Christofer, Crista, Cristos, Kristopher

Christos
(Greek) form of Christopher
Chris, Kristos

Chito
(American) fast-food eater; hungry
Cheetoh, Chitoh

Choicey
(American) word name; picky
Choicie, Choisie

Chonito
(Spanish) friend
Chonit, Chono

Chopo
(American) cowhand
Chop, Choppy

Choto
(Spanish) kid
Shoto

Chotto
(Last name as first name)

Chubby
(American) oversized
Chubbee, Chubbey, Chubbi, Chubbie

Chuck
(German) rash
Chuckee, Chuckey, Chuckie, Chucky

Chucky
(German) impulsive
Chuckey, Chucki, Chuckie

Chunky
(American) word name; large
Chunk, Chunkey, Chunki

Churchill
(English) bright
Church

Chutar, Chuter
(Spanish) aiming for goals

Cicero
(Latin) strong speaker
Cice

Cicil, Cecil
(English) shy
Cice

Cid
(Spanish) leader; lord
Ciddie, Ciddy, Cyd, Sid

Cimarron
(Place name) cowboy
Cimaronn

Cinco
(Spanish) fifth child
Cinko, Sinko

Ciro
(Italian) lordly
Ciroh, Cirro, Cyro

Cirrus
(Latin) thoughtful; cloud formation
Cerrus, Cirrey, Cirri, Cirrie, Cirry, Cirus, Serrus, Serus

Cisco
(American) clever
Sisco, Sysco

Citronella
(American) oil from fragrant grass; pungent
Cit, Citro, Cytronella, Sitronella

Civille
(American) form of place name Seville

Clance
(Irish) form of Clancy; redhead; aggressive
Clancy, Clanse, Klance, Klancy

Clair
(English) renowned
Claire, Clare

Clancy
(Irish) lively; feisty redhead
Clance, Clancey, Clancie

Claran
(Latin) bright
Clarance, Claransi, Claranse, Clare, Claren, Clarence, Clary, Klarense

Clarence
(Latin) intelligent
Clarance, Clare, Clarens, Clarense, Clarons, Claronz, Clarrence, Klarence, Klarens

Clarinett
(Invented) plays the clarinet
Clare, Clarinet, Clary, Klare, Klari

Clark
(French) personable; scholar
Clarke

Claude
(Latin); slow-moving; lame
Claud, Claudey, Claudie, Claudy, Klaud, Klaude

Claus, Klaus
(Greek) victorious
Klaas

Claven
(English) endorsed
Klaven

Clawdell
(American) form of Claudell
Clawd

Claxton
(English) townie
Clax, Klax

Clay
(English) firm; short for Claybrook and Clayton; reliable
Claye, Klae, Klay

Claybey
(American) southern; earthly
Claybie, Klaybee

Clayborne
(English) earthly
Clabi, Claybie, Klay

Claybrook
(English) sparkling smile
Claibrook, Clay, Claybrooke, Clayie

Clayton
(English) stodgy
Clay, Claytan, Clayten

Cleary
(Irish) smart
Clear, Clearey, Clearie

Cleavon
(English) daring
Cheavaughn, Cleavaughn, Cleave, Cleevaughan, Cleevon

Clem
(Latin) casual
Cleme, Clemmey, Clemmie, Clemmy, Clim

Clement
(Scottish) gentle
Clem, Clemmyl

Clemente
(Spanish) pleasant
Clemen, Clementay

Clements
(Latin) forgiving man
Clem, Clement, Clemmants, Clemment

Clemer
(Latin) mild
Clemmie, Clemmy, Klemer, Klemmie, Klemmye

Clemmie
(Latin) mild
Clem, Klem, Klemmee, Klemmy

Clenzy
(Spanish) forgiving; cleansed
Clense, Clensy, Klenzy

Cleopatrick
(African-American) combo of Cleopatra and Patrick
Cleo, Cleopat, Kleo, Kleopatrick, Pat, Patrick

Cleophas
(Greek) seeing glory; known
Cle, Cleofus, Cleoph, Klee, Kleofus, Kleophus

Cleon
(Greek) famed man
Clee, Cleone, Kleon

Cletus
(Greek) creative; selected
Clede, Cledus, Cletis

Cleve
(English) precarious; cliff
Clive

Cleveland
(English) daring
Cleavelan, Cleve, Clevon, Clevy, Cliveland

Cliff
(English) short for Clifford; dashing
Clif, Cliffey, Cliffie, Cliffy

Clifford
(English) dashing
Cleford, Cliff, Cliffy, Clyford

Clifton
(English) risk-taker
Cliff, Clifftan, Clifften, Cliffy

Clint
(English) short for Clinton; bright
Clent, Clynt, Klint

Clinton
(English) curious; bright; cliff in town
Clenton, Clint, Clinten, Clynton, Klinten, Klinton

Clive
(English) daring; living near a cliff
Cleve, Clyve

Clooney
(American) dramatic
Cloone, Cloonie, Cloony, Clune, Cluney, Clunie, Cluny

Clotaire
(French) famous
Clotie, Klotair, Klotie

Clovis
(German) famed warrior
Clove, Cloves, Clovus, Klove, Kloves, Klovis

Cloyd
(American) form of Floyd; cloying
Cloy, Cloye, Kloy, Kloyd

Clyde
(Welsh) adventurer
Clide, Clydey, Clydie, Clydy, Clye, Klyde, Klye

Clydell
(American) countrified
Clidell, Clydel

Clydenestra
(Spanish) form of Clyde
Clyde

Coal
(American) word as a name
Coale, Koal

Cobb
(English) cozy
Cob, Cobbe

Coben
(Last name as first name) creative
Cob, Cobb, Cobe, Cobee, Cobey, Cobi, Coby, Kob, Kobee, Koben, Kobi, Koby

Coby
(American) friendly
Cob, Cobe, Cobey, Cobie

Coca
(American) excitable
Coka, Cokey, Cokie, Koca, Koka

Cochise
(Native American) warrior
Cocheece, Cochize

Coco
(French) brash
Coko, Koko

Cody
(English) comforting
Coday, Code, Codee, Codey, Codi, Codie

Cog
(American) short for Cogdell; necessary
Kog

Cogdell
(Last name as first name) needed
Cogdale

Cohn
(American) winner
Kohn

Cokie
(American) bright
Cokey, Coki, Cokie, Cokki, Kokie

Colbert
(English) cool and calm
Colbey, Colbi, Colbie, Colburt, Colby, Cole

Colborn
(English) intimidating; cold brook
Colbey, Colborne, Colburn, Colby, Cole

Colby
(English) bright; secretive; dark farm
Colbey, Colbi, Colbie, Cole, Colie

Colden
(English) haunting
Coldan, Coldun, Cole

Cole
(Greek) lively; winner
Coal, Coley, Colie, Kohl, Kole

Coleman
(English) lively; peacemaker
Cole, Colemann, Kohlman

Colgate
(English) passway
Colgait, Colgaite, Kolgate

Colin
(Irish) young and quiet; peaceful; the people's victor
Colan, Cole, Colen, Collin, Collyn

Colley
(English) dark-haired
Col, Colli, Collie

Collier
(English) hard-working; miner
Colier, Collie, Colly, Colyer

Collin
(Scottish) shy
Collen, Collie, Collon, Colly

Collins
(Irish) shy; holly
Collens, Collie, Collons, Colly, Kolly

Colson
(English) precocious; son of Nicholas
Cole, Colsan, Colsen

Colt
(English) frisky; horse trainer
Colty, Kolt, Koltt

Colten, Colton
(English) dark town; mysterious
Cole, Collton, Colt, Coltan, Coltawn, Kol

Colter
(English) keeping the colts
Colt, Coltor, Colty

Colum
(Latin) peaceful; dove
Colm, Kolm, Kolum

Columbus
(Latin) peaceful (discovered America)
Colom, Colombo, Columbe

Comanche
(Native American) tribe; wild-spirited; industrious
Comanch, Komanche

Como
(Place name) handsome
Comoh

Comus
(Greek) humorous
Comes, Comas, Commus, Komus

Conall
(Scottish) highly regarded
Conal

Conan
(Irish) worthy of praise
Conen, Connie, Conny, Conon

Conant
(Irish) topnotch
Conent, Connant

Concord
(English) agreeable
Con, Concor, Conny, Koncord, Konny

Cong
(Chinese) bright

Conlan
(Irish) winner
Con, Conland, Conlen, Connie, Conny

Conk, Konk
(Invented) from conch (mollusk of the ocean); jazzy
Conch, Conkee, Conkee, Conkey, Conky, Kanch, Konkey, Konkey

Connell
(Irish) strong
Con, Conal, Connall, Connel, Connelle, Connie, Conny

Connery
(Scottish) daring
Con, Conery, Connarie, Connary, Connie, Conny

Connie
(Irish) short for Connor, Connery, Conrad
Con, Conn, Connee, Conney, Conni, Conny

Connor
(Scottish) brilliant
Con, Conn, Conner, Conor, Kon, Konnor

Conrad
(German) optimist
Con, Connie, Conny, Conrade, Konrad

Conrado
(Spanish) bright advisor
Conrad, Conrod, Conrodo

Conridge
(Last name as first name) advisor
Con, Conni, Connie, Conny, Ridge

Conroy
(Irish) wise writer
Conrie, Conroye, Conry, Roy, Roye

Constantine
(Latin) consistent
Con, Conn, Consta, Constance, Constant, Constantyne

Conway
(Irish) vigilant
Con, Connie, Kon, Konway

Cooke
(Latin) cook
Cook, Cookie, Cooky

Coolidge
(Last name as first name) wary
Cooledge

Cooper
(English) handsome; maker of barrels
Coup, Couper, Koop, Kooper, Kouper

Cope
(English) able
Cape

Corbet
(Latin) dark
Corb, Corbett, Corbit, Corbitt, Korb, Korbet

Corbin
(Latin) dark and brooding
Corban, Corben, Corby

Corbitt
(Last name as first name) brooding
Corbet, Corbett, Corbie, Corbit, Corby

Corby
(Latin) dark
Corbey, Korbee, Korby, Korry

Corcoran
(Irish) ruddy-skinned
Corkie, Corky

Cord
(Origin unknown) soap opera macho man
Corde, Kord

Cordel
(French) practical
Cordel, Cordell, Cordelle, Cordie, Cordill, Cordy

Cordero
(Spanish) gentle
Cordara, Cordaro, Cordarro, Kordarro, Kordero

Corey
(Irish) laughing
Core, Corie, Corry, Cory, Korey, Korrie, Kory

Corin
(Latin) combative
Coren, Dorrin, Koren, Korrin

Cork
(Place name) city in Ireland
Corkee, Corkey, Corki, Corky, Kork

Corky
(American) casual
Corkee, Corkey, Korky

Corn
(Latin) form of Cornelius; horn; yellow-haired
Korn

Cornelius
(Greek) a temptation
Coarn, Conny, Corn, Corni, Cornie, Corny, Kornelius, Neel, Neely, Neil, Neiley

Cornell
(French) fair
Corne, Cornelle, Corny, Kornell

Corrigan
(Irish) aggressive
Coregan, Corie, Correghan, Corrie, Corry, Koregan, Korrigan

Cort
(German) eloquent
Corte, Court, Kort

Cortez
(Spanish) victorious; explorer
Cortes

Corvin
(English) friend
Corwin, Corwynn, Korry, Korvin

Corwin
(English) heart's delight
Corrie, Corry, Corwan, Corwann, Corwyn, Corwynne

Cory
(Latin) humorous
Coarie, Core, Corey, Corrie, Kohry, Kori

Cosgrove
(Irish) winner
Cosgrave, Cossy, Kosgrove, Kossy

Cosma
(Greek) universal
Cos, Kosma

Cosmas
(Greek) universal
Cos, Kosmas, Koz

Cosmo
(Greek) in harmony with life
Cos, Cosimon, Cosmos, Kosmo

Cosner
(English) organized; handsome
Cosnar, Kosner

Costas
(Greek) constant
Costa, Costah

Cotton
(Botanical name) casual
Cottan

Coty
(French) comforter
Cotey, Coti, Cotie, Koty

Coug
(American) short for cougar; fierce
Cougar, Koug, Kougar

Coulter
(English) dealing in colts; horseman
Colter, Coult, Kolter, Koulter

Counsel
(Latin) advisor
Consel, Council, Kounse, Kounsell

Courtnay
(English) sophisticated
Cort, Corteney, Court, Courtney, Courtny

Covell
(English) warm
Covele, Covelle

Covet
(American) word as name; desires
Covett, Covette, Kovet

Covington
(English) distinctive
Covey, Coving, Kovey, Kovington

Cowan
(Irish) cozy
Cowen, Cowie, Cowy

Cowboy
(American) western

Cowell
(English) brash; frank
Kowell

Cowey
(Irish) reclusive
Cowee, Cowie, Kowey

Coye
(English) outdoorsman
Coy, Coyey, Coyie

Coylie
(American) coy
Coyl, Koyl, Koylie

Coystal
(American) coy
Coy, Koy, Koystal

Crad
(American) practical
Cradd, Krad, Kradd

Crago
(Last name as first name) macho
Crag, Craggy, Krago

Craig
(Irish) brave climber
Crai, Craigie, Cray, Craye, Crayg, Creg, Cregge, Kraig

Crandal
(English) open
Cran, Crandall, Crandell, Crane

Crawford
(English) flowing
Crafe, Craford, Craw, Fordy

Crayton
(English) substantial
Craeton, Cray, Creighton

Creed
(American) believer
Crede, Creede, Creyd, Kreed

Creighton
(English) sophisticated
Criton

Crey, Creigh
(English) short for Creighton; slight
Craedie, Cray, Creydie

Creshaun
(African-American) inspired
Creshawn, Kreshaun

Cresp
(Latin) man with curls
Crisp, Crispen, Crispun, Crispy, Cryspin, Kresp, Krisp, Krispin, Krispyn

Crew
(American) word as name; sailor
Krew

Crispin
(Latin) man with curls
Chrispy, Crespen, Crispo, Crispy, Krispin, Krispo

Crispo
(Latin) curly-haired
Crisp, Krispo

Cristo
(Place name, Spanish) from Count of Monte Cristo
Kristo

Cristian
(Greek) form of Christian
Kristian

Criten
(American) shortened version of Critendon; critical
Critan, Kriten

Critendon
(Last name as first name) critical
Crit, Criten, Krit, Kritendon

Crofton
(Irish) comforter
Croft, Croften

Cromwell
(Irish) giving
Chromwell, Crom, Crommie

Crosby
(Irish) easygoing
Crosbee, Crosbie, Cross,
Krosbie, Krosby

Croston
(English) by the cross
Cro, Croton, Kroston

Cruze
(Spanish) cross
Cruise, Cruse, Kruise,
Kruze

Cuba
(Place name) distinctive;
spicy
Cubah, Cueba, Kueba,
Kuba

Cucuta
(Place name) city in
North Colombia; sharp
Cucu

Cuernavaca
(Place name) city in
Mexico; cowhorn
Vaca

Cuke
(American) zany
Kook, Kooky, Kuke

Culkin
(American) child actor
Culki, Kulkin

Cull
(American) selective
Cullee, Cullie, Cully,
Kulley

Cullen
(Irish) attractive
Culen, Cull, Cullan,
Cullen, Cullie, Cully,
Kullen, Kully

Culley
(Irish) secretive
Cull, Cullie, Cully, Kull,
Kully

Culver
(English) peaceful
Colver, Cull, Culley, Culli,
Cully

Culverado
(American) peaceful
Cull, Cullan, Culver,
Culvey, Kull

Cummings
(Literature) poetic
Cumming, Kummings

Cuney
(Last name as first
name) serious
Cune, Kune, Kuney

Cunning
(Irish) from surname
Cunningham;
wholesome
Cuning

Cunningham
(Irish) milk-pail town;
practical
Cuningham

Curb
(American) word as a
name; dynamic
Kurb

Curbey
(American) form of
Kirby; high-energy
Curby

Curley
(American) cowboy
Curly, Kurly

Curran
(Irish) smiling hero
Curan, Curr, Curren,
Currey, Currie, Curt

Currie
(English) messenger;
courteous
Kurrie

Curt
(French) short for Curtis;
kind
Kurt

Curtis
(French) gracious; kind-
hearted
Curdi, Curdis, Curt,
Curtey, Curtice, Curtie,
Curtiss, Curty, Kurt

Custer
(Last name as first
name) watchful;
stubborn
Cust, Kust, Kuster

Cutler
(English) wily
Cutlar, Cutlur, Cuttie,
Cutty

Cutsy
(English) from Cutler;
knife-man
Cutlar, Cutler, Cuttie,
Cutty, Kutsee, Kutsi,
Kutsy

Cuttino
(African-American)
athletic
Kuttino

Cuyler
(American) form of
Schuyler; protective
Kuyler

Cy
(Greek) shining example
Cye, Si

Cyll
(American) bright
Syll, Cyl

Cyprien
(French) religious
Cyp, Cyprian

Cyprus
(Place name) outgoing

Cyrano
(Greek) shy heart
Cyranoh, Cyre, Cyrie,
Cyrno, Cyry

Cyril
(Greek) regal
Ciril, Cyral, Cyrell, Cyrille

Cyrus
(Persian) sunny
Cye, Syrus

Cyrx
(American) conniving
Cyrxie

Czeslaw
(Polish) honorable
Slav, Slavek

Dabney
(Place name) careful;
funny
Dab, Dabnee, Dabnie,
Dabny

Dacias
(Latin) place name;
brash
Dace, Daceas, Dacey,
Dacy, Dayce, Daycie

Dada
(African) curly-haired

Dade
(Place name) county in
Florida; renegade
Daide, Dayde

Dag
(Scandinavian) sunny
Dagg, Dagny

Daggan
(Scandinavian) day

Dagny
(Scandinavian) day
Dag

Dagoberto
(Spanish) day
Dagobert
Dagwood
(English) comic
Dag, Dawood, Woody
Dairus
(Invented) daring
Daras, Dares, Darus
Dakarai
(African) happy
Dakarrai, Dakk
Dakota
(Native American)
friendly
*Dack, Dak, Dakodah,
Dakotah, Kota*
Dakote
(Place name) from
Dakota (states North
and South Dakota)
Dako
Dalai
(Indian) peaceful
Dalee
Dalanee
(Invented) form of
Delaney
Dalaney, Dalani
Dale
(English) natural
Dail, Day, Dayl, Dayle

Dalen
(English) up-and-coming
*Dalan, Dalin, Dallen,
Dallin, Dalyn*
Daley
(Irish) organized
Dailey, Daily, Dale
Dalgus
(American) loving the
outdoors
Dalhart
(Place name) city in
Texas
Dal
Dallas
(Place name) good old
boy; city in Texas
Dall, Dallice, Dallus
Dallin
(English) valley-born;
fine
Dal, Dallen
Dalsten
(English) smart
Dal, Dalston
Dalt
(English) abundant
Dall, Daltt, Daltey
Dalton
(English) farmer
Dall, Daltan, Dalten

Dalvis
(Invented) form of Elvis;
sassy
*Dal, Dalves, Dalvus,
Dalvy*
Damacio
(Spanish) calm; tamed
*Damas, Damasio,
Damaso, Damazio*
Damarcus
(African-American)
confident
*D'Marcus, Damarkes,
Damarkus, Demarcus*
Damary
(Greek) tame
Damaree, Damarie
Damascus
(Place name) capital of
Syria; dramatic
Damas, Damask
Damaso
(Spanish) taming
Damas
Damean
(American) form of
Damian; tamed
*Dama, Daman, Damas,
Damea*
Dameetre
(Invented) form of
Dmitri; audacious
Dimitri

Damian
(Greek) fate; (Latin)
demon
*Dame, Damean,
Dameon, Damey,
Damien, Damion,
Damyean, Damyon,
Damyun*

Damon
(Greek) dramatic;
spirited
Damonn, Damyn,

Dan
(Hebrew) short for
Daniel; spiritual
Dahn, Dannie, Danny

Dana
(Scandinavian) light-
haired
Danah, Dane, Dayna

Dandre, DeAndre
(American) light
*Dan, Dandrae, Dandray,
DeAndrae, DeAndray,
Diondrae*

Dane
(English) man from
Denmark; light
*Daine, Daney, Danie,
Danyn, Dayne, Dhane*

Daneck
(American) well-liked
*Danek, Danick, Danik,
Danike, Dannick*

Danely
(Scandinavian) Danish
Dainely, Daynelee

Dang
(Vietnamese) worthy

Dangelo
(Italian) angelic
Danjelo

Danger
(American) word as a
name; dangerous
Dang, Dange, Dangery

Daniel
(Hebrew) judged by
God; spiritual
*Dan, Dann, Danney,
Danni, Dannie, Danniel,
Danny, Danyel, Danyell,
Danyyell*

Daniele
(Hebrew) form of Daniel
Danyel, Danyell

Danne
(Biblical) from Daniel;
faithful
Dann

Danner
(Last name as first
name) rescued by God
Dan, Dann, Danny

Danno
(Hebrew) kind
Dannoh, Dano

Danny
(Hebrew) short for
Daniel; spiritual
*Dan, Dann, Dannee,
Danney, Danni, Dannie*

Danon
(French) remembered
*Danen, Danhann,
Dannon, Danton*

Dante
(Latin) enduring
*Dan, Danne, Dantey,
Dauntay, Dayntay,
Dontay*

Dantre
(African-American)
faithful
*Dantray, Dantrae,
Dontre, Dantrey, Dantri,
Dantry, Don, Dont,
Dontrey, Dontri*

Dantrell
(African-American)
spunky
*Dantrele, Dantrill,
Dantrille*

Danube
(Place name) flowing;
river
Dannube, Danuube

Daquan
(African-American)
rambunctious
Dakwan, Dequan

Darbrie
(Irish) free man; light-hearted
Dar, Darb, Darbree, Darbry

Darby
(Irish) free spirit
Dar, Darb, Darbee, Darbie, Darre

Darce
(Irish) dark
Darcy, Dars, Darsy, D'Arcy

Darcel
(French) dark
Dar, Darce, Darcelle, Darcey, Darcy, Darsy

Darcy
(French) slow-moving
Darce, Darse, Darsey, Darsy

Dare
(Irish) short for Darroh; dark
Dair, Daire, Darey

Darian
(American) inventive
Dari, Darien, Darion, Darrian, Darrion, Derreynn

Darin
(Irish) great
Daren, Darren, Darrie, Daryn

Dario
(Spanish) rich
Darioh, Darrey

Darion
(Irish) great potential
Dare, Darien, Darrion, Daryun

Darius, Darrius
(Greek) affluent
Dare, Dareas, Dareus

Dark
(Slavic) short for Darko; macho
Dar, Darc

Darko
(Slavic) macho
Dark

Darlen
(American) darling
Darlan, Darlun

Darnell
(English) secretive
Dar, Darn, Darnel, Darnie, Darny

Darold
(American) clever
Dare, Darrold, Darroll, Derold

Daron
(Irish) great
Darren, Dayron

Darrell
(French) loved man
Darel, Darol, Darrel, Darrey, Daryl, Derrel, Derrell

Darren
(Irish) great man
Daren, Darin, Darryn, Derron, Derry

Darrett
(American) form of Garrett; efficient
Dare, Darry

Darroh, Darrow
(English) armed; bright
Dare, Daro, Darrie, Darro, Darrohye, Darrow

Darrti
(American) fast; deer
Dart, Darrt

Darryl
(French) darling man
Darrie, Daryl, Derrie, Deryl, Deryll

Dart
(Place name) decisive
Darte, Dartt

Darton
(English) swift; deer

Darwin
(English) dearest friend
Dar, Darwen, Darwinne, Darwon

Daryn
(American) form of Darren
Darynn, Deryn

Dash
(American) speedy; dashing
Dashy

Dashawn
(African-American) unusual
D'Sean, D'Shawn, Dashaun, Deshaun, Deshawn

Dashell
(African-American) dashing
Dashiell

Dasher
(American) dashing; fast
Dash

Davao
(Place name) city in the Philippines; exotic
Davo

Dave
(Hebrew) short for David; loved
Davey, Davi, Davie, Davy

Daven
(American) form of Dave; dashing
Davan

Davey
(Hebrew) short for David; loved
Dave, Davee, Davi, Davie, Davy

Davian
(Hebrew) dear one
Daveon, Davyon

David
(Hebrew) beloved
Davad, Dave, Daved, Davee, Daven, Davey, Davi, Davide, Davie, Davy, Davydd

David-Drue
(American) combo of David and Drue; sweet and loved
David-Drew, David-Dru, David Drue

Davidpaul
(American) beloved
David-Paul

Davidson
(English) son of David
Davidsen, Davison

Davin
(Scandinavian) smart
Dave, Daven, Dayven

Davins
(American) from David; smart
Davens

Davis
(Welsh) David's son; heart's child
Dave, Daves, Davies

Davon
(American) sweet
Davaughan, Davaughn, Dave, Davone, Devon

Davonnae
(African-American) from David; loved
Davawnae, Davonae

Davonte
(African-American) energetic
D'Vontay, Davontay, Devonta

Daw
(English) quiet
Dawe, Dawes

Dawber
(Last name as first name) funny
Daw, Dawb, Dawbee, Dawbey, Dawby, Daws

Dawk
(American) spirited
Dawkins

Daws
(English) dedicated
Daw, Dawsen, Dawz

Dawson
(English) David's son; loved
Dawsan, Dawse, Dawsen, Dawsey, Dawsin

Dax
(French) unique; water-loving
Dacks, Daxie

Day
(English) calm
Daye

Dayton
(English) the town of David; planner
Daeton, Day, Daye, Daytawn, Deytawn, Deyton

Deacon
(Greek) giving
Decon, Deecon, Dekawn, Deke, Dekie, Dekon

Deagan
(Last name as first name) capable
Degan

Deal
(Last name as first name) wheeler-dealer
Deale

Dean
(English) calming
Deane, Deanie, Deany, Deen, Dene, Dino

Deangelo
(Italian) sweet; personable
D'Angelo, Dang, Dange, DeAngelo, Deanjelo, Deeanjelo, DiAngelo, Di-Angelo

Deans
(English) sylvan; valley
Dean, Deaney, Deanie

Deanthony
(African-American) rambunctious
Deanthe, Deanthoney, Deanthonie, Deeanthie, Dianth

Deanza
(Spanish) smooth
Denza

Dearing
(Last name as first name) endearing
Dear

Dearon
(American) dear one
Dear

Deason
(Invented) cocky
Deace, Deas, Dease, Deasen, Deasun

Debonair
(French) with a beautiful air; elegant and cultured
Debonaire, Debonnair, Debonnaire

Debythis
(African-American) strange
Debiathes

Decatur
(American) place name; special
Dec, Decatar, Decater, Deck

Deccan
(Place name) region in India; scholar
Dec, Dek

Deck
(Irish) short for Declan; strong; devout
Decky

Declan
(Irish) strong; prayerful
Dec, Deck, Dek, Deklan, Deklon

Deddrick
(American) form of Deidrich; substantial
Dead, Dedrik

Dedeaux
(French) sweet
Dede, Dee

Dedric
(German) leader
Dedrick, Deidrich

Dee
(American) short for names that start with D
D, De

Deek
(American) short for
Deacon; leader
Deke

Deepak
(Sanskrit) light of
knowledge
Depak, Depakk, Dipak

Deeter
(American) friendly
Deter

DeFoy
(French) child of Foy
Defoy, Defoye

Degraf
(French) child of Graf
DeGraf

Deidrich
(German) leader
Dedric, Dedrick, Deed,
Deide, Deidrick, Diedrich

Deinorus
(African-American)
vigorous
Denorius, Denorus

Deion
(Greek) form of
Dion/Deone (god of
wine); fun-loving;
charismatic
Dee

Dejuan
(African-American)
talkative
Dejuane, Dewaan,
Dewan, Dewaughan,
Dewon, Dwon, Dwonn,
Dwonne

Deke
(Hebrew) from Dekel;
brilliant; sturdy tree
Deek, Dekel

Del
(English) valley; laid-
back and helpful
Dail, Dell, Delle

Delaney
(Irish) challenging
Del, Delainie, Delanie,
Delany, Dell

Delano
(Irish) dark
Del, Delaynoh, Dell

Delbert
(English) sunny
Bert, Berty, Del, Delburt,
Dell

Delete
(Origin unknown)
ordinary
Delette

Delfino
(Spanish) dolphin;
sealoving
Define, Fino

Delgado
(Spanish) slim

Delius
(Greek) from Delos
Deli, Delia, Delos

Delmar
(Last name as first
name) friendly
Delm

Delmer
(American) country
Del, Delmar, Delmir

Delmis
(Spanish) friend
Del, Delms

Delmore
(French) seagoing
Del, Delmer, Delmoor,
Delmoore

Delmy
(American) from French
Delmore; seagoing
Delmi

Delroy
(French) royal; special
Del, Dell, Dellroy, Delroi,
Roi, Roy

Delsi
(American) easygoing
Delci, Delcie, Dels,
Delsee, Delsey, Delsy

Delt
(American) fraternity boy
Delta

Delton
(English) friend
Delt, Deltan, Delten

Delvan
(English) form of Delwin;
friend
Del, Dell, Delven, Delvun

Delvin
(English) good friend
*Del, Dell, Delly, Delven,
Delvyn*

Delwin
(English) good friend
*Del, Dell, Dellwin,
Delwyn*

Delwinse
(English) friend
*Del, Delwen, Delwince,
Delwins, Delwy*

Demarco
(Italian) daring
*D'Marco, Deemarko,
Demarkoe, Demie,
Demmy, Dimarco*

Demarcus
(American) zany; royal
*DeMarcus, Demarkes,
DeMarkus, Demarkus,
Demarquiss, DeMarquiss*

Demario
(Italian) bold
*D'Mareo, D'Mario,
Demarioh, Demarrio,
Demie, Demmy, Dimario*

Demarques
(African-American) son
of Marques; noble
*Demark, Demarkes,
Demarquis, Demmy*

Demete
(American) from Greek
Demetrius; a saint
Deme, Demetay

Demetrice
(Greek) form of
Demetrius; fertile

Demetrick
(African-American)
earthy
*Demetrik, Demi,
Demitrick*

Demetrios
(Greek) earth-loving
*Demeetrius, Demetreus,
Demetri, Demetrious,
Demetris, Demi, Demie*

Demetrius
(Greek) form of Demeter,
goddess of fertility
*Dem, Demetri, Demmy,
Demos*

Demitri
(Greek) fertile; earthy
*Demetrie, Demetry,
Demi, Demie, Demitry,
Dmitri*

Demond
(African-American)
worldly
Demonde

Demos
(Greek) of the people
Demas, Demmos

Demosthenes
(Greek) orator; eloquent
Demos

Demps
(Irish) form of Dempsey;
sturdy
Demps, Dempse, Dempz

Dempsey
(Irish) respected; judge
*Dem, Demi, Demps,
Dempsie, Dempsy*

Denard
(Last name as first
name) envied
*Den, Denar, Denarde,
Denny*

Denby
(Scandinavian) place
name; adventurous
*Danby, Denbee, Denbie,
Denney, Dennie, Denny*

Deni
(English) form of
Dionysius, god of revelry
and wine; festive
Denni

Denis
(Greek) reveler
Den, Denese, Dennis

Denk
(American) sporty
Denky, Dink

Denman
(English) dark; valley-dweller
Den, Deni, Denmin, Denney, Denni, Dennie, Dennman, Denny, Dinman

Dennis
(Greek) reveler
Denes, Deni, Denis, Deniss, Denni, Dennies, Denniz, Denny, Deno, Dino

Dennisen
(English) Dennis's son; partier
Dennison, Dennizon

Denny
(Greek) short for Dennis; fun-loving
Den, Denee, Deni, Denney, Denni

Denton
(English) place name; valley settlement; happy
Dent, Dentan, Denten, Dentie, Dentin

Denver
(Place name) capital of Colorado; climber
Den, Denny

Denzel
(English) sensual
Den, Denny, Densie, Denz, Denze, Denzell, Denzelle, Denzil, Denzille, Denzylle, Dinzie

Deondray
(African-American) romantic
Deandre, Deeon, Deondrae, Deondrey, Deone

Deone, Dion
(Greek) short for Dionysius, god of wine; fun-loving; charismatic
Deion, Deonah, Deonne

Deonté
(French) outgoing
De'On, Deontae, Deontay, Deontie, Diontay, Diontayye

Deordre
(African-American) outgoing
Deordray

Deotis
(African-American) combo of De and Otis; scholar
Deo, Deoh, Deotus

Depp
(American) movie-star surname; theatrical
Dep

Derald
(American) combo of Harold and Derrell; content
Deral, Dere, Derry, Deruld

Derek
(German) ruler; bold heart
Darrick, Derak, Dere, Deric, Deriqk, Derk, Derrek, Derrick, Derryck, Dirk, Dyrk

Derlin
(English) from Derland, deer land; sly
Derl, Derlan, Derland, Derlen, Derlyn, Durland, Durlin

Dermod
(Irish) from Dermot; guileless; thoughtful
Dermud

Dermond
(Irish) unassuming
Dermon, Dermun, Dermund, Derr

Dermot
(Irish) unabashed; giving
Der, Dermod, Derree, Derrey, Derri

Dermott
(Irish) guileless; freedom-loving
Derie, Derm, Dermot, Derrie

Deron
(African-American) variation on Darren; smart
Dare, Daron, DaRon, Darone, Darron, Dayron, Dere

Derrell
(French) another form of Darrell; loved
Dere, Derrel, Derrill

Derri
(American) breezy
Derree, Derry

Derrick
(German) bold heart
Derak, Derick

Derry
(Irish) red-haired
Dare, Darry, Derrey, Derri, Derrie

Derward, Durward
(Last name as first name) clunky
Der, Derr, Derwy, Dur, Durr, Ward

Derwin
(English) bookish
Derwynn, Durwen, Durwin

Deseo
(Spanish) desire
Des, Desi, Dezi

Deshawn
(African-American) brassy
D'Sean, D'Shawn, Dashaun, Dashawn, Deshaun, Deshaune, Deshawnn, Deshon

Deshea
(American) confident
Desh, DeShay, Deshay, Deshie

Deshon
(African-American) bold; open
Desh, Deshan, Deshann

Desiderio
(Italian, Spanish) desirable
Des, Desi, Desie

Desire
(American) word as name; desirable
Des, Desi, Desidero

Desmee
(Irish) form of Desmond; from Munster
Desi, Dessy, Dezme, Dezmee, Desmey, Dezmie, Dezmo, Dezzy

Desmond
(Irish) from Munster; profound
Des, Desi, Desmon, Desmund, Dezmond, Dizmond

Desmun
(Irish) form of Desmond; profound
Des, Dez

Desperado
(Spanish) renegade
Des, Desesperado, Dessy, Dezzy

Destin
(Place name) city in Florida; destiny; fate
Desten, Destie, Deston, Destrie

Detroy
(African-American) outgoing
Detroe

Detton
(Last name as first name) decisive
Deet, Dett

Deuce
(American) two in cards;
second child
Doos, Duz

DeUndre
(African-American) child
of Undre
*Deundrae, DeUndray,
Deundry*

Devann
(American) divine child
DeVanne, Deven

Devaughan
(American) bravado
*Devan, Devaughn,
Devonne*

Devender
(American) poetic
*Devander, Deven,
Devendar*

Deverell
(American) special
*Dev, Devee, Deverel,
Deverelle, Devie, Devy*

Devin
(Irish) poetic; writer
*Dev, Devan, Deven,
Devon, Devvy, Devyn*

Devine
(Latin) divine
Dev, Devinne

Devinson
(Irish) poetic
*Dev, Devan, Devee,
Deven, Davin, Devy*

Devland
(Irish) courageous
*Dev, Devland, Devlen,
Devlin, Devy*

Devlin
(Irish) courageous
*Dev, Devlan, Devland,
Devlen, Devy*

Devon
(Irish) writer
*Deavon, Dev, Devin,
Devohne, Devond,
Devonn, Devy*

Devonte
(African-American)
variation on Devon;
outgoing
Devontae, Devontay

Dewayne
(American) spirited
*Dewain, Dewaine,
Duwain, Dwain*

Dewey
(Welsh) valued
Dew, Dewie, Dewy, Duey

Dewitt
(English) fair-haired
*Dewie, DeWitt, Wittie,
Witty*

DeWittay
(African-American) witty
*Dewitt, De Witt, Witt,
Witty*

Dewon
(African-American)
clever
Dejuan, Dewan

Dex
(Latin) from Dexter;
right-handed; hearty
Dexe

Dexee
(American) short for
Dexter; lucky
Dex, Dexey, Dexi, Dexie

Dexter
(Latin) skillful; right-
handed
*Decster, Dex, Dext,
Dextah, Dextar, Dextor*

Diablo
(Spanish) devil

Diamon
(American) luminous
Dimon, Dimun, Diamund

Diamond
(English) bright; gem
*Dimah, Dime, Dimond,
Dimont*

Diaz
(Spanish) rowdy
Dias, Diazz

Dice
(English) risk-taking
*Dicey, Dies, Dize, Dyce,
Dyse*

Dick
(German) short for Richard; ruler who dominates
Dickey, Dicki, Dickie, Dicky, Dik

Dickens
(Literature) articulate

Diedrich
(German) form of Dedrick; ruler
Dedric, Dedrick, Deed, Died, Dietrich

Diego
(Spanish) untamed; wild
Deago, Deagoh, Dee, Diago

Diesel
(American) movie-star name
Dees, Deez, Desel, Dezsel, Diezel

Dieter
(German) prepared
Detah, Deter

Digby
(Irish) man of simplicity

Dijon
(Place name) France; mustard
Dejawn

Dill
(Irish) loyal
Dillard, Dilly

Dillion
(Irish) from Dillon; loyal

Dillon
(Irish) loyal
Dill, Dillan, Dillen, Dilly, Dilon, Dylan, Dylanne

Dimas
(Spanish) frank

Dimitri, Dmitri
(Russian) fertile; flourishing
Demetry, Demi, Demitri, Demitry

Dino
(Italian) short for Dean
Dean, Deanie, Deano, Deinoh, Dinoh

Dinos
(Greek) short for Constantine; proud
Dean, Dino, Dinohs, Dynos

Dinose
(American) form of Dino; joyful
Denoze, Dino, Dinoce, Dinoz, Dinoze

Dins
(American) climber
Dinse, Dinz

Dinsmore
(Irish) guarded
Dinnie, Dinny, Dins

Diogenes
(Greek) honest man
Dee, Dioge, Dioh

Dion
(Greek) short for Dionysius, god of wine; reveler
Deon, Dio, Dionn

Dionisio
(Spanish) from Dionysius, god of wine and revelry; reveler
Dionis, Dioniso, Dionysio

Dionysus
(Greek) joyous celebrant; god of wine
Dee, Deonysios, Dion, Dionysius

Dirk
(Scandinavian) leader
Derk, Dirke, Dirky, Durk,

Diron
(American) form of Darren; great
Diran, Dirun, Dyronn

Dit
(Hungarian) short for Ditrik

Dix
(American) energetic
Dex

Dixie
(American) southerner
Dix, Dixee, Dixey, Dixi

Dixon
(English) Dick's son; happy
Dickson, Dix, Dixie, Dixo

Doan
(English) hills; quiet
Doane, Doe

Dobes
(American) unassuming
Dobe, Doe

Dobie
(American) reliable; southern
Dobe, Dobee, Dobey, Dobi

Dobromir
(Polish) good
Dobe, Dobry, Doby

Dobry
(Polish) good
Dobe, Dobree, Dobrey

Doc, Dock
(American) short for doctor; physician
Dok

Dodd
(English) swaggering; has a small-town sheriff feel
Dod

Dodge
(English) swaggering

Dody
(Greek) God's gift
Doe

Dog
(American) animal as name; good buddy
Daug, Dawg, Dogg, Doggie, Doggy

Doherty
(Irish) rash
Doh, Doughertey

Dolan
(Irish) dark
Dolen

Dolf
(German) short for Rudolph; wolf
Dolfe, Dolfie, Dolfy, Dolph, Dophe

Dolgen
(American) tenacious
Dole, Dolg, Dolgan, Dolgin

Dolon, Dolton
(Irish) brunette
Dole, Dolen

Dom
(Latin) short for Dominic, saint; of the Lord
Dome, Dommie, Dommy

Domenico
(Italian) confident
Dom, Domeniko

Domingo
(Spanish) Sunday-born boy
Demingo, Dom, Domin, Dominko

Dominic
(Latin) child of the Lord; saint
Dom, Domenic, Dominick

Dominique
(French) spiritual
Dom, Dominick, Dominike, Domminique

Domino
(Latin) winner
Domeno, Dominoh, Domuno

Don
(Scottish) short for Donald; powerful
Dahn, Doni, Donn, Donney, Donni, Donnie, Donny

Donaciano
(Spanish) dark
Dona, Donace, Donae, Donase

Donahue
(Irish) fighter
Don, Donohue

Donald
(Scottish) world leader; powerful
Don, Donal, Doneld, Donild, Donn, Donney, Donni, Donnie, Donny

Donatello
(Italian) giving
Don, Donatelo,
Donetello, Donny, Tello

Donatien
(French) generous
Don, Donatyen, Donn,
Donnatyen

Dong
(Chinese) from the east

Donnell
(Irish) courageous
Dahn, Don, Donel,
Donell, Donhelle,
Donnie, Donny

Donnelly
(Irish) righteous
Donalee, Donally,
Donelli, Donely, Donn,
Donnellie, Donnie

Donnis
(American) from Donald;
dark; regal
Don, Donnes, Donnus

Donny
(Irish) fond leader
Donney, Donni, Donnie

Donovan
(Irish) combative
Don, Donavan,
Donavaughn, Donavyn,
Donivin, Donny,
Donovon

Don Quixote
(Literature) an original

Dont
(American) dark; giving
Don, Dontay

Dontae
(African-American)
capricious
Dontay, Donté

Dontave
(African-American) wild
spirit
Dontav, Donteve

Donton
(American) confident
Don, Donnee, Dont,
Dontie

Dontrell
(African-American) jaded
Dontray, Dontree,
Dontrel, Dontrelle,
Dontrey, Dontrie, Dontrill

Donyale
(African-American) regal;
dark
Donyel, Donyelle

Donyell
(African-American) loyal
Donny, Danyel, Donyal

Donzell
(African-American) form
of Denzel
Dons, Donsell, Donz,
Donzelle

Doocey
(American) clever
Dooce, Doocee, Doocie,
Doos

Dooley
(Irish) shy hero
Doolee, Dooli, Dooly

Dorian
(Greek) the sea's child;
mysterious; youthful
forever
Dora, Dore, Dorean,
Dorey, Dorie, Dorien,
Dory

Dorman
(Last name as first
name) practical
Dor, Dorm

Dorral
(Last name as first
name) vain
Dorale, Dorry

Dorset
(Place name) county in
England
Dorsett, Dorzet

Dotan
(African) hardworking
Dotann

Dov
(Hebrew) bear

Doug
(Scottish) short for
Douglas; strong
*Dougie, Dougy, Dug,
Dugy*

Douglas
(Scottish) powerful;
dark river
*Doug, Douggie, Dougie,
Douglace, Douglass,
Douglis*

Dovie
(American) peaceable
*Dove, Dovee, Dovey,
Dovi, Dovy*

Dowd
(American) serious
Doud, Dowdy, Dowed

Doyal
(American) form of
Doyle; dark and unusual
Doile, Doyl, Doyle

Doyle
(Irish) deep; dark
*Doil, Doy, Doyal, Doye,
Doyl*

Doylton
(Last name as first
name) pretentious
Doyl, Doyle

Dracy
(American) form of
Stacy; secretive
*Dra, Drace, Dracee,
Dracey, Draci, Drase,
Drasee, Drasi*

Dradell
(American) serious
Drade, Dray

Drake
(English) dragon-like;
fire-breathing
Drago, Drakie, Drako

Draper
(English) precise; maker
of drapes
Draiper, Drape

Dravey
(American) groovy
Dravee, Dravie, Dravy

Drew
(Welsh) wise; well-liked
Dru

Drexel
(American) thoughtful
Drex

Dries
(Dutch)
Dre

Driscoll
(Irish) pensive
Drisk, Driskell

Dru
(English) wise; popular
Drew, Drue

Drummond
(Scottish) practical
*Drum, Drumon,
Drumond*

Drury
(French) loving man
*Drew, Drewry, Drure,
Drurey, Drurie*

Dryden
(English) writer; calm
Driden, Drydan, Drydin

Drystan
(Welsh) form of Tristan;
mourning
Drestan, Dristan, Drystyn

Duane
(Irish) dark man
*Dewain, Dewayne,
Duain, Duwain,
Duwaine, Duwayne,
Dwain, Dwaine, Dwayne*

Dub
(Irish) short for Dublin;
friendly
Dubby

Dublin
(Place name) city in
Ireland; trendy

Duc
(Vietnamese) honest

Dude
(American) cool guy
Dudley
(English) compromiser;
rich; stuffy
Dud, Dudd, Dudlee,
Dudlie, Dudly
Dueart
(American) kind
Art, Duart, Due, Duey
Duff
(Scottish) dark
Duf, Duffey, Duffie, Duffy
Duffy
(Scottish) dark
Duff
Dugan
(Irish) dark man
Doogan, Dougan,
Duggie, Duggy, Dugin
Duke
(Latin) leader of the
pack
Dook, Dukey, Dukie
Dumisani
(African) leader
Dumont
(French) monumental
Dummont, Dumon,
Dumonde, Dumonte,
Dumontt
Dunbar
(Irish) castle-dweller
Dunbarr

Dunbaron
(American) dark
Baron, Dunbar
Duncan
(Scottish) spirited
fighter
Dunc, Dunk, Dunkan,
Dunne
Dunia
(American) dark
Dunya
Dunk
(Scottish) form of
Duncan; dark;
combative
Dunc, Dunk
Dunlavy
(English) sylvan
Dunlave
Dunley
(English) meadow-
loving; sylvan
Dunlea, Dunlee,
Dunleigh, Dunli, Dunly,
Dunnlea
Dunmore
(Scottish) guarded
Dun, Dunmohr,
Dunmoore
Dunn
(Irish) neutral
Dun, Dunne

Dunphy
(American) dark; serious
Dun, Dunphe, Dunphee,
Dunphey
Dunstan
(English) well-girded
Dun, Duns, Dunse,
Dunsten, Dunstin,
Dunston
Dunstand
(English) form of
Dunstan; protected
Dunsce, Dunse, Dunst,
Dunsten, Dunstun
Duran
(Last name as first
name) lasting; musical
Durand, Durante, Durran
Durand
(Latin) from Durant;
lasting; dependable
Duran, Durayn
Durant
(Latin) lasting; alluring
Duran, Durand, Durante,
Durr, Durrie, Durry
Durban
(Place name) city in
South Africa
Durb, Durben
Durham
(Last name as first
name) supportive
Duram

Duro

(Place name) Palo Duro Canyon; enduring
Dure

Durrell

(English) protective
Durel, Durell, Durr, Durrel, Durry

Durwin

(English) dear friend
Durwen, Durwinn

Durwood, Durward

(English) vigilant; home-loving
Derrwood, Derwood, Durr, Durrwood, Durwould

Duster

(American) form of Dusty; deliberate
Dust, Dustee, Dustey, Dusti, Dusty

Dustin

(German) bold and brave
Dust, Dustan, Dusten, Dustie, Dusty, Dustyn

Dusty

(German) short for Dustin; brave
Dust, Dustee, Dustey, Dusti, Dustie

Dusty-Joe

(American) cowboy
Dustee, Dusti, Dusty, Dustyjoe, Joe

Dutch

(Dutch) from Holland; optimistic
Dutchie, Dutchy

Duval

(French) valley; peaceful
Dovahl, Duv, Duvall, Duvalle

Dwain

(American) form of Dwayne; country; dark
Dwaine

Dwan

(African-American) fresh
D'wan, D'Wan, Dewan, Dwawn, Dwon

Dwanae

(African-American) dark; small
Dwannay

Dwayne

(American) country
Duane, Duwane, Dwaine

Dweezel

(American) creative
Dweez

Dwight

(English) intelligent; white
Dwi, Dwite

Dwyer

(Irish) wise
Dwire, Dwyyer

Dyer

(English) creative
Di, Dier, Dyar, Dye

Dylan

(Welsh) sea god; creative
Dill, Dillan, Dillon, Dilloyn, Dilon, Dyl, Dylahn, Dylen, Dylin

Dynell

(African-American) seaman; gambler
Dinell, Dyne

Dyron

(African-American) mercurial; sea-loving
Diron, Dyronn, Dyronne

Dyson

(English) sea-loving
Dieson, Dison, Dysan, Dysen, Dysun, Dyzon

Dyvet

(English) worker; dyes
Dye

Eagle
(Native American) sharp-eyed
Eagal, Egle

Eamon
(Irish) form of Edmund; thriving; protective
Amon, Emon

Earl
(English) promising; noble
Earle, Earley, Earlie, Early, Eril, Erl

Early
(English) punctual
Earl, Earlee, Earley

Earnest
(English) genuine
Earn, Earnie, Ern, Ernie

Earon
(American) form of Aaron
Earonn

Earvin
(English) sea-loving
Dervin, Ervin

Easey
(American) easygoing
Easy, Ezey

Easton
(English) outdoorsy; east town
Easten

Eaton
(English) wealthy
Etawn, Eton

Ebby
(Hebrew) short for Ebenezer; rock; reliable
Ebbey, Ebbi

Ebenezer
(Hebrew) base of life; rock
Eb, Ebbie, Ebby, Eben, Ebeneezer, Ebeneser

Eberhardt
(German) brave
Eb, Eber, Eberhard

Eckhardt
(German) iron-willed
Eck, Eckhard, Eckhart, Ekhard

Ed
(English) short for Edward
Edd, Eddie, Eddy, Edy

Edan
(Scottish) fiery
Edon

Edcell
(English) focused; wealthy
Ed, Edcelle, Eds, Edsel

Eddie
(English) short for Edward
Eddee, Eddey, Eddy

Eden
(Hebrew) delight
Eadon, Edin, Edon, Edye, Edyn

Edenson
(Hebrew) delight
Edence, Edens, Edensen

Edgar
(English) success
Ed, Eddie, Edghur, Edgur

Edgardo
(English) successful
Edgar, Edgard, Edgardoh

Edge
(American) cutting edge; trendsetter
Eddge, Edgy

Edilberto
(Spanish) noble
Edilbert

Edison
(English) Edward's son; smart
Ed, Eddie, Edisen, Edyson

Edmond
(English) protective
Ed, Edmon, Edmund
Edmund
(English) protective
Ed, Eddie, Edmond
Edrick
(English) rich leader;
(American) laughing
Ed, Edri, Edrik, Edry
Edsel
(English) rich
Ed, Eddie, Edsil, Edsyl
Eduardo
(Spanish) flirtatious
Ed, Eddie, Edwardo
Edward
(English) prospering;
defender
*Ed, Eddey, Eddi, Eddie,
Eddy, Edwar, Edwerd*
Edwin
(English) prosperous
friend
Ed, Edwinn, Edwynn
Efrain
(Hebrew) fertile
Efren
Efrim
(Hebrew) short for
Ephraim
Ef, Efrem, Efrum

Efton
(American) form of
Ephraim; (Hebrew)
fruitful
Ef, Eft, Eften, Eftun
Egan
(Irish) spirited
Eggie, Egin, Egon
Egbert
(English) bright sword
*Egber, Egburt, Eggie,
Eggy*
Egborn
(English) ready; born of
Edgar
*Eg, Egbornem, Egburn,
Eggie*
Eghert
(German) smart
Eghertt, Eghurt
Egmon
(German) protective
*Egmond, Egmont,
Egmun, Egmund,
Egmunt*
Egeus
(American) word as
name; protective
Aegis, Egis
Egypt
(Place name)
Elam
(Hebrew) from Eliam;
God-centered;
distinctive

Elan
(French) finesse
Elann, Elon
Elbis
(American) exalted
*Elb, Elbace, Elbase,
Elbus*
Elbridge
(American) presidential
Elb, Elby
Elder
(English) older sibling
El, Eldor
Eldon
(English) place name;
charitable
El, Elden, Eldin
Eldorado
(Place name) city in
Arkansas (El Dorado)
El, Eld, Eldor
Eldread
(English) wise advisor
El, Eldred, Eldrid
Eldridge
(English) supportive
Eldredge
Elgin
(English) elegant
Elgen
Elegy
(Spanish) memorable
Elegee, Elegie, Elgy

Elendor
(Invented) special
Elen, Elend

Eli
(Hebrew) faithful man;
high priest
El, Elie, Eloy, Ely

Elian
(Spanish) spirited
Eliann, Elyan

Elias
(Greek) spiritual
El, Eli, Eliace, Elyas

Eliezer
(Origin unknown) of God

Elijah
(Hebrew) religious; Old
Testament prophet
El, Elie, Elija

Elijah-Blue
(American) combo of
Elijah and Blue; devout
Elijah-Bleu, Elijah-Blu

Eliseo
(Spanish) daring
Elizeo

Ellard
(German) brave man
Ell, Ellarde, Ellee, Ellerd

Ellery
(English) dominant
El, Ell, Ellary, Ellerie, Ellie

Elliott
(English) God-loving
Elie, Elio, Ell, Elliot

Ellis
(English) form of Elias;
devout
Ellice, Ells

Ellis-Marcelle
(American) combo of
Ellis and Marcelle;
achiever
*Ellis, Ellismarcelle,
Marcelle*

Ellison
(English) circumspect
*Ell, Ellason, Ellisen, Ells,
Ellyson*

Elman
(American) protective
El, Elle, Elmen, Elmon

Elmer
(English) famed
*Ell, Elm, Elmar, Elmir,
Elmo, Elmoh*

Elmo
(Greek) gregarious
Ellmo, Elmoh

Elmot
(American) lovable
Elm

Elmore
(English) radiant
*Elm, Elmie, Elmoor,
Elmor*

Elsworth
(Last name as first
name) pretentious
Ells, Ellsworth

Elof
(Swedish) the one heir
Loff

Eloi
(French) chosen one
Eloie, Eloy

Elonzo
(Spanish) sturdy; happy
El, Elon, Elonso

Elroy
(French) giving
Elroi, Elroye

Elsden
(English) spiritual
Els, Elsdon

Elson
(English) from Elston;
affluent
Elsen

Elston
(English) sophisticated
Els, Elstan, Elsten

Elton
(English) settlement;
famous
*Ell, Ellton, Elt, Eltan,
Elten*

Elvin
(English) friend of elves
El, Elv, Elven

Elvind
(American) form of
Elvin/Alvin; friend of
elves
Elv

Elvis
(Scandinavian) wise; musical
El, Elvyse, The King

Elwen
(English) friend of elves
Elwee Elwy, Elwyn, Elwynn, Elwynt

Elwond
(Last name as first name) steady
Ellwand, Elwon, Eldwund

Elwood
(English) old wood; everlasting
Ell, Elwoode, Elwould, Woodie, Woody, Woodye

Ely
(Hebrew) lifted up
Eli

Emanuel
(Hebrew) with God
Em, Eman, Emanuele

Emberto
(Italian) pushy
Berty, Embert, Emberte

Emerson
(German) Emery's son; able
Emers, Emersen

Emery
(German) hardworking leader
Em, Emeri, Emerie, Emmerie, Emory, Emrie

Emil
(Latin) ingratiating
Em, Emel, Emele

Emilio
(Italian) competitive; (Spanish) excelling
Emil, Emile, Emilioh, Emlo

Emjay
(American) reliable
Em-J, Em-Jay, M.J., MJ

Emmanuel
(Hebrew) with God
Em, Eman, Emmanuele

Emmett
(Hebrew) truthful; sincere
Emit, Emmet, Emmitt

Emory
(German) industrious leader
Emmory, Emori, Emorie

Emuel
(Hebrew) form of Emmanuel (God with us); believer
Emanuel, Imuel

Eneas
(Hebrew) much-praised
Ennes, Ennis

Engelbert
(German) angel-bright
Bert, Bertie, Berty, Engelber, Inglebert

Enlai
(Chinese) thankful

Enoch
(Hebrew) dedicated instructor
En, Enoc, Enok

Enos
(Hebrew) mortal
Enoes

Enrick
(Spanish) cunning
Enric, Enrik

Enrico
(Italian) ruler
Enrike, Enriko

Enrique
(Spanish) charismatic ruler
Enrika, Enrikae, Enriqué, Quiqui

Enzo
(Italian) fun-loving

Ephraim
(Hebrew) fertile
Eff, Efraim, Efram, Efrem

Erasmus
(Greek) beloved
Eras, Erasmas, Erasmis

Erazmo
(Spanish) loved
Erasmo, Eraz, Ras, Raz

Erhardt
(German) strong-willed
Erhar, Erhard, Erhart, Erheart

Eric, Erik
(Scandinavian) powerful leader
Ehrick, Erek, Erick, Eryke

Erin
(Irish) peace-loving
Aaron, Aron, Erin, Eryn

Erlan
(English) aristocratic
Earlan, Earland, Erland, Erlen, Erlin

Ernest
(English) sincere
Earnest, Ern, Ernie, Erno, Ernst, Erny, Ernye

Ernesto
(Spanish) sincere
Ernie, Nesto, Nestoh

Ernie
(English) short for Ernest
Ernee, Erney, Erny

Erol
(American) noble
Eral, Eril, Errol

Eros
(Greek) sensual
Ero

Erose
(Greek) from the word eros; sensual; resolute
Eroce

Erskine
(Scottish) high-minded
Ers, Ersk, Erskin

Ervin
(English) sea-loving
Earvin, Erv, Ervan, Erven, Ervind, Ervyn

Ervine
(English) sea-lover
Ervene, Ervin

Esau
(Hebrew) rough-hewn
Es, Esa, Esauw, Esaw

Esaul
(American) combo of Esau and Saul; hairy
Esau, Esaw, Esawle, Saul

Esmé
(French) beloved
Es, Esmae, Esmay

Esmond
(French) handsome
Esmand, Esmon, Esmund

Esmun
(American) kind
Es, Esman, Esmon

Esperanza
(Spanish) from esperance; (English) hopeful
Esper, Esperance, Esperence

Essex
(Place name) dignified
Ess, Ez

Esteban
(Spanish) royal; friendly
Estabon, Estebann, Estevan

Estes
(Place name) eastern; open
Estas, Este, Estis

Estridge
(Last name as first name) fortified
Es, Estri, Estry

Etereo
(Spanish) heavenly; spiritual
Etero

Ethan
(Hebrew) firm will
Eth, Ethen, Ethin, Ethon

Etheal
(English) of good birth
Ethal

Ethelbert
(German) principled
Ethelburt, Ethylbert

Euclid
(Greek) brilliant
Euclide, Uclid

Eugene
(Greek) blue-blood
Eugean, Eugenie, Ugene

Eural
(American) form of Ural
Mountains; upward
Eure, Ural, Ury

Eurby
(Last name as first
name)
Erby, Eurb

Eurskie
(Invented) dorky
Ersky

Eusebio
(Spanish) devoted to
God
*Eucebio, Eusabio,
Eusevio, Sebio, Usibo*

Eustace
(Latin) calming
Eustice, Eustis, Ustace

Eustacio
(Spanish) calm;
visionary
*Eustacio, Eustase,
Eustasio, Eustazio,
Eustes, Eustis*

Evan
(Irish) warrior
*Ev, Evann, Evanne, Even,
Evin*

Evander
(Greek) manly;
champion
Evand, Evandar, Evandir

Evanus
(American) form of Evan;
heroic
*Evan, Evin, Evinas,
Evinus*

Evaristo
(Spanish) form of Evan;
heroic
Evariso, Evaro

Eve
(Invented) form of Yves
Eeve

Evelyn
(American) writer
Ev, Evlinn, Evlyn

Everard
(German) tough
Ev, Evrard

Everett
(English) strong
*Ev, Everet, Everitt, Evret,
Evrit*

Everhart
(Scandinavian) vibrant
Evhart, Evert

Everly
(American) singing
*Everlee, Everley, Everlie,
Evers*

Evetier
(French) good

Evett
(American) bright
*Ev, Evatt, Eve, Evidt,
Evitt*

Evon
(Welsh) form of Evan;
warrior
*Even, Evin, Evonne,
Evonn, Evyn*

Ewan
(Scottish) youthful spirit
Ewahn, Ewon

Ewand
(Welsh) form of Evan;
warrior
Ewen, Ewon

Ewanell
(American) form of
Ewan; hip
Ewanel, Ewenall

Ewart, Ewert
(English) shepherd;
caring
Ewar, Eward

Ewing
(English) law-abiding
Ewin, Ewyng

Excell
(American) competitive
Excel, Exsel, Exsell

Exia
(Spanish) demanding
Ex, Exy

Eza
(Hebrew) from Ezra; helpful
Esri

Ezekiel
(Hebrew) God's strength
Eze, Ezek, Ezekhal, Ezekial, Ezikiel, Ezkeil

Ezequiel
(Spanish) devout

Ezra
(Hebrew) helpful; strong
Esra, Ezrah

Ezzie
(Hebrew) from the name Ezra; helpful
Ez

Faber
(German) grower
Fabar, Fabir, Fabyre

Faberto
(Latin) form of Fabian; grower; deals in beans
Fabe, Fabey, Fabian, Fabien, Fabre

Fabian
(Latin) grower; singer
Fab, Fabean, Fabeone, Fabie

Fabio
(Italian) seductive; handsome
Fab, Fabioh

Fable
(American) storyteller
Fabal, Fabe, Fabel, Fabil

Fabrizio
(Italian) fabulous

Fabryce
(Latin) crafty
Fab, Fabby, Fabreese, Fabrese, Fabrice

Fabulous
(American) vain
Fab, Fabby, Fabu

Faddis
(American) loner; deals in beans
Faddes, Fadice, Fadis

Faddy
(American) faddish
Fad, Faddey, Faddi

Fadil
(Arabic) giving

Fagan
(Irish) fiery
Fagane, Fagen, Fagin, Fegan

Fahd
(Arabic) fierce; panther; brave
Fahad

Fahim
(Arabic) intelligent

Fairbanks
(English) place name; forceful
Fairbanx, Farebanks

Fairfax
(English) full of warmth
Fairfacks, Farefax, Fax, Faxy

Faisal
(Arabic) authoritative
Faisel, Faizal, Fasel, Fayzelle

Faladrick
(Origin unknown)
Faldrick, Faldrik

Falcon
(American) bird as name; dark; watchful
Falk, Falkon

Falk
(Hebrew) falcon
Falke

Fam
(American) family-oriented
Fammy

Famous
(American) word as name; ambitious
Fame

Fannin
(English) happy
Fane

Far
(English) traveler
Farr

Faran
(American) sincere
Fahran, Faren, Faron, Feren, Ferren

Fargo
(American) jaunty
Fargouh

Farley
(English) open
Farl, Farlee, Farleigh, Farlie, Farly, Farlye

Farnham
(English) windblown; field
Farnhum, Farnie, Farnum, Farny

Farquar
(French) masculine

Farr
(English) adventurer
Far

Farrar
(French) distinguished
Farr

Farrell
(Irish) brave
Farel, Farell, Faryl

Farren
(English) mover
Faran, Faron, Farrin, Farron

Farris
(Arabic) rider; (Irish) rock, reliable
Fare, Farice, Faris

Faulkner
(English) disciplinarian
Falcon, Falconner, Falkner, Falkoner

Faust
(Latin) lucky
Fauston

Favian, Favion
(Latin) knowing
Fav

Fawcett
(American) audacious
Fawce, Fawcet, Fawcette, Fawcie, Fawsie, Fowcett

Faysal
(Arabic) judgmental

Federico
(Spanish) peaceful and affluent
Federik

Fedrick
(American) form of Cedrick; wandering
Fed, Fedric, Fedrik

Felipe
(Spanish) horse-lover
Felepe, Filipe, Flippo

Felix
(Latin) joyful
Felixce, Filix, Phelix, Philix

Felman
(Last name as first name) smart
Fel, Fell

Fenner
(English) capable
Fen, Fenn, Fynner

Fenton
(English) nature-loving
Fen, Fenn, Fennie, Fenny

Fentress
(English) natural
Fentres, Fyntres

Feo
(Native American)
confident
Feeo, Feoh

Ferdinand
(German) adventurer
*Ferdie, Ferdnand, Ferdy,
Fernand*

Fergus
(Irish, Scottish)
topnotch
*Feargus, Ferges, Fergie,
Fergis, Fergy*

Ferguson
(Irish) bold; excellent
*Fergie, Fergs, Fergus,
Fergusahn, Fergusen,
Fergy, Furgs, Furgus*

Ferlin
(American) countrified
Ferlan

Fermin
(Spanish) strong-willed
Fer, Fermen, Fermun

Fernando
(Spanish) bold leader
*Ferd, Ferdie, Ferdinando,
Ferdy, Fernand*

Ferrell
(Irish) hero
Fere, Ferrel, Feryl

Festive
(American) word as
name; joyful
Fest, Festas, Festes

Festus
(Latin) happy
Festes

Fidel
(Latin) faithful
Fidele, Fidell, Fydel

Fidencio
(Spanish)
Fidence, Fidens, Fido

Field
(English) outdoorsman
Fields

Fielding
(English) outdoorsman;
working the fields

Fien
(American) elegant
Fiene, Fine

Fiero
(Spanish) fiery

Fife
(Scottish) bright-eyed
Fyfe, Phyfe

Fiji
(Place name) Fiji Islands;
islander
Fege, Fegee, Fijie

Fikry
(American) industrious
Fike, Fikree, Fikrey

Filbert
(English) genius
Fil, Filb, Bert, Phil

Filip
(Greek) horse-lover;
(Belgium) form of Philip
Fil, Fill

Filmer
(English) from Filmore;
famed
Fill, Filmar

Filmore
(English) famed
*Fill, Fillie, Fillmore, Filly,
Fylmore*

Finian
(Irish) fair
Fin, Finean, Finn, Fynian

Finley
(Irish) magical
Fin, Finny, Fynn, Fynnie

Finn
(Scandinavian) fair-
haired; from Finland
Fin, Finnie, Finny

Finnegan
(Irish) fair
*Finegan, Finigan, Finn,
Finny*

Finton
(Irish) magical, fair
Finn, Finny, Fynton

Fish, Fishel
(Hebrew) fish
Fysh

Fitz
(French) bright young man; son
Fitzy

Fitzgerald
(English) bright young man; Gerald's son

Fitzmorris
(Last name as first name) son of Morris
Fitz, Morrey, Morris

Fitzsimmons
(English) bright young man; Simmons's son

Flabia
(Spanish) light-haired
Flavia

Flag
(American) patriotic
Flagg

Flavean
(Flavian) form of Flavian

Flavian
(Greek) blond
Flovian

Flavio
(Italian) shining
Flav, Flavioh

Fleada
(American) introvert
Flayda

Flemming
(English) from Flanders; confident
Fleming, Flyming

Fletcher
(English) kind-hearted; maker of arrows
Fletch, Fletchi, Fletchie, Fletchy

Flint
(English) stream; nature-lover
Flinn, Flintt, Flynt, Flynnt

Florian
(Latin) flourishing
Florean, Florie

Floyd
(English) practical; hair of gray
Floid

Flynn
(Irish) brash
Flin, Flinn, Flinnie, Flinny, Flyne

Flynt
(English) flowing; stream
Flint, Flinte, Flinty, Flynte

Foley
(Last name as first name) creative
Folee, Folie

Folker
(German) watchful
Folke, Folko

Fontayne
(French) giving; fountain
Font, Fontaine, Fontane, Fountaine

Fonzie
(German) short for Alphonse
Fons, Fonsi, Fonz, Fonzi

For
(American) word as a name
Fore

Foran
(American) form of foreign; exotic
Foren, Forun

Forbes
(Irish) wealthy
Forb

Ford
(English) strong
Feord, Forde, Fyord

Fordan
(English) river crossing; inventive
Ford, Forday, Forden

Foreign
(American) word as name; foreigner
Foran

Forend
(American) forward
Fore, Foryn, Forynd

Forest
(French) nature-loving
Forrest, Fory, Fourast

Forester
(English) protective; of the forest
Forrester, Forry

Fortune
(French) fortunate man
Fortounay, Fortunae

Fost
(Latin) form of Foster; worthwhile
Foste, Fostee, Fosty

Foster
(Latin) worthy
Fauster, Fostay

Fowler
(English) hunter; traps fowl
Fowller

Francesco
(Italian) flirtatious
Fran, Francey, Frankie, Franky

Francis
(Latin) free spirit; from France
Fran, Frances, Franciss, Frank, Franky, Frannkie, Franny, Frans

Francisco
(Spanish) free spirit; from Latin Franciscus; Frenchman
Chuco, Cisco, Francisk, Franco, Frisco, Paco, Pancho

Francista
(Spanish) from Franciscus; Frenchman; free
Cisco, Cisto, Francisco, Franciscus, Fransico

Franco
(Spanish) defender; spear
Francoh, Franko

Francois
(French) smooth; patriot; Frenchman
Frans, Franswaw, French, Frenchie, Frenchy

Frank
(English) short for Franklin; outspoken; landowner
Franc, Franco, Frankee, Frankey, Frankie, Franko, Franky

Frankie
(English) outspoken; landowner
Frankee, Frankey, Franky

Franklin
(English) outspoken; landowner
Francklin, Franclin, Frank, Frankie, Franklinn, Franklyn, Franklynn, Franky

Frasier
(English) attractive; man with curls
Frase, Fraser, Fraze, Frazer

Fred
(German) short for Frederick; plainspoken leader
Fredde, Freddo, Freddy, Fredo

Freddie
(German) short for Frederick; plainspoken leader
Freddee, Freddey, Freddi, Freddy

Freddis
(German) from the name Frederick; friendly
Freddus, Fredes, Fredis

Frederic
(French) peaceful king
Fred, Freddy

Frederick
(German) plainspoken leader; peaceful
Fred, Freddy, Frederic, Fredrich, Fredrik

Freeman
(English) free man
Free, Freedman, Freman

Frieder
(German) peaceful leader
Frie, Fried, Friedrich, Friedrick

Friederich, Friedrich
(German) form of Frederick; leader of peace
Fridrich

Frisco
(American) short for Francisco; free
Cisco, Frisko

Fritz
(German) short for Frederick and Friedrich
Firzie, Firzy, Frits, Fritts, Fritzi, Fritzie, Fritzy

Frost
(English) cold; freeze

Fructuoso
(Spanish) fruitful
Fru, Fructo

Fuddy
(Origin unknown) bright-eyed
Fuddie, Fudee, Fudi

Fulbright
(German) brilliant; full of brightness
Fulbrite

Fuller
(English) tough-willed
Fuler

Fullerton
(English) strong
Fuller, Fullerten

Fulton
(English) fresh mind; field by the town

Funge
(Last name as first name) stodgy
Funje, Funny

Furlo
(American) macho
Furl

G

Gabbana
(Italian) creative
Gabi

Gabe
(Hebrew) short for Gabriel; devout
Gabbee, Gabbi, Gabby, Gabi, Gabie, Gaby

Gabino
(Spanish) strong believer
Gabby, Gabi

Gable
(French) dashing

Gabriel
(Hebrew) God's hero; devout
Gabby, Gabe, Gabi, Gabreal, Gabrel, Gabriele, Gabrielle, Gabryel

Gad
(Hebrew) lucky; audacious
Gadd

Gaddis
(American) hard to please; picky
Gad, Gaddes, Gadis

Gael
(English) speaks Gaelic; independent

Gaetano
(Italian) from the city of Gaeta; Italian
Gaetan, Geitano, Guytano

Gagan
(French) form of Gage; dedicated
Gage

Gage
(French) dedicated

Gailen
(French) healer; physician
Galan, Galen, Galun

Galbraith
(Irish) sensible
Gal

Galbreath
(Irish) practical man
Galbraith, Gall

Gale
(English) cheerful
Gael, Gail, Gaile, Gaille, Gayle

Galen
(Greek) calming; intelligent
Gaelin, Gailen, Gale, Galean, Galey, Gaylen

Galileo
(Italian) from Galilee; inventor
Galilayo

Gallagher
(Irish) helpful
Galagher, Gallager, Gallie, Gally

Gallant
(American) word as a name; savoir-faire
Gael, Gail, Gaila, Gaile, Gayle

Gallman
(Last name as first name) lively
Galman

Galo
(Spanish) enthusiastic
Gallo

Galloway
(Irish) outgoing
Gallie, Gally, Galoway, Galway

Gamberro
(Spanish) hooligan
Gami

Gamble
(Scandinavian) mature wisdom
Gam, Gamb, Gambel, Gambie, Gamby

Gammon
(Last name as first name) game
Gamen, Gamon, Gamun

Ganon
(Irish) fair-skinned
Gannon, Ganny

Ganso
(Spanish) goose; goofy
Gans, Ganz

Ganya
(Russian) strong

Garcia
(Spanish) strong
Garce, Garcey, Garsey

Gard
(English) guard
Garde, Gardey, Gardi, Gardie, Gardy, Guard

Gardner
(English) keeper of the garden
Gar, Gard, Gardener, Gardie, Gardiner, Gardnyr, Gardy

Gareth
(Irish) kind, gentle
Gare

Garfield
(English) armed
Gar, Garfeld

Garin
(American) form of
Darin; kind
Gare, Gary

Garland
(French) adorned
*Gar, Garlan, Garlend,
Garlind, Garlynd*

Garn
(American) prepared
Gar, Garnie, Garny, Garr

Garner
(French) guard
Gar, Garn, Garnar, Garnir

Garnett
(English) armed; spear
Gar, Garn, Garnet, Garny

Garon
(American) gentle
Garonn, Garonne

Garonzick
(Last name as first
name) secure
*Gare, Garon, Garons,
Garonz*

Garr
(English) short for
Garnett and Garth;
giving
Gar

Garrett
(Irish) brave; watchful
*Gare, Garet, Garitt,
Garret, Garritt, Gary,
Gerrot*

Garrick
(English) ruler with a
spear; brave
*Garey, Garic, Garick,
Garik, Garreck, Gary,
Gerrick, Gerrieck*

Garrison
(French) prepared
*Garris, Garrish, Garry,
Gary*

Garth
(Scandinavian) sunny;
gardener
*Gar, Gare, Garry, Gart,
Garthe, Gary*

Garthay
(Irish) from Gareth;
gentle
Garthae

Garv
(English) peaceful
Garvey, Garvy

Garvy
(Irish) peacemaker
Garvey

Garwood
(English) natural
*Garr, Garwode,
Garwoode, Woody*

Gary
(English) strong man
Gare, Garrey, Garri

Gaspare
(Italian) treasure-holder
Casper, Gasp, Gasparo

Gaston
(French) native of
Gascony; stranger
Gastawn, Gastowyn

Gate
(English) open
Gait

Gaudy
(American) word as
name; colorful
Gaudin, Gaudy

Gavard
(Last name as first
name) creative
Gav, Gaverd

Gavin
(English) alert; hawk
*Gav, Gaven, Gavinn,
Gavon, Gavvin, Gavyn*

Gawain
(Hebrew) archangel
*Gawaine, Gawayne,
Gwayne*

Gaylin
(Greek) calm
*Gaelin, Gayle, Gaylen,
Gaylon*

Gaylord
(French) high-energy
Gallerd, Galurd, Gaylar,
Gayllaird, Gaylor

Gaynor
(Irish) spunky
Gainer, Gaye, Gayner

Gayton
(Irish) fair
Gayten, Gaytun

Geary
(English) flexible
Gearey

Genaro
(Latin) dedicated
Genaroe, Genaroh

Gene
(Greek) noble
Geno, Jene, Jeno

General
(American) military rank
as name; leader

Geno
(Italian) spontaneous

Genoah
(Place name) Genoa,
Italy
Genoa, Jenoa, Jenoah

Genovese
(Italian) spontaneous;
from Genoa, Italy
Genno, Geno, Genovise,
Genovize

Gent
(American) short for
gentleman; mannerly
Gynt, Jent, Jynt

Gentil
(Spanish) charming
Gentilo

Gentry
(American) high
breeding
Genntrie, Gent, Gentree,
Gentree, Gentrie

Geo
(Greek) form of George;
good
Gee

Geoff
(English) short for
Geoffrey; peaceful
Jeff

Geoffrey
(English) peaceful
Geffry, Geoff, Geoffie,
Geoffry, Geoffy, Geofry,
Jeff

George
(Greek) land-loving;
farmer
Georg, Georgi, Georgie,
Georgy, Jorg, Jorge

Georgio
(Italian) earth-worker
Giorgio, Jorgio, Jorjeo,
Jorjio

Georgios
(Greek) land-loving

Georgy
(Greek) short for George
Georgee, Georgi,
Georgie

Gerald
(German) strong; ruling
with a spear
Geralde, Gerrald, Gerre,
Gerry

Gerard
(French) brave
Gerord, Gerr, Gerrard

Gerber
(Last name as first
name) particular
Gerb

Gere
(English) spear-wielding;
dramatic
Gear

Gerhard
(German) forceful
Ger, Gerd

Germain
(French) growing; from
Germany
Germa, Germaine,
Germane, Germay,
Germayne, Jermaine

German
(German) from Germany

Gerod
(English) form of Gerard; brave
Garard, Geraldo, Gerard, Gerarde, Gere, Gererde, Gerry, Gerus, Giraud, Jerade, Jerard, Jere, Jerod, Jerott, Jerry

Geronimo
(Italian, Native American) wild heart
Geronimoh

Gerry
(English) short for Gerald
Gerr, Gerre, Gerree, Gerrey, Gerri, Gerrie

Gershom
(Biblical) exile

Gervaise
(French) man of honor
Gerv, Gervase, Gervay

Gervasio
(Spanish) aggressive
Gervase, Gervaso, Jervasio

Gervis, Jervis
(German) honored
Gerv, Gervace, Gervaise, Gervey, Jervaise

Geter
(Origin unknown) hopeful
Getterr, Getur

Ghalby
(Origin unknown) winning
Galby

Ghassan
(Arabic) in the prime of life

Giacomo
(Italian) replacement; musical
Como, Gia

Giancarlo
(Italian) combo of Gian and Carlo; magnetic
Carlo, Carlos, Gia, Gian, Giannie, Gianny

Giann
(Italian) believer in a gracious God
Ghiann, Giahanni, Gian, Gianni, Giannie, Gianny

Gianni
(Italian) calm; believer in God's grace
Giannie, Gianny

Gibbs
(English) form of Gibson; spunky
Gib, Gibb, Gibbes

Gibson
(English) smiling
Gib, Gibb, Gibbie, Gibbson, Gibby, Gibsan, Gibsen, Gibsyn

Gid
(Hebrew) form of Gideon; warrior; Bible distributor
Gidd, Giddee, Giddi, Giddy

Gideon
(Hebrew) power-wielding
Giddy, Gideone, Gidion, Gidyun

Gidney
(English) strong
Gidnee, Gidni

Giglio
(Italian) form of the word gigolo
Gig

Gifford
(English) generous-hearted
Giff, Gifferd, Giffie, Giffy

Gilbert
(English) intelligent
Gil, Gilber, Gilburt, Gill, Gilly

Gilberto
(Spanish) bright
Bertie, Berty, Gil, Gilb, Gilburto, Gillberto, Gilly

Gilby
(Irish) blond
Gilbie, Gill, Gillbi

Gilchrist
(Irish) open
Gill

Gildo
(Italian) macho
Gil, Gill, Gilly

Giles
(French) protective
Gile, Gyles

Gilford
(English) kind-hearted
Gill, Gillford, Guilford

Gill
(Hebrew) happy man
Gil, Gilli, Gillie, Gilly

Gilles
(French) miraculous
Geal, Zheal, Zheel

Gillespie
(Irish) humble
Gilespie, Gill, Gilley, Gilli, Gilly

Gilley
(American) countrified
Gill, Gilleye, Gilli, Gilly

Gillian
(Irish) devout
Gill, Gilley, Gilly, Gillyun

Gilman
(Irish) serving well
Gilley, Gilli, Gillman, Gillmand, Gilly, Gilmand, Gilmon

Gilmer
(English) riveting
Gelmer, Gill, Gillmer, Gilly

Gilmore
(Irish) riveting
Gill, Gillmore, Gilmohr

Gilon
(Hebrew) joyful
Gill

Ginder
(American) form of gender; vivacious
Gin, Gind, Gindyr, Jind, Jinder

Gino
(Italian) of good breeding; outgoing
Geeno, Geino, Ginoh

Giordano
(Italian) delivered
Giorgie, Jiordano

Giorgio
(Italian) earthy; creative
George, Georgeeo, Georgo, Jorge, Jorgio

Giovanni
(Italian) jovial; happy believer
Geovanni, Gio, Giovani, Giovannie, Giovanny, Vannie, Vanny, Vonny

Gitel
(Hebrew) good

Giulio
(Italian) youth

Giuseppe
(Italian) capable
Beppo, Giusepe, Gusepe

Given
(Last name as first name) gift
Givens, Gyvan, Gyven, Gyvin

Gizmo
(American) playful
Gis, Gismo, Giz

Glad
(American) happy
Gladd, Gladde, Gladdi, Gladdie, Gladdy

Gladwyn
(English) friend who has a light heart
Glad, Gladdy, Gladwin, Gladwynn

Glancy
(American) form of Clancy; ebullient
Glance, Glancee, Glancey, Glanci

Glanville
(French) serene

Glasgow
(Place name) city in Scotland

Glenard
(Irish) from a glen;
nature-loving
Glen, Glenerd, Glenn,
Glennard, Glenni,
Glennie

Glen
(Irish) natural wonder
Glenn

Glendon
(Scottish) fortified in
nature
Glen, Glend, Glenden,
Glenn, Glynden

Glenn
(Irish) natural wonder
Glen, Glenni, Glennie,
Glenny, Glynn, Glynny

Gloster
(Place name) form of
Gloucester, city area in
England
Gobi
(Place name) audacious
Gobee, Gobie

Gobind
(Sanskrit) the name of a
Hindi deity
Govind

Gockley
(Last name as first
name) peaceful
Gocklee

Goddard
(German) staunch in
spirituality
Godard, Godderd,
Goddird

Godfrey
(Irish) peaceful
Godfree, Godfrie, Godfry

Godwin
(English) close to God
Godwinn, Godwyn,
Godwynn

Gohn
(African-American)
spirited
Gon

Goldo
(English) golden
Golo

Goliath
(Hebrew) large
Goliathe

Gomer
(English) famed fighter
Gomar, Gomher, Gomor

Gong
(American) forceful

Gonz
(Spanish) form of
Gonzalo; wild wolf
Gons, Gonz, Gonza,
Gonzales, Gonzalez

Gonzales
(Spanish) feisty
Gonzalez

Gonzalo
(Spanish) feisty wolf
Gonz, Gonzoloh

Goode
(English) good
Good, Goodey, Goody

Goran
(Croatian) good

Gordon
(English) nature-lover;
hill
Gord, Gordan, Gorden,
Gordi, Gordie, Gordy

Gordy
(English) short for
Gordon
Gordee, Gordi, Gordie

Gore
(English) practical; pie-
shaped land

Gorgon
(Place name) form of
Gorgonzola, Italy
Gorgan, Gorgun

Gorham
(English) sophisticated;
name of a silver
company
Goram

Gorky
(Place name)
amusement park in
Russia in the novel
Gorky Park; mysterious
*Gork, Gorkee, Gorkey,
Gorki*

Gorman
(Irish) small man
Gormann, Gormen

Grady
(Irish) hardworking
Grade, Gradee, Gradey

Graham
(English) wealthy; grand
house
*Graeham, Graeme,
Grame*

Granbel
(Last name as first
name) grand and
attractive
Granbell

Granderson
(Last name as first
name) grand
Grand, Grander

Grange
(French) lonely; on the
farm
*Grainge, Granger,
Grangher*

Granison
(Last name as first
name) son of Gran;
grandiose
Gran, Grann

Granite
(American) rock; hard
Granet

Grant
(English) expansive
Grandt, Grann, Grannt

Granville
(French) grandiose
*Grann, Granvel,
Granvelle, Gravil*

Gravette
(Origin unknown) grave
Gravet

Gray
(English) hair of gray
Graye, Grey

Graylon
(English) gray-haired
*Gray, Grayan, Graylan,
Graylin*

Grayson
(English) son of man
with gray hair
Gray, Grey, Greyson

Graz
(Place name) city in
Austria

Graziano
(Italian) dearest
Graciano, Graz

Greenlee
(English) outdoorsy
Green, Greenlea, Greenly

Greeley
(English) careful
Grealey, Greel, Greely

Greenwood
(English) untamed;
forest
*Greene, Greenwoode,
Greenwude, Grenwood*

Greg
(Latin) short for Gregory;
vigilant
Gregg, Greggie, Greggy

Gregoire
(French) watchful
Gregorie

Gregor
(Greek) cautious
Greger, Gregors, Greig

Gregorio
(Greek) careful

Gregory
(Greek) cautious
*Greg, Greggory, Greggy,
Gregori, Gregorie,
Gregry*

Grenville
(New Zealand)
outdoorsy
Granville, Gren

Griffin
(Latin) unconventional
Greffen, Griff, Griffee,
Griffen, Griffey, Griffie,
Griffon, Griffy

Griffith
(Welsh) able leader
Griff, Griffee, Griffey,
Griffie, Griffy

Grigori
(Russian) watchful
Grig, Grigor

Grimm
(English) grim; dark
Grim, Grym

Gris
(German) gray
Griz

Griswald
(German) bland
Greswold, Gris, Griswold

Grover
(English) thriving
Grove

Gruver
(Origin unknown)
ambitious
Gruever

Guerdon
(English) combative

Guido
(Italian) guiding
Guidoh, Gwedo, Gweedo

Guillermo
(Spanish) attentive
Guilermo, Gulermo

Gundy
(American) friendly
Gundee

Gunn
(Scandinavian) macho;
gunman
Gun, Gunner

Gunnar
(Scandinavian) bold
Gunn, Gunner, Gunnir

Guntersen
(Scandinavian) macho;
gunman
Gun, Gunth

Gunther
(Scandinavian) able
fighter
Funn, Gunnar, Gunner,
Guntar, Gunthar,
Gunthur

Gunyon
(American) tough;
gunman
Gunn, Gunyun

Gus
(Scandinavian) short for
Gustav
Guss, Gussi, Gussy,
Gussye

Gustachian
(American) pretentious
Gus, Gussy, Gust

Gustaf
(German) armed; vital
Gus, Gusstof, Gustav,
Gustovo

Gustav, Gustave
(Scandinavian) vital
Gus, Gussie, Gussy,
Gusta, Gustaf, Gustaff,
Gusti, Gustof, Gustoff

Gustavo
(Spanish) vital; gusto
Gus, Gustaffo, Gustav

Gusto
(Spanish) pleasure
Gusty

Gustus
(Scandinavian) royal
Gus, Gustaf, Gustave,
Gustavo

Guth
(Irish) short for Guthrie;
in the wind
Guthe, Guthry

Guthrie
(Irish) windy; heroic
Guthree, Guthry

Guy
(French) assertive;
(German) leader
Guye

Guwayne
(American) combo of
Guy and Wayne
Guwain, Guwane, Guy,
Gwaine, Gwayne

Guzet
(American) bravado
Guzz, Guzzett, Guzzie

Gweedo
(Invented) form of Guido

Gwent
(Place name)

Gwill
(American) dark-eyed
Gewill, Guwill

Gwynn
(Welsh) fair
Gwen, Gwyn

Gyth
(American) capable
Gith, Gythe

Habib
(Arabic) well loved
Habeeb

Habie
(Origin unknown) jovial
Hab

Hackman
(German) fervent; hacks wood
Hackmann

Haddy
(English) short for Hadley; sylvan
Had, Haddee, Haddey, Haddi

Hadley
(English) lover of nature; meadow with heather
Haddleye, Hadlee, Hadlie, Hadly

Hagan
(German) defender
Hagen, Haggan, Haggin

Hakim, Hakeem
(Arabic) brilliant
Hakeam, Hakym

Hal
(English) home ruler

Haldane
(German) fierce; person who is half Danish
Haldayn, Haldayne

Hale
(English) heroic
Halee, Haley, Hali

Halen
(Swedish) portal to life
Hailen, Hale, Haley, Hallen, Haylen, Haylin

Haley
(Irish) innovative
Hail, Hailee, Hailey, Hale, Halee, Hayley

Hall
(English) solemn

Halmer
(English) robust

Halse
(English) on the island
Halce, Halsi, Halsy, Halzee, Halzie

Halsey
(English) isolated; island

Halwell
(English) special
Hallwell, Halwel, Halwelle

Hamaker
(Last name as first name) industrious
Ham

Hamid
(Arabic) grateful
Hameed

Hamidi
(Arabic and African)
praiseworthy
Ham, Hamedi, Hameedi,
Hamm, Hammad

Hamil
(English) rough-hewn
Hamel, Hamell, Hamill,
Hamm

Hamilton
(English) benefiting
Hamelton, Hamil,
Hammilton

Hamlet
(German, French)
conflicted; small village;
Shakespearean hero
Ham, Hamlette, Hamlit,
Hamm

Hamlin
(German) homebody
Hamaline, Hamelin,
Hamlen, Hamlyn

Hammond
(English) ingenious
Ham, Hamm, Hammon,
Hamond

Hamp
(American) fun-loving
Ham, Hampton

Hampton
(English) distinctive
Ham, Hamm, Hamp,
Hampt

Hank
(English) short for
Henry; ruler; cavalier
Hankey, Hanks, Hanky

Hanley
(English) natural;
meadow high
Han, Hanlee, Hanleigh,
Hanly

Hannes
(Scandinavian) short
form of Johannes; giving
Hahnes

Hannibal
(Slavic) leader
Hanibal, Hanibel, Hann

Hans
(Scandinavian) believer;
warm
Hahns, Hanz, Hons

Hansa
(Scandinavian)
traditional; believer in a
gracious Lord
Hans

Hansel
(Scandinavian) gullible;
open
Hans, Hansie, Hanzel

Hansen
(Scandinavian) warm;
Hans's son
Han, Handsen, Hans,
Hansan, Hanson,
Hanssen, Hansson, Hanz

Hardin
(English) lively; valley of
hares
Hardee, Harden

Harding
(English) fiery
Harden, Hardeng

Harean
(African) aware

Harford
(English) jolly
Harferd

Hargrove
(English) fruitful

Hark
(American) word as
name; behold
Harko

Harlan
(English) army land;
athletic
Hal, Harl, Harlen, Harlon,
Harlynn

Harlemm
(African-American) from
Harlem; dancer
Harl, Harlam, Harlem,
Harlems, Harlum, Harly

Harley
(English) wild-spirited
Harl, Harlee, Harly

Harlow
(English) bold
Harlo, Harloh

Harmon
(German) dependable
Harm, Harman, Harmen

Harold
(Scandinavian) leader of an army
Hal, Harald, Hareld, Harry

Harper
(English) artistic and musical; harpist
Harp

Harpo
(American) jovial
Harpoh, Harrpo

Harris
(English) dignified
Haris, Harriss

Harrison
(English) Harry's son; adventurer
Harrey, Harrie, Harris, Harrisan, Harrisen, Harry

Harrod
(Hebrew) victor
Harod, Harry

Harry
(English) home ruler
Harree, Harrey, Harri, Harrie, Harye

Hart
(English) giving
Harte

Hartley
(English) wilderness wanderer
Hartlee, Hartleigh, Hartly

Hartman
(German) strong-willed
Hart, Hartmann, Harttman

Hartsey
(English) lazing on the meadow; sylvan
Harts, Hartz

Harun
(Arabic) highly regarded

Harv
(German) able combatant
Har

Harvey
(German) fighter
Harv, Harvi, Harvie, Harvy

Harwin
(American) safe
Harwen, Harwon

Hasan
(Arabic) attractive

Hasani
(African) good

Hashim
(Arabic) force for good
Hasheem

Hask
(Hebrew) from Haskell, form of Ekekial; smart
Haske

Haskell
(Hebrew) ingratiating
Hask, Haskel, Haskie, Hasky

Hassan
(Arabic) good-looking
Hasan

Hastings
(English) leader
Haste

Haswell
(English) dignified
Has, Haz

Hattan
(Place name) from Manhattan; sophisticate
Hatt

Havard
(American) form of Harvard; guardian
Hav

Haven
(English) sanctuary
Haiv, Hav

Hawke
(English) watchful;
falcon
Hauk, Hawk
Hayden
(English) respectful
Haden, Hadon, Hay,
Haydyn
Hayes
(English) open
Haies, Hay, Haye
Hayman
(English) hedging
Hay
Hayne
(English) working
outdoors
Haine, Haines, Haynes
Hayward
(English) creative; good
work ethic
Hay
Hayword
(English) open-minded
Haword, Hayward,
Haywerd
Hearn
(English) optimistic
Hearne, Hern
Heath
(English) place name;
open space; natural
Heathe, Heith, Heth

Heathcliff
(English) mysterious
Heaton
(English) high-principled
Heat, Heatan, Heaten
Hector
(Greek) loyal
Hec, Heco, Hect, Hectar,
Hecter, Tito
Hedley
(English) natural
Heinrich
(German) form of Henry;
leader
Hein, Heine, Heinrick,
Heinrik
Heinz
(German) advisor
Heinze
Helgi
(Scandinavian) happy
Helge
Helio
(Hispanic) bright
Heller
(German) brilliant
Hellerson
(German) brilliant one's
son; smart
Helley
Helmar
(German) protected;
smart
Helm, Helmer, Helmet,
Helmut

Helmut
(German, Polish)
brave
Hender
(German) ruler;
illustrious
Hend
Henderson
(English) reliable
Hender, Hendersen,
Hendersyn
Hendrik
(German) home ruler
Heinrich, Hendrick,
Henrick, Hindrick
Henley
(English) surprising
Henlee, Henly, Henlye,
Hinley
Henning
(Scandinavian) ruler
Henrik
(Norwegian) leader
Henric, Henrick
Henry
(German) leader
Hank, Harry, Henree,
Henri
Herb
(German) energetic
Herbi, Herbie, Herby,
Hurb

Herbert
(German) famed warrior
Herb, Herbart, Herberto,
Herbie, Herbirt, Herby,
Hurb, Hurbert

Hercule
(French) strong
Hercuel, Harekuel,
Herkuel

Hercules
(Greek) grand gift
Herc, Herk, Herkules

Heriberto
(Spanish)
Herbert, Heribert

Herman
(Latin) fair fighter
Herm, Hermahn,
Hermann, Hermie,
Hermon, Hermy

Hermes
(Greek) courier of
messages
Hermez

Hermod
(Scandinavian)

Hernando
(Spanish) bold
Hernan

Herndon
(English) nature-loving
Hern, Hernd

Hershall
(Hebrew) from Hershel;
deer; swift
Hersch, Herschel, Hersh,
Herzl, Heshel, Hirschel,
Hirsh, Hirshel

Herschel, Hershel
(Hebrew) fast; deer
Hersch, Hersh, Hershell,
Hershelle, Herzl, Hirchel,
Hirsch, Hirshel

Hershey
(Hebrew) deer; swift;
sweet
Hersh, Hershel, Hirsh

Hertzel
(Hebrew) form of
Herschel; deer; swift
Hert, Hertsel, Hyrt

Hervey
(American) form of
Harvey; ardent and
studious
Herv, Herve, Hervy

Herzon
(American) from
Hershel; fast
Herz, Herzan, Herzun

Hesperos
(Greek) evening star
Hesperios, Hespers

Hess
(Last name as first
name) bold
Hes, Hys

Hewitt
(German) smart
Hew, Hewet, Hewett,
Hewie, Hewit, Hewy,
Hugh

Hiawatha
(Native American)
Iroquois chief
Hia

Hickok
(American) Wild Bill
Hickok, U.S. marshal

Hieronymos
(Greek) alternate of
Jerome
Heronymous

Hilarion
(Greek) cheery; hilarious
Hilary, Hill

Hilary
(Latin) joyful
Hilaire, Hill, Hillarie,
Hillary, Hillery, Hilly,
Hilorie

Hildebrand
(German) combative;
sword
Hill, Hilly

Hillel
(Hebrew) praised;
devout
Hilel, Hill

Hillery
(Latin) form of Hilary;
pleasant
Hill

Hilliard
(German) brave;
settlement on the hill
Hill, Hillard, Hillierd,
Hilly, Hillyerd, Hylliard

Hilton
(English) sophisticated
Hillton, Hiltawn, Hiltyn,
Hylton

Hines
(Last name as first
name) strong
Hine, Hynes

Hippocrates
(Greek) philosopher
Hipp

Hiram
(Hebrew) most admired
Hi, Hirom, Hirym

Hiro
(Japanese) giving

Hirsh
(Hebrew) deer; swift
Hersh, Hershel, Hirschel,
Hirshel

Hitchcock
(English) creative;
spooky
Hitch

Hobart
(German) haughty
Hobb, Hobert, Hoebard

Hobson
(English) helpful backer
Hobb, Hobbie, Hobbson,
Hobby, Hobsen

Hodge
(English) form of Roger;
vibrant
Hodges

Hodgie
(English) nickname for
Hodge
Hodgy

Hogan
(Irish) high-energy;
vibrant
Hogahn, Hoge, Hoghan

Hogue
(Last name as first
name) youth
Hoge

Hojar
(American) wild spirit
Hobar, Hogar

Hoke
(Origin unknown)
popular

Holbrook
(English) place name;
educated
Brooke, Brookie, Brooky,
Holb, Holbrooke

Holden
(English) quiet; gracious
Holdan, Holdin, Holldun

Holder
(English) musical
Hold, Holdher, Holdyer

Holegario
(Spanish) superfluous
Holegard

Hollis
(English) flourishing
Hollace, Hollice, Hollie,
Holly

Holloway
(Last name as first
name) jovial
Hollo, Hollway, Holoway

Hollywood
(Place name) cocky;
showoff
Holly, Wood

Holm
(English) natural;
woodsy
Holms

Holmes
(English) safe haven
Holmm, Holmmes

Holt
(English) shaded view
Holte, Holyte

Homer
(Greek) secure
Hohmer, Home, Homere,
Homero

Honchy
(American) form of honcho; leader
Honch, Honchee, Honchey, Honchi

Hondo
(African) warring

Honesto
(Spanish) truthful
Honesta, Honestoh

Honorato
(Spanish) full of honor
Honor, Honoratoh

Honoré
(Latin) man who is honored
Honor, Honoray

Hood
(Last name as first name) easygoing; player
Hoode, Hoodey

Hoolihan
(American) hooligan
Hool, Hoole, Hooli

Hoop
(American) ball player
Hooper, Hoopy

Hopper
(Last name used as first name) creative

Horace
(Latin) poetic
Horaace, Horase, Horice

Horatio
(Latin) poetic; dashing
Horate, Horaysho

Horst
(German) deep; thicket
Hurst

Horstman
(German) profound
Horst, Horstmen, Horstmun

Horston
(German) thicket; sturdy
Horst

Horton
(English) brash
Horten, Hortun

Hosea
(Hebrew) prophet

Hosie
(Hebrew) from Hosea; prophet
Hosaya, Hose

Houston
(English) Texas city; rogue; hill town
Houst, Hust, Huston

How
(American) word as a name
Howe, Howey, Howie

Howard
(English) well-liked
How, Howerd, Howie, Howurd, Howy

Howart
(Origin unknown) admired
Howar

Howe
(German) high-minded
How, Howey, Howie

Howell
(Welsh) outstanding
Howel, Howey, Howie, Howill

Howlan
(English) living on a hill; high

Hoyt
(Irish) spirited
Hoit, Hoye

Huang
(Chinese) rich

Hubbard
(German) fine
Hubberd, Hubert, Hubie

Hubert
(German) intellectual
Bert, Bertie, Burt, Hubart, Huberd, Hue, Huebert, Hugh

Hubie
(English) short for Hubert
Hube, Hubee, Hubey, Hubi

Hud
(English) charismatic
cowboy
Hudd

Hudson
(English) Hugh's son;
charismatic adventurer
Hud, Hudsan, Hudsen

Huelett
(American) bright;
southern
*Hu, Hue, Huel, Hugh,
Hulette*

Hugh
(English) intelligent
*Hue, Huey, Hughey,
Hughi, Hughie, Hughy*

Hughdonald
(American) combo of
Hugh and Donald;
southern
*Huedonald, Hughdon,
Hughdonal, Hughdonn*

Hughie
(English) intelligent;
lucky in parentage
Hughee, Hughi, Hughy

Hugo
(Latin) spirited heart

Huland
(English) bright
Hue, Huel, Huey, Hugh

Hull
(Place name) spirited;
confident

Humberto
(Spanish) brilliant
*Hum, Humb, Humbert,
Humbie*

Humphrey
(German) strong
peacemaker
*Hum, Hump, Humphry,
Humprey*

Hunn
(German) combative
Hun

Hunt
(English) active

Hunter
(English) hunter;
adventurer
Hunt

Hunting
(English) hunter
Huntyng

Huntler
(English) hunter
Huntt

Huntley
(English) hunter
*Hunt, Hunter, Huntlea,
Huntlee, Huntlie, Huntly*

Hurley
(Irish) the tide; flowing
*Hurlea, Hurlee, Hurli,
Hurly*

Husky
(American) big
*Husk, Huskee, Huskey,
Huski*

Hussein
(Arabic) attractive man
*Husain, Husane, Husein,
Hussain*

Hutch
(American) safe haven
*Hut, Hutchey, Hutchie,
Hutchy*

Hutter
(Last name as first
name) tough
*Hut, Hutt, Huttey, Huttie,
Hutty*

Hutton
(English) sophisticated
*Hutt, Huttan, Hutten,
Hutts*

Huxley
(English) outdoorsman
*Hux, Huxel, Huxle,
Huxlee, Huxlie*

Hyatt
(English) secure
Hy, Hye, Hyett, Hyut

Hyde
(English) special; a hyde
is 120 acres
Hide, Hy

Hyghner
(Last name as first name) lofty goals
High, Highner, Hygh

Hyll
(Origin unknown) open-minded
Hy, Hye, Hyell

Hyman
(Hebrew) life
Hy, Hymie

Iagan
(Scottish) fire

Iago
(Spanish) feisty villain
Iagoh

Ian
(Scottish) believer; handsome
Iain, Ean, Eon, Eyon

Ibu
(Japanese) creative

Icarus
(Mythology) ill-fated
Ikarus

Ich
(Hebrew) short for Ichabod; has-been
Ick, Ickee, Ickie, Icky

Ichabod
(Hebrew) glory in the past; slim
Ich, Icha, Ickabod, Ika, Ikabod, Ikie

Iggy
(Latin) short for Ignatius; spunky
Iggee, Iggey, Iggi, Iggie

Ignace
(French) fiery
Iggy, Ignase

Ignatius
(Latin) firebrand
Ig, Iggie, Iggy, Ignashus, Ignatious, Ignnatius

Igor
(Russian) warrior

Ike
(Hebrew) short for Isaac and Eisenhower; friendly
Ika, Ikee, Ikey, Ikie

Immanuel
(Hebrew) honored
Emmanuel, Imanuel

Indiana
(Place name) U.S. state; rowdy; dashing
Indio, Indy

Indore
(Place name) city in India
Indor

Ingelbert
(German) combative
Ing, Inge, Ingelbart, Ingelburt

Ingmar
(Scandinavian) fertile
Ing, Inge, Ingemar, Ingmer

Ingmer
(Scandinavian) short for
Ingemar; famed
*Ing, Ingamar, Ingemar,
Ingmar*

Ingra
(English) short for
Ingram; kind-hearted
Ingie, Ingrah, Ingrie

Ingram
(English) angelic; kind
*Ing, Ingraham, Ingre,
Ingrie, Ingry*

Innad
(Syrian)
Inad

Innis
(Irish) isolated
Ines, Inis, Innes

Ira
(Hebrew) cautious
Irae, Irah

Iram
(English) smart
Irem, Irham, Irum

Iranga
(Sri Lanken) special

Irv
(English) short for Irving

Irvin
(English) attractive
Irv, Irvine

Irving
(English) attractive
Irv, Irve, Irveng, Irvy

Irwin
(English) practical
*Irwen, Irwhen, Irwie,
Irwinn, Irwy, Irwynn*

Isaac
(Hebrew) laughter
*Isaak, Isack, Izak, Ize,
Izek, Izzy*

Isadore
(Greek) special gift
*Isador, Isedore, Isidore,
Issy, Izzie, Izzy*

Isai
(Hebrew) believer

Isaiah
(Hebrew) saved by God
*Isa, Isay, Isayah, Isey,
Izaiah, Izey*

Isak
(Scandinavian) laughter
Isac

Ishmael
(Hebrew) outcast son of
Abraham in the Bible
Hish, Ish, Ishmel, Ismael

Isidore
(Greek, French) gift
Isi, Izzie

Isidoro
(Spanish) gift
*Cedro, Cidro, Doro,
Izidro, Sidro, Ysidor*

Isidro
(Greek) gift
Isydro

Israel
(Hebrew) God's prince;
conflicted
Israyel, Issy, Izzy

Isser
(Slavic) creative

Ivan
(Russian) believer in a
gracious God; reliable
one
Ivahn, Ive, Ivey, Ivie

Ivar
(Scandinavian) Norse
god

Ive
(English) able
Ivee, Ives, Ivey, Ivie

Ives
(American) musical
Ive

Ivor
(Scandinavian)
outgoing; ready
Ivar, Ive, Iver, Ivy

Izaak
(Polish) full of mirth

Izac
(Slavic) spicy; happy
*Isaac, Izak, Izie, Izze,
Izzee*

Izador
(Spanish) gift
*Dorrie, Dory, Isa, Isador,
Isadoro, Isidoros,
Isodore, Iza, Izadoro*

Izzy
(Hebrew) friendly
Issie, Issy, Izi, Izzee, Izzie

Jabal
(Place name) short for
Japalpur (city in India);
attractive

Jabari
(African-American) brave

JaBee
(American) combo of Jay
and B
J.B., Jabee, Jaybe, Jaybee

Jaber
(American) form of
Arabic Jabir; comforting
Jabar, Jabe, Jabir

Jabir, Jabbar
(Arabic) supportive

Jabon
(American) wild
Jabonne

Jace
(American) audacious
Jase, Jhace

Jacee
(American) combo of Jay
and C
*J.C., Jacey, JayC, Jaycee,
Jaycie, Jaycy*

Jacek
(Polish) hyacinth;
growing
Jack, Yahcik

Jacett
(Invented) jaunty
Jaycett

Jacinto
(Spanish) hyacinth;
fragrant
Jacint

Jack
(Hebrew) believer in a
gracious God;
personality-plus
*Jackee, Jackie, Jacko,
Jacky, Jax*

Jackie
(English) personable
*Jackee, Jackey, Jacki,
Jacky, Jaki*

Jackson
(English) Jack's son; full
of personality
*Jackee, Jackie, Jacks,
Jacsen, Jakson, Jax,
Jaxon*

Jacob
(Hebrew) replacement; best boy
Jaccob, Jacobe, Jacobee, Jake, Jakes, Jakey, Jakob

Jacobo
(Spanish) warm
Jake, Jakey

Jacques
(French) romantic; ingenious
Jacquie, Jacue, Jaques, Jock, Jok

Jadaan
(Last name as first name)
Jada, Jadan, Jade, Jay

Jadall
(Invented) punctual
Jada, Jade

Jade
(Spanish) valued (jade stone)
Jadee, Jadie, Jayde

Jadee
(American) combo of Jay and D
J.D., Jadee, JayD, Jaydy

Jadney
(Last name as first name)
Jad

Jadon, Jadyn
(American) devout; ball-of-fire
Jade, Jadin, Jadun, Jaeden, Jaiden, Jaydie, Jaydon

Jaegel
(English) salesman
Jaeg, Jaeger, Jael

Jaeger
(German) outdoorsman
Jaegir, Jagher, Jagur

Jael
(Hebrew) climber

Jaffey
(English) form of Jaffe
Jaff

Jagan, Jago
(English) confident
Jagen, Jagun

Jagger
(English) brash
Jagar, Jager, Jaggar, Jagir

Jaggerton
(English) brash
Jag, Jagg

Jagit
(Invented) brisk
Jaggett, Jaggit, Jagitt

Jaguar
(Spanish) fast
Jag, Jagg, Jaggy, Jagwar, Jagwhar

Jai
(American) adventurer
Jay

Jaime
(Spanish) follower
Jaimey, Jaimie, Jamee, Jaymie

Jair
(Hebrew) teacher
Jairo

Jairo
(Origin unknown)
Jaero, Jairoh

Jaison
(American) form of Jason
Jaizon

Jaja
(African) praise-worthy

Jakar
(Place name) from Jakarta, Indonesia
Jakart, Jakarta, Jakarte

Jake
(Hebrew) short for Jacob
Jaik, Jakee, Jakey, Jakie

Jakob
(Hebrew) form of Jacob
Jakab, Jake, Jakeb, Jakey, Jakie, Jakobe, Jakub

Jaleel, Jalil
(Arabic) handsome

Jalen
(American) vivacious
Jalon, Jaylen, Jaylin, Jaylon

Jamail
(Arabic) good-looking
Jahmil, Jam, Jamaal, Jamahal, Jamal, Jamil, Jamile, Jamy

JaMarcus
(African-American) combo of Jay and Marcus; attractive
Jamarcus, Jamark, Jamarkus

Jamari
(African-American) attractive

Jamarr
(African-American) attractive; formidable
Jam, Jamaar, Jamar, Jammy

Jamel
(Arabic) form of Jamal
Jameel, Jamele, Jimelle

James
(English) dependable; steadfast
Jaimes, Jamsey, Jamze, Jaymes, Jim, Jimmy

Jameson
(English) able; James's son
Jamesan, Jamesen, Jamesey, Jamison, Jamsie

Jamie
(English) short for James
Jaimie, Jamee, Jamey, Jay, Jaymsey

Jamin
(Hebrew) favored son
Jamen, James, Jamie, Jamon, Jaymon

Jamisen
(American) form of James/Jamie; lively
Jami, Jamie, Jamis, Jamison

Jan
(Dutch) form of John; believer
Jaan, Jann, Janne

Jan-Erik
(Slavic) combo of Jan and Erik; reliable
Jan-Eric

Janson
(Scandinavian) Jan's son; hardworking
Jan, Janne, Janny, Jansahn, Jansen, Jansey

Jantz
(Scandinavian) short for Jantzen
Janson, Janssen, Janz, Janzon

Janus
(Latin) Roman god of beginnings and endings; optimistic; born in January
Jan

Jaquawn
(African-American) rock
Jakka, Jaquan, Jaquie, Jaqwen, Jock

Jard
(American) form of Jared; longlasting
Jarra, Jarrd, Jarri, Jerd, Jord

Jared
(Hebrew) descendant; giving
Jarad, Jarod, Jarode, Jarret, Jarrett, Jerod, Jerrad, Jerrod

Jarek
(Slavic) fresh
Jarec

Jarell
(Scandinavian) giving
Jare, Jarelle, Jarey, Jarrell, Jerrell

Jaren
(Hebrew) vocal
Jaron, Jayrone, J'ron

Jarenal
(American) form of
Jaren; longlasting
*Jaranall, Jaret, Jarn,
Jaronal, Jarry, Jerry*

Jareth
(American) open to
adventure
Jarey, Jarith, Jarth, Jary

Jarred
(Hebrew) form of Jared
*Jared, Jere, Jerod, Jerred,
Jerud*

Jarrell
(English) jaunty
*Jare, Jarell, Jarrel, Jarry,
Jerele, Jerrell*

Jarrett
(English) confident
*Jare, Jaret, Jarret, Jarry,
Jerot, Jerret, Jerrett,
Jurett, Jurette*

Jarrod
(Hebrew) form of Jared
Jare, Jarod, Jarry, Jerod

Jarvey
(German) celebrated
*Garvey, Garvy, Jarvee,
Jarvi, Jarvy*

Jarvis
(German) athletic
*Jarv, Jarvee, Jarves,
Jarvey, Jarvhus, Jarvie,
Jarvus, Jarvy*

Jary
(Spanish) form of Jerry;
leader
Jaree

Jashon
(African-American)
combo of Jason and the
letter h

Jason
(Greek) healer; man on a
quest
*Jace, Jacey, Jaisen, Jase,
Jasen, Jasey, Jasyn,
Jayson, Jaysun*

Jason-Joel
(American) combo of
Jason and Joel; popular
Jasonjoel, Jason Joel

Jasper
(English) guard; country
boy
*Jasp, Jaspur, Jaspy,
Jaspyr*

Jaster
(English) form of Jasper;
vigilant
Jast

Jathan
(Invented) combo of
Jake and Nathan;
attractive
*Jae, Jath, Jathe, Jathen,
Jathun, Jay*

Javaris
(African-American) ready
Javares, Javarez

Javier
(Spanish) affluent;
homeowner
Havyaire, Javey, Javiar

Javon
(Hebrew) hopeful
*Javan, Javaughn, Javen,
Javonn, Javonte*

Javonte
(African-American)
jaunty
*Javaughantay, Javawnte,
Ja-Vonnetay, Ja-Vontae*

Jawon
(African-American) shy
*Jawaughn, Jawaun,
Jawuane, Jowon*

Jax
(American) form of
Jackson; fun
Jacks

Jay
(English) short for a
name starting with J;
colorful
Jai, Jaye

Jaya
(American) jazzy
Jay, Jayah

Jaydon
(American) bright-eyed
Jayde, Jayden, Jaydey, Jaydi, Jaydie, Jaydun, Jaydy

Jaylin
(American) combo of Jay and Lin

Jaymes
(American) form of James
Jaimes, James

JayR
(American) actor
J.R.

Jayson
(Greek) form of Jason

Jazz
(American) jazzy
Jazze, Jazzee, Jazzy

Jean
(French) form of John; kind
Jeanne, Jeannie, Jene

Jean-Baptiste
(French) combo of Jean and Baptiste; John the Baptist; religious
John-Baptiste

Jean-Claude
(French) combo of Jean and Claude; gracious

Jean-Francois
(French) combo of Jean and Francois; smooth

Jean-Michel
(French) combo of Jean and Michel; godly

Jean-Paul
(French) combo of Jean and Paul; small and giving

Jean-Philippe
(French) combo of Jean and Philippe; handsome

Jean-Pierre
(French) combo of Jean and Pierre; giving and dependable

Jeb
(Hebrew) jolly
Jebb, Jebby

Jebediah
(Hebrew) close to God
Jeb, Jebadiah, Jebby, Jebedyah

Jecori
(American) exuberant
Jekori

Jed
(Hebrew) helpful
Jedd, Jeddy, Jede

Jediah
(Hebrew) God's help
Jedi, Jedyah

Jedidiah
(Hebrew) close to God
Jed, Jeddy, Jeddyah, Jedidyah

Jeevan
(African-American) form of Jevon; lively
Jevaughn, Jevaun

Jeff
(English) short for Jeffrey or Jefferson
Geoff, Jeffie, Jeffy

Jefferson
(English) dignified
Jeff, Jeffarson, Jeffersen, Jeffursen, Jeffy

Jeffery
(English) alternate for Jeffrey; peaceful
Jeffrey, Jeffrie, Jeffry, Jefry

Jeffrey
(English) peaceful
Geoffrey, Jeff, Jeffree, Jeffrie, Jeffry, Jeffy, Jefree

Jelani
(African-American) trendy
Jelanee, Jelaney, Jelanne

Jem
(English) short for James
Jemmi, Jemmy, Jemmye, Jemy

Jemarr
(African-American) worldly
Jemahr

Jemonde
(French) man of the world
Jemond

Jenkins
(English) from the surname
Jenkin, Jenks, Jenky, Jenx, Jinx

Jep
(American) easygoing
Jepp

Jerald
(English) form of Gerald; merry
Jere, Jereld, Jerold, Jerrie, Jerry

Jeramy
(Hebrew) exciting
Jeramah, Jeramie, Jere, Jeremy

Jere
(Hebrew) short for Jeremy
Jeree, Jerey

Jeremiah
(Hebrew) prophet uplifted by God; farsighted
Jeramiah, Jere, Jeremyah, Jerome, Jerry

Jeremie
(Hebrew) loquacious
Jeremee, Jeremy

Jeremy
(English) talkative
Jaramie, Jere, Jeremah, Jereme, Jeremey, Jerrey, Jerry

Jericho
(Arabic) nocturnal
Jerako, Jere, Jerico, Jeriko

Jerick
(American) form of Jericho; tenacious
Gericho, Jereck, Jerik, Jero, Jerok, Jerrico

Jeril
(American) form of Jarrell; leader
Jerill, Jerl, Jerry

Jerma
(American) form of Germain; man of Germany
Jermah, Jermane, Jermayne

Jermain, Jerman
(French) from Germany
German, Germane, Germanes, Germano, Germanus, Jermaine, Jermane, Jermayn, Jermayne

Jermaine
(German) form of Germaine
Germain, Germaine, Jere, Jermain, Jermane, Jermene, Jerry

Jermey
(American) short for Jermaine; friendly
Jermy

Jermon
(African-American) dependable
Jermonn

Jernigan
(Last name as first name) spontaneous
Jerni, Jerny

Jero
(American) jaunty
Jeroh, Jerree, Jerri, Jerro, Jerry

Jerod
(Hebrew) form of Jerrod and Jarrod

Jerome
(Latin) holy name; blessed
Jarome, Jere, Jerohm, Jeromy, Jerree, Jerrome, Jerry, Jirome

Jerone
(English) hopeful
Jere, Jerohn, Jeron, Jerrone

Jeronimo
(Italian) form of Gerome;
Geronimo, Apache
Indian chief; excited
Gerry, Jero, Jerry

Jerral
(American) form of
Gerald/Jerald; exciting
Jeral, Jere, Jerry

Jerrell
(American) exciting
*Jarell, Jerre, Jerrel, Jerrie,
Jerry*

Jerrett
(Hebrew) form of Jarrett
*Jeret, Jerete, Jerod, Jerot,
Jerret*

Jerry
(German) strong
*Gerry, Gery, Jerre, Jerri,
Jerrie, Jerrye*

Jerse, Jersey
(Place name) calm; rural
Jerce, Jercey, Jerzy

Jesmar
(American) from Jesse;
Biblical
Jess, Jessie, Jezz, Jezzie

Jesper
(American) easygoing
Jesp, Jess

Jesse, Jessie
(Hebrew) wealthy
*Jess, Jessee, Jessey,
Jessi, Jessye*

Jessup
(Last name as first
name) rich
Jess, Jessa, Jessie, Jessy

Jesuan
(Spanish) devout

Jesus
(Hebrew) saved by God
*Hesus, Jesu, Jesuso,
Jezus*

Jesus-Amador
(Spanish) combo of
Jesus and Amador;
loving the Lord
*Jesusamador, Jesus
Amador*

Jesus-Angel
(Spanish) combo of
Jesus and Angel; angel
of God
Jesusangel, Jesusangelo

Jetal
(American) zany
*Jetahl, Jetil, Jett, Jettale,
Jetty*

Jethro
(Hebrew) fertile
Jeto, Jett, Jetty

Jeton
(French) a chip for
gamblers; wild spirit
*Jet, Jetawn, Jets, Jett,
Jetty*

Jett
(American) wild spirit
Jet, Jets, Jetty, The Jet

Jettie
(American) from mineral
name Jett; wild spirit
Jette, Jettee, Jetti

Jevan
(African-American)
spirited
*Jevaughn, Jevaun, Jevin,
Jevon*

Jevon
(African-American)
spirited
Jevaun

Jhonatan
(African) spiritual
Jhon, Jon

Ji
(Chinese) organized;
orderly

Jim
(Hebrew) short for
James
*Jem, Jihm, Jimi, Jimmee,
Jimmy*

Jimbo
(American) cowhand; endearment for Jim
Jim, Jimb, Jimbee, Jimbey, Jimby

Jimbob
(American) countrified
Gembob, Jim Bob, Jim-Bob, Jymbob

Jimmy
(English) short for James
Jim, Jimi, Jimmey, Jimmi, Jimmye, Jimy

Jimmydee
(American) combo of Jimmy and Dee; southern boy
Jimmy D, Jimmy Dee, Jimmy-Dee

Jimmy-John
(American) country boy
Jimmiejon, Jimmyjohn, Jimmy-Jon, Jymmejon

Jin
(Chinese) golden

Jinan
(Place name) city in China
Jin

Jing
(Chinese) unblemished; capital

Joab
(Hebrew) praising God; hovering
Joabb

Joachim
(Hebrew) a king of Judah; powerful; believer
Akim, Jakim, Yachim, Yakim

Joaquin
(Spanish) bold; hip
Joakeen, Joaquin, Juakeen, Jwaqueen

Job
(Hebrew) patient
Jobb, Jobe, Jobi, Joby

Joby
(Hebrew) patient; tested
Job, Jobee, Jobi

Jock
(Hebrew) grace in God; athlete
Jockie, Jocky

Jody
(Hebrew) believer in Jehovah; combo of Joe and Dee
Jodee, Jodey, Jodie, Jodye, Joe

Joe
(Hebrew) short for Joel and Joseph
Jo, Joey, Joeye, Joie

Joebob
(American) combo of Joe and Bob
J.B., Jobob, Joe-Bob

Joedan
(American) combo of Joe and Dan
Jodan, Jodin, Jodon, Joe-Dan, Joedanne

Joel
(Hebrew) prophet in the Bible
Joelie, Joell, Jole, Joly

Joemac
(American) combo of Joe and Mac
J.M., Joe-Mac, Joe-Mack, Jomack

Joey
(Hebrew) short for Joel and Joseph
Joee, Joie

Johann
(German) spiritual musician
Johan, Johane, Yohann, Yohanne, Yohon

Johannes
(Hebrew) form of John, the Biblical name
Johan, Jon

John
(Hebrew) honorable; Biblical name
Jahn, Jhan, Johne, Johnne, Johnni, Johnnie, Johnny, Johnnye, Jon

Johnnie, Johnny
(Hebrew) endearment for John; honorable man
Gianni, Johnie, Jonni, Jonny

Johnny-Dodd
(American) country sheriff
Johnniedodd, Johnny Dodd

Johnpaul
(American) combo of John and Paul
John Paul, John-Paul, Jonpaul

Johnny-Ramon
(Spanish) renegade
Johnnyramon, Johnny Ramon

Johnson
(English) John's son; credible
Johnsen, Johnsonne, Jonsen, Jonson

JoJo
(American) friendly; popular
Jo-Jo

Jomar
(African-American) helpful
Joemar, Jomarr

Jon
(Hebrew) alternative for John
Jonni, Jonnie, Jonny, Jony

Jonah
(Hebrew) peacemaker
Joneh

Jonas
(Hebrew) capable; active
Jon

Jonathan, Johnathan
(Hebrew) gracious
Johnathon, Jonathon

Jordahno
(Invented) form of Giordano

Jordan
(Hebrew) descending
Jorden, Jordon, Jordun, Jordy, Jordyn

Jon-Eric
(American) combo of Jon and Eric
Joneric, Jon Eric, John-Eric

Jon-Jason
(American) combo of Jon and Jason
Johnjace, John-Jaison, John-Jazon, Jon Jason, Jonjason, Jon-Jayson

Jonjay
(American) combo of Jon and Jay; jaunty; believer
Jonjae, Jon Jay, Jon-Jay

Jonmarc
(American) combo of Jon and Marc
Jon Marc, Jon-Marc, John Mark

Jonnley
(American) form of Jon; believer
Jonn, Jonnie

Jordy
(Hebrew) from Jordan

Jorge
(Spanish) form of George; farmer
Jorje, Quiqui

Jorgen
(Scandinavian) farmer
Jorgan

Jos
(Place name) city in Nigeria

José
(Spanish) asset; favored
Joesay, Jose, Pepe, Pepito

Josef, Joseph
(Hebrew) asset; supported by Jehovah
Jodie, Joe, Joey, Josep, Josephe, Jozef, Yusif

Josh, Joshua
(Hebrew) saved by the Lord; devout
Joshuam, Joshyam, Josue, Jozua

Joshuah
(Hebrew) devout

Josia
(Hebrew) form of Josiah; supported by the Lord
Josea

Josiah
(Hebrew) Jehovah bolsters
Josyah

Joss
(English) form of Joseph; cool
Josslin, Jossly

Josue
(Spanish) devout

Jourdain
(French) flowing
Jordane, Jorden

Jovan
(Slavic) gifted
Jovahn, Jovohn

Jovani, Jovanni
(Italian) Roman god Jove; jovial
Jovani, Jovanni, Jovanny, Jovany

Jove
(Mythology) Roman sky god

Juanantonio
(Spanish) combo of Juan and Antonio; believer in a gracious God
Juan Antonio, Juan-Antonio

Jozef
(Polish) supported by Jehovah; asset
Joe, Joze

Juan
(Spanish) devout; lively
Juann, Juwon

Juancarlos
(Spanish) combo of Juan and Carlos; debonair

Juan-Fernando
(Spanish) combo of Juan and Fernando; believer in a gracious God
Juanfernand, Juanfernando, Juan Fernando

Juanjose
(Spanish) combo of Juan and Jose; active

Juanmiguel
(Spanish) combo of Juan and Miguel; hopeful

Juanpablo
(Spanish) combo of Juan and Pablo; believer
Juan Pablo, Juan-Pablo

Jubilo
(Spanish) rejoicing; jubilant
Jube

Judas
(Latin) Biblical traitor

Judd, Jud
(Latin) secretive

Jude
(Latin) form of Judas; disloyal
Judah

Judge
(English) judgmental
Judg

Judson
(Last name as first name) mercurial
Judsen

Judule
(American) form of Judah; judicious
Jud, Judsen, Judsun

Jules
(Greek) young Adonis
Jewels, Jule

Julian
(Greek) gorgeous
Juliane, Julien, Julyon, Julyun

Julio
(Spanish) handsome;
youthful
Huleeo, Hulie, Julie

Julius
(Greek) attractive
Juleus, Jul-yus, Jul-yuz

Ju-Long
(Chinese) powerful

Jumbe
(African) strong
Jumbey, Jumby

Juneau
(Place name) capital of
Alaska
Juno, Junoe

Junior
(Latin) young son of the
father, senior
Junnie, Junny, Junyer

Junius
(Latin) youngster
Junie, Junnie, Junny

Jupiter
(Roman) god of thunder
and lightning; guardian
Jupe

Jura
(Place name) mountain
range between France
and Switzerland
Jurah

Jurass
(American) from Jurassic
Period of dinosaurs;
daunting
Jurases, Jurassic

Jus
(French) just
Just, Justice, Justis

Juste
(French) law-abiding
Just, Zhuste

Justice
(Latin) just
*Jusees, Just, Justice,
Justiz, Justus, Juztice*

Justie
(Latin) honest; fair
Jus, Justee, Justey, Justi

Justin
(Latin) fair
*Just, Justan, Justen,
Justun, Justyn, Justyne*

Justino
(Spanish) fair
Justyno

Justiz
(American) judging; fair
Justice, Justis

Juvenal
(Latin) young
Juve

Juventino
(Spanish) young
*Juve, Juven, Juvey, Tino,
Tito*

Juwon
(African-American) form
of Juan; devout; lively
Jujuane, Juwan, Juwonne

Kacy
(American) happy
K.C., Kace, Kacee, Kase, Kasee, Kasy, Kaycee

Kade
(American) exciting
*Cade, Caden, K.D.
Kadey, Kaid, Kayde, Kydee*

Kadeem
(Arabic) servant
Kadim

Kaden
(American) exciting
Cade, Caden, Kadan, Kadon, Kadyn, Kaiden

Kaeto
(American)
Cato, Cayto, Caytoe, Kato

Kahil
(Turkish) ingénue;
(Arabic) friend; (Greek)
handsome
Cahill, Kaleel, Kalil, Kayhil, Khalil

Kai
(Hawaiian, African)
attractive

Kaid
(English) round; happy
Caiden, Cayde, Caydin, Kaden, Kadin, Kaid

Kailin
(Irish) sporty
Kailyn, Kale, Kalen, Kaley, Kalin, Kallen, Kaylen

Kale
(American) healthy;
vegetable
Kail, Kayle, Kaylee, Kayley, Kaylie

Kalgan
(Place name) city in
China
Kal

Kalunga
(African) watchful; the
personal god of the
Mbunda of Angola

Kamal, Kamil
(Arabic) perfect
Kameel

Kamau
(African) quiet soldier
Kamall

Kameron
(Scottish) form of
Cameron
Kameren, Kammeron, Kammi, Kammie, Kammy, Kamran, Kamrin, Kamron

Kamon
(American) form of
Cayman; place name:
Cayman Islands;
alligator
Cayman, Caymun, Kame, Kammy, Kayman, Kaymon

Kance
(American) combo of
Kane and Chance;
attractive
Cance, Cance, Cans, Kaince, Kans, Kanse, Kaynce

Kane
(American, English)
sterling spirit
Kain, Kaine, Kaney, Kanie, Kayne

Kang
(Korean) healthy

Kaniel, Kanel
(Hebrew) confident;
supported by the Lord;
hopeful
Kane, Kan-El, Kanelle, Kaney

Kano
(Place name) city in Nigeria
Kan, Kanoh

Kant
(German) philosopher
Cant

Kaper
(American) capricious
Cape, Caper, Kahper, Kape

Kapp
(Greek) short for the surname Kaparos
Kap, Kappy

Kareem
(Arabic) generous
Karehm, Karem, Karim, Karreem, Krehm

Karey
(Greek) form of Cary or Carey
Karee, Kari, Karrey, Karry

Karl
(German) manly; forceful
Karll, Karlie

Karolek
(Polish) form of Charles; grown man
Karol

Karr
(Scandinavian)
Carr

Kasey
(Irish) form of Casey
Kasi, Kasie

Kasper
(German) reliable
Caspar, Casper, Kasp, Kaspar, Kaspy

Kass
(German) standout among men
Cass, Kasse

Kassidy
(Irish) form of Cassidy
Kass, Kassidi, Kassidie, Kassie

Kavan
(Irish) good-looking
Cavan, Kaven, Kavin

Kay
(Greek) joyful
Kai, Kaye, Kaysie, Kaysy

Kayle
(Hebrew) faithful
Kail, Kayl

Kayven
(Irish) handsome
Cavan, Kavan, Kave

Kazan
(Greek) creative
Kaz

Kazimierz
(Polish) practical
Kaz

Keane
(German) attractive
Kean, Keen, Keene, Kiene

Keanu (Hawaiian) cool breeze over mountains
Keahnu

Kearn
(Irish) outspoken
Kearny, Kern, Kerne, Kerney

Kearney
(Irish) sparkling
Kearn, Kearns, Kerney, Kirney

Keaton
(English) nature-lover
Keaten, Keats, Keatt, Keatun, Keton

Keats
(Literature) poetic
Keatz

Kecalf
(American) inventive
Keecalf

Kechel
(African-American)
Kach, Kachelle

Kedrick
(American) form of Kendrick
Ked, Keddy, Kedric, Kedrik

Kee-Bun
(Taiwanese)
Keebun
Keefe
(Irish) handsome
Keaf, Keafe, Keef, Kief
Keegan
(Irish) ball-of-fire
Keagin, Kegan, Kege, Keghun
Keeley
(Irish) handsome
Kealy, Keelee, Keelie, Keely, Keilie
Keen
(German) smart
Kean, Keane, Keene, Keeney, Kene
Keenan
(Irish) bright-eyed
Kenan
Keeney
(American) incisive
Kean, Keane, Keaney, Keene, Kene
Keirer
(Irish) dark
Kerer
Keiron
(Irish) dark
Keiren, Keronn
Keith
(English) witty
Keath, Keeth, Keithe

Keithen
(Scottish) gentle
Keith
Kel
(Irish) fighter; energetic
Kell
Kelby
(English) snappy; charming
Kel, Kelbey, Kelbi, Kelbie, Kelbye, Kell, Kelly
Kelcy
(English) helpful
Kelci, Kelcie, Kelcye, Kelsie
Kell
(English) fresh-faced
Kel, Kelly
Kellen
(Irish) strong-willed
Kel, Kelen, Kelin, Kell, Kellan, Kellin, Kelly, Kelyn
Keller
(Last name as first name) bountiful
Kel, Keler, Kelher, Kell, Kylher
Kelly
(Irish) able combatant
Keli, Kellee, Kelley, Kelli

Kelsey
(Scandinavian) unique among men
Kel, Kells, Kelly, Kels, Kelsi, Kelsie, Kelsye, Kelzie, Kelzy
Kelts
(Origin unknown) energetic
Kel, Kelly, Kelse, Kelsey, Keltz
Kelvin
(English) goal-oriented
Kelvan, Kelven, Kelvun, Kelvynn, Kilvin
Kemper
(American) high-minded
Kemp, Kempar
Ken
(Scottish) short for Kenneth; cute
Kenn, Kenny, Kinn
Kendall
(English) shy
Ken, Kend, Kendahl, Kendal, Kendoll, Kendy, Kindal
Kendan
(English) strong; serious
Ken, Kend, Kenden
Kenel
(Invented) form of Kendall; hopeful
Kenele

Kenlee
(American) combo of
Ken and Lee
Kenley
(English) distinguished
Kenlee, Kenlie, Kenly
Kennard
(English) courageous;
selfless
*Ken, Kenard, Kennar,
Kenny*
Kennedy
(Irish) leader
Kennedie, Kennidy
Kenner
(English) capable
Kennard
Kennet
(Scandinavian) good-
looking
Kenet, Kennete
Kenneth
(Scottish) handsome;
(Irish) good-looking
*Ken, Keneth, Kenith,
Kennath, Kennie, Kenny*
Kenny
(Scottish) short for
Kenneth
*Kennee, Kenney, Kenni,
Kennie*
Kent
(English) fair-skinned

Kentlee
(Last name as first
name) dignified
*Ken, Kenny, Kent,
Kentlea, Kentleigh,
Kently*
Kenton
(English) from Kent
Kenyon
(Irish) dear blond boy
*Ken, Kenjon, Kenny,
Kenyawn, Kenyun*
Keon
(American) unbridled
enthusiasm
Keonne
Keontay
(African-American)
outrageous
Keon, Keontae, Keontee
Kerm
(Irish) form of Kermit;
guileless
Kurm
Kermit
(German) droll
*Kerm, Kermee, Kermet,
Kermey, Kermi, Kermie,
Kermy*
Kernis
(Invented) dark;
different
Kernes

Kerr
(Scandinavian) serious
Kerre, Kurr
Kerry
(Irish) dark
Kere, Keri, Kerrey, Kerrie
Kerstie
(American) spunky
Kerstee, Kersty
Kerwyn
(Irish) energetic
*Kerwen, Kerwin, Kerwun,
Kir, Kirs, Kirwin*
Keshawn
(African-American)
friendly
*Kesh, Keshaun,
Keyshawn, Shawn*
Keshon
(African-American)
sociable
Kesh
Keshua
(African-American) form
of the girl name Kesha
Keshe
Kesley
(American) derivative of
Lesley; active
Keslee, Kesli, Kezley
Kesse
(American) attractive
*Kessee, Kessey, Kessi,
Kessie*

Ketchum
(Place name) city in Idaho
Catch, Ketch, Ketcham, Ketchim

Kevin
(Irish) handsome; gentle
Kev, Kevahngn, Kevan, Keven, Kevvie, Kevvy

Key
(English) key
Keye, Keyes

Keyohtee
(Invented) form of Quixote

Khalid
(Arabic) everlasting
Khalead, Khaled, Khaleed

Khalil
(Arabic) good friend

Khambrel
(American) articulate
Kambrel, Kham, Khambrell, Khambrelle, Khambryll, Khamme, Khammie, Khammy

Khevin
(American) form of Kevin; good-looking
Khev

Khouri
(Arabic) spiritual
Couri, Khory, Khourae, Kori

Khyber
(Place name) pass on border of Pakistan and Afghanistan
Kibe, Kiber, Kyber

Kibo
(Place name) mountain peak (highest peak of Kilimanjaro); spectacular
Kib

Kiefer
(American) talented
Keefer, Kefer

Kiel
(Place name) city in North Germany

Kieran
(Irish) handsome brunette
Keiran, Kier, Kieren, Kierin, Kiers, Kyran

Kiev
(Place name) capital city of Ukraine

Killi
(Irish) form of Killian; fighter
Killean, Killee, Killey, Killyun

Killian
(Irish) effervescent
Killee, Killi, Killie, Killyun, Kylian

Kim
(English) enthusiastic
Kimmie, Kimmy, Kimy, Kym

Kimball
(Greek) inviting
Kim, Kimb, Kimbal, Kimbie, Kymball

Kincaid
(Scottish) vigorous
Kincaide, Kinkaid

King
(English) royal leader

Kingsley
(English) royal nature
King, Kings, Kingslea, Kingslee, Kingsleigh, Kingsly, Kins

Kingston
(English) gracious
King, Kingstan, Kingsten

Kinsey
(English) affectionate; winning
Kensey, Kinsie

Kip
(English) focused
Kipp, Kippi, Kippie, Kippy

Kipling
(Literature) adventurous
Kiplen

Kirby
(English) brilliant
Kerb, Kirb, Kirbee,
Kirbey, Kirbie, Kyrbee,
Kyrby

Kirk
(Scandinavian) believer
Kirke, Kurk

Kirkwood
(English) heavenly
Kirkwoode, Kurkwood

Kirvin
(American) form of
Kevin; good-looking
Kerven, Kervin, Kirv,
Kirvan, Kirven

Kit
(Greek) mischievous
Kitt

Klaus
(German) wealthy
Klaes, Klas, Klass

Klay
(English) form of Clay;
reliable
Klaie, Klaye

Kleber
(Last name as first
name) serious
Klebe

Klev
(Invented) form of Cleve
Kleve

Knight
(English) protector
Knighte, Nighte

Knoll
(American) flamboyant
Noll

Knowles
(English) outdoorsman
Knowlie, Knowls, Nowles

Knox
(English) bold

Knut
(Scandinavian)
aggressive
Knute

Kobe
(Hebrew) cunning
Kobee, Kobey, Kobi,
Koby

Kody
(English) brash
Kodee, Kodey, Kodi,
Kodye

Kohler
(Origin unknown)

Kolton
(Origin unknown)

Komic
(Invented) funny
Com, Comic, Kom

Konnor
(Irish) another spelling
of Connor
Konnar, Konner

Konrad
(German) bold advisor
Khonred, Kon, Konn,
Konny, Konraad,
Konradd, Konrade

Konstantin
(Russian) forceful
Kon, Konny, Kons,
Konstance, Konstantine,
Konstantyne

Konstantinos
(Greek) steadfast
Constance, Konstance,
Konstant, Tino, Tinos

Korey
(Irish) lovable
Kori, Korrey, Korrie

Kornelius
(Latin) another spelling
of Cornelius
Korne, Kornellius,
Kornelyus, Korney,
Kornnelyus

Korrigan
(Irish) another spelling
of Corrigan
Koregan, Korigan, Korre,
Korreghan, Korri,
Korrigon

Kort
(German) talkative

Kory
(Irish) another spelling for Corey
Kori, Korre, Korrey, Korrye

Koshy
(American) jolly
Koshee, Koshey, Koshi

Koster
(American) spiritual
Kost, Kostar, Koste, Koster

Kraig
(Irish) another spelling for Craig
Krag, Kragg, Kraggy

Kricker
(Last name as first name) reliable
Krick

Kris
(Greek) short for Kristian and Kristopher
Krissy, Krys

Krishna
(Hindi) pleasant
Krishnah

Krister
(Scandinavian) religious

Kristian
(Greek) another form of Christian
Kris, Krist, Kristyan

Kristo
(Greek) short for Kristopher

Kristopher
(Greek) bearer of Christ
Kris, Krist, Kristo, Kristofer

Krystyn
(Polish) Christian
Krys, Krystian

Krzysztof
(Polish) bearing Christ
Kreestof

Kubrick
(Last name as first name) creative
Kubrik

Kurt
(Latin) wise advisor
Curt, Kurty

Kurtis
(Latin) form of Curtis
Kurt, Kurtes, Kurtey, Kurtie, Kurts, Kurtus, Kurty

Kutty
(English) knife-wielding
Cutty

Kwame
(African) Saturday's child
Kwamee, Kwami

Kwintyn
(Polish) fifth child
Kwint, Kwintin, Kwynt

Kyan
(Japanese)
Kyann

Kyle
(Irish) serene
Kiel, Kiyle, Kye, Kyl, Kyley, Kylie, Kyly

Kyle-Evan
(American) combo of Kyle and Evan
Kyle Evan

Kyler
(English) peaceful
Kieler, Kiler, Kye

Kylerton
(American) form of Kyle
Kylten

Kyzer
(American) wild spirit
Kaizer, Kizer, Kyze

Labarne
(American) form of
Laban; (Hebrew) white
Labarn

Labaron
(French) the baron
LaBaron, LaBaronne

LaBryant
(African-American) son
of Bryant; brash
*Bryant, La Brian, La
Bryan, Labryan,
Labryant*

Lachlan
(Scottish) feisty
*Lacklan, Lackland,
Laughlin, Lock, Locklan*

Ladarius
(Origin unknown)

Ladd
(English) helper; smart
Lad, Laddee, Laddey

Laddie
(English) youthful
*Lad, Ladd, Laddee,
Laddey, Laddy*

Ladisiao
(Spanish) helpful
Laddy

Lael
(Hebrew) Jehovah's
Lale

Lafaye
(American) cheerful
*Lafay, Lafayye, Laphay,
Laphe*

Lafayetta
(Spanish) from the
French name Lafayette;
bold
Lafay

Lafayette
(French) ambitious
Lafayet, Lafayett

Lafe
(American) punctual
Laafe, Laife, Laiffe

Lagos
(Place name) city in
Nigeria
Lago

Lagrand
(African-American) the
grand
Grand, Grandy, Lagrande

Laird
(Scottish) rich
Layrd, Layrde

Lalo
(Latin) singer of a lullaby
Laloh

Lamalcom
(African-American) son
of Malcolm; kingly
*LaMalcolm, LaMalcom,
Mal, Malcolm, Malcom*

Lamar
(Latin) renowned
Lamahr, Lamarr

Lamber
(German) form of
Lambert; ingratiating
Lambur

Lambert
(German) bright
*Lamb, Lamber, Lambie,
Lamburt, Lammie,
Lammy*

Lamond
(French) worldly
*Lamon, Lamonde,
Lemond*

Lamont
(Scandinavian) lawman
Lamon

Lance
(German) confident
Lanse, Lantz, Lanz

Lancelot
(French) romantic
*Lance, Lancelott,
Launcelot, Launcey*

Lander
(English) landed
Land

Landers
(English) wealthy
Land, Landar, Lander, Landor

Landis
(English) owning land; earthy
Land, Landes, Landice, Landise, Landly, Landus

Lando
(American) masculine
Land

Landon
(English) place name; plain; old-fashioned
Land, Landan, Landen

Landry
(French) entrepreneur
Landré, Landree

Lane
(English) secure
Laine, Laney, Lanie, Lanni, Layne

Lang
(English) top
Lange

Langdon
(English) longwinded
Lang, Langden, Langdun

Langford
(English) healthy
Lanford, Langferd

Langham
(Last name as first name) long
Lang

Langley
(English) natural
Lang, Langlee, Langli, Langly

Langston
(English) longsuffering
Lang, Langstan, Langsten

Langton
(English) long
Lange

Lanny
(American) popular
Lann, Lanney, Lanni, Lannie

Lansing
(Place name) city in Michigan
Lance, Lans

Laramie
(French) pensive
Laramee

Lare
(American) wealthy
Larre, Layr

Largel
(American) intrepid
Large

Lariat
(American) word as name; roper
Lare, Lari

Larkin
(Irish) brash
Lark, Larkan, Larken, Larkie, Larky

Larndell
(American) generous
Larn, Larndelle, Larndey, Larne

Larne
(Place name) district in Northern Ireland
Larn, Larney, Larny

Larnell
(American) giving
Larne

Laron
(American) outgoing
Larron, Larrone

Larrmyne
(American) boisterous
Larmie, Larmine, Larmy, Larmyne

Larry
(Latin) extrovert
Lare, Larrey, Larri, Larrie, Lary

Lars
(Scandinavian) short for Lawrence and Laurens
Larrs, Larse, Larsy

Lashaun
(African-American)
enthusiastic
Lashawn, La-Shawn,
Lashon, Lashond

Lasisch
(Origin unknown)

Laskey
(Last name as first
name) jovial
Lask, Laski

Lassen
(Place name) a peak in
California in the Cascade
Range
Lase, Lasen, Lassan,
Lassun

Lassit
(American) broad-
minded
Lasset, Lassitte

Lassiter
(American) witty
Lassater, Lasseter,
Lassie, Lassy

Lathrop
(English) home-loving
Lathrap, Latrope, Laye,
Laythrep

Latimer
(English) interprets;
philanthropic
Latymer

Latorris
(African-American)
notorious
LaTorris

Latravious
(African-American)
healthy
Latrave

Latty
(English) giving
Lat, Latti, Lattie

Laurence
(Latin) glorified
Larence, Laurance,
Laurans, Laure, Lorence

Laurens
(German) brilliant
Larrie, Larry, Laure,
Laurins, Lorens, Lors

Laurent
(French) martyred
Laurynt

Lavaughn
(African-American) perky
Lavan, Lavon, Lavonn,
Levan, Levaughn

Lavaughor
(African-American)
laughing
Lavaugher, Lavawnar

Lawford
(English) dignified
Laford, Lauford, Lawferd

Lawrence
(Latin) honored
Larrie, Larry, Laurence,
Lawrance, Lawrunce

Lawson
(English) Lawrence's
son; special
Law, Laws, Lawsan,
Lawsen

Layshaun
(African-American) merry
Laysh, Layshawn

Laysy
(Last name as first
name) sophisticated
Lay, Laycie, Laysee

Layt
(American) fascinating
Lait, Laite, Late, Layte

Layton
(English) musical
Laytan, Laytawn, Layten

Lazar
(Hebrew) from Lazarus;
helped by God
Lazare, Lazaro, Lazear,
Lazer

Lazarus
(Greek) renewed
Lasarus, Lazerus,
Lazoros

Leamon
(American) powerful
Leamm, Leamond,
Leemon

Leand
(Greek) from Leander;
leonine
Leander

Leander
(Greek) ferocious;
lion-like
Anders, Leann, Leannder

Lear
(Greek) royal
Leare, Leere

Learly
(Last name as first
name) terrific
Learley

Leather
(American) word as
name; tough
Leath

Leavery, Leautry
(American) giving
*Leautree, Leautri, Levry,
Lo, Lotree, Lotrey, Lotri,
Lotry*

Lectoy
(American) form of
Lecter and Leroy; good-
old-boy
Lec, Lecto, Lek

Lee
(English) loving
Lea, Lee, Leigh

Leeander
(Invented) form of
Leander

Leenoris
(African-American) form
of Lenore; respected
Lenoris

Leeodis
(African-American)
combo of Lee and Odis;
carefree
Lee-Odis, Leotis

Leeron
(African-American)
combo of Lee and Ron
Leerawn

Leibel
(Hebrew) lion

Leif
(Scandinavian) loved
one
Laif, Leaf, Leife

Leighton
(Last name as first
name) hearty
*Laytan, Layton,
Leighten, Leightun*

Leland
(English) protective
*Leeland, Leighlon,
Leiland, Lelan, Lelond*

Leldon
(American) form of
Eldon; bookish
Leldun

Lemar
(American) form of
Lamar; famed landowner
Lemarr

Lemetrias
(African-American) form
of Lemetrius
Lem

Lemon
(American) fruit; tart
Lemonn, Lemun, Limon

Len
(German) short for
Leonard
Lennie, Lynn

Lenard
(American) form of
Leonard; heart of a lion
Lenerd

Lennart
(Scandinavian) brave
Lenn, Lenne

Lennon
(Irish) renowned; caped
Lenn, Lennan, Lennen

Lennox
(Scottish) authoritative
*Lennix, Lenocks, Lenox,
Linnox*

Lenny
(German) short for
Leonard
*Lenn, Lenney, Lenni,
Lennie, Leny, Linn*

Lenton
(American) religious
Lent, Lenten, Lentun

Lenvil
(Invented) typical
Lenval, Level

Leo
(Latin) lion-like; fierce

Leocadio
(Spanish) lion-hearted
Leo

Leoliver
(American) combo of Leo
and Oliver; audacious
Leo

Leon
(Greek) tenacious
Lee, Leo, Leone, Leonn

Leonard
(German) courageous
*Lee, Leo, Leonar,
Leonerd, Leonord, Lynar,
Lynard, Lynerd*

Leonardo
(Italian) lion-hearted
Leo

Leoncio
(Spanish) lion-hearted
Leon, Leonce, Leonse

Leondras
(African-American)
lionine
*Leon, Leondre,
Leondrus, Leonid*

Leonidus
(Latin) strong
*Leon, Leone, Leonidas,
Leonydus*

Leopaul
(American) combo of Leo
and Paul; brave; calm
Leo-Paul

Leopold
(German) brave
Lee, Leo

Leoti
(American) outdoorsy
Lee, Leo

Leovardo
(Spanish) form of
Leonardo; brave
Leo, Leovard

Lepoldo
(Spanish) form of
Leopold; brave
Lee, Lepold, Poldo

Lerey
(American) form of Larry
Lerrie, Lery

Leroy
(French) king; royal
*Leeroy, Leroi, Le-Roy,
Roy, Roye*

Les
(English) short for Leslie
Lez, Lezli

Leshawn
(African-American)
cheery
*Lashawn, Leshaun,
Le-Shawn*

Leslie
(Scottish) fortified
*Lee, Les, Lesley, Lesli,
Lezlie, Lezly*

Lesner
(Last name as first
name) serious
Les, Lez, Lezner

Lester
(American) large
persona
Les, Lestor

Lev
(Russian) lionine

Levar
(American) softspoken
Levarr

Levi
(Hebrew) harmonious
Lev, Levey, Levie, Levy

Levonne
(African-American)
forward-thinking
Lavonne, Leevon, Levon

Lew
(Polish) lion-like
Leu

Leward
(French) contentious
Lewar, Lewerd

Lew-Gene
(American) combo of
Lew and Gene;
renowned fighter
Lou-Gene

Lewie
(French) form of Louie
Lew, Lewee, Lewey, Lewy

Lewis
(English) different
spelling for Louis
*Lew, Lewey, Lewie,
Lewus, Lewy*

Lex
(English) short for
Alexander; mysterious
*Lexa, Lexe, Lexi, Lexie,
Lexy*

Li
(Chinese) strong man

Liam
(Irish) protective;
handsome
Leam, Leeam, Leeum

Liang
(Chinese) good man

Liberio
(Spanish) liberated
Libere, Lyberio

Liberty
(American) freedom-
loving
Lib

Librada
(Italian, Spanish) free

Lictor
(Invented) form of
Lecter; disturbed
Lec, Lek

Lidon
(Hebrew) judge

Lieven
(Belgium)
Lieve

Lillo
(American) triple-threat
talent
Lilo

Limo
(Invented) from the word
limousine; sporty
Lim

Linc, Link
(English) short for
Lincoln; leader
Links

Lincoln
(English, American)
quiet
Linc, Link

Lindberg
(German) blond good
looks
*Lin, Lind, Lindburg,
Lindie, Lindy, Lyndberg,
Lyndburg*

Linden
(Botanical) tree
Lindun

Lindoh
(American) sturdy
Lindo, Lindy

Lindsay, Lindsey
(English) natural
*Lind, Lindsee, Linz,
Linzee, Lyndsey, Lyndzie,
Lynz, Lynzie*

Lindy
(German) form of
Lindberg; daring
Lind

Linley
(English) open-minded
*Lin, Linlee, Linleigh,
Lynlie*

Linnard
(German) form of
Leonard; bold
Linard, Lynard

Lino
(American) form of Linus
Linus

Linus
(Greek) blond
Linas, Line, Lines

Linwood
(American) open

Lionel
(French) fierce
Li, Lion, Lionell, Lye,
Lyon, Lyonel, Lyonell

Lister
(Origin unknown)
intelligent

Litton
(English) centered
Lyten, Lyton, Lytton

Livingston
(English) comforting
Liv, Livey, Livingstone

Llano
(Place name) river in
Texas; flowing
Lano

Llewellyn
(English) fiery; fast
Lew, Lewellen, Lewellyn

Lloyd
(English) spiritual; joyful
Loy, Loyd, Loydde, Loye

Lobo
(Spanish) wolf
Loboe, Lobow

Lochlain
(Irish) assertive
Lochlaine, Lochlane,
Locklain

Lock
(English) natural
Locke

Lodge
(English) safe haven

Loey
(American) daring
Loie, Lowee, Lowi

Lofton
(Last name as first
name) lofty
Loften

Logan
(Irish) eloquent
Logen, Loggy, Logun

Lombardi
(Italian) winner
Bardi, Bardy, Lom,
Lombard, Lombardy

London
(English) ethereal;
capital of Great Britain
Londen

Lonnie
(Spanish) short for
Alonzo
Lonney, Lonni, Lonny

Loocho
(Invented) form of Lucho

Lorance
(Latin) form of
Lawrence; longsuffering;
patient
Lorans, Lorence

Lord
(English) regal
Lorde

Lordlee
(English) regal
Lordly, Lords

Loredo
(Spanish) smart cowboy
Lorado, Loredoh, Lorre,
Lorrey

Loren
(Latin) hopeful; winning
Lorin, Lorrin

Lorens
(Scandinavian) form of
Laurence

Lorenzo
(Spanish, Italian)
bold and spirited
Larenzo, Loranzo, Lore,
Lorence, Lorenso,
Lorentz, Lorenz, Lorrie,
Lorry

Loring
(German) brash
Looring, Lorrie, Louring

Lorne
(Latin) grounded
Lorn, Lorny

Lorry
(English) form of Laurie
Lore, Lorri, Lorrie, Lorry,
Lory

Lot
(Hebrew) furtive
Lott

Lothario
(German) lover
*Lotario, Lothaire,
Lotherio, Lothurio*

Lou
(German) short for Louis
Lew

Louie, Louey
(German) short for Louis

Louis
(German, French)
powerful ruler
*Lew, Lewis, Lou, Louie,
Lue, Luie, Luis*

Loundis
(American) visionary
*Lound, Loundas,
Loundes, Lowndis*

LouVon
(American) combo of
Lou and Von; searching
*Lou Von, Louvaughan,
Louvawn, Lou-Von*

Lovell
(English) brilliant
Lovall, Love, Lovelle

Lovett
(Last name as first
name) loving
Lovat, Lovet

Low
(American) word as a
name; lowkey
Lowey

Lowell
(English) loved
Lowall, Lowel

Lowry
(Last name as first
name) leader
Lowree, Lowrey

Loys
(American) loyal
Loyce, Loyse

Luc
(French) light; laidback
Lucca, Luke

Luca
(Italian) light-hearted
Louca, Louka, Luka

Lucas
(Greek) patron saint of
doctors/artists; creative
*Lucca, Luces, Luka,
Lukas, Luke, Lukes,
Lukus*

Lucho
(Spanish) lucky; light

Lucian
(Latin) soothing
Lew, Luciyan, Lushun

Luciano
(Italian) light-hearted
Luca, Lucas, Luke

Lucious
(African-American) light;
delicious
Luceous, Lushus

Lucius
(Latin) sunny
Lucca, Luchious, Lushus

Lucky
(American) lucky
Luckee, Luckey, Luckie

Ludie
(English) glorious
Ludd

Ludlow
(German) respected
Ludlo, Ludloe

Ludovic
(Slavic) smart; spiritual
*Luddovik, Lude, Ludovik,
Ludvic, Vick*

Ludwig
(German) talented
*Ludvig, Ludweg,
Ludwige*

Luigi
(Italian) famed warrior
Lui, Louie

Luis
(Spanish) outspoken
Luez, Luise, Luiz

Lujo
(Spanish) luxurious
Luj

Luka, Luca
(Italian, Croatian)
easygoing
Luke

Lukah
(Invented) form of Luca
Lukas
(Greek) light-hearted;
creative
Lucus
Luke
(Latin) worshipful
Luc, Lucc, Luk, Lukus
Lumer
(American) light
Lumar, Lume, Lumur
Luna
(Spanish) moon
Lunn
(Irish) smart and brave
Lun, Lunne
Lusk
(Last name as first
name) hearty
*Lus, Luske, Luskee,
Luskey, Luski, Lusky*
Luther
(German) reformer
Luthar, Luth, Luthur
Luthus
(American) form of
Luther; prepared and
armed
Luth, Luthas
Lyal
(English) form of Lyle;
islander
Lye

Lyle
(French) unique
Lile, Ly, Lyle
Lyman
(English) meadow-man;
sportsman
Lyndall
(English) nature-lover
Lynd, Lyndal, Lyndell
Lyndon
(English) verbose
*Lindon, Lyn, Lynd,
Lyndonn*
Lynge
(Scandinavian) sylvan
nature
Lynn
(English) water-loving
Lin, Linn, Lyn, Lynne
Lynshawn
(African-American)
combo of Lyn and
Shawn; helpful
*Linshawn, Lynnshaw,
Lynshaun*
Lyon
(Place name) in France
Lyone
Lysande
(Greek) freewheeling
Lyse
Lysander
(Greek) lover
Lysand

Lyulf
(German) haughty;
combative
Lyulfe, Lyulff

Mac, Mack
(Irish, Scottish) short for "Mc" or "Mac" surname; friendly
Mackee, Macki, Mackie, Macky

Macaffie
(Scottish) charming
Mac, Mack, Mackey, McAfee, McAffee, McAffie

Macario
(Spanish) blessed
Macareo, Makario

Macarlos
(Spanish) manly
Carlos

Macauley
(Scottish) righteous; dramatic
Mac, Macaulay, McCauley

Macbey
(American) form of Mackey
Mackbey, Makbee, Makbi

Mackenzie
(Irish) giving
Mackenzy, Mackinsey, Makinzie, McKenzie

Maclain
(Irish) natural wonder
McLain, McLaine, McLean

Macon
(Place name) creative; southern
Makon

Macy
(French) lasting; wealthy
Mace, Macee, Macey, Macye

Madan
(Hindi) god of love; loving

Maddox
(English) giving
Maddocks, Maddy, Madox

Madhav
(Hindi) sweet
Madhu

Madison
(English) good
Maddison, Maddy, Madisan, Madisen, Son

Madock
(American) giving
Maddock, Maddy, Madoc

Madras
(Place name) city in India

Magee
(Irish) practical; lively
Mackie, Maggy, McGee

Magic
(American) magical
Majic

Magnus
(Latin) outstanding
Maggy, Magnes

Maguire
(Irish) subtle
Macky, Maggy, McGuire

Mahan
(American) cowboy
Mahahn, Mahand, Mahen, Mayhan

Mahir
(Arabic) skilled

Mahmud
(Arabic) remarkable

Main
(Place name) river in Gemany; leader
Mainess, Mane, Maness

Majeed
(Arabic) majestic
Majid

Majid
(Arabic) glorious

Major
(Latin) leading
*Mage, Magy, Majar,
Maje, Majer*

Makale
(Invented) form of
Mikhail

Maks
(Russian) short for
Maksimilian

Maksimilian
(Russian) competitor
Maksim

Makya
(Native American)
hunter

Malachi
(Hebrew) angelic;
magnanimous
*Malachy, Malakai,
Malaki, Maleki*

Malcolm
(Scottish) peaceful
*Mal, Malkalm, Malkelm,
Malkolm*

Maldon
(French) strong and
combative
Maldan, Malden

Malfred
(German) feisty
Malfrid, Mann

Malik
(Arabic) angelic
Malic

Malla-Ki
(Invented) form of
Malachi

Mallin
(English) rowdy warrior
*Malen, Malin, Mallan,
Mallen, Mallie, Mally*

Mallory
(French) wild spirit
*Mal, Mallie, Malloree,
Mallorie, Mally, Malory*

Maloney
(Irish) religious
*Mal, Malone, Malonie,
Malony*

Malvin
(English) open-minded
*Mal, Malv, Malven,
Malvyne*

Mandell
(German) tough; almond
*Mandee, Mandel,
Mandela, Mandie,
Mandy*

Manfred
(English) peaceful
*Manferd, Manford,
Mannfred, Mannie,
Manny, Mannye*

Manfredo
(Italian) strong
peacefulness

Manila
(Place name) capital of
Philippines
Manilla

Maninder
(Hindi) masculine;
potent

Manley
(English) virile; haven
*Man, Manlee, Manlie,
Manly*

Manning
(English) heroic
Man, Maning, Mann

Mannix
(Irish) spiritual
Manix, Mann, Mannicks

Manny
(Spanish) short for
Manuel
Manney, Manni, Mannie

Manolo
(Spanish) from Spanish
shoe designer Manolo
Blahnik; cutting-edge

Mansfield
(English) outdoorsman
*Manesfeld, Mans,
Mansfeld*

Manu
(Hindi) father of people;
masculine

Manuel
(Hebrew, Spanish) gift
from God
*Mann, Mannuel, Manny,
Manual, Manuelle*

Manus
(American) strong-willed
*Manes, Mann, Mannas,
Mannes, Mannis,
Mannus*

Manvel
(French) great town;
hardworking
*Mann, Manny, Manvil,
Manville*

Marc, Mark
(French) combative
*Markee, Markey,
Markeye, Markie Mark,
Markie, Marko, Marky*

Marc-Anthony
(French) combo of Marc
and Anthony
*Marcantony, Mark-
Anthony, Markantony*

Marcel
(French) singing God's
praises
Marcell, Mars, Marsel

Marcellus
(Latin) romantic;
persevering
*Marcel, Marcelis,
Marcey, Marsellus,
Marsey*

Marcial
(Spanish) martial;
combative
Mars

Marco
(Italian) tender
*Marc, Mark, Markie,
Marko, Marky*

Marconi
(Italian) inventive; tough

Marcos
(Spanish) outgoing
*Marco, Marko, Markos,
Marky*

Marco-Tulio
(Spanish) fighter;
substantial
Marco Tulio, Marcotulio

Marcoux
(French) aggressive;
manly
Marce, Mars

Marcus
(Latin) combative
*Marc, Mark, Markus,
Marky*

Marcus-Anthony
(Spanish) valuable;
aggressive
*Marc Anthony,
Marc-Antonito,
Marcus-Antoneo,
Marcusantonio,
Markanthony, Taco,
Tonio, Tono*

Marek
(Polish) masculine

Marguez
(Spanish) noble
Marguiz

Mariano
(Italian) combative;
manly
Mario

Marin
(French) ocean-loving
Maren, Marino, Maryn

Mario
(Italian) masculine
*Marioh, Marius, Marrio,
Morio*

Marion
(Latin) suspicious
Mareon, Marionn

Marjuan
(Spanish) contentious
*Marhwon, Marwon,
Marwond*

Markell
(African-American)
personable
Markelle

Markham
(English) homebody
*Marcum, Markhum,
Markum*

Markos
(Greek) warring; masculine
Marc, Mark

Marl
(English) rebel
Marley, Marli

Marley
(English) secretive
Marlee, Marleigh, Marly

Marlin
(English) opportunistic; fish
Marllin

Marlo, Marlow
(English) hill by a lake; optimistic
Mar, Marl, Marlowe

Marlon
(French) wizard; strange
Marlan, Marlen, Marlin, Marly

Marmaduke
(English) haughty
Duke, Marmadook, Marmahduke

Marmion
(French) famed
Marmeonne, Marmyon

Marq
(French) noble
Mark, Marque, Marquie

Marquise
(French) noble
Mark, Markese, Marky, Marq, Marquese, Marquie, Marquis

Mars
(Latin) warlike (god of war)
Marrs, Marz

Marsdon
(English) comforting
Marr, Mars, Marsden, Marsdyn

Marsh
(English) handsome
Marr, Mars, Marsch, Marsey, Marsy

Marshall
(French) giving care
Marsh, Marshal, Marshel, Marshell, Marsy

Marston
(English) personable
Mars, Marst, Marstan, Marsten

Martin
(Latin) combative; from Mars
Mart, Marten, Marti, Martie, Marton, Marty

Marty
(Latin) short for Martin
Mart, Martee, Martey, Marti, Martie, Martye

Marv
(English) short for Marvin; good friend
Marve, Marvy

Marvin
(English) steadfast friend
Marv, Marven, Marvy

Masa
(African) centered

Mashawn
(African-American) vivacious
Masean, Mashaun, Mayshawn

Maslen
(American) promising
Mas, Masline, Maslyn

Mason
(French) ingenious; reliable; stonemason
Mace, Mase

Masood
(Iranian)

Massey
(English) doubly excellent
Maccey, Masey, Massi

Massimo
(Italian) great
Masimo, Massey, Massimmo

Mateo
(Italian) gift
Mateus
(Italian) God's gift
Mathau
(American) spunky
*Mathou, Mathow,
Mathoy*
Mather
(English) leader; army;
strong
Mathar
Mathias
(German) form of
Matthew; dignified
*Mathies, Mathyes, Matt,
Matthias, Matty*
Matias
(Spanish) gift from God
Mathias, Matios, Mattias
Matlock
(American) rancher
Lock, Mat, Matt
Matson
(Hebrew) son of
Matthew
*Matsan, Matsen, Matt,
Matty*
Matt
(Hebrew) short for
Matthew
Mat, Matte

Matthew
(Hebrew) God's gift
*Math, Matheu, Mathieu,
Matt, Mattie, Mattsy,
Matty*
Matti
(Scandinavian) form of
Matthias; God's gift
Mat, Mats
Matts
(Swedish) gift from God
Matty
(Hebrew) short for
Matthew
Mattey, Matti
Mauri
(Latin) short for
Maurice; dark
Maurice
(Latin) dark
*Maur, Maurie, Maurise,
Maury, Moorice, Morice,
Morrie, Morry*
Mauricio
(Italian) dark
Mari, Mauri, Maurizio
Maurizio
(Italian) dark
*Marits, Miritza, Moritz,
Moritza, Moritzio*
Maury
(Latin) short for
Maurice; dark
Mauree, Maurey

Maverick
(American)
unconventional
*Mav, Mavarick,
Mavereck, Mavreck,
Mavvy*
Mavis
(French) bird; thrush;
free
Mavas, Mavus
Max
(Latin) best
*Mac, Mack, Macks,
Maxey, Maxie, Maxx,
Maxy*
Maxime
(French) greatest
Max, Maxeem, Maxim
Maximilian
(Latin) most wonderful
*Max, Maxemillion,
Maxie, Maxima,
Maximillion,
Maxmyllyun, Maxy*
Maximino
(Spanish) maximum;
tops
*Max, Maxem, Maxey,
Maxi, Maxim, Maxy*
Maxinen
(Spanish) maximum
Max, Maxanen, Maxi

Maxwell
(English) full of excellence
Maxe, Maxie, Maxwel, Maxwill, Maxy

Mayer
(Hebrew) smart
Mayar, Maye, Mayor, Mayur

Maynard
(English) reliable
Mayne, Maynerd

Mayo
(Irish) nature-loving
Maio, Maioh, May, Mayes, Mayoh, Mays

Mayon
(Place name) volcano in the Philippines
May, Mayan, Mays, Mayun

Maz
(Hebrew) aid
Maise, Maiz, Mazey, Mazi, Mazie, Mazy

McCoy
(Irish) jaunty; coy
Coye, MacCoy

McDonald
(Scottish) open-minded
Mac-D, Macdonald

McFarlin
(Last name as first name) son of Farlin; confident
Far, Farr

McGowan
(Irish) feisty
Mac-G, Mcgowan

McGregor
(Irish) philanthropic
Macgregor

McKinley
(Last name as first name) son of Kinley; holding his own
Kin, Kinley, McKinlee

McLin
(Irish) careful
Mac, Mack

Mead
(English) outdoorsman
Meade, Meede

Meallan
(Irish) sweet
Maylan, Meall

Medford
(French) natural; comical
Med, Medfor

Meir
(Hebrew) teacher
Mayer, Myer

Mel
(Irish) short for Melvin
Mell

Melbourne
(Place name) city in Australia; serene
Mel, Melborn, Melbourn, Melburn, Melburne

Melburn
(English) sylvan; outdoorsy
Mel, Melbourn, Melburne, Milbourn, Milburn

Meldon
(English) destined for fame
Melden, Meldin, Meldyn

Meldric
(English) leader
Mel, Meldrik

Melecio
(Spanish) cautious
Melesio, Melezio, Mesio

Melroy
(American) form of Elroy
Mel

Melton
(English) nature; natural
Mel, Meltan

Melville
(French) mill town
Mel, Mell, Melvil, Melvill

Melvin
(English) friendly
Mel, Melvine, Melvon,
Melvyn, Milvin

Melvis
(American) form of Elvis;
songbird
Mel, Melv

Memphis
(Place name) city in
Tennessee
Memphus

Mercer
(English) affluent
Merce, Mercur, Murcer

Meredith
(Welsh) protector
Merdith, Mere,
Meredyth, Meridith,
Merrey

Merlin
(English) clever
Merl, Merlan, Merle,
Merlinn, Merlun, Murlin

Merrick
(English) bountiful
seaman
Mere, Meric, Merik,
Merrack, Merrik

Merrie
(English) giving
Merey, Meri, Merri

Merrill
(French) renowned
Mere, Merell, Merill,
Merrell, Merril, Meryll

Merritt
(Latin) worthy
Merid, Merit, Merret,
Merrid

Merv
(Irish) short for Mervin;
bold
Murv

Mervin
(Irish) bold
Merv, Merven, Mervun,
Mervy, Mervyn, Murv,
Murvin

Meshach
(Hebrew) fortunate
Meeshak, Meshack,
Meshak

Mesquite
(American) rancher;
spiny shrub
Meskeet

Meyer
(Hebrew) brilliant
Maye, Meier, Mye, Myer

Meyshaun
(African-American)
searching
Maysh, Mayshaun,
Mayshawn, Meyshawn

Michael
(Hebrew) spiritual
patron of soldiers
Mical, Michaelle, Mickey,
Mikael, Mike, Mikey,
Mikiee, Miko

Michel
(French) fond
Mich, Michelle, Mike,
Mikey

Michelangelo
(Italian) God's
angel/messenger;
artistic
Michel, Michelanjelo,
Mikalangelo, Mike,
Mikel, Mikelangelo

Michon
(French) form of Michel;
God-like
Mich, Michonn, Mish,
Mishon

Mickel
(American) form of
Michael; friend
Mick, Mikel

Mickey
(American) enthusiastic
Mick, Micki, Mickie,
Micky, Miki, Myck

Mickey-Lee
(American) friendly
Mickey Lee, Mickeylee,
Mickie-Lee

Miga
(Spanish) persona; essence

Miguel
(Spanish) form of Michael
Megel, Migel, Migelle

Miguelangel
(Spanish) angelic
Miguelanjel

Mihir
(Hindi) sunny

Mika
(Hebrew) form of Micah
Mikah, Mikie, Myka, Mykie, Myky

Mikael
(Scandinavian) warrior
Michael, Mikel, Mikkel

Mike
(Hebrew) short for Michael
Meik, Miik, Myke

Mikhail
(Russian) god-like; graceful
Mika, Mikey, Mikkail, Mykhey

Mikolas
(Greek) form of Nicholas; bright
Mick, Mickey, Mickolas, Mik, Miko, Mikolus, Miky

Milagros
(Spanish) miracle
Milagro

Milam
(Last name as first name) uncomplicated
Mylam

Milan
(Place name) city in Italy; smooth
Milano

Milburn
(Scottish) volatile
Milbyrn, Milbyrne, Millburn

Miles
(German) forgiving
Mile, Miley, Myles, Myyles

Miley
(American) reliable; forgiving
Mile, Miles, Mili, Mily, Myles, Myley

Milford
(English) from a calm (mill) setting; country
Milferd, Milfor

Millard
(Latin) old-fashioned
Milard, Mill, Millerd, Millurd, Milly

Miller
(English) practical
Mille, Myller

Mills
(English) safe
Mill, Milly, Mylls

Milo
(German) soft-hearted
Miles, Milos, Mye, Mylo

Milos
(Slavic) kind
Mile, Miles, Myle, Mylos

Milton
(English) innovative
Melton, Milt, Miltey, Milti, Miltie, Milty, Mylt, Mylton

Mimi
(Greek) outspoken
Mims

Miner
(Last name as first name) hard-working; miner
Mine, Miney

Mingo
(American) flirtatious
Ming-O, Myngo

Mirlam
(American) great
Mir, Mirsam, Mirtam

Misael
(Hebrew) godlike

Misha
(Russian) short for
Mikhail
Mitchell
(English) optimistic
Mitch, Mitchel,
Mitchelle, Mitchie,
Mitchill, Mitchy, Mitshell,
Mytchil
Modesto
(Spanish) modest
Modysto
Modred
(Greek) unafraid
Modrede, Modrid
Moe
(American) short for
names beginning with
Mo or Moe; easygoing
Mo
Moey
(Hebrew) easygoing
Moe, Moeye
Mohammad
(Arabic) praiseworthy
Mohamad, Mohamid,
Mohamud, Muhammad
Mohan
(Hindi) compelling
Mohana
(Sanskrit) handsome
Mohann

Mohawk
(Place name) river in
New York
Mohsen
(Austrian)
Mosen
Moises
(Hebrew) drawn from
the water
Moe
Mojave
(Place name) desert in
California; towering man
Mohave, Mohavey
Moline
(American) narrow
Moleen, Molene
Momo
(American) rascal
Monahan
(Irish) believer
Mon, Monaghan,
Monehan, Monnahan
Money
(American) word as
name; popular
Muney
Monico
(Spanish) form of
Monaco; player
Mon

Monroe
(Irish) delightful;
presidential
Mon, Monro, Munro,
Munroe
Montague
(French) forward-
thinking
Mont, Montagew,
Montagu, Montegue,
Monty
Montana
(Spanish) U.S. state;
sports icon
Mont, Montane,
Montayna, Monty
Monte
(Spanish) short for
Montgomery and
Montague; handsome
Mont, Montee, Monti,
Monts, Monty
Monteague
(African-American)
combo of Monty and
Teague; creative
Mont, Montegue, Monti,
Monty
Montgomery
(English) wealthy
Mongomerey, Monte,
Montgomry, Monty

Montraie
(African-American) fussy
Mont, Montray,
Montraye, Monty

Montrel
(African-American)
popular
Montrell, Montrelle,
Monty

Montrose
(French)
high-and-mighty
Mont, Montroce,
Montros, Monty

Monty
(English) short for
Montgomery and
Montague
Monte, Montee, Montey,
Monti

Moody
(American) expansive
Moodee, Moodey,
Moodie

Moon
(African) dreamer

Mooney
(American) dreamer
Moon, Moonee, Moonie

Moore
(French) dark-haired
Mohr, Moores, More

Mooring
(Last name as first
name) centered
Moring

Moose
(American) large guy
Moos, Mooz, Mooze

Mordecai
(Hebrew) combative
Mord, Morde, Mordekai,
Morducai, Mordy

Morell
(French) secretive
More, Morelle, Morey,
Morrell, Mourell, Murell

Morey
(Latin) dark
Morrie, Morry

Morgan
(Celtic) confident
seaman
Morg, Morgen, Morghan

Morlen
(English) outdoorsy
Morlan, Morlie, Morly

Moroni
(Place name) city in
Comoros; joyful
Maroney, Maroni,
Marony, Moroney,
Morony

Morris
(Latin) dark
Maurice, Moris, Morse,
Mouris

Morrley
(English) outdoors-
loving
More, Morlee, Morley,
Morly, Morrs

Morse
(English) bright code-
maker
Morce, Morcey, Morry,
Morsey

Mortimer
(French) deep
Mort, Mortemer, Mortie,
Morty, Mortymer

Morton
(English) sophisticated
Mort, Mortan, Mortun,
Morty

Moses
(Hebrew) appointed for
special things
Mosa, Mose, Mosesh,
Mosie, Mozes, Mozie

Moshe
(Hebrew) special
Mosh, Moshie

Moss
(Irish) giving
Mossy

Motee
(Paskistani)

Motor
(American) word as
name; speedy; active
Mote

Mottel
(Hebrew) from Max;
fighter
Mozam
(Place name) from
Mozambique
Moze
Mudge
(Last name as first
name) friendly
Mud, Mudj
Muhammad
(Arabic) form of
Mohammed; praised
Muhamed, Muhammed
Mukul
(Hindi) bird; beginnings
Mundo
(Spanish) short for
Edmundo; prosperous
Mun, Mund
Mungo
(Scottish) loved;
congenial
*Mongo, Mongoh,
Munge, Mungoh*
Murcia
(Place name) region in
Spain
Mursea
Murdoch
(Scottish) rich
*Merdock, Merdok, Murd,
Murdock, Murdok,
Murdy*

Murfain
(American) bold spirit
*Merfaine, Murf, Murfee,
Murfy, Murphy*
Murff
(Irish) short for Murphy;
feisty
Merf, Murf
Murl
(English) nature-lover;
sea
Murphy
(Irish) fighter
*Merph, Merphy, Murfie,
Murph*
Murray
(Scottish) sea-loving;
sailor
*Mur, Muray, Murrey,
Murry*
Murrell
(English) nature-lover;
sea
Mycheal
(African-American)
devoted
Mysheal
Myles
(German) form of Miles
Mylos
(Slavic) kind
Milos

Myrle
(American) able
*Merl, Merle, Myrie,
Myryee*
Myron
(Greek) notable
Mi, Miron, My, Myrayn
Myrzon
(American) humorous
Merzon, Myrs, Myrz

Nabil
(Arabic) of noble birth; honored
Nabeel, Nobila

Nada
(Arabic) morning dew; giver
Nadah

Nadir
(Arabic) rare man

Nahir
(Hebrew) light
Nahor

Nando
(Spanish) short for Fernando

Nanson
(American) spunky
Nance, Nanse, Nansen, Nansson

Napoleon
(German) lion of Naples; domineering
Nap, Napo, Napoleone, Napolion, Napolleon, Nappy

Narciso
(Spanish) form of Greek Narcissus, who fell in love with his reflection; vain
Narcis

Narcissus
(Greek) self-loving; vain
Narciss, Narcissah, Narcisse, Nars

Nasario
(Spanish) dedicated to God
Nasar, Nasareo, Nassario, Nazareo, Nazarlo, Nazaro, Nazor

Nash
(Last name as first name) exciting
Nashe, Nashey

Nasser
(Arabic) winning
Nasir, Nassar, Nasse, Nassee, Nassor

Nat
(Hebrew) short for Nathaniel
Natt, Natte, Nattie, Natty

Nate
(Hebrew) short for Nathan and Nathaniel
Natey

Natividad
(Spanish) a child born at Christmastime

Nathan
(Hebrew) short for Nathaniel; magnanimous
Nat, Nate, Nathen, Nathin, Natthaen, Natthan, Natthen, Natty

Nathaniel
(Hebrew) God's gift to mankind
Nat, Nate, Nathan, Nathaneal, Nathanial, Nathe, Nathenial

Nation
(American) patriotic

Nato
(American) gentle
Nate, Natoe, Natoh

Navarro
(Spanish) place name; wild spirit
Navaro, Navarroh, Naverro

Neal
(Irish) winner
Nealey, Neall, Nealy, Neel, Neelee, Neely, Nele

Neander
(Greek) from Neanderthal
Ander, Nean, Neand

Nebraska
(Place name) U.S. state
Neb

Ned
(English) short for
Edward; comforting
Neddee, Neddie, Neddy

Nedrun
(American) difficult
*Ned, Nedd, Neddy,
Nedran, Nedro*

Neely
(Scottish) winning
Neel, Neels

Nehemiah
(Hebrew) compassionate
Nehemyah, Nemo

Nellie
(English) short for
Nelson; singing
*Nell, Nellee, Nelli, Nells,
Nelly*

Nelson
(English) broad-minded
*Nell, Nels, Nelsen,
Nelsun, Nilsson*

Neptune
(Latin) god of the sea
*Neptoon, Neptoone,
Neptunne*

Nero
(Latin) unyielding
Neroh

Nery
(Spanish) daring
*Neree, Nerey, Nerrie,
Nerry*

Nesto
(Greek) adventurer
Nestoh, Nestoro

Nestor
(Greek) wanderer
*Nest, Nester, Nestir,
Nesto, Nesty*

Netar
(African-American)
bright
Netardas

Netzer
(American) form of
Nestor
Net

Nevada
(Place name) U.S. state
Nev, Nevadah

Neville
(French) innovator
*Nev, Nevil, Nevile,
Nevvy, Niville*

Newbie
(American) novice
New, Newb

Newell
(English) fresh face in
the hall
*New, Newall, Newel,
Newy, Nywell*

Newlin
(Welsh) able; new pond
Newl, Newlynn, Nule

Newman
(English) attractive
young man
*Neuman, New,
Newmann*

Newt
(English) new

Newton
(English) bright; new
mind
New, Newt

Neyman
(American) son of Ney;
bookish
Ney, Neymann, Neysa

Nicah
(Greek) victorious
Nik, Nike

Nicholas
(Greek) winner; the
people's victor
*Nichelas, Nicholus, Nick,
Nickee, Nickie, Nicklus,
Nickolas, Nicky, Nikolas,
Nyck, Nykolas*

Nichols
(English) kind-hearted
Nicholes, Nick, Nicky,
Nikols

Nick
(English) short for
Nicholas
Nic, Nik

Nicklaus
(Greek) form of Nicholas
Nicklaws, Niklus

Nicky
(Greek) short for
Nicholas
Nick, Nickee, Nickey,
Nicki, Nik, Nikee, Nikki

Nico
(Italian) victor

Nicolas
(Italian) form of
Nicholas; victorious
Nic, Nico, Nicolus

Niels
(Scandinavian)
victorious
Neels

Nigel
(English) champion
Nigie, Nigil, Nygelle

Nike
(Greek) winning
Nykee, Nykie, Nyke

Nikita
(Russian) not yet won
Nika

Niklas
(Scandinavian) winner
Niklaas, Nils, Klaas

Nikolai
(Russian) winning
Nika

Nikolas
(Greek) form of Nicholas
Nik, Nike, Niko, Nikos,
Nyloas

Nikos
(Greek) victor
Nicos, Niko, Nikolos

Niles
(English) smooth
Ni, Nile, Niley, Nyles,
Nyley

Nimrod
(Hebrew) renegade
Nimrodd, Nymrod

Nino
(Spanish) child; young
boy

Ninyun
(American) spirited
Ninian, Ninion, Ninyan,
Nynyun

Nissan
(Hebrew) omen
Nisan, Nissyn

Niven
(Last name as first
name) smooth

Nix
(American) negative
Nicks, Nixy

Nixon
(English) audacious
Nickson, Nixen, Nixun

Noah
(Hebrew) peacemaker
Noa, Noe, Nouh

Noam
(Hebrew) sweet man
Noahm, Noe

Noble
(Latin) regal
Nobe, Nobee, Nobel,
Nobie, Noby

Noe
(Spanish) quiet;
(Polish) comforter
Noeh, Noey

Noel
(French) born on
Christmas
Noelle, Noelly, Nole,
Nollie

Noey
(Spanish) form of Noah;
he who wanders
Noe, Noie

Nolan
(Irish) outstanding;
noble
*Nole, Nolen, Nolline,
Nolun, Nolyn*

Nolden
(American) noble
Nold

Nolly
(Scandinavian) hopeful
*Nole, Noli, Noll, Nolley,
Nolleye, Nolli, Nollie*

Norb
(Scandinavian)
innovative
*Noberto, Norbie, Norbs,
Norby*

Norbert
(German) bright north
Norb, Norbie, Norby

Nordin
(Nordic) handsome
*Nord, Nordan, Norde,
Nordee, Nordeen, Nordi,
Nordun, Nordy*

Norman
(English) sincere; man of
the North
*Norm, Normen, Normey,
Normi, Normie, Normon,
Normun, Normy*

Norshawn
(African-American)
combo of Nor and
Shawn
*Norrs, Norrshawn,
Norshaun*

North
(American) directional
Norf, Northe

Norton
(English) dignified man
of the North
Nort, Nortan, Norten

Norval
(English) from the North
Norvan

Norville
(French) resident of a
northern village; warm-
hearted
*Norvel, Norvil, Norvill,
Norvyl*

Norshell
(African-American) brash
Norshel, Norshelle

Norwin
(English) friendly
*Norvin, Norwen,
Norwind, Norwinn*

Nowell
(Last name as first
name) dependable
Nowe

Nowey
(American) knowing
Nowee, Nowie

Nueces
(Place name) Nueces
River

Nuell
(American) form of
Newell (last name); in
charge
Nuel

Nuey
(Spanish) short for
Nueva
Nui, Nuie

Nunry
(Last name as first
name) giving
Nunri

Nuys
(Place name) from Van
Nuys, California
Nies, Nyes, Nys

Nye
(Welsh) focused
Ni, Nie, Nyee

Nyle
(American) form of
Niles/Nile; smooth
Nyl, Nyles

Oak
(English) sturdy
Oake, Oakie

Oakley
(English) sturdy; strong
Oak, Oakie, Oakly, Oklie

Obadiah
(Hebrew) serving God
Obadyah, Obediah, Obee, Obie, Oby

Obbie
(Biblical) from Biblical prophet Obadiah; serving God
Obey, Obi, Obie

Obedience
(American) strict
Obie

Oberon
(German) strong-bearing
Obaron, Oberahn, Oberone, Oburon

Obey
(American) short for Obadiah
Obe, Obee, Obie, Oby

Ocean
(Greek) ocean; child born under a water sign
Oceane

Ocie
(Greek) short for Ocean
Osie

Octavio
(Latin) eight; able
Octavioh

Ode
(Greek) poetry as a name; poetic
Odee, Odie

Odell
(American) musical
Dell, Odall, Ode, Odey, Odyll

Oder
(Place name) river in Europe
Ode

Odin
(Scandinavian) Norse god of magic; soulful
Odan, Oden

Odisoose
(Invented) form of Odysseus
Ode

Odysseus
(Greek) wanderer
Ode, Odey, Odie

Ogdon
(English) literate
Og, Ogdan, Ogden

Ogle
(American) word as name; leer; stare
Ogal, Ogel, Ogll, Ogul

Ojay
(American) brash
O.J., Oojai

Okan
(Turkish)
Oke

Okie
(American) man from Oklahoma
Okey, Okeydokey

Olaf
(Scandinavian) watchful
Olay, Ole, Olef, Olev, Oluf

Olajuwon
(Arabic) honorable
Olajuwan, Olujuwon

Olan
(Scandinavian) royal ancestor
Olin, Ollee

Olav
(Scandinavian) traditional
Ola, Olov, Oluf

Ole
(Scandinavian) watchful
Olay

Oleg
(Russian) holy; religious
Olag, Ole, Olig

Oliver
(Latin) loving nature
Olaver, Olive, Ollie, Olliver, Olly, Oluvor

Olivier
(French) eloquent
Oliveay

Ollie
(English) short for Oliver
Olie, Ollee, Olley, Olly

Omaha
(Place name) city in Nebraska

Omar
(Arabic) spiritual
Omahr, Omarr

Omie
(Italian) homebody
Omey, Omi, Omye

Onesimo
(Spanish) number one
Onie

Onofrio
(German) smart
Ono, Onofreeo, Onofrioh

Oo
(Korean)

Oren
(Hebrew) from Owen; sturdy (tree)

Orenthiel
(American) sturdy as a pine
Ore, Oren

Orenthiem
(American) sturdy as a pine
Orenth, Orenthe

Orestes
(Greek) leader
Oresta, Oreste, Restie, Resty

Oriol
(Spanish) best
Orioll

Orion
(Greek) fiery hunter
Oreon, Ori, Orie, Ory

Orlando
(Spanish) famed; distinctive
Orl, Orland, Orlie, Orlondo, Orly

Orme
(English) kind
Orm

Ormond
(English) kind-hearted
Ormand, Ormande, Orme, Ormon, Ormonde, Ormund, Ormunde

Orran
(Irish) green-eyed
Ore, Oren, Orin

Orrick
(English) sturdy as an oak
Oric, Orick, Orreck, Orrik

Orrie
(American) short for Orson; solid
Orry

Orson
(Latin) strong as a bear
Orsan, Orsen, Orsey, Orsun

Orth
(English) honest
Orthe

Orval
(American) form of Orville; bold
Orvale

Orville
(French) brave
Orv, Orvelle, Orvie, Orvil

Orway
(American) kind
Orwaye

Osborne
(English) strong-spirited
Osborn, Osbourne, Osburn, Osburne, Ossie, Oz, Ozzie, Ozzy

Osburt
(English) smart
Osbart, Osbert, Ozbert, Ozburt

Oscar
(Scandinavian) divine
Ozkar

Oscard
(Greek) fighter
Oscar, Oskard

Osgood
(English) good man
Osgude, Ozgood

Osiel
(Spanish)

Oslo
(Place name) capital of
Norway
Os, Oz

Osman
(Spanish) verbose
*Os, Osmen, Osmin,
Ossie, Oz, Ozzie*

Osmond
(English) singing to the
world
*Os, Osmonde, Osmund,
Ossie, Oz, Ozzy*

Osrec
(Scandinavian) leader
Os, Ossie

Ossie
(Hebrew) powerful
Os, Oz, Ozzy

Osvaldo
(German) divine power
Osvald, Oswaldo

Oswald
(English) divine power
*Oswalde, Oswold,
Oswuld, Oszie, Oz*

Othell
(African-American)
thriving
Oth, Othey, Otho

Othello
(Spanish) bold
Otello, Othell

Otis
(Greek) intuitive
*Oates, Odis, Otes, Ottes,
Ottis*

Otoniel
(Spanish) fashionable
Otonel

Otto
(German) wealthy
Oto, Ott, Ottoh

Ottway
(German) fortunate
Otwae, Otway

Overton
(Last name as first
name) leader
Ove, Overten

Ovidio
(Spanish) from Ovid
(Roman poet); creative
Ovido

Owen
(Welsh) well-born; high-
principled
Owan, Owin, Owwen

Ox
(American) animal;
strong
Oxy

Oxford
(English) scholar; ox
crossing
Fordy, Oxferd, Oxfor

Oz
(Hebrew) courageous;
unusual

Ozell
(English) strong
Ozel

Oziel
(Spanish) strong

Ozzie
(English) short for
Oswald
Oz, Ozzee, Ozzey, Ozzy

Pablo
(Spanish) strong;
creative
Pabel, Pabo, Paublo

Packer
(Last name as first
name) orderly
Pack

Paco
(Spanish) energetic
*Pak, Pakkoh, Pako,
Paquito*

Paddy
(Irish) short for Patrick;
noble; comfortable
*Paddey, Paddi, Paddie,
Padee*

Page
(French) helpful
Pagey, Paige, Payg

Pago
(Place name) Pago Pago
Pay

Palladin
(Greek) confrontational;
wise
*Palidin, Palladyn,
Palleden, Pallie, Pally*

Palmer
(English) open
*Pallmar, Pallmer, Palmar,
Palmur*

Pampa
(Place name) city in
Texas

Pan
(Greek mythology) god
of forest and shepherds
Pann

Panama
(Place name) canal
connecting North and
South America; rounder
Pan

Pancho
(Spanish) short for
Francisco; jaunty
Panchoh, Ponchito

Pantaleon
(Spanish) pants;
trousers; manly
Pant, Pantalon

Paolo
(Italian) form of Paul;
small and high-energy
Paoloh, Paulo

Paquito
(Spanish) dear Paco

Paris
(English) lover; France's
capital
Pare, Paree, Parris

Park
(English) calming
Parke, Parkey, Parks

Parker
(English) manager
Park, Parks

Parnell
(French) ribald
Parne, Parnel, Parnelle

Parnelli
(Italian) frisky
Parnell

Paros
(Place name) Greek
island; charming
Par, Paro

Parr
(English) protective
Par, Parre

Parrish
(French) separate and
unique; district

Parry
(Welsh) young son
Parrie, Pary

Parryth
(American) up-and-coming
Pareth, Parre, Parry, Parythe

Pascal
(French) boy born on Easter or Passover; spiritual
Pascalle, Paschal, Paskalle, Pasky

Pasquale
(Italian) spiritual
Pask, Paskwoll, Pasq, Pasquell, Posquel

Pastor
(English) clergyman
Pastar, Paster

Pat
(English) short for Patrick; noble
Pattey, Patti, Patty, Pattye, Pattee

Patrick
(Irish) aristocrat
Paddy, Patric, Patrik, Patriquek, Patryk, Pats, Patsy

Patriot
(American) patriotic

Patterson
(English) intellectual
Paterson, Pattersen, Pattersun, Pattersund

Patton
(English) brash warrior
Patten, Pattun, Patun, Peyton

Paul
(Latin) small; wise
Pauley, Paulie, Pauly

Pauli
(Italian) dear Paul
Paulee, Pauley, Paulie, Pauly

Paulo
(Spanish) form of Paul

Paulos
(Greek) small

Paulus
(Latin) small
Paul, Paulie, Paulis, Pauly

Pavel
(Russian) inspired
Pasha

Pawel
(Polish) believer
Pawl

Pax
(Latin) peace-loving
Paks, Paxy

Payne
(Latin) countryman
Paine, Payn

Payton
(English) soldier's town
Pate, Payten, Paytun, Peyton

Peader
(Scottish) rock or stone; reliable
Peder, Peter

Pearson
(English) dark-eyed
Pearse, Pearsen, Pearsun, Peerson

Pecos
(Place name) Pecos River in Texas; cowboy
Peck, Pekos

Pedro
(Spanish) audacious
Pedra, Pedrin, Pedroh

Pelly
(English) happy
Peli, Pelley, Pelli

Pelon
(Spanish) joyful

Pembroke
(French) sophisticated
Brookie, Pemb, Pembrooke, Pimbroke

Penn
(German) strong-willed
Pen, Pennee, Penney, Pennie, Penny

Pepin
(German) ardent
Pepen, Pepi, Pepp, Peppi, Peppy, Pepun

Pepper
(Botanical) livewire
Pep, Pepp, Peppy
Per
(Scandinavian) secretive
Percival
(French) mysterious
Parsival, Percey, Percy,
Perseval, Purcival, Purcy
Percy
(French) short for
Percival
Percee, Percey, Perci,
Percie
Perfecto
(Spanish) perfect
Perfek
Pericles
(Greek) fair leader
Periklees, Perry
Perine
(Latin) adventurer
Perrin, Perrine, Perry,
Peryne
Perk
(American) perky
Perkey, Perki, Perky
Perkins
(English) political
Perk, Perkens, Perkey
Peron
(Spanish)

Perry
(English) tough-minded
Parry, Perr, Perrey, Perri,
Perrie
Perryman
(Last name as first
name) nature-lover
Perry
Perth
(Place name) capital of
Western Australia
Purth
Perun
(Hindi) from the name
Perunkulam
Pete
(English) easygoing
Petey, Petie
Peter
(Greek) dependable;
rock
Per, Petar, Pete, Petee,
Petey, Petie, Petur
Petra
(Place name) city in
Arabia; dashing
Peyton
(English) form of Payton
Pey, Peyt
Pharis
(Irish) heroic
Farres, Farrus, Pharris

Phelps
(English) droll
Felps, Filps
Phex
(American) kind
Fex
Phil
(Greek) short for Phillip
Fill, Phill
Philander
(Greek) lover of many;
infidel
Filander, Phil, Philandyr
Philemon
(Greek) kisser
Filemon, Philamon
Philip
(Greek) outdoorsman;
horse-lover
Felipe, Filipp, Flippo,
Phil, Phillie, Phillippe,
Philly
Philippe
(French) form of Philip
Felipe, Filippe, Philipe
Philo
(Greek) lover
Filo
Phineas
(English) far-sighted
Fineas, Finny, Pheneas,
Phineus, Phinny

Phoenix
(Greek) bird of immortality; everlasting
Fee, Feenix, Fenix, Nix

Pierce
(English) insightful; piercing
Pearce, Peerce, Peers, Peersey, Percy, Piercy, Piers

Pierre
(French) socially adroit
Piere

Pietro
(Italian) reliable
Pete

Pilar
(Spanish) basic
Pilarr

Pin
(Vietnamese) joyful

Pincus
(American) dark
Pinchas, Pinchus, Pinkus

Pinechas
(Hebrew) form of Paul; dark

Piney
(American) living among pines; comfortable
Pine, Pyney

Pinkston
(Last name as first name) different
Pink, Pinky

Pio
(Italian) pious

Pip
(German) ingenious
Pipp, Pippin, Pippo, Pippy

Pitch
(American) word as name; musical

Pitt
(English) swerving dramatically

Pittman
(English) blue-collar worker

Placid
(Latin) calm
Plasid

Placido
(Italian) serene songster
Placeedo, Placidoh, Placydo

Plato
(Greek) broad-minded
Plata, Platoh

Playtoh
(Invented) form of Plato

Plutarco
(Greek) nefarious

Pluto
(Greek) universal

Poet
(American) writer
Poe

Pollard
(German) close-minded
Pollar, Pollerd, Polley

Polo
(Greek) adventurer
Poloe, Poloh

Ponce
(Spanish) fifth; wanderer
Poncey, Ponse

Ponnuswamy
(Hindi)

Pontius
(Latin) the fifth

Pony
(Scottish) dashing
Poney, Ponie

Poogie
(American) snuggly
Poog, Poogee, Poogi, Poogs, Pookie

Poole
(Place name) area in England
Pool

Pope
(Greek) father
Po

Porter
(Latin) decisive
Poart, Port, Portur, Porty

Powder
(American) cowboy
Powd, Powe

Powell
(English) ready

Prairie
(American) rural man or rancher
Prair, Prairey, Prairi, Prairy

Preemoh
(Invented) form of Primo

Prentice
(English) learning
Prenticce, Prentis, Prentiss, Printiss

Presley
(English) songbird; meadow of the priest
Preslee, Preslie, Presly

Preston
(English) spiritual
Prestyn

Price
(Welsh) vigorous
Pricey, Pryce

Priestley
(English) cottage of the priest
Priestlea, Priestlee, Priestly

Primerica
(American) form of America; patriotic
Prime

Primitivo
(Spanish) primitive
Primi, Tito, Tivo

Primo
(Italian) topnotch
Preemo, Primoh, Prymo

Prince
(Latin) regal leader
Preenz, Prins, Prinz, Prinze

Prop
(American) word as name; fun-loving
Propp

Prosper
(Italian) having good fortune
Pros

Pryor
(Latin) spiritual director
Pry, Prye

Purvin
(English) helpful
Pervin

Purvis
(French) provider
Pervis, Purviss

Putnam
(English) fond of water
Puddy, Putnum, Puttie, Putty

Quaddus
(African-American) bright

Quannell
(African-American) strong-willed
Kwan, Kwanell, Kwanelle, Quan, Quanelle, Quannel

Quaronne
(African-American) haughty
Kwarohn, Kwaronne, Quaronn

Quashawn
(African-American) tenacious
Kwashan, Kwashaun, Kwashawn, Quasha, Quashie, Quashy

Quenby
(English) giving
Quenbee, Quenbie, Quenbey

Quentin
(Latin) fifth
Kwent, Quent, Quenton, Quint, Quintin, Quinton, Qwent, Qwentin, Qwenton

Quick
(American) fast; remarkable

Quiessencia
(Spanish) essential; essence
Quiess, Quiessence

Quigley
(Irish) loving nature
Quiglee, Quiggly, Quiggy

Quincy
(French) fifth; patient
Quensie, Quincee, Quinci, Quincie

Quinn
(Irish) short for Quinton; bright
Kwen, Kwene, Quenn, Quin

Quintavius
(African-American) fifth child
Quint

Quintin
(Latin) planner
Quenten, Quint, Quinton

Quintus
(Spanish) fifth child
Quin, Quinn, Quint

Quiqui
(Spanish) friend; short for Enrique
Kaka, Keke

Quito
(Spanish) lively
Kito

Quoitrel
(African-American) equalizer
Kwotrel, Quoitrelle

Quon
(Chinese) bright; light

Rabbit
(Literature) character in
Rabbit Run; fast
Rab

Rad
(Scandinavian) helpful;
confident
Radd

Raddy
(Slavic) cheerful
*Rad, Radde, Raddie,
Radey*

Radford
(English) helpful
*Rad, Raddey, Raddie,
Raddy, Radferd*

Radimir
(Polish) joyful

Radley
(English) sways with the
wind
Radlea, Radlee, Radleigh

Rady
(Filipino)

Raekwon
(African-American)
proud
Raykwonn

Rael
(African)

Rafael
(Hebrew, Spanish)
renewed
*Rafaelle, Rafayel,
Rafayelle, Rafe, Raphael,
Raphaele*

Rafe
(Irish) tough
Raff, Raffe, Raif

Rafferty
(Irish) wealthy
*Rafarty, Rafe, Raff,
Raferty, Raffarty,
Raffertie, Raffety*

Rafi
(Arabic) musical; friend
Rafee, Raffy

Raheem
(Arabic) having empathy
Rahim

Rahman
(Arabic) full of
compassion
Raman, Rahmahn

Rahn
(American) form of Ron;
kind
*Rahnney, Rahnnie,
Rahnny*

Rain
(English) helpful; smart
*Raine, Rainey, Rainey,
Raini, Rains, Raney,
Rayne*

Rainer
(German) advisor
Rainor, Rayner, Raynor

Rainey
(German) generous
*Rain, Raine, Raney,
Raynie*

Rainier
(Place name)
distinguished

Raj
(Sanskrit) with stripes
Rajiv

Rajab
(Arabic) glorified

Rajoseph
(American) combo of
Ra and Joseph
Raejoseph

Rakesh
(Hindi) king

Raleigh
(English) jovial
*Ralea, Ralee, Raleighe,
Rawlee, Rawley, Rawlie*

Ralf
(American) form of Ralph
Raulf

Ralph
(English) advisor to all
*Ralf, Ralphie, Ralphy,
Raulf, Rolf*

Ralphie
(English) form of Ralph
Ralphee, Ralphi

Ram
(Sanskrit) compelling;
pleasant
Ramm

Rambo
(Movie name) daring;
action-oriented
Ram

Ramiro
(Spanish) all-knowing
judge
*Rameero, Ramero,
Ramey, Rami*

Ramone
(Spanish) wise
advocate; romantic
*Ramond, Raymond,
Romon*

Ramp
(American) word as
name; hyper
Ram, Rams

Rams
(English) form of
Ramsey; boisterous;
strong
Ramm, Ramz

Ramsey
(English) savvy
*Rams, Ramsay, Ramsy,
Ramz, Ramzee, Ramzy*

Rance
(American) renegade
Rans, Ranse

Rancye
(American) form of
Rance
Rancel, Rancy

Rand
(Place name) ridge of
gold-bearing rock in
South Africa

Randal
(English) secretive
*Randahl, Randel,
Randey, Randull, Randy*

Randolph
(English) protective
*Rand, Randolf,
Randolphe, Randy*

Randy
(English) short for
Randall or Randolph
*Randee, Randey, Randi,
Randie*

Rangarajan
(Hindi) charming

Ranger
(French) vigilant
Rainge, Range, Rangur

Rani
(Hebrew) joyful
Ran, Ranie, Rannie

Rank
(American) word as
name
Ran

Ransom
(Latin) wealthy
*Rance, Ranse, Ransome,
Ransum, Ransym*

Raoul
(Spanish) confidant
Raul, Raulio

Raphael
(Hebrew) archangel in
the Bible; painter
Rafael, Rafe, Rapfaele

Rashad
(Arabic) wise
*Rachad, Rashaud,
Rashid, Rashod, Roshad*

Rasheed
(Arabic) intelligent

Rashid
(Arabic) focused

Rasputin
(Russian) a Russian
mystic
Rasp

Raudel
(African-American)
rowdy
Raudell, Rowdel

Raul
(French) sensual
Rauly, Rawl

Raven
(American) bird; dark
and mysterious
*Rave, Ravey, Ravy,
Rayven*

Ravi
(Hindi) sun god
Ravee

Rawle
(French) form of Raul;
sensitive

Rawleigh
(American) form of
Raleigh
Rawlee, Rawli

Ray
(French) royal; king
Rae, Raye, Rayray

Rayce
(American) form of
Raymond; advisor
Rays, Rayse

Rayfield
(English) woodsy;
capable
Rafe, Ray, Rayfe

Raymond
(English) strong
*Ramand, Ramond, Ray,
Raymie, Raymonde,
Raymun, Raymund,
Raymy*

Raymont
(American) combo of
Ray and Mont;
distinguished
*Raemon, Raymon,
Raymonte*

Raynaldo
(Spanish) form of
Renaldo; innovative
*Ray, Rayni, Raynie,
Raynoldo*

Raynard
(French) judge; sly
*Ray, Raynaud, Renard,
Renaud, Rey, Reynard,
Reynaud*

Rayner
(French) form of
Raymond; counselor
Ray, Rayne

Rayshan
(African-American)
inventive
*Ray, Raysh, Raysha,
Rayshun*

Rayshawn
(African-American)
combo of Ray and
Shawn
*Raeshaun, Rayshaun,
Rayshie, Rayshy*

Reace, Rhys
(Welsh) passionate
*Reece, Rees, Rees,
Reese*

Read
(English) red-haired
Reade, Reed, Reid

Reagan
(Irish) kingly
*Ragan, Raghan, Reagen,
Reegan, Regan*

Reaner
(Last name as first
name) even-tempered
Rean, Rener

Rebel
(American) outlaw
Reb, Rebbe, Rebele

Red
(English) man with red
hair
Redd, Reddy

Redford
(English) handsome man
with ruddy skin
*Readford, Red, Reddy,
Redferd, Redfor*

Redmon
(German) protective
*Redd, Reddy, Redmond,
Redmun, Redmund*

Reece
(Welsh) vivacious
Rees, Reese, Reez

Reed
(English) red-haired
Read, Reede, Reid

Rees
(Welsh) form of the
name Rhys; ardor
Reece, Reese, Reez, Rez
Reese
(Welsh) vivacious
Reis, Rhys
Reeves
(English) giving
Reave, Reaves, Reeve
Regal
(American) debonair
Regall
Regent
(Latin) word as name;
royal; grand
Reggie
(English) short for
Reginald; wise advisor
*Reg, Reggey, Reggi,
Reggye*
Reginald
(English) wise advisor
*Reg, Reggie, Reginal,
Regineld*
Regine
(French) artistic
Regeen
Regis
(Latin) king; gilded
talker
Reggis
Reid
(English) red-haired
Reide

Reilly
(Irish) daring
Rilee, Riley, Rilie
Reinhart
(German) brave-hearted
*Reinhar, Reinhardt,
Rhinehard, Rhinehart*
Remi
(French) fun-loving
*Remee, Remey, Remmy,
Remy*
Remington
(Last name as first
name) intellectual
Rem, Remmy
Remuda
(Spanish) herd of
horses, or changing
horses (a relay); rancher
Rem, Remmie, Remmy
Remus
(Latin) fast
*Reemus, Remes,
Remous*
Renard
(French) smart
Renardt
Renato
(Italian) born again
Renata, Renate
Renaud
(English) powerful
Renny

René
(French) born again
*Renee, Rennie, Renny,
Re-Re*
Renfro
(Welsh) calm
*Renfroe, Renfrow,
Renphro, Rinfro*
Renny
(French) able
Renney, Renni, Rennye
Reno
(Place name)
Reen, Reenie, Renoh
ReShard
(African-American)
rough
Reshar, Reshard
Resugio
(Spanish) form of
Refugio
Resuge
Rett
(Literature) form of
Rhett, from *Gone With
the Wind*
Rhett
Reuben
(Hebrew) religious;
(Spanish) creative
*Rube, Rubey, Rubie,
Rubin, Ruby, Rubyn*
Rev
(Invented) ramped up
Revv

Revin

(American) distinctive

Revan, Revinn, Revun

Rex

(Latin) kingly

Rexe

Rexford

(American) form of Rex; noble

Rex, Rexferd, Rexfor, Rexy

Rey

(Spanish) short for Reynaldo

Ray, Reye, Reyes

Reynard

(French) brilliant

Raynard, Rayne, Renardo

Reynold

(English) knowledgeable tutor

Ranald, Ranold, Reinold, Renald, Renalde, Rey, Reye, Reynolds

Reza

(Iranian) content

Rhene

(American) smiley

Reen, Rheen

Rhett

(American) romantic

Rhet, Rhette

Rhodes

(Greek) lovely

Rhoades, Rodes

Rhodree

(Welsh) ruler

Rodree, Rodrey, Rodry

Rhyon

(American) form of Ryan

Rhyan, Rhyen

Ricardo

(Spanish) snappy

Recardo, Ric, Riccardo, Ricky

Rice

(English) rich

Ryes

Rich

(English) affluent

Richie, Ritchie

Richard

(English) wealthy leader

Rich, Richerd, Richey, Richi, Richie, Rickie, Ricky, Ritchie

Richardean

(American) combo of Richard and Dean; unusual

Richard Dean, Richard-Dean, Richardene

Richey

(German) ruler

Rich, Richee, Richie, Ritch, Ritchee, Ritchee, Ritchey

Richie

(English) short for Richard

Richey, Richi, Ritchey, Ritchie

Richmond

(German) rich and protective

Rich, Richie, Richmon, Richmun, Ricky, Ritchmun

Richter

(Last name as first name) hopeful

Rick, Ricky, Rik, Rikter

Rick

(German) short for Richard; friendly

Ric, Rickey, Ricki, Rickie, Ricky, Rik

Rico

(Italian) spirited; ruler

Reco, Reko, Ricko, Rikko, Riko

Ricotoro

(Spanish) combo of Rico and Toro; brave bull

Ricky, Rico-Toro, Rikotoro, Toro

Ridge

(English) on the ridge; risk-taker

Ridley
(English) ingenious
*Redley, Rid, Ridley,
Ridlie, Ridly, Rydley*

Rigby
(English) high-energy
Rigbie, Rigbye, Rygby

Rigoberto
(Spanish) strong
Bert, Berto, Rigo

Rike
(American) form of Nike;
high-spirited
*Rikee, Rykee, Rykie,
Ryky*

Rilee
(American) form of Riley
Rilea, Rileigh

Rileigh
(American) form of Riley
Ryleigh

Riley
(Irish) brave
*Reilly, Rylee, Ryley, Rylie,
Ryly*

Ringo
(English) funny
Ring, Ringgoh, Ryngo

Rio
(Spanish) water-loving
Reeo

Rione
(Spanish) flowing
Reo, Reone, Rio

Rio Grande
(Spanish) a river in Texas
Rio, Riogrande

Rip
(English) serene
Ripp, Rippe

Ripley
(English) serene
Riplee

Ris
(English) outdoorsman;
smart
*Rislea, Rislee, Risleigh,
Riz, Rizlee*

Risley
(English) smart and
quiet
*Rislee, Risleye, Rizlee,
Rizley*

Ritch
(American) leader
*Rich, Richee, Richey,
Ritch, Ritchal, Ritchee,
Ritchi*

Ritchie
(English) form of Richie
Ritchee, Ritchey, Ritchy

Rito
(American) spunky
Reit

Ritt
(German) debonair
Rit, Rittie, Rittly

Ritter
(German) debonair
Riter, Rittyr

River
(Place name) hip
Riv, Ryver

Roam
(American) wanderer
*Roamey, Roamy, Roma,
Rome*

Roarke
(Irish) ruler
Roark, Rork, Rourke

Rob
(English) short for
Robert; smart
Robb

Robbie
(English) short for
Robert; smart
*Robbee, Robbey, Robbi,
Robby*

Robert
(English) brilliant;
renowned
*Bob, Bobbie, Bobby,
Rob, Robart, Robbie,
Robby, Roberto, Robs,
Roburt*

Roberto
(Spanish) form of
Robert; bright and
famous
Berto, Rob, Robert, Tito

Roberts
(Last name as first name) luminous
Rob, Robards, Robarts, Roburts

Robert-Lee
(American) patriotic
Bobbylee, Robby Lee, Robert Lee, Robert-E-Lee, Robertlee

Robeson
(English) Rob's son; bright
Roberson, Robison

Robin
(English) gregarious
Robb, Robbin, Robby, Robyn

Roble
(Last name as first name) divine
Robel, Robl, Robley

Robson
(English) sterling character
Robb, Robbson, Robsen

Rocco
(Italian) tough
Roc, Rock, Rockie, Rocko, Rocky, Rok, Rokee, Rokko, Roko

Rochester
(English) guarded
Roche

Rock
(American) hardy
Roc, Rocky, Rok

Rocket
(American) word as a name; snappy
Rokket

Rockleigh
(English) dependable; outdoorsy
Rocco, Rock, Rocklee, Rockley, Rocky, Roklee

Rockwell
(American) spring of strength
Rock, Rockwelle, Rocky

Rocky
(English) hardy; tough
Rocco, Rock, Rockee, Rockey, Rocki, Rockie

Rod
(English) brash
Rodd, Roddy

Rodas
(Spanish) Spanish name for the Rhone River in France
Rod, Roda

Roddy
(German) short for Roderick; effective
Roddee, Roddi, Roddie

Rodel
(American) generous
Rodell, Rodey, Rodie

Rodeo
(Spanish) roundup; cowboy
Rodayo, Roddy, Rodyo

Roderick
(German) effective leader
Roddy, Roddyrke, Roderic, Roderik, Rodreck, Rodrick, Rodrik

Rodger
(German) form of Roger
Rodge, Roge

Rodman
(German) hero
Rodmin, Rodmun

Rodney
(English) open-minded
Rod, Roddy, Rodnee, Rodni, Rodnie

Rodolfo
(Spanish) spark
Rod, Rudolfo, Rudolpho

Rodree
(American) leader
Rodrey, Rodri, Rodry

Rodrigo
(Spanish) feisty leader
Rod, Roddy, Rodrego, Rodriko

Rodriguez
(Spanish) hot-blooded
Rod, Roddy, Rodreguez, Rodrigues

Roe
(English) deer

Rogelio
(Spanish) aggressive
Rojel, Rojelio

Roger
(German) famed warrior
Rodge, Rodger, Roge, Rogie, Rogyer

Roi
(French) form of Roy

Roland
(German) renowned
Rolend, Rollan, Rolland, Rollie, Rollo, Rolund

Rolando
(Spanish) famous
Rolan

Role
(American) word as name; brash
Roel, Roll

Rolf
(German) kind advisor
Rolfee, Rolfie, Rolfy, Rolph

Rollie
(English) short for Roland
Rollee, Rolley, Rolli, Rolly

Rollins
(German) form of Roland; dignified
Rolin, Rolins, Rollin, Rolyn

Roman
(Latin) fun-loving
Romen, Romey, Romi, Romun, Romy

Rome
(Place name)
Romeo

Romeo
(Italian) romantic lover
Romah, Rome, Romeoh, Romero, Romey, Romi, Romy

Romer
(American) form of Rome
Roamar, Roamer

Romney
(Welsh) roamer
Rom, Romnie

Romulo
(Spanish) man from Rome
Romo

Romulus
(Latin) presumptuous
Rom, Romules, Romulo

Ron
(English) short for Ronald; kind
Ronn

Ronald
(English) helpful
Ron, Ronal, Ronel, Ronney, Ronni, Ronnie, Ronuld

Rondel
(French) poetic
Ron, Rondal, Rondell, Rondie, Rondy

Ronford
(English) distinguished
Ronferd, Ronnforde

Roni
(Hebrew) joyful
Rone, Ronee

Ronnie
(English) short for Ronald
Ronnee, Ronney, Ronni, Ronny

Roone
(Irish) distinctive; bright face
Rooney, Roune

Rooney
(Irish) man with red hair
Rooni, Roony

Roose
(Last name as first name) high-energy
Rooce, Roos, Rooz, Ruz

Roosevelt
(Dutch) strong leader
Rooseveldt, Rosevelt, Rosy, Velte

Rooster
(American) animal as name; loud
Roos, Rooz

Roper
(American) roper
Rope

Rory
(German) strong
Roree, Rorey, Roreye, Rorie

Rosano
(Italian) rosy prospects; romantic

Roscoe
(English) woods; nature-loving
Rosco, Roskie, Rosko, Rosky

Roser
(American) redhead; outgoing
Rozer

Roshaun
(African-American) loyal
Roshawn

Rosk
(American) swift
Roske

Rosling
(Scottish) redhead; explosive
Roslin, Rosy, Rozling

Ross
(Latin) attractive
Rossey, Rossie, Rossy

Rossa
(American) exuberant
Ross, Rosz

Rossain
(American) hopeful
Rossane

Roswell
(English) fascinating
Roswel, Roswelle, Rosy, Rozwell, Well

Roth
(German) man with red hair
Rothe, Rauth

Roupen
(American) quiet
Ropan, Ropen, Ropun

Rover
(English) wanderer
Rovar, Rovey, Rovur, Rovy

Rowan
(English) red-haired; adorned
Rowe, Rowen

Rowdy
(English) athletic; loud
Roudy, Rowdee, Rowdi, Rowdie

Rowe
(English) outgoing
Roe, Row, Rowie

Rowell
(English) rocker
Roll, Rowl

Roy
(French) king
Roi

Royal
(French) king
Roy, Royall, Royalle, Roye

Royalton
(French) king
Royal, Royallton

Royce
(English) affluent
Roy, Royse

Roycie
(American) form of Royce; kind
Rory, Roy, Royce, Royse, Roysie

Royden
(English) outdoors; regal
Roy, Roydin

Rube
(Spanish) short for Ruben
Rubino

Ruben
(Spanish) form of Reuben
Rube, Ruby

Rudeger
(German) friendly
Rudger, Rudgyr, Rudigar, Rudiger, Rudy

Rudo
(African) loving

Rudolf
(German) wolf
Rodolf, Rudy

Rudolph
(German) wolf
Rodolf, Rodolph, Rud, Rudee, Rudey, Rudi, Rudolpho, Rudy

Rudow
(German) lovable

Rudy
(German) short for Rudolph
Rude, Rudee, Rudey, Rudi

Rudyard
(English) closed off
Rud, Rudd, Ruddy

Rueban
(American) form of Ruben; talented
Ruban

Rufino
(Spanish) redhead

Rufus
(Latin) redhead
Fue, Rufas, Rufes, Ruffie, Ruffis, Ruffy, Rufous

Rugby
(English) braced for contact
Rug, Rugbee, Rugbie, Ruggy

Rulon
(Native American) spirited
Rulonn

Runako
(African) attractive

Rune
(German) secretive
Roone, Runes

Rush
(English) loquacious
Rusch

Rusk
(Spanish) innovator
Rusck, Ruske, Ruskk

Russ
(French) short for Russell; dear

Russell
(French) man with red hair; charmer
Russ, Russel, Russy, Rusty

Rustin
(English) redhead
Rustan, Ruston, Rusty

Rusty
(French) short for Russell
Rustee, Rustey, Rusti

Rutherford
(English) dignified
Ruthe, Rutherfurd, Rutherfyrd

Rutilio
(Spanish)

Rutledge
(English) substantial
Rutlidge

Ryan
(Irish) royal; good-looking
Rhine, Rhyan, Rhyne, Ryane, Ryann, Ryanne, Ryen, Ryun

Ryder
(English) outdoorsy (man who rides horses)
Rider, Rye

Ryerson
(English) fit outdoorsman
Rye

Ryland
(English) excellent
Rilan, Riland, Rye, Rylan

Rylandar
(English) farmer
Rye, Rylan, Ryland

Ryne
(Irish) form of Ryan;
royal
Rine, Ryn, Rynn

Ryszard
(Polish) courageous
leader
Reshard

Sabene
(Latin) optimist
Sabe, Sabeen, Sabin,
Sabyn, Sabyne

Saber
(French) armed; sword
Sabar, Sabe, Sabre

Saddam
(Arabic) powerful ruler
Saddum

Sadler
(English) practical
Sadd, Saddle, Sadlar,
Sadlur

Sae
(American) talkative
Saye

Saeed
(African) lucky

Sagaz
(Spanish) clever
Saga, Sago

Sage
(Botanical) wise
Saje

Saginaw
(Place name) city in
Michigan
Sag, Saggy

Saied
(Arabic) fortunate

Sal
(Italian) short for
Salvador and Salvatore
Sall, Sallie, Sally

Salado
(Spanish) funny
Sal

Salehe
(Africa) good

Salford
(Place name) city in
England

Salim
(Arabic) safe; peaceful
Saleem

Salt
(American) word as
name; salt-of-the-earth
Salty

Salute
(American) patriotic

Salvador
(Spanish) savior;
spirited
Sal, Sally, Salvadore

Salvatore
(Italian) rescuer; spirited
Sal, Sallie, Sally,
Salvatori, Salvatorre

Sam
(Hebrew) short for
Samuel; wise
Samm, Sammey, Sammi,
Sammy

Sami
(Lebanese) high

Samir
(Arabic) special
Sameer, Samere

Sammy
(Hebrew) wise
Samie, Sammee, Sammi,
Sammie, Samy

Samos
(Place name) casual

Samson
(Hebrew) strong man
Sam, Sampson

Samuel
(Hebrew) man who
heard God; prophet
Sam, Samael, Sammeul,
Sammie, Sammo,
Sammuel, Sammy,
Samual

Sanborn
(English) one with
nature
Sanborne, Sanbourn,
Sandy

Sancho
(Latin) genuine
Sanch, Sanchoh

Sander
(Greek) savior of
mankind; nice
Sandor

Sanders
(English) kind
Sandars, Sandors,
Saunders

Sandy
(English) personable
Sandee, Sandey, Sandi

Sanford
(English) negotiator
Sandford, Sandy,
Sanferd, Sanfor

Sanorelle
(African-American)
honest
Sanny, Sano, Sanorel,
Sanorell

Sansone
(Italian) strong

Santana
(Spanish) saintly
Santa, Santanah,
Santanna, Santee

Santiago
(Spanish) sainted;
valuable
Sandiago, Santego,
Santiagoh, Santy, Tago

Santos
(Italian) holy; blessed
Sant, Santo

Sarday
(American) extrovert
Sardae, Sardaye

Sargent
(French) officer/leader
Sarge, Sergeant

Sasha
(Russian) helpful
Sacha, Sash

Sasson
(Hebrew) happy

Satchel
(American) unique
Satch

Saunder
(English) defensive;
focused
Saunders

Saul
(Hebrew) gift
Sawl, Saulie, Sol, Solly

Savage
(Last name as first
name) wild
Sav

Saville
(French) stylish
Savelle, Savile, Savill

Savoy
(Place name) region in
France
Savoe

Sawyer
(English) hardworking
Saw, Sawyrr

Saxe
(English) short for Saxon
Sax, Saxee, Saxey, Saxie

Saxon
(English) swordfighter;
feisty
*Sackson, Sax, Saxan,
Saxe, Saxen*

Sayre
(Welsh) skilled
Saye, Sayer, Sayers

Scafell
(Place name) mountain
in England

Scanlon
(Irish) devious
*Scan, Scanlin, Scanlun,
Scanne*

Scant
(American) word as
name; too little
Scanty

Scardino
(Italian)

Schaffer
(German) watchful
Schaffur, Shaffer

Schelde
(Place name) river in
Europe; calm
Shelde

Schmidt
(German) hardworking;
blacksmith
Schmit

Schneider
(German) stylish; tailor
Sneider, Snider

Schuyler
(Dutch) protective
Skylar, Skyler

Scorpio
(Latin) lethal
Scorp, Scorpioh

Scott
(English) from Scotland;
happy
Scot, Scotty

Scotty
(English) happy
Scottee, Scottey, Scotti

Scully
(Irish) vocal
Scullee, Scullie

Seabrook
(English) outdoorsy
Seabrooke

Seamus
(Gaelic) replacement;
bonus
Seemus, Semus

Sean
(Hebrew, Irish) grace in
God
*Seann, Shaun, Shaune,
Shawn*

Searcy
(English) fortified
Searcee, Searcey

Searles
(English) fortified
*Searl, Searle, Serles,
Serls*

Sebastian
(Latin) dramatic;
honorable
*Bastian, Seb, Sebashun,
Sebastion, Sebastuan,
Sebo*

Sebe
(Latin) short for
Sebastian
*Seb, Sebo, Seborn,
Sebron, Sebrun*

Sedg
(American) classy
Sedge

Seger
(English) singer
*Seager, Seeger, Sega,
Segur*

Segundo
(Spanish) second child

Sekani
(African) laughing

Selestino
(Spanish) heavenly
*Celeste, Celestino, Celey,
Sele, Selestyno*

Selvon
(American) gregarious
Sel, Selman, Selv, Selvaughn, Selvawn

Sender
(Hebrew) form of Alexander; protective

Senior
(French) older
Sennyur, Senyur, Sinior

Sennen
(English) old

Seraphim
(Hebrew) full of fire
Sarafim, Saraphim, Serafim, Serephim

Sergeant
(French) officer; leader
Sarge, Sargent

Sergei
(Russian) handsome
Serg, Serge, Sergie, Sergy, Surge

Sergio
(Italian) handsome
Serge, Sergeeo, Sergeoh

Seth
(Hebrew) chosen
Sethe

Seven
(American) dramatic; seventh child
Sevene, Sevin

Several
(American) word as name; multiplies
Sevral, Sevrull

Severo
(Italian) unbending; severe

Sevester
(American) form of Sylvester
Seveste, Sevy

Seward
(English) guarding the sea
Sew, Sewerd, Sward

Sexton
(English) church-loving
Sextan, Sextin, Sextown

Seymour
(French) prayerful
Seamore, See, Seye, Seymore

Shade
(English) mysterious
Shadee, Shadey, Shady

Shadow
(English) mystique
Shade

Shadrach
(Biblical) Godlike; brave
Shad, Shadd, Shadrack, Shadreck, Shadryack

Shakir
(Arabic) appreciative
Shakee, Shakeer

Shalom
(Hebrew) peaceful
Sholem, Sholom

Shaman
(Russian) mystical
Shamain, Shamon, Shayman

Shamus
(Irish) seizing
Shamuss

Shance
(American) form of Chance; open
Shan, Shanse

Shand
(English) loud
Shandy

Shandee
(English) noisy
Shandi, Shandy

Shane
(Irish) easygoing
Shain, Shay, Shayne

Shannon
(Irish) wise
Shana, Shanan, Shane, Shann, Shannen, Shanon

Shaq
(Arabic) short for
Shaquille
Shack, Shak

Shaquille
(Arabic) handsome
*Shak, Shakeel, Shaq,
Shaquil, Shaquill*

Sharif
(Arabic) truthful
Shareef, Sheref

Shaun
(Irish) form of Sean
*Seanne, Shaune,
Shaunn*

Shaw
(English) safe; in a tree
grove
Shawe

Shawn
(Irish) form of Sean
*Shawnay, Shawne,
Shawnee, Shawney*

Shawnell
(African-American)
talkative
Shaunell

Shawner
(American) form of
Shawn

Shawon
(African-American)
optimistic
*Shawan, Shawaughn,
Shawaun*

Shay
(Irish) short for Shamus;
bolstering
Shai

Shayde
(Irish) confident
Shaedy, Sheade

Shaykeen
(African-American)
successful
Shay, Shaykine

Shayshawn
(American) combo of
Shay and Shawn; able
*Shaeshaun, Shaeshawn,
Shayshaun*

Shea
(Irish) vital
Shay

Sheehan
(Irish) clever
Shehan, Shihan

Sheen
(English) bright and
shining; talented
Shean, Sheene

Shelby
(English) established
*Shel, Shelbee, Shelbey,
Shelbie, Shell, Shelly*

Sheldon
(English) quiet
*Shel, Sheld, Shelden,
Sheldin, Shell, Shelly*

Shem
(Hebrew) famous

Shen
(Chinese) introspective

Sheng
(Chinese) winning

Shep
(English) watchful
Shepp, Sheppy

Sheridan
(Irish) wild-spirited
*Sharidan, Sheridon,
Sherr, Sherrey, Shuridun*

Sherlock
(English) fair-haired;
smart
Sherlocke, Shurlock

Sherm
(English) worker; shears
Shermy

Sherman
(English) tough-willed
*Cherman, Shermann,
Shermy, Shurman*

Sherwood
(English) bright options
*Sherwoode, Shurwood,
Woodie, Woody*

Shevon
(African-American) zany
*Shavonne, Shevaughan,
Shevaughn*

Shiloh
(Hebrew) gift from God; charmer
Shile, Shilo, Shy, Shye

Shipley
(English) meadow of sheep
Ship

Shiva
(Hindi) of great depth and range; life/death
Shiv

Shon
(American) form of Shawn
Sean, Shaun, Shonn

Shontae
(African-American) hopeful
Shauntae, Shauntay, Shawntae, Shontay, Shontee, Shonti, Shontie, Shonty

Shorty
(American) small in stature
Shortey, Shorti

Shuu
(Japanese) responsible

Si
(Hebrew) short for Simon
Sy

Sid
(French) short for Sidney
Cyd, Siddie, Siddy, Syd

Sidney
(French) attractive
Ciddie, Cidnie, Cyd, Cydnee, Sidnee, Sidnie, Syd, Sydney

Sidor
(Russian) gifted
Isidor, Sydor

Siegfried
(German) victor
Siegfred, Sig, Sigfred, Sigfrid, Siggee, Siggie, Siggy

Sierra
(Spanish) dangerous
See-see, Serra, Siera, Sierrah

Sig
(German) short for Sigmund and Siegfried
Siggey, Siggi, Sigi, Syg

Sigga
(Scandinavian) from Siegfried; peaceful; winning
Sig

Sigmund
(German) winner
Siegmund, Sig, Siggi, Siggy, Sigi, Sigmon, Sigmond

Silas
(Latin) saver
Si, Siles, Silus

Silous
(American) form of Silas; brooding
Si, Silouz

Silvano
(Latin) of the woods; unique
Silvan, Silvani, Silvio, Sylvan

Silver
(Spanish) form of Silva; outgoing
Sylver

Simcha
(Hebrew) joyful

Simeon
(French) listener
Si, Simone, Sy

Simms
(Hebrew) good listener
Sims

Simon
(Hebrew) good listener; thoughtful
Si, Siman, Simen, Simeon, Simmy, Sye, Symon, Syms

Simpson
(Hebrew) simplistic
Simpsen, Simpsun, Simson

Sinclair
(French) prayerful
Clair, Sinc, Sinclare, Synclaire

Sindbad
(Literature) daring
Sinbad
Singer
(Last name as first
name) vocalist
Synger
Sisto
(American) cowboy
Sisyphus
(Greek) in mythology,
a cruel king
Six
(American) number as
name
Syx
Skeeter
(English) fast
Skeater, Skeet, Skeets
Skeetz
(American) zany
Skeet, Skeeter, Skeets
Skilling
(English) masterful
Skillings
Skip
(American) short for
Skipper
Skipp, Skyp, Skyppe
Skippy
(American) fast
*Skippee, Skippie,
Skyppey*

Skye
(Dutch) goal-oriented
Sky
Skylar
(Dutch) protective
*Skilar, Skye, Skyeler,
Skylir*
Slade
(English) quiet child
Slaid, Slayd, Slayde
Sladkey
(Slavic) glorious
Sladkie
Slam
(American) friendly
Slams, Slamz
Slavek
(Polish) smart; glorious
Slavec, Slavik
Slawomir
(Slavic) great glory;
famed
Slavek, Slavomir
Sloan
(Irish) sleek
Sloane, Slonne
Slocum
(Last name as first
name) happy
Slo, Slocom, Slocumb
Slover
(Last name as first
name)
Slove

Smith
(English) crafty;
blacksmith
*Smid, Smidt, Smit,
Smitt, Smitti, Smitty*
Smokey
(American) smokin'
Smoke, Smokee, Smoky
Snake
(Place name) U.S. river
So
(Vietnamese) smart
Socorro
(Spanish) helpful
Sokorro
Socrates
(Greek) philosophical;
brilliant
*Socratez, Socratis,
Sokrates*
Sol
(Hebrew) short for
Solomon
Solly
Solly
(Hebrew) short for
Solomon
*Sollee, Solley, Solli,
Sollie*
Solomon
(Hebrew) peaceful and
wise
*Salamon, Sol, Sollie,
Solly, Soloman*

Somerset
(English) talented
Somer, Somers, Sommerset, Summerset

Sommar
(English) summer
Somer, Somers, Somm, Sommars, Sommer

Son
(English) boy
Sonni, Sonnie, Sonny

Sonny
(English) boy
Son, Sonney, Sonni, Sonnie

Sonteeahgo
(Invented) form of Santiago

Soren
(Scandinavian) good communicator
Soryn

Sorrel
(French) reddish-brown horse; horse lover
Sorre, Sorrell, Sorrey

Sound
(American) word as a name; dynamic

Spanky
(American) outspoken; stubborn
Spank, Spankee, Spankie

Sparky
(Latin) ball of fire; joyful
Spark, Sparkee, Sparkey, Sparki, Sparkie

Speers
(English) good with spears; swift-moving
Speares, Spears, Spiers

Spence
(English) short for Spencer
Spens, Spense

Spencer
(English) giver; provides well
Spence, Spencey, Spenser, Spensor, Spensy

Spider
(American) scary
Spyder

Spike
(American) word as name
Spiker

Spiker
(English) go-getter
Spike, Spikey, Spyk

Spiro
(Greek) breath of fresh air
Spi, Spiroh, Spiros, Spy, Spyro

Springer
(English) fresh
Spring

Sprague
(French) high-energy

Spud
(English) energetic

Spurgeon
(Botanical) from the shrub spurge; natural
Spurge

Spunk
(American) spunky; lively
Spunki, Spunky

Spurs
(American) boot devices used to spur horses; cowboy
Spur

Squire
(English) land-loving
Squirre, Skwyre

Stacey
(English) hopeful
Stace, Stacee, Stacy, Stase, Stasi

Stafford
(English) dignified
Staff, Staffard, Stafferd, Staffi, Staffie, Staffor, Staffy

Stamos
(Greek) reasonable
Stammos, Stamohs

Stan
(Latin) short for Stanley

Standish
(English) farsighted
Standysh

Stanford
(English) dignified
Stan, Stanferd, Stann

Stanislaus
(Latin) glorious
Staneslaus, Stanis, Stanislus, Stann, Stanus

Stanislav
(Russian) glory in leading
Slava, Stasi

Stanley
(English) traveler
Stan, Stanlea, Stanlee, Stanli, Stanly

Stanton
(English) stone-hard
Stan

Stark
(German) high-energy
Starke, Starkey

Starling
(English) singer; bird
Starlling

Starr
(English) bright star
Star, Starri, Starrie, Starry

Stavros
(Greek) winner
Stavrohs, Stavrows

Steadman
(English) landowner; wealthy
Steadmann, Sted, Stedmann

Steele
(English) hardworking
Steel, Stille

Stefan
(Scandinavian) crowned; (German) chosen one
Stefawn, Steff, Steffan, Steffie, Steffon, Steffy, Stefin, Stephan

Stefano
(Italian) crowned
Stef, Steffie, Steffy, Stephano, Stephanos

Stehlin
(Last name as first name) genius
Staylin, Stealan, Stehlan

Steinbeck
(Last name as first)

Stellan
(Swedish)

Sten
(Scandinavian) stone
Stene, Stine

Steph
(English) short for Stephen; victorious
Stef, Steff, Steffy

Stephan
(Greek) form of Stephen; victorious

Stephanos
(Greek) crowned; martyr
Stef, Stefanos, Steph, Stephanas

Stephen
(Greek) victorious
Stephan, Stephon, Stevee, Steven, Stevey, Stevi, Stevie, Stevy

Stephene
(French) form of Stephen; wearing a crown
Stef, Steff, Steph

Sterling
(English) worthwhile

Stern
(German) bright; serious
Stearn, Sterns

Stetson
(American) cowboy
Stetsen, Stetsun, Stettson

Steubing
(Last name as first name)
Steuben, Stu, Stuben, Stubing

Steve
(Greek) short for Steven and Stephen; victorious
Stevie

Steven
(Greek) victorious
Stevan, Steve, Stevey, Stevie

Stevie
(English) short for Steven, Stephen
Stevee, Stevey, Stevi, Stevy

Stewart
(English) form of Stuart; steward or keeper
Stewert, Stu, Stuie

Stig
(Scandinavian) upwardly mobile
Stigg, Styg, Stygg

Stiles
(English) practical
Stile, Stiley, Styles

Sting
(English) spike of grain

Stobart
(German) harsh
Stobe, Stobey, Stoby

Stock
(American) macho
Stok

Stockard
(English) dramatic
Stock, Stockerd, Stockord

Stocker
(English) foundation
Stock

Stoli
(Russian) celebrant

Stone
(English) athletic
Stonee, Stoney, Stonie, Stony

Stonewall
(English) fortified
Stone, Stoney, Wall

Stoney
(American) form of Stone; friendly
Stonee, Stoni, Stonie

Storm
(English) impetuous; volatile
Storme, Stormy

Stowe
(English) secretive
Stow, Stowey

Strato
(Invented) strategic
Strat, Stratt

Stratton
(Scottish) home-loving
Straton, Strattawn

Stretch
(American) easygoing
Stretcher

Strike
(American) word as name; aggressive
Striker

Strom
(German) water-lover
Strome, Stromm

Strother
(Irish) strict
Strothers, Struther, Struthers

Struther
(Last name as first name) flowing
Strother, Strothers, Struthers

Stu
(English) short for Stuart
Stew, Stue, Stuey

Stuart
(English) careful; watchful
Stewart, Stu, Stuey

Studs
(American) cocky
Studd, Studds

Sture
(Scandinavian) difficult
Sturah

Styles
(English) practical
Stile, Stiles, Style

Stylianos
(Greek) stylish
Styli

Sugar-Ray
(American) strong
Sugar Ray

Sullivan
(Irish) dark-eyed; quiet
*Sullavan, Sullie,
Sullivahn, Sully*

Sully
(Irish) melancholy; quiet
*Sull, Sullee, Sulley,
Sullie*

Sultan
(American) bold
Sultane, Sulten, Sultin

Sumney
(American) ethereal
*Summ, Summy, Sumnee,
Sumnie*

Sutherland
(Scandinavian) sunny;
southerner
Southerland

Sutter
(English) southern
Sutt, Suttee, Sutty

Sutton
(English) sunny;
southerner

Sven
(Scandinavian) young
boy
Svein, Svend, Swen

Swain
(English) rigid; leading
the herd
Swaine, Swayne

Sweeney
(Irish) hero
Schwennie, Sweeny

Swift
(English) fast
Swifty

Swindell
(English) polished
*Schwindell, Swin,
Swindel*

Sy
(Latin) short for Silas,
Sylas, *Si*

Sydney
(French) form of Sidney
Cyd, Syd, Sydie

Sylvain
(Latin) reclusive
Syl

Sylvan
(Spanish) nature-loving
*Silvan, Syl, Sylvany,
Sylvin*

Sylvester
(Latin) forest dweller;
heavyduty
Sil, Silvester, Sly, Syl

Symms
(Last name as first
name) landowner

Symotris
(African-American) lucky
*Sym, Symetris,
Symotrice, Syms*

Tab
(German) intelligent
Tabbey, Tabby

Tad
(Greek) short for Thaddeus
Taddee, Taddey, Taddie, Taddy

Tadeusz
(Polish) praise-worthy
Tad, Taduce

Taff
(American) sweet
Taf, Taffee, Taffey, Taffi, Taffy

Taft
(English) flowing
Tafte, Taftie, Taffy

Tahoe
(Place name) Lake Tahoe, Nevada
Taho

Taj
(Sanskrit) royal; crowned

Tal
(Hebrew) worrier
Tallee, Talley, Talli, Tally

Talbot
(French) skillful
Tal, Talbott, Tally

Talmadge
(English) natural; living by lakes
Tal, Tally, Tamidge

Talon
(French) wily
Tallie, Tallon, Tally, Tawlon

Tam
(Hebrew) truthful
Tammy

Tamarius
(African-American) stubborn
Tam, Tamerius, Tammy, T'Marius

Tammy
(English) short for Thomas and Tamarius
Tammee, Tammie, Tammey

Tan
(Japanese) high achiever

Tane
(Polynesian) sky god; fertile
Tain

Tankie
(American) big
Tank, Tankee, Tanky

Tanner
(English) tanner of skins
Tan, Tann, Tannar, Tanne, Tannor, Tanny

Tannie
(English) tanner of skins
Tann, Tanney, Tanny

Taos
(Place name) town in New Mexico
Tao, Tayo

Tap
(American) word as name
Tapp, Tappi, Tappy

Tariq
(African-American) conquerer
Tarik

Tarleton
(English) stormy
Tally, Tarlton

Tarrance
(Latin) smooth
Terance, Terrance, Terry

Tarri
(American) form of Terry
Tari, Tarree, Tarrey, Tarry

Taryll
(American) form of Terrell
Tarell

Tate
(English) happy
Tait, Tatey, Tayt

Tatry
(Place name) mountains
in Poland
Tate, Tatree, Tatri

Taurean
(African-American)
reclusive; quiet
Taureen

Taurus
(Astrological sign)
macho
Tar, Taur, Tauras, Taures

Tavares
(African-American)
hopeful
Tavarus

Tavarius
(African-American)
fun-loving
*Tav, Taverius, Tavurius,
Tavvy*

Tavish
(Scottish) upbeat
Tav, Taven, Tavis

Tay
(Scottish) river in
Scotland; jaunty
Tae, Taye

Taylor
(English) tailor
*Tailor, Talor, Tayler,
Tayley*

Tayton
(American) form of
Payton
*Tate, Taye, Tayte, Tayten,
Taytin*

Teague
(Irish) bard; poet
Teaguey, Tege

Ted
(English) short for
Theodore
*Teddee, Teddey, Teddi,
Teddy*

Teddy-Blue
(American) smiley
*Blu, Blue, Teddie-Blue,
Teddy, Teddyblu,
Teddy-Blu, Teddyblue*

Tedrick
(African-American) form
of Cedrick
Ted, Tedrik

Tedshawn
(American) combo of Ted
and Shawn
Teddshawn, Tedshaun

Tedwayne
(American) combo of Ted
and Wayne; friendly
Ted Wayne, Ted-Wayne

Tegan
(Irish) form of Teague;
literary figure
*Tege, Tegen, Tegun,
Teige*

Teller
(English) relates stories;
storytelling
Tellie, Telly

Telvis
(American) form of Elvis
Telly

Tempest
(French) stormy; volatile
Tempie, Tempy, Tempyst

Temple
(Latin) spiritual
Tempie, Templle, Tempy

Templeton
(English) from religious
place
*Temp, Tempie, Temple,
Temps*

Ten
(American) word as
name; tenth

Tennant
(American) capable
Tenn

Tennessee
(Native American) able
fighter; U.S. state
Tenns, Tenny

Tennyson
(English) storyteller
*Tenie, Tenn, Tenneyson,
Tenny, Tennysen*

Teodoro
(Spanish) God's gift
Tedoro, Teo, Teodore, Theo

TeQuarius
(African-American) secretive
Teq, Tequarius, Tequie

Terard
(Invented) form of Gerard
Terar, Tererd, Terry

Termell
(Invented) form of Terrell; militant
Termel

Terrance
(Latin) calm
Terance, Terence, Terre, Terree, Terrence, Terrie, Terry

Terrelle
(German) thunderous; outspoken
Terel, Terele, Terell, Teril, Terille, Terral, Terrale, Terre, Terrel, Terril, Terrill, Terrille, Terry, Tirill, Tirrill, Tyrel, Tyril

Terry
(English) short for Terrence
Terree, Terrey, Terri, Terrie

Teva
(Hebrew) natural
Tevah

Tevaughn
(African-American) tiger
Tev, Tevan, Tevaughan, Tivan, Tivaughan

Tevey
(Hebrew) good
Tev, Tevi, Tevie

Tevin
(African-American) outgoing
Tev, Tevan, Tivan

Tevis
(American) flamboyant
Tev, Tevas, Teves, Teviss, Tevy

Tex
(American) from Texas; cowboy
Texas, Texx

Texas
(American) from Texas; cowboy
Tex

Thad
(Greek) short for Thaddeus; brave
Thadd, Thaddy

Thaddeus
(Greek) brave
Thad, Thaddius, Thaddy, Thadeus, Thadius

Thady
(Irish) thankful
Thad, Thaddee, Thaddie, Thaddy, Thads

Thane
(English) protective
Thain, Thayn

Thanus
(American) landowner; wealthy
Thainas, Thaines

Thatcher
(English) practical
Thatch, Thatchar

Thayer
(English) protected; sheltered
Thay, Thayar

Themba
(African) hopeful

Theo
(Greek) Godlike

Theodore
(Greek) God's gift; a blessing
Teddy, Theeo, Theo, Theodor, Theos

Theodoros
(Greek) God's gift
Theo, Theodor

Theophilos
(Greek) loved by God
Theo

Therman
(Scandinavian)
thunderous
Thur, Thurman, Thurmen

Theron
(Greek) industrious
Therron, Theryon

Thierno
(American) humble
Therno, Their

Thomas
(Greek) twin; lookalike
*Thom, Thomes, Thommy,
Thomus, Tom, Tomas,
Tommi, Tomus*

Thompson
(English) prepared
*Thom, Thompsen,
Thompsun, Thomson,
Tom, Tommy*

Thor
(Scandinavian)
protective; god of
thunder
Thorr, Tor

Thorin
(Scandinavian) form of
Thor; god of thunder
Thorrin, Thors

Thorne
(English) complex
*Thorn, Thornee, Thorney,
Thornie, Thorny*

Thornston
(Scandinavian)
protected
Thornse, Thors

Thornton
(English) difficult
Thorn, Thornten

Thorpe
(English) homebody
Thor, Thorp

Thrace
(Place name) region in
southeast Europe
Thrase

Thurman
(Last name as first
name) popular
*Thurmahn, Thurmen,
Thurmie, Thurmy*

Thurmond
(Norse) sheltered
Thurman, Thurmon

Thurston
(Scandinavian) thunders
*Thor, Thors, Thorst,
Thorsten, Thur, Thurs,
Thursten, Torsten,
Torston*

Thurstron
(Scandinavian) volatile
*Thorst, Thorsten,
Thorstin, Thurs,
Thurstran*

Tiago
(Hispanic) brave
Ti, Tia

Tige
(American) easygoing
Tig, Tigg

Tiger
(American) ambitious;
strong
*Tig, Tige, Tigur, Tyg,
Tyge, Tyger, Tygur*

Tillery
(German) ruler
Till, Tiller

Tilton
(English) prospering
Till, Tillie, Tylton

Tim
(Greek) short for
Timothy
Timmy, Tym

Timber
(American) word as
name
*Timb, Timby, Timmey,
Timmi, Timmy*

Timmy
(Greek) truthful
*Timi, Timmee, Timmey,
Timmie*

Timon
(Literature) from
Shakespeare's *Timon of
Athens*; wealthy man
Tim

Timothy
(Greek) reveres God
Tim, Timathy, Timmie, Timmy, Timothey, Timothie, Timuthy

Tinks
(American) coy
Tink, Tinkee, Tinki, Tinky, Tynks, Tynky

Tino
(Spanish) respected
Tyno

Tinsley
(English) personable
Tensley, Tins, Tinslee, Tinslie, Tinsly

Tip
(American) small boy
Tipp, Tippee, Tippey, Tippi, Tippy, Typp

Tisa
(African) ninth child

Titan
(Greek) powerful giant
Titun, Tityn

Tito
(Latin) honored
Teto, Titoh

Titus
(Latin) heroic
Titas, Tite, Tites

Tobes
(Hebrew) form of Tobias; believing the Lord is good
Tobee, Tobi, Tobs

Tobias
(Hebrew) believing the Lord is good
Tobi, Toby, Tobyas, Tovi

Tobin
(Hebrew) form of Tobias; believing the Lord is good
Toban, Toben, Tobun, Toby, Tobyn

Toby
(Hebrew) short for Tobias; believing the Lord is good
Tobe, Tobee, Tobey, Tobie, Toto

Todd
(English) sly; fox
Tod, Toddy

Todros
(Hebrew) gifted; treasure
Todos

Togo
(Place name) country in West Africa; jaunty

Toks
(American) carefree

Tolan
(American) studious
Tolen, Toll

Tolbert
(English) bright prospects
Talbart, Talbert, Tolbart, Tolburt, Tollee, Tolley, Tollie, Tolly

Toledo
(Place name) city in Ohio; casual
Tol, Tolly

Tom
(English) short for Thomas; twin
Thom, Tommy

Tomas
(Spanish) form of Thomas

Tomasso
(Italian) doubter
Maso, Tom

Tommie
(Hebrew, English) short for Thomas
Tomee, Tommee, Tommey, Tommi, Tomy

Toni
(Greek, Italian, American, English) soaring
Tonee, Toney, Tonie

Tor
(Scandinavian) thunder; brash
Thor, Torr, Torri, Torrie, Torry

Tord
(Dutch) peaceful

Toribio
(Spanish) strong; bullish

Torkel
(Scandinavian) protective

Torn
(Last name as first name) whirlwind
Torne, Tornn

Toro
(Spanish) bull

Toronto
(Place name) jaded
Torontoe

Torq
(Scandinavian) form of Thor, god of thunder
Tork

Torr
(English) tower; tall
Torre

Torrence
(Latin) smooth
Torence, Torey, Tori, Torr, Torrance, Torrie, Tory

Torri
(English) calming
Toree, Tori, Torre, Torree, Torrey, Torry

Tova
(Hebrew) good
Tov

Townie
(American) jovial
Townee, Towney, Towny

Toyah
(Place name) town in Texas; saucy
Toy, Toya, Toye

Trace
(French) careful
Trayse

Tracy
(French) spunky
Trace, Tracee, Tracey, Traci

Trae
(American) form of Trey; third

Trahan
(English) handsome
Trace, Trahahn, Trahain, Trahane, Trahen

Trampus
(American) talkative
Amp, Tramp, Trampy

Trap
(American) word as name; masculine
Trapp, Trappy

Traves
(American) traversing different roads
Trav, Travus, Travys

Travers
(English) helpful

Travis
(English) conflicted
Tavers, Traves, Travess, Travey, Travus, Travuss

Travon
(African-American) brash
Travaughn

Trayton
(English) third
Tray, Trey

Tremayne
(French) protector
Tramaine, Treemayne, Trem, Tremain, Tremaine, Tremane, Tremen

Trent
(Latin) quick-minded
Trente, Trenty, Trint, Trynt

Trenton
(Latin) fast-moving
Trent, Trentan, Trenten, Trentin

Treva
(Irish) wise
Trevan

Trevan
(African-American)
outgoing
Trevahn, Trevann

Trevon
(African-American)
studious
Trevaughan

Trevor
(Irish) wise
Trever, Trevur, Treve

Trey
(English) third-born;
creatively brilliant
Trae, Tray, Tre, Treye

Trigg
(American) short for
Trigger; horse or trigger-
finger
Trig, Trygg

Trinee
(Spanish) musical
Triney, Trini

Trinity
(Latin) triad
Trinitie

Trip
(English) wanderer
Tripe, Tripp

Tripsy
(English) dancing
Trippsie, Tryppsi

Tristan
(English) impulsive
*Trestan, Trestyn, Trist,
Tristen, Tristie, Triston,
Tristy, Tristyn*

Triste
(French) sad love affair
Tristan

Trivett
(Last name as first
name)
Trevett, Triv

Trivin
(American) form of
Devin; clever
Trevin

Trocky
(American) manly
Trockey, Trockie

Troy
(French) good-looking
Troi, Troye, Troyie

Troylane
(American) combo of
Troy and Lane
Troy Lane, Troy-Lane

Trudell
(English) remarkable for
honesty
Trude, True

True
(English) truthful
Tru

Truitt
(English) honest
Tru, True, Truett, Truitte

Truk
(Place name) islands in
the West Pacific; tough
Truck

Truman
(English) honest man
*Tru, True, Trueman,
Trumann*

Trusdale
(English) truthful
Dale, Tru, True

Tu
(Vietnamese) fourth

Tucker
(English) stylish
Tuck, Tucky, Tuckyr

Tucks
(English) short for
Tucker; fanciful
Tuk

Tullis
(Latin) important
Tull, Tullice, Tullise, Tully

Tully
(Irish) short for Tullis;
interesting
Tull, Tulley, Tulli, Tullie

Tulsa
(Place name) cowboy;
rancher
Tune
(American) dancer;
musical
Toone, Tuney
Tung
(Chinese, Vietnamese)
dignified; wise
Turk
(English) tough
Terk, Turke
Turone
(African-American) form
of Tyrone
Ture, Turrey, Turry
Turner
(Latin) skilled
Turn
Tut
(Arabic) brave
Tuttie, Tutty
Tuvia
(Hebrew) good
Tuvyah
Twain
(English) dual-faceted
Twaine, Tway, Twayn
Ty
(English) short for Tyler
Ti, Tie, Tye
Tyce
(American) lively
Tice

Tygie
(American) energetic
Tygee, Tygey, Tygi
Tyler
(English) industrious
*Tile, Tiler, Ty, Tye, Tylar,
Tyle, Tylir, Tylor*
Tyonne
(African-American) feisty
Tye, Tyon
Typhoon
(Weather name) volatile
*Tifoon, Ty, Tyfoon,
Tyfoonn*
Tyr
(Scandinavian) Norse
god; daring warrior
Tyre
(English) thunders
Tyr
Tyree
(African-American)
courteous
Ty, Tyrae, Tyrie, Tyry
Tyreece
(African-American)
combative
Tyreese
Tyrell
(African-American)
personable
*Trelle, Tyrel, Tyrelle, Tyril,
Tyrrel*

Tyron
(African-American) self-
reliant
Tiron, Tyronn
Tyrone
(Greek) self-starter;
autonomous
*Terone, Tirone, Tirus, Ty,
Tyronne, Tyroon, Tyroun*
Tyroneece
(African-American) ball-
of-fire
Tironeese, Tyronnee
Tys
(American) fighter
*Thysen, Tyes, Tys, Tyse,
Tysen*
Tyson
(French) son of Ty
*Tison, Tyse, Tysen,
Tysson, Tysy*

Udall
(English) certain; valley of trees
Eudall, Udahl, Udawl, Yudall

Ugo
(Italian) bright mind

Ukel
(American) player
Ukal, Uke, Ukil

Ukraine
(Place name) republic

Ulan
(Place name) city in Russia, Ulan Ude
Ulane

Uldarico
(Spanish)

Ulff
(Scandinavian) wolf; wild
Ulf, Ulv

Ulices
(Latin) form of Ulysses; wanderer
Uly

Ulissus
(Invented) form of Ulysses

Ulrich
(German) ruling; powerful
Ulrek, Ulriche, Ulrick

Ulysses
(Latin) forceful
Ule, Ulesses, Ulises, Ulisses

Umi
(African) life

Unique
(American)
Uneek, Unik

Upton
(English) highbrow writer
Uppton, Uptawn, Upten, Uptown

Urban
(Latin) city dweller
Urb, Urbain, Urbaine, Urbane, Urben, Urbin, Urbun, Urby

Uri
(Hebrew) short for Uriel; light

Uriah
(Hebrew) bright; led by God
Uri, Urie, Uryah

Urias
(Hebrew) Lord as my light; old-fashioned
Uri, Uria, Urius

Uriel
(Hebrew) light; God-inspired

Urvano
(Spanish) city boy
Urbano

Urvine
(Place name) form of Irvine, California
Urveen, Urvene, Urvi

Ury
(Hispanic) God-loving

Usher
(Latin) decisive

Utah
(Place name) U.S. state

Vadim
(French) creative
Vadeem

Vaduz
(Place name) city in Germany

Vail
(English) serene
Vaile, Vale, Valle

Val
(Latin) short for Valery and Valentine; strong
Vall

Valenti
(Italian) strong; romantic
Val, Valence, Valentin, Valentyn

Valentin
(Russian) healthy; strong
Val, Valeri

Valentine
(Latin) robust
Val, Valentyne, Valyntine

Valentino
(Italian) strong; healthy
Val

Valeri
(Russian) athletic; strong
Val, Valerian, Valerio, Valry

Van
(Dutch) from the family of...
Vann

Vance
(English) brash
Vans, Vanse

Vander
(Greek) short for Evander
Vand

Vandiver
(American) quiet
Van, Vand, Vandaver, Vandever

Vandwon
(African-American) covert
Vandawon, Vandjuan

Vanya
(Russian) right
Van, Yard, Yardy

Varkey
(American) boisterous

Varlan
(American) tough
Varland, Varlen, Varlin

Varma
(Hindi) fruitful

Varner
(Last name as first name) formidable
Varn

Vas
(Slavic) protective
Vaston, Vastun, Vasya

Vashon
(American) delightful
Vashaun, Vashonne

Vassil
(Bulgarian) king
Vass

Vaughn
(Welsh) compact
Vaughan, Vaunie, Von

Veejay
(American) talkative
V.J., Vee-Jay, Vejay

Vegas
(Place name) from Las Vegas, Nevada
Vega

Vejis
(Invented) form of Regis; outgoing
Veejas, Veejaz, Vejas, Vejes

Velle
(American) tough
Vell, Velley, Velly, Veltree

Velvet
(American) smooth
Vel, Velvat, Velvit

Venancio
(Spanish)
Ventura
(Spanish) good fortune
Vergel
(Spanish) writer
Vergele, Virgil
Verile
(German) macho
*Verill, Verille, Verol,
Verrill*
Vern
(Latin) short for Vernon
Verne, Vernie, Verny
Vernados
(Greek) hearty
Verner
(German) resourceful
*Vern, Verne, Vernir,
Virner*
Verniamin
(Greek) form of
Benjamin; son of the
right hand
Vernon
(Latin) fresh and bright
Verne, Vernen, Verney
Verona
(Italian) man of Venice
Verone
Vic
(Latin) short for Victor
Vick, Vickey, Vik

Vicente
(Spanish) winner
Vic, Vicentay, Visente
Victor
(Latin) winner
*Vic, Vickter, Victer, Vikki,
Viktor, Vitorio*
Vidalo
(Spanish) vibrant
Vidal
Viggo
(Scandinavian)
exuberant
Viggoa, Vigo
Vigile
(American) vigilant
Vegil, Vigil
Vilmos
(Italian) happy
Villmos
Vin
(Italian) short for
Vincent
*Vinn, Vinney, Vinni,
Vinnie*
Vince
(English) short for
Vincent
Vee, Vence, Vins, Vinse
Vincent
(Latin) victorious
*Vencent, Vincente,
Vinciente, Vinn, Vinny*

Vincenzo
(Italian) conquerer
Vincenze, Vinnie, Vinny
Vinson
(English) winning
attitude
*Venson, Vince, Vinny,
Vins*
Virgil
(Latin) holding his own
*Verge, Vergil, Virge,
Virgie, Virgy*
Vitale
(Italian) vital
Vitas
(Latin) lively
Vidas, Vite
Vito
(Italian) short for
Vittorio; lively; victor
Veto, Vite
Vittorio
(Italian) victorious
*Vite, Vito, Vitor, Vitorio,
Vittore*
Vivar
(Greek) alive
Viv
Vlad
(Russian) short for
Vladimir

Vladimir
   (Russian) glorious
   leader
   *Vlada, Vladameer,
   Vladamir, Vlademar,
   Vlakimar*
Vladja
   (Russian) short for
   Vladislav
Volf
   (Hebrew) form of Will;
   bold
Volker
   (German) prepared to
   defend
   Volk
Von
   (German) bright
   Vaughn, Vonn, Vonne
Vonzie
   (American) form of
   Fonzie; personable
   *Vons, Vonze, Vonzee,
   Vonzey, Vonzi*

Waclaw
   (Polish) glorified
Wade
   (English) mover;
   crossing a river
   Wadie, Wayde
Wadell
   (English) southerner
   Waddell, Wade
Waden
   (American) form of
   Jaden; fun
   Wade, Wedan
Wadsworth
   (English) homebody
   Wadswurth
Wagner
   (German) musical;
   practical
   *Wagg, Waggner,
   Waggoner, Wagnar,
   Wagnur*
Wagon
   (American) conveyance
   Wag, Wagg, Waggoner

Wait
   (American) word as
   name; patient
   Waite
Wake
   (Place name) island in
   the Marshall Islands
Waldemar
   (German) famous leader
   Valdemar
Walden
   (English) calming
   *Wald, Waldan, Waldin,
   Waldo, Waldy*
Waldo
   (German) short for
   Oswald; zany
   Wald, Waldoh, Waldy
Walenty
   (Polish) strong
Wales
   (English) from Wales in
   England
   *Wails, Wale, Waley, Wali,
   Waly*
Walker
   (English) distinctive
   Walk, Wally
Wallace
   (English) from Wales;
   charming
   *Wallas, Walley, Walli,
   Wallice, Wallie, Wally*

Walls
(American) walled
Walen, Wally, Waltz, Walz

Wally
(English) short for Walter
Wall, Walley, Walli, Wallie

Walsh
(English) inquisitive
Walls, Welce, Welch, Wells, Welsh

Walter
(German) army leader
Walder, Wallie, Wally, Walt, Waltur, Walty

Walton
(English) shut off; protected
Walt, Walten, Waltin

Ward
(English) vigilant; alert
Warde

Warden
(English) watchful
Warde, Wardie, Wardin, Wardon

Ware
(English) aware; cautious
Warey, Wary

Waring
(English) dashing
Wareng, Warin, Warring

Wark
(American) watchful

Warner
(German) protective
Warne

Warren
(German) safe haven
Waren, Warron, Warry, Worrin

Warwen
(American) defensive
Warn, Warwun, Warwun

Warwick
(English) lavish
War, Warweck, Warwyc, Warwyck, Wick

Washburn
(English) bountiful
Washbern, Washbie, Washby

Washington
(English) leader
Wash, Washe, Washing

Watkins
(English) able
Watkens, Wattie, Wattkins, Watty

Watson
(English) helpful
Watsen, Watsie, Watsun, Watsy, Wattsson

Wave
(American) word as a name
Waive, Wave, Wayve

Waverley
(Place name) city in New South Wales
Waverlee, Waverli, Waverly

Way
(English) landed; smart
Waye

Wayling
(English) the right way
Waylan, Wayland, Waylen, Waylin

Waylon
(English) country boy
Way, Wayland, Waylen, Waylie, Waylin, Waylond, Waylun, Wayly

Wayman
(English) traveling man
Way, Waym, Waymon, Waymun

Waymon
(American) knowing the way
Waymond

Wayne
(English) wheeler-dealer
Wain, Way, Wayn, Waynne

Webb
(English) intricate mind
Web, Webbe

Weber
(German) intuitive
Webb, Webber

Webster
(English) creative
Web, Webstar, Webstur

Weebie
(American) wily
Weebbi

Weido
(Italian) bright;
personable
Wedo

Welby
(German) astute
Welbey, Welbi, Welbie,
Wellby

Welford
(English) unusual
Walferd, Wallie, Wally

Wellington
(English) nobility
Welling

Wells
(English) place name;
unique
Well, Wellie, Welly

Welsh
(English) form of Walsh
Welch, Wellsh

Wendell
(German) full of
wanderlust
Wend, Wendall, Wendel,
Wendey, Wendie,
Wendill, Wendull, Wendy

Went
(American) ambitious
Wente, Wentt

Wes
(English) short for
Wesley
Wess, Wessie, Wessy

Wesley
(English) bland
Wes, Weslee, Weslie,
West, Westly, Wezlee,
Wezley

Wesson
(American) from the
West
Wess, Wessie

West
(English) westerner
Weste, Westt

Westie
(American) capricious
West, Westee, Westey,
Westt, Westy

Westleigh
(English) western
Westlea, Westlie, Wezlee

Westoll
(American) open
West, Westall

Weston
(English) good neighbor
West, Westen, Westey,
Westie, Westy, Westin

Wether
(English) light-hearted
Weather, Weth, Wethar,
Wethur

Wheat
(Invented) fair-haired
Wheatie, Wheats,
Wheaty, Whete

Wheel
(American) important
player
Wheele

Wheeler
(English) likes cars;
wheel maker
Weeler, Wheel, Wheelie,
Wheely

Wheeless
(English) off track
Whelus

Wheelie
(American) bigwig
Wheeley, Wheels,
Wheely

Whistler
(English) melodic
Whis, Whistlar, Whistle,
Whistlerr

Whit
(English) short for
Whitman
Whitt, Wit

Whitey
(English) fair-skinned
White

Whitman
(English) man with white hair
Whit, Whitty, Witman

Whitney
(English) likes white spaces
Whit, Whitnee, Whitnie, Whitt, Whittney, Witt

Whitson
(English) son of Whit
Whitt, Witt

Whittaker
(English) outdoors-loving
Whitaker, Whitt, Witaker, Wittaker

Wick
(American) burning
Wic, Wik, Wyck

Wilbert
(German) smart
Wilburt

Wilbur
(English) fortified
Wilbar, Wilber, Willbur

Wilburn
(German) brilliant
Bernie, Wil, Wilbern, Will

Wilder
(English) wild man
Wildar, Wilde, Wildey

Wiles
(American) tricky
Wyles

Wiley
(English) cowboy
Wile, Willey, Wylie

Wilfred
(German) peacemaker
Wilferd, Wilford, Will, Willfred, Willfried, Willie, Willy

Wilfredo
(Italian) peaceful

Wilhelm
(German) resolute; determined
Wilhem

Wilkins
(English) affectionate
Welkie, Welkins, Wilk, Wilkie, Willkins

Will
(English) short for William; likable
Wil, Wyll

Willard
(German) courageous
Wilard, Willerd

William
(English) staunch protector
Will, Willeam, Willie, Wills, Willy, Willyum, Wilyam

Willie
(German) short for William; protective
Will, Willey, Willeye, Willi, Willy

Willis
(German) youthful
Willace, Willece, Willus

Wilmer
(German) resolute; ambitious
Willmer, Wilmyr, Wylmer

Wilson
(English) extraordinary
Willson, Wilsen, Wilsun

Wilt
(English) talented
Wiltie

Wilton
(English) practical and open
Wilt, Wiltie, Wylten, Wylton

Winchell
(English) meandering
Winchie, Winshell

Wind
(American) word as name; breezy
Windy

Windell
(German) wanderer
Windelle, Windyll

Windsor
(English) royal
Win, Winnie, Winny,
Winsor, Wyndsor,
Wynser

Wings
(American) soaring; free
Wing

Winkel
(American) bright;
conniving
Wink, Winky

Winlove
(Filipino) winning favor

Winslow
(English) friendly
Winslo, Wynslo,
Wynslow

Winsome
(English) gorgeous;
winsome
Wins, Winsom, Winz

Winston
(English) dignified
Win, Winn, Winnie,
Winny, Winstan,
Wynsten, Wynston

Winter
(English) born in winter
Win, Winnie, Winny,
Wintar, Wintur, Wynter,
Wyntur

Winthrop
(English) winning; stuffy
Win, Winn, Winnie,
Winny, Wintrop

Wintle
(French)

Wiss
(American) carefree
Wissie, Wissy

Witold
(Polish) lively

Witt
(Slavic) lively
Witte

Witty, Witte
(American) humorous
Wit, Witt, Wittey, Wittie

Wize
(American) smart
Wise, Wizey, Wizi, Wizie

Wladymir
(Polish) famous ruler

Wladyslaw
(Polish) good leader
Slaw

Wohn
(African-American)

Wojtek
(Polish) comforter;
warrior

Wolf
(German) short for
Wolfgang
Wolff, Wolfy

Wolfe
(German) wolf; ominous
Wolf, Wolff, Wulf, Wulfe

Wolfgang
(German) talented; a
wolf walks
Wolf, Wolff, Wolfy,
Wulfgang

Wolley
(American) form of Wally
Wolly

Wood
(English) short for
Woodrow
Woode, Woody

Woodery
(English) woodsman
Wood, Wooderree,
Woodree, Woodri,
Woodry, Woods,
Woodsry, Woody

Woodfin
(English) attractive
Wood, Woodfen,
Woodfien, Woodfyn,
Woodie, Woody

Woodrow
(English) special
Wood, Woodrowe,
Woody

Woodward
(English) watchful
Wood, Woodie,
Woodwerd, Woody

Woody
(American) jaunty
Woodey, Woodi, Woodie

Woolsey
(English) leader
Wools, Woolsi, Woolsie, Woolsy

Worcester
(English) secure

Word
(American) word as name; talkative
Words, Wordy, Wurd

Worden
(American) careful
Word, Wordan, Wordun

Wordsworth
(English) poetic
Words, Worth

Worsh
(American) from the word worship; religious
Wor

Worth
(English) deserving
Werth, Worthey, Worthie, Worthy, Wurth

Worthington
(English) fun; worthwhile
Worth, Worthey, Worthing, Worthingtun, Wurthington

Wrangle
(American) cowboy
Wrang, Wrangler, Wrangy

Wren
(American) leader of men
Ren, Rin, Rinn, Wrenn

Wright
(English) clear-minded; correct
Right, Rite, Wrighte, Write

Wulf
(Hebrew) wolf
Wolf

Wyatt
(French) ready for combat
Wy, Wyat, Wyatte, Wye

Wyclef
(American) trendy
Wycleff

Wycliff
(English) edgy
Cliffie, Cliffy, Wicliff, Wyclif, Wycliffe

Wydee
(American) form of Wyatt; fighter
Wy, Wydey, Wydie

Wylie
(English) charmer
Wiley, Wye, Wylee

Wymann
(English) contentious
Wimann, Wye, Wyman

Wynne
(English) dear friend
Winn, Wynn

Wyshawn
(African-American) friendly
Shawn, Shawny, Why, Whysean, Wieshawn, Wye, Wyshawne, Wyshie, Wyshy

Wyton
(English) fair-haired crowd-pleaser
Wye, Wytan, Wyten, Wytin

Wyze
(American) sizzle; capable
Wise, Wye, Wyse

X

Xander
(Greek) short for Alexander
Xan, Xande, Xandere, Xandre

Xanthus
(Greek) golden-haired child

Xavier
(Arabic) shining
Zavey, Zavier

Xaxon
(American) happy
Zaxon

Xen
(African-American) original
Zen

Xeno
(Greek) gracious
Xenoes, Zene, Zenno, Zenny, Zeno, Zenos

Xerxes
(Persian) leader
Xerk, Xerky, Zerk, Zerkes, Zerkez

Xyle
(American) helpful
Zye, Zyle

Xyshaun
(African-American) zany
Xye, Zye, Zyshaun, Zyshawn

Y

Yadon
(Last name as first name) different
Yado, Yadun

Yael
(Hebrew) teacher
Yail, Yaley, Yalie

Yancy
(American) vivacious
Yanci, Yancie, Yancy, Yanzie

Yank
(American) Yankee
Yanke

Yannis
(Greek) believer in God
Yannie

Yarden
(Hebrew) flowing
Yard, Yardan, Yarde, Yardene, Yardun

Yardley
(English) adorned; separate
Yard, Yarde, Yardie, Yardlea, Yardlee, Yardly, Yardy

Yash
(Hindi)
Yates
(English) smart; closed
Yate, Yattes, Yeats
Yeats
(English) gates
Yen
(Chinese) calming;
capable
Yeoman
(English) helping
*Yeomann, Yo, Yoeman,
Yoman, Yoyo*
Yimer
(Scandinavian) giant
Yoav
(Hebrew) form of Joab
Yoel
(Hebrew) form of Joel
Yohann
(German) form of Johann
Yohan, Yohn
Yonah
(Hebrew) form of Jonah
York
(English) affluent
*Yorke, Yorkee, Yorkey,
Yorki, Yorky*
Yorker
(English) rich
York, Yorke, Yorkur
Yosef
(Hebrew) form of Joseph
Yose, Yoseff, Yosif

Young
(English) fledgling
Jung, Younge
Yovan
(Slavic) form of Jovan
Yu
(Chinese) shiny; smart
Yuan
(Chinese) circle
Yuke
(American) short for
Yukon
Yukon
(Place name)
individualist
Yule
(English) Christmas-born
Yuel, Yuley, Yulie
Yuma
(Place name) city in
Arizona; cowboy
Yumah
Yuri
(Russian) dashing
*Yurah, Yure, Yurey, Yurie,
Yurri, Yury*
Yuris
(Latin) farmer
Yures, Yurus
Yves
(French) honest;
handsome
Eve, Ives

Yvonn
(French) attractive
Von, Vonn, Yvon

Z

Zab
(American) slick
Zabbey, Zabbi, Zabbie, Zabby

Zac
(Hebrew) short for Zachariah; Lord remembers
Zacary, Zach, Zachary, Zachry

Zacary
(Hebrew) form of Zachary
Zac, Zacc, Zaccary, Zaccry, Zaccury

Zaccheus
(Hebrew) unblemished
Zac, Zacceus, Zack

Zace
(American) pleasure-seeking
Zacey, Zacie, Zase

Zach
(Hebrew) short for Zachary
Zac, Zachy

Zachariah
(Hebrew) Lord remembers
Zac, Zacaryah, Zachary, Zachey, Zachi, Zachie, Zachy, Zack, Zechariah, Zhack

Zacharias
(Hebrew) devout
Zacharyas

Zachary
(Hebrew) spiritual
Zacary, Zacchary, Zach, Zackar, Zackarie, Zak, Zakari, Zakri, Zakrie, Zakry

Zack
(Hebrew) short for Zachary
Zacky, Zak

Zade
(Arabic) flourishing; trendy
Zaid

Zadok
(Hebrew) unyielding
Zadek, Zaydie, Zadik, Zayd

Zain
(American) zany
Zane, Zayne

Zakary
(Hebrew) form of Zachary

Zaki
(Arabic) virtuous
Zak

Zale
(Greek) strong
Zail, Zaley, Zalie

Zander
(Greek) short for Alexander
Zande, Zandee, Zandey, Zandie, Zandy

Zandy
(American) high-energy
Zandee, Zandi

Zane
(English) debonair
Zain, Zay, Zayne, Zaynne

Zano
(American) unique
Zan

Zappa
(American) zany
Zapah, Zapp

Zartavious
(African-American) unusual
Zar, Zarta

Zashawn
(African-American) fiery
Zasean, Zash, Zashaun, Zashe, Zashon, Zashone

Zavier
(Arabic) form of Xavier

Zbigniew
(Polish) free of malice; calming

Zeb
(Hebrew) short for Zebediah
Zebe

Zebby
(Hebrew) believer; rambunctious
Zabbie, Zeb, Zebb, Zebbie

Zebediah
(Hebrew) gift from God
Zeb, Zebadia, Zebb, Zebbie, Zebby, Zebi, Zebidiah

Zechariah
(Hebrew) form of Zachariah
Zeke

Zed
(Hebrew) energetic
Zedd, Zede

Zedekiah
(Hebrew) believing in a just God
Zed, Zeddy, Zedechia, Zedechiah

Zeevy
(American) sly
Zeeve, Zeevi, Zeevie

Zeffy
(American) explosive
Zeff, Zeffe, Zeffi, Zeffie

Zeke
(Hebrew) friendly; outgoing
Zeek, Zekey, Zeki

Zelig
(Hebrew) holy; happy
Zel

Zen
(Japanese) spiritual

Zeno
(Greek) philosophical; stoic
Zeney, Zenie, Zenno, Zeny

Zenon
(Greek, Polish) godlike

Zent
(American) zany
Zynt

Zephyr
(Greek) breezy
Zefar, Zefer, Zeffer, Zefur

Zero
(Arabic) nothing
Zeroh

Zerond
(American) helpful
Zerre, Zerrie, Zerry, Zerund

Zeshon
(African-American) zany
Zeshaune, Zeshawn

Zeus
(Greek) vibrant
Zues

Zevi
(Hebrew) brisk
Zevie

Zhivago
(Russian) dashing; romantic
Vago

Zhong
(Chinese) middle brother; loyal

Zia
(Hebrew) in motion
Zeah, Ziah

Zie
(American) compelling
Zye, Zyey

Ziggy
(American) zany

Zigmand
(American) form of Sigmund
Zig, Ziggy

Zikomo
(African) grateful

Zino
(Greek) philosopher
Zeno

Zion
(Hebrew) sign
Zeione, Zi, Zione, Zye

Ziv
　(Hebrew) energetic
　Zeven, Zevy
Ziven
　(Polish) lively
　Ziv
Ziya
　(Turkish)
Zol
　(American) jaunty
　Zoll
Zoma
　(American) loquacious
　Zome
Zorba
　(Greek) pleasure seeker
　Zorbah, Zorbe
Zorby
　(Greek) tireless
　Sorby, Zorb, Zorbie
Zorshawn
　(African-American) jaded
　Zahrshy, Zorsh, Zorshie,
　Zorshon, Zorshy
Zuberi
　(African) powerful
Zvon
　(Croatian) short for
　Zvonimir
　Zevon, Zevonn
Zyke
　(American) high-energy
　Zykee, Zyki, Zykie, Zyky

A

Aaliyah
(Hebrew) moving up
Aliya

Aamori
(African) good

Abay
(Native American) growing
Abai, Abbay, Abey, Abeye

Abayomi
(African) giving joy

Abby
(English) happy
Abbee, Abbey, Abbie, Abbye

Abella
(French) vulnerable; capable
Abela, Abele, Abell, Bela, Bella

Abery
(Last name as first name) supportive
Abby, Aberee, Abrie, Abry

Abia, Abiah
(Arabic) excellent
Ab, Aba, Abbie

Abigail
(Hebrew, English, Irish) joyful
Abagail, Abbegayle, Abbey, Abbie, Abby, Abegail, Abey, Abigal, Abigayle, Gail, Gayle

Abilene
(Place name) Texas town; southern girl
Abalene, Abi, Abiline, Aby

Abiola
(Spanish) God-loving
Abby, Abi, Biola

Abra
(Hebrew) form of Abraham; strong and exemplary
Aba, Abbee, Abbey, Abbie, Abby

Abrianna
(American) insightful
Abryanna, Abryannah

Abrielle
(American) form of Abigail; rejoices
Abby, Abree, Abrey, Abrie, Abriella, Abryelle

Acacia
(Greek) everlasting; tree
Akaysha, Cacia, Cacie, Case, Casey, Casha, Casia, Caysha, Kassy, Kaykay

Accalia
(Latin) stand-in
Accal, Accalya, Ace, Ackie

Achantay
(African-American) reliable
Achantae, Achanté

Ada
(German) noble; joyful
Adah, Addah, Adeia, Aida

Adaani
(French) pretty; noble
Adan, Adane, Adani, Daani, Dani

Adabelle
(American) combo of Ada and Belle; noble beauty
Ada, Adabel, Addabel, Belle

Adaeze
(African) prepared
Adaese

Adair
(Scottish) innovative
*Ada, Adare, Adayr,
Adayre, Adda*

Adalia
(Spanish) spunky
*Adahlia, Adailya,
Adallyuh, Adaylia*

Adara
(Greek) lovely
Adarah, Adrah

Addison
(English) awesome
*Addeson, Addie,
Addison, Addy, Addyson,
Adeson, Adison*

Addy
(English) nickname for
Addison; distinctive;
smiling
*Addee, Addie, Addy,
Addye, Adie, Ady*

Adeen
(American) decorated
*Addy, Adeene, Aden,
Adene, Adin*

Adelaide
(German) calming;
distinguished
*Ada, Adalaid, Adalaide,
Adelade, Adelaid, Laidey*

Adeline
(English) sweet
*Adaline, Adealline,
Adelenne, Adelina,
Adelind, Adlin, Adline*

Adelita
(Spanish) form of Adela;
noble
*Adalina, Adalita,
Adelaina, Adelaine,
Adeleta, Adey, Audilita,
Lita, Lite*

Adelka
(German) form of
Adelaide; noble
*Addie, Addy, Adel,
Adelkah, Adie*

Adelle
(German) giving
Adel, Adell, Addy

Adelpha
(Greek) beloved sister
Adelfa, Adelphe

Adena
(Hebrew) precious
*Ada, Adenna, Adina,
Adynna, Deena, Dena*

Adia
(African) God's gift

Adina
(Hebrew) high hopes
*Addy, Adeen, Adeena,
Adine, Deena, Dena,
Dina*

Adisa
(Hispanic) friendly
Adesa, Adissa

Adiva
(Arabic) gracious

Adjanys
(Hispanic) lively
Adjanice, Adjanis

Adline
(German) reliable
*Addee, Addie, Addy,
Adleen, Adlene, Adlyne*

Adonia
(Greek) beauty
*Adona, Adonea,
Adoniah, Adonis*

Adora
(Latin) adored child
*Adorae, Adoray, Dora,
Dore, Dorey, Dori,
Dorree, Dorrie, Dorry*

Adra
(Greek) beauty

Adria
(Latin) place name
Adrea

Adrianna
(Greek, Latin) rich;
exotic
*Addy, Adree, Adriana,
Adrie, Adrin, Anna*

Adrienne
(Latin) wealthy
Adreah, Adreanne, Adrenne, Adriah, Adrian, Adrien, Adrienn, Adrin, Adrina

Aereale
(Hebrew) form of Ariel; light and sprite
Aereal, Aeriel, Areale

Aeronwenn
(Welsh) white; aggressor
Awynn

Afton
(English) confident
Aft, Aftan, Aften, Aftie

Africa
(Place name) continent
Afrika

Afua
(African) baby born on Friday
Afuah

Agafi
(Greek) form of Agnes; pure
Ag, Aga, Agafee, Agaffi, Aggie

Agapi, Agape
(Greek) love
Agapay, Agappe

Agasha
(Greek) form of Agatha; longsuffering
Agashah, Agashe

Agate
(English) gemstone; precious girl
Agatte, Aget, Aggey, Aggie

Agatha
(Greek) kind-hearted
Agath, Agathah, Agathe, Aggey, Aggie, Aggy

Agatta
(Greek) form of Agatha; honorable and patient
Ag, Agata, Agathi, Aggie, Agi, Agoti, Agotti

Agave
(Botanical) strong-spined; genus of plants
Ag, Agavay, Aggie, Agovay

Agentina
(Spanish) form of Argentina; colorful
Agen, Agente, Tina

Aggie
(Greek) kind-hearted
Aggee, Aggy

Agnes
(Greek) pure
Ag, Aggie, Aggnes, Aggy, Agnas, Agnes, Agness, Agnie, Agnus, Nessie

Ahvanti
(African) focused
Avanti

Aida
(Arabic) gift
Aeeda, Ayeeda, Ieeda

Aidan
(Irish) from the male name Aidan; fiery
Aden, Aiden

Aileen
(Irish, Scottish) fair-haired beauty
Aleen, Alene, Alenee, Aline, Allee, Alleen, Allene, Allie, Ally

Ailey
(Irish) form of Aileen; light and friendly
Aila, Ailee, Ailie, Ailli, Allie

Aimee
(French) beloved
Aime, Aimey, Aimme, Amee, Amy

Aimee-Lynn
(American) combo of Aimee and Lynn; lovable
Aimee Lynn, Aimeelin, Aimeelynn

Aimer
(German) leader; loved
Aimery, Ame, Amie

Ainsley
(Scottish) meadow;
outdoorsy
*Ainslea, Ainslee,
Ainsleigh, Ainslie, Anes,
Anslie, Aynslee, Aynsley*

Aintre
(Irish) joyous estate
*Aintree, Aintrey, Antre,
Antry*

Aisha
(Arabic, African) life;
lively
*Aeesha, Aiesha,
Aieshah, Ayeesha,
Ayisha, Ieashia, Ieeshah,
Iesha*

Aislinn
(Irish) dreamy
Aisling, Aislyn, Aislynn

Alabama
(Place name) western
Bama

Alaine
(Gaelic) lovely
*Alaina, Alaiyne, Alenne,
Aleyna, Aleyne, Allaine,
Allayne*

Alala
(Roman mythology)
sister of Mars; protected
Alalah

Alana
(Scottish) pretty girl
*Alahna, Alahnah, Alaina,
Alainah, Alanah, Alanna,
Alannah, Allana, Allie,
Ally*

Alanis
(French) shining star
Alannis

Alason
(German) form of Alison;
noble; bright
Ala, Alas

Alaygrah
(Invented) form of
Allegra; frisky
Alay, Allay

Alaytheea
(Invented) form of
Aleithea; honest
Alay, Thea, Theea

Alberta
(French) bright-eyed
*Alb, Albertah, Albie,
Albirta, Alburta, Bertie,
Berty*

Albertine
(English) form of Albert;
bright
*Albertyne, Albie,
Albyrtine, Teeny*

Albie
(American) casual
Albee, Albey, Alby, Albye

Alcina
(Greek) magical; strong-
willed
*Alcee, Alcie, Als, Alsena,
Alsie. Cina, Seena, Sina*

Aldona
(American) sweet
Aldone

Alea
(Arabic) excellent
*Alaya, Aleah, Aleeah,
Alia, Ally*

Aleah
(American) combo of
Allie and Leah
Alayah, Alayja

Aleeza, Aliza
(Hebrew) joy

Alegria
(Spanish) beautiful
movement
Allegria

Aleksandra
(Polish, Russian) helpful

Alessa
(Italian) helper
Alesa

Alessandra
(Italian) defender of
mankind
Aless, Alessa

Alessia, Allyshia
(Italian) nice
Alesha, Alyshia

Alethea
(Greek) truthful
Alathea, Aleethia, Aletha, Aletie, Altheia, Lathea, Lathey

Aletta
(Greek) carefree
Aleta, Aletta, Eletta, Letti, Lettie, Letty

Alexa
(Greek) short for Alexandra
Alecksa, Aleksah, Alex, Alexia

Alexakai
(American) combo of Alexa and Kai; merry
Alexikai, Lexi, Kai

Alexandra
(Greek, English, Scottish, Spanish) regal protector
Alejandra, Alejaundro, Alex, Alexandrah, Alexandria, Alexis, Alezandra, Allesandro, Ally, Lex, Lexi, Lexie

Alexandrine
(French) helpful
Alexandrie, Alex, Ally, Lexi, Lexie

Alexia
(Greek) helpful, bright
Alexea, Alexiah, Alixea, Lex, Lexey, Lexie, Lexy

Alexis
(Greek) short for Alexandra; helpful; pretty
Aleksus, Alexius, Alexus, Alexys, Lex, Lexey, Lexi, Lexie, Lexis, Lexus

Alfonsith
(German) aggressive
Alf, Alfee, Alfey, Alfey, Alfie, Alfonsine, Allfrie, Alphonsine, Alphonsith

Alfre
(English) short for Alfreda; seer
Alfree

Alfreda
(English) wise advisor
Alfi, Alfie, Alfred, Alfredah, Alfrede, Alfredeh, Freda, Freddy

Ali
(Greek) short for Alexandra; defending
Aley, Allee, Alley, Ally

Alianet
(Spanish) honest; noble
Alia, Aliane

Alice
(Greek) honest
Alece, Alicea, Alise, Alliss, Ally, Allys, Alyse, Alysse, Lisie, Lisy, Lysse

Aliceann
(American) combo of Alice and Ann; well-born; southern feel
Alice Ann, Alicean, Alice-Ann

Alicia
(Greek) delicate; lovely
Alisha

Alida
(Greek) stylish
Aleda, Aleta, Aletta, Alidah, Alita, Lee, Lida, Lita, Lyda

Alina
(Scottish, Slavic) fair-haired
Alene, Aline, Allene, Allie, Ally, Allyne, Lena, Lina

Alisa
(Hebrew) happy
Alissa, Allisa, Allissdh, Alyssa

Alisha
(Greek) happy; truthful
Aleesha, Alesha, Alicia, Ally, Allyshah, Lesha, Lisha

Alison
(Scottish) noble
Alisen

Alissa
(Greek) pretty
Alesa, Alessa, Alise, Alissah, Allee, Allie, Ally, Allyssa, Alyssea

Alita
(Native American) sparkling

Alka
(Polish) distinctive
Alk, Alkae

Allegra
(Italian) snappy
Aligra, All, Allagrah, Allie, Alligra, Ally

Allena
(Greek) outstanding
Alena, Alenah, Allana, Allie, Ally

Allene
(Greek) wonderful
Alene, Alyne

Allessandra
(Italian) kind-hearted
Allesandra

Allie
(Greek) smiling
Ali, Allee, Alli, Ally, Allye

Allison
(English) kind-hearted
Alison, Allie, Allisan, Allisen, Allisun, Ally, Allyson, Sonny

Allura
(Hispanic) alluring
Alura

Allyson
(English) another form of Allison
Alisaune, Allysen, Allysun, Alyson

Allysse
(Greek) smooth
Allice, Allyce, Allyss

Alma
(Latin) good; soulful
Almah, Almie, Almy

Almeria
(Arabic) princess
Alma, Almara, Almaria, Almer, Almurea, Als

Almirah, Almira
(Spanish, Arabic) princess
Allmeerah, Elmira, Mira

Alodie
(Origin unknown) thriving
Alodee

Aloha
(Hawaiian) love

Alona
(Jewish) sturdy oak
Allona

Alondra
(Spanish) bright
Alond, Alondre, Alonn

Alouette
(French) birdlike
Allie, Allo, Allou, Allouetta, Alou, Alowette

Aloyse, Aloise
(German) renowned
Aloice, Aloyce

Alpha
(Greek) first; superior
Alf, Alfa, Alfie, Alph, Alphah, Alphie

Alston
(English) a place for a noble
Allie, Ally, Alstan, Alsten, Alstun

Alta
(Latin) high place; fresh

Altea
(Polish) healer

Althaea
(Latin, Italian) healing

Althea
(Greek, English) demure; healer
Althe, Althey, Althia, Althie, Althy, Thea, They

Alva
(Spanish) fair; bright
Alvah

Alvada
(American) evasive
Alvadah, Alvayda

Alverna
(English) truthful friend
(elf friend)
Alver, Alverne,
Alvernette

Alvernise
(English) form of
Alverne; honest (elf
friend)
Alvenice

Alvina
(English) beloved;
friendly
Alvee, Alveena, Alvie,
Alvine, Alvy

Alvita
(Latin) charismatic

Alyda
(French) soaring
Aleda, Alida, Alita, Lida,
Lyda

Alysia
(Greek) compelling
Aleecia, Alesha, Alicia,
Alish, Alycia

Alyssa
(Greek) flourishing
Alissa, Allissa, Allissae,
Ilyssah, Lissa, Lyssa,
Lyssy

Amabe
(Latin) loved
Ama

Amabelle
(American) loved
Amabel, Amahbel

Amada
(Latin, Spanish) loved
one
Ama, Amadah

Amal
(Arabic) optimistic
Amahl

Amalina
(German) worker
Am, Ama, Amaleen,
Amaline, Amalyne

Amanda
(Latin, English, Irish)
lovable
Amand, Amandah,
Amandy, Manda,
Mandee, Mandi, Mandy

Amandra
(American) variant of
Amanda; lovely
Amand, Mandee, Mandi,
Mandra, Mandree,
Mandry, Mandy

Amara
(Greek, Italian) unfading
beauty
Am, Amarah, Amareh,
Amera, Amura, Mara

Amarillo
(Place name) a city in
Texas; cowgirl
Ama, Amari, Amarilla,
Amy, Rillo

Amaris
(Hebrew) beloved;
dedicated
Amares

Amaryllis
(Greek) fresh flower
Ama, Amarillis

Amber
(French) gorgeous and
golden; semiprecious
stone
Ambar, Amberre, Ambur,
Amburr

Amber-Dee
(American) combination
of Amber and Dee;
golden jewel;
spontaneous
Amber D, Amber Dee

Amberkalay
(American) combo of
Amber and Kalay;
beautiful energy
Amber-Kalé, Amber-Kalet

Amberlee
(American) combo of
Amber and Lee
Amberlea, Amberleigh,
Amberley, Amberli,
Amberly, Amburlee

Amberlyn
(American) combo of
Amber and Lyn
*Amberl, Amberlin,
Amberlynn, Amlynn*

Amboree
(Last name as first
name) precocious
Ambor, Ambree

Ambrosette
(Greek) eternal
*Amber, Ambie, Ambro,
Ambrosa, Ambrose*

Ambrosia
(Greek) eternal
*Ambroze, Ambrozeah,
Ambrozia*

Amelia
(German) industrious
*Amalee, Amaylyuh,
Amele, Ameleah, Ameli,
Amelie, Amelya, Amilia*

Amera
(Arabic) of regal birth
Ameera, Amira

America
(American) patriotic
*Amer, Amerca, Americah,
Amerika, Amur*

Amethyst
(Greek) precious gem
Amathist, Ameth

Amica
(Latin) good friend
Ameca, Ami, Amika

Amici
(Italian) friend
Amicie, Amie, Amisie

Amiga
(Spanish) friend
Amigah

Amina
(Arabic) trustworthy
Amena, Amine

Amity
(Latin) a good friend
Amitee, Amitey, Amiti

Amor
(Spanish) love
Amora, Amore

Amora
(Spanish) love

Amorelle
(French) lover
*Amoray, Amore, Amorel,
Amorell*

Amoretta
(French) little love

Amorita
(Spanish) loved

Amy
(Latin) loved one
*Aimee, Amey, Ameyye,
Ami, Amie, Amye, Amye*

Amykay
(American) combo of
Amy and Kay
Amikae

Amylynn
(American) combo of
Amy and Lynn
*Ameelyn, Amilynn,
Amylyn*

Amyrka
(Spanish) lively
*Amerka, Amurka, Amyrk,
Amyrrka*

Anabelle, Anabella
(American) combo of
Ana and Belle; lovely
*Anabel, Anabell,
Annabelle*

Anabril
(Spanish) merciful;
pretty
*Anabrelle, Anna,
Annabril*

Anais
(French) variant of Anne;
graceful

Anala
(Hindi) fiery

Analia
(Hebrew) gracious;
hopeful
*Ana, Analea, Analeah,
Analiah, Analya*

Analeese
(Scandinavian) gracious
*Analece, Analeece,
Annaleese*

Analicia
(Spanish) combo of Ana and Licia; gracious sweetheart
Analice, Analicea, Analisha, Licia

Analisa
(American) combo of Ana and Lisa; lovely
Analise, Annalisa, Anna-Lisa

Analy
(American) graceful; gracious
Analee, Anali

Analynne
(American) combo of Ana and Lynne
Analinn, Analynn, Annalinne, Annalynn

Anand
(Hindi) joyful; profound
Anan, Ananda

Anastasiya
(Greek, Russian) reborn; royal
Anastasia, Anastasya

Anastay
(Greek) born again; renewed
Ana, Anastae, Anastie

Anatola, Anatole
(Greek, French) dawn
Anatol

Anayancy
(Spanish) combo of Ana and Yancy; buoyant
Ana Yancy, Anayanci, Anayancie, Ana-Yancy

Anders
(Scandinavian) stunning
Andars, Andie, Andurs, Andy

Andi
(English) casual
Andee, Andie

Andraa
(Greek, French) feminine
Andrah

Andrea
(Greek) feminine
Andee, Andi, Andie, Andra, Andrae, Andre, Andreah, Andreena

Andreanne
(American) combo of Andrea and Anne
Andreane, Andrie, Andry

Andree
(Greek) strong woman
Andrey, Andrie, Andry

Andrenna
(Scottish) pretty; gracious
Andreene, Adrena

Andrianna
(Greek) feminine
Andree, Andy

Andromeda
(Greek) beautiful star
Andromedah

Anemone
(Greek) breath of fresh air

Anewk
(Invented) form of Anouk

Angel
(Latin) sweet; angelic
Angelle, Angie, Anjel, Annjell

Angela
(Greek) divine; angelic
Angelena, Angelica, Angelina, Angelle, Angie, Gela, Nini

Angelia
(American) angelic messenger
Angelea, Angeliah

Angelica
(Latin) angelic messenger
Angie, Anjeleka, Anjelica, Anjelika, Anjie

Angelina
(Latin) angelic
Ange, Angelyna, Angie, Anje, Anjelina, Anjie

Angeline
(American) angelic
Angelene, Angelline

Angelique
(Latin, French) angelic
Angel, Angeleek,
Angelik, Angie, Anjee,
Anjel, Anjelique

Angelle
(Latin) angelic
Ange, Angell, Anje,
Anjell, Anjelle,

Angie
(Latin) angelic
Angey, Angi, Angye,
Anjie

Aniece
(Hebrew) gracious
Ana, Anesse, Ani, Anice,
Annis, Annissa

Aniela
(Polish) sent by God
Ahneela

Anik, Anika
(Hebrew) hospitable
Anec, Anecca, Aneek,
Aneeka, Anic, Anica,
Annika

Anissa
(Greek) a completed
spirit
Anisa, Anise, Anyssa,
Anysse

Anita
(Spanish) gracious
Aneda, Aneeta, Anitta

Anitra
(Invented, from
literature) combo of
Anita and Debra
Anetra, Anitrah, Annitra

Anjali
(Hindi) pretty; honored
Anjaly

Anjana
(Hindi) merciful; pretty
Anjann

Anjelica
(Latin) angelic
Anjelika

Anjeliett
(Spanish) little angel
Anjel, Anjeli, Jelette,
Jeliett, Jeliette, Jell, Jelly

Anjul
(French) jovial
Angie, Anjewel, Anji,
Anjie, Anjool

Ann
(Hebrew) loving;
hospitable
Aine, An, Ana, Anna,
Anne, Annie, Ayn

Ann-Dee
(American) variant of
Andy; graceful
Andee, Andey, Andi,
Andy, Ann Dee, Anndi

Anna
(English, Italian,
German, Russian,
Polish) gracious
Ana, Anae, Anah, Annah,
Anne, Anuh

Annairis
(American) combo of
Anna and Iris; sweet
Anairis, Ana-Iris, Anna
Iris

Annamaria
(Italian) combo of Anna
and Maria; merciful and
holy
Anamaria, Anna-Maria,
Annamarie

Anna-Pearl
(American) Anna and
Pearl; dated
Anapearl, Anna Pearl,
Annapearl

Anneliese
(Scandinavian) gracious;
(German) religious
Aneliece, Aneliese

Annella
(Scottish) graceful
Anell, Anella, Anelle

Annemarie
(German) combo of Anne
and Marie
Anmarie, Ann Marie,
Anne-Marie, Annmarie

Annette
(American) vivacious;
giving
*Anette, Ann, Anne,
Annett, Annetta, Annie,
Anny*

Anne-Louise
(American) combo of
Anne and Louise; sweet
*Anlouise, Ann Louise,
Annelouise, Annlouise,
Ann-Loweez*

Annie
(Hebrew, Irish) gracious;
hip
*Ann, Annee, Anney,
Anni, Anny*

Annika
(Scandinavian) gracious
Anika

Anninka
(Russian) gracious;
graceful

Annissa
(Greek) gracious;
complete
*Anissa, Anni, Annie,
Annisa*

Anouk
(French) form of Ann

Anshaunee
(African-American)
combo of Ann and
Shaunee; happy
*Annshaunee,
Anshawnee*

Ansley
(English) happy in the
meadow
*Annesleigh, Ans, Anslea,
Anslee, Ansleigh, Ansli,
Anslie*

Anstass
(Greek) resurrected;
eternal
*Ans, Anstase, Stace,
Stacey, Stass, Stassee*

Anstice
(Greek) everlasting
*Anst, Steece, Steese,
Stice*

Antigone
(Greek) impulsive;
defiant

Antique
(Word as name) old soul
Anteek, Antik

Antoinette
(Latin) quintessential;
(French) feminine form
of Antoine
*Antoine, Antoinet,
Antwanett, Antwonette,
Antwonette, Toinette,
Tonette*

Antonia
(Latin) perfect
*Antone, Antonea,
Antoneah*

Antonian
(Latin) valuable
*Antoinette, Antonetta,
Toni, Tonia, Tonya*

Antwanette
(African-American) form
of Antoinette; prized
Antwan, Antwanett

Anya
(Russian) grace

Aphra
(Hebrew) earthy;
sentimental
*Af, Affee, Affey, Affy,
Afra, Aphree, Aphrie*

Aphrodite
(Greek) goddess of love
and beauty
Afrodite, Aphrodytee

Apolinaria
(Spanish) form of Greek
god Apollonia; martyr
Apolinara

Apollonia
(Greek) sun goddess
*Apolinia, Apolyne,
Appollonia*

Apple
(Botanical) fruit; quirky
Apel, Appell

April
(Latin) month of the
year; springlike
*Aprel, Aprile, Aprille,
Apryl*

Aqua
(Spanish) colorful
Akwa

Arabella
(Latin) answer to a
prayer; beauty
*Arabel, Arabelle, Arbel,
Arbella, Bella, Belle,
Orabele, Orabella*

Araceli
(Latin) heavenly
Ara, Aracelli, Ari

Aracelle
(Spanish) flamboyant;
heavenly
*Ara, Aracel, Aracell,
Araseli, Celi*

Arachne
(Greek) weaver; spider

Araminta
(English) unique;
precious dawn
*Ara, Arama, Aramynta,
Minta*

Araylia
(Latin) golden
Araelea, Aray, Rae, Ray

Arbra
(American) form of Abra;
sensitive
Arbrae

Arcelia
(Spanish) treasured
*Arcey, Arci, Arcilia, Arla,
Arlia*

Arcelious
(African-American)
treasured
*Arce, Arcel, Arcelus, Arcy,
Arselious*

Archon
(American) capable
*Arch, Archee, Archi,
Arshon*

Ardath
(Hebrew) ardent
*Ardee, Ardie, Ardith,
Ardon*

Ardele
(Latin) enthusiastic;
dedicated
*Ardell, Ardella, Ardelle,
Ardine*

Arden
(Latin) ardent; sincere
*Ardan, Ardena, Ardin,
Ardon*

Ardiana
(Spanish) ardent
Ardi, Ardie, Diana

Ardie
(American) enthusiastic;
special
Ardee, Ardi

Areika
(Spanish) pure
*Areka, Areke, Arika,
Arike*

Arekah
(Greek) virtuous; loving

Arelie
(Latin) golden girl
Arelee, Arely, Arlea

Aretha
(Greek) virtuous;
vocalist

Aretta
(Greek) virtuous
Arette, Arie

Argentina
(Place name) confident;
land of silver
*Arge, Argen, Argent,
Argenta, Argie, Tina,
Tinee*

Arianda
(Greek) helper
Ariand

Aridatha
(Hebrew) flourishing
Ar, Arid, Datha

Arisca
(Greek) form of Arista;
best; delight
Ariska, Ariske, Arista

Argosy
(French) bright
Argosee, Argosie

Argus
(Greek) bright
Arguss

Argyle
(French, American)
complicated
*Argie, Argile, Argy,
Argylle*

Aria
(Italian) melody; solo
Ariah

Ariadne
(Greek) faithful
*Ariadna, Aryana,
Aryanna*

Ariana
(Greek) devout;
(Welsh) treasured silver
*Ana, Ari, Aria, Arianah,
Arianna, Arri, Arriannah*

Ariane
(Greek) very gracious
Arianne, Aryahn

Arianne
(French) kind
Ana, Ari, Ariann

Ariel
(French, Hebrew)
heavenly singer
Aeriel, Airey, Arielle

Aries
(Latin) zodiac sign of the
ram; contentious
Arees

Arista
(Greek) wonderful

Aristelle
(Greek) wonder
Aristela, Aristella

Aritha
(Greek) virtuous
Arete, Aretha

Arizona
(Place name) cowgirl
Zona

Arketta
(Invented) outspoken
Arkett, Arkette, Arky

Arlea
(Greek) heavenly
*Airlea, Arlee, Arleigh,
Arlie, Arly*

Arleana
(American) form of
Arlene; dedicated
Arlena, Arlina

Arlena
(Irish) dedicated
*Arlana, Arlen, Arlenna,
Arlie, Arlina, Arlyna,
Arrlina, Lena, Lina,
Linney*

Arlene
(Irish) dedicated
*Arlee, Arleen, Arlie,
Arline, Arlyne, Arlynn,
Lena, Lina*

Arlette
(French) loyal
Arlet

Armanda
(French) disciplined

Armani, Armonie
(French) fashionable
*Armanee, Armanie,
Armond, Armonee,
Armoni*

Armida
(Latin) armed; prepared
Armi, Armid, Army

Arnette
(English) little eagle;
observant
*Arn, Arnee, Arnet,
Arnett, Ornette*

Arosell
(Last name as first
name) loyal
Arosel

Arpine
(Romanian) dedicated
Arpyne

Arthlese
(Irish) rich
Arth, Arthlice, Artis

Artriece
(Irish) stable
Artee, Artreese, Arty

Arvis
(American) special
Arvee, Arvess, Arvie, Arviss, Arvy

Asabi
(African) outstanding

Asha, Ashra
(Hebrew) lucky
Ashah

Ashandra
(African-American) dreamer
Ashan, Ashandre

Ashanti
(African) place name; graceful
Ashantay, Anshante

Ashantia
(American) outgoing
Ashantea, Ashantiah

Asharaf
(Hindi) wishful
Asha, Ashara

Ashby
(English) farm of ash trees
Ashbee

Ashland
(Irish) dreamlike
Ashelyn, Ashlan, Ashleen, Ashlin, Ashlind, Ashline, Ashlinn

Ashlei
(English) variant of Ashley; pretty
Ashee, Ashie, Ashly, Ashy

Ashley
(English) woodland sprite; meadow of ash trees
Ash, Ashie, Ashlay, Ashlea, Ashlee, Ashleigh, Ashli, Ashlie, Ashly

Ashlyn
(English) natural

Ashonika
(African-American) pretty
Ashon, Ashoneka, Shon

Ashton
(English) place name; from an eastern town; sassy
Ashe, Ashten, Ashtun, Ashtyn

Asia
(Greek) reborn; continent
Ashah, Asiah, Asya, Aysia, Azhuh

Asma
(Arabic) exalted; loyal

Asmay
(Origin unknown) special
Asmae, Asmaye

Asp
(Greek) short for Aspasia; witty

Aspasia
(Greek) witty
Aspashia

Aspen
(Place name) earth mother
Azpen

Asra
(Hindi) pure
Azra

Astera
(Greek) star-like
Asteria, Astra, Astree, Astrie

Astra
(Greek) star
Astrah, Astrey

Astrid
(Scandinavian, German)
beautiful goddess
*Aster, Asti, Astred, Astri,
Atty, Estrid*

Asysa
(Arabic) lively
Aesha, Asha, Aysah

Atalanta
(Greek) athletic; fleet-
footed
Addi, Atlante, Attie

Athalia
(Hebrew) ambitious

AthaSue
(American) combo of
Atha and Sue; sweet and
discriminating
Atha, Athasue, Atha-Sue

Athelean
(Greek) eternal;
precocious
Athey, Athi

Athene
(Chinese) wise

Athena
(Greek) wise woman;
goddess of wisdom in
mythology
*Athene, Athenea, Athina,
Xena, Zena*

Athie
(Hebrew) wise
Athee, Athey, Athy

Atifa
(Arabic) compassionate
Ateefah

Aubrey
(German) noble being;
(French) blonde leader
*Aubery, Aubey, Aubrea,
Aubree, Aubreye, Aubrie,
Aubry*

Auburne
(American) tough-
minded
*Aubee, Aubey, Aubi,
Aubie, Auburn, Auby*

Audie
(French) rich; (American)
daring
*Audee, Audey, Audi,
Audy, Audye*

Audra
(English) exciting
Audrah, Audray

Audrey
(Old English) strong and
regal
*Audi, Audie, Audra,
Audree, Audreen,
Audreye, Audri,
Audrianna, Audrianne,
Audrie, Audrina, Audry*

Augusina
(Latin) great
*Agustico, Agustin,
Augusine, Augustine,
Gusty, Tina, Tino*

Augusta
(Latin) revered
*Augustah, Auguste,
Augustia, Augustyna,
Austina*

Augustine
(Latin) dignified;
worthwhile
*Augestinn, Augusta,
Augustina, Augustyna,
Augustyne, Austie,
Austina, Austine, Tina*

Aunjanue
(French) sparkling

Aunshaunte
(African-American)
believer
*Anshauntay,
Aunshauntay,
Aunshawntay,
Aunshawnte, Shauntae,
Shauntay, Shaunte*

Aura
(Greek) breeze
Arra

Aurease
(Latin) excellent, golden
*Auree, Aureese, Aurey,
Auriece, Aury*

Aurelia, Aurelie
(Latin) dawn goddess
*Arelia, Aura, Auralea,
Aurel, Auria, Auriel,
Aurielle*

Auriel
(Latin) gold
Auriol

Aurora
(Latin) morning glow
Aurorah, Aurore, Rory

Aurysia
(Latin) gold
Arys, Arysia, Aurys

Austen
(Literature) austere
Austyn

Austeena
(American) statuesque
Austeenah, Austie, Austina

Austine, Austin
(Latin) respected
Austen, Austene, Austine

Autra
(Latin) gold
Aut

Autumn
(Latin) joy of changing seasons

Ava
(Latin) pretty; delicate bird
Avah, Eva

Avalon
(Celtic) paradise

Avalynne
(American) combo of Ava and Lynne
Avaline, Avalinn, Avalynn, Avelinn

Avena
(Latin) basic; oat field

Avengelica
(Spanish) avenging
Angelica, Avenga, Avengele, Gelica

Averil
(French) flighty
Ava, Averile, Aviril

Avery
(French) flirtatious
Avary, Averee, Averi, Averie

Avis
(Latin) little bird

Aviana
(Latin) fresh

Avianca
(Latin) fresh

Avisae
(American) springlike
Ava, Avas, Aves, Avi

Aviva
(Hebrew) springlike
Avivah

Avolonne
(African-American) happy
Avalonn, Ave, Avelon, Avlon, Avo, Avolon, Avolunne

Avon
(English) graceful
Avaughn, Avaugn, Avonn, Avonne

Avrit
(Hebrew) fresh
Avie, Avree, Avret, Avrie

Axelle
(French) serene
Axel, Axell

Aya
(Hebrew) bird in flight

Ayan
(Hindi) pure
Ayun

Ayanna
(Hindi) innocent
Ayunna

Ayeisha
(Arabic) feminine
Aeesha, Aieshah, Asha, Ayeeshea, Ayisa, Iasha, Yeisha, Yeishee, Yisha, Yishie

Ayla
(Hebrew) strong as an oak

Aylee
  (Hebrew) light
Ayleen
  (Hebrew) light-hearted
  Aylene
Aylin
  (Spanish) strong
  Aylen
Aylwin
  (Welsh) beloved
  Ayle, Aylwie
Aynona
  (Hebrew) form of Anne;
  graceful
  *Ayn, Aynon, Aynonna,
  Aynonne*
Azenet
  (Spanish) sungod's gift
  Aza, Azey
Azucena
  (Spanish) lily pure
  Azu, Azuce, Azucina
Azura, Azure
  (French) blue-eyed
  Azuhre, Azzura

Babe
  (Latin) little darling;
  baby
Babette
  (French) little Barbara
Babianne
  (American) combo of
  Babi and Anne; fun-
  loving
  *Babi, Babiane, Babyann,
  Biann, Bianne*
Babs
  (American) short for
  Barbara; lively
Bachi
  (Japanese) happy
  *Bachee, Bachey, Bachie,
  Bochee*
Baden, Boden
  (German) friendly
  Bodey
Badger
  (Irish) badger
  Badge
Baek
  (Origin unknown)
  mysterious

Bagent
  (Last name as first
  name) baggage
  Bage
Bagula
  (German) enthused
  Baggy
Bahama
  (Place name) sun-loving
  Baham
Bahati
  (African) lucky girl
  Baha, Bahah
Bahir
  (Arabic) striking
  Bah, Baheer, Bahi
Bai
  (Chinese) outgoing
Baiben
  (Irish) sweet; exotic
  *Babe, Babe, Bai, Baib,
  Baibe, Baibie, Baibin*
Bailey
  (English) bailiff
  Bailee, Baylee, Baylie
Bailon
  (American) variant of
  Bailey; dancing; happy
  Bai, Baye, Baylon
Bain
  (American) thorn; pale
  Baine, Bane, Bayne
Baird
  (Irish) ballad singer
  Bayrde

Baldree
(German) brave; loquacious
Baldry

Bali
(Place name) exotic

Ballou
(American) outspoken
Bailou, Balou

Balvino
(Spanish) powerful
Balvene, Balveno

Bambi
(Italian) childlike; baby girl
Bambee, Bambie, Bamby

Bamp
(American) vivid
Bam, Bampy

Banessa
(American) combo of B and Vanessa; hopeful
B'Nessa, Banesa, Benessa

Bano
(Persian) bride
Bannie, Banny, Banoah, Banoh

Bao
(Chinese) adorable; creative

Bao-Jin
(Chinese) precious gold

Baptista
(Latin) one who baptizes
Battista

Barb
(Latin) short for Barbara

Barbara
(Greek, Latin) unusual stranger
Babette, Babina, Babs, Barb, Barbie, Barbra, Bobbie, Bobi

Barbro
(Swedish) extraordinary
Bar, Barb, Barbar

Barcelona
(Place name) exotic
Barce, Lona

Barcie
(American) sassy
Barsey, Barsi

Barrett
(Last name as first name) happy girl
Bari, Barret, Barrette, Barry, Berrett

Barrie
(Irish) markswoman Feminine form of the masculine Barry
Bari, Barri, Barry

Barron
(Last name as first name) bright
Bare, Baron, Barrie, Beren, Beron

Basey
(Last name as first name) beauty
Bacie, Basi

Baseylea
(American) combo of Basey and Lee; pretty
Basey, Basilea, Basilee, Leelee

Basimah
(Arabic) smiling

Bastienna
(French) from male name Bastien; clever
Bastee, Bastienne

Bathsheba
(Hebrew) beautiful daughter of Sheba
Sheba

Bathshira
(Arabic) happy; seventh

Batia, Batya
(Hebrew) daughter of God
Batea

Batice
(American) warrior; attractive
Bateese, Batese, Batiece, Batty

Bay
(Vietnamese) Saturday's child; patient; unique
Bae, Baye

Bayo
(African) bringing joy

Baynes
(American) from male name Baines; confident
Bain, Baines, Bayne

Bayonne
(Greek) joyful victor
Bay, Baye, Bayonn, Bayonna, Bayunn

Bea
(American) short for Beatrice

Beata
(German) blessed
Bayahta

Beatrice
(Latin) blessed woman, joyful
Beat, Beata, Beatrise, Bibi, Treece, Trice

Beatrix
(Latin) happy

Beatriz
(American) joy

Bebe
(French) baby
Babee, Baby, Bebee

Becca
(Hebrew) short for Rebecca; lively
Bekka

Bechet
(French)

Becky
(English) short for Rebecca; spunky
Becki, Beki

Bedelia
(Irish) form of Bridget; powerful

Beegee
(American) laidback; calm
B.G., Begee, Be-Gee

Bee-Sun
(Filipino) nature-loving; glad
Bee Sun

Bego
(Hispanic) spunky
Beago

Begonia
(Botanical) flower

Behorah
(Invented) friend
Be, Behi, Behie, Behora

Beige
(American) simple; calm
Bayge

Beige-Dawn
(American) clear morning
Bayge-Dawn, Beige Dawn

Beila
(Spanish) beautiful

Beilarosa
(Spanish) combo of Beila and Rosa; beautiful rose
Beila, Beila-Rosa, Beila-Rose, Beiliarose, Rose

Bela
(Czech) white
Belah

Belanie
(Invented) combo of B and Melanie; lovely
Bela, Belan, Belanee, Belaney, Belani, Belle

Belann, Belan
(Spanish) pretty
Bela, Belana, Belane, Belanna

Belem
(Spanish) pretty
Bel, Beleme, Bella

Belgica
(American) white
Belgika, Belgike, Belgyke, Bellgica

Belia
(Spanish) beauty
Belea, Beliano, Belya, Belyah

Belicia
(Spanish) believer
Belia

Belinda
(Latin, Spanish)
beautiful serpent
Belynda

Belita
(Spanish) pretty little
one; (French) beauty

Bella
(Italian) beautiful

Bellace
(Invented) pretty
Bellase, Bellece, Bellice

Belle
(French) beautiful
Bele, Bell

Bellina
(French) beautiful

Belva
(Latin) beautiful view

Belvia
(Invented) practical
*Bell, Belva, Belve,
Belveah*

Bendite
(Latin) well blessed
*Ben, Bendee, Bendi,
Bennie, Benny, Binni*

Benecia
(Latin) short for Benedicta

Benedicta
(Latin) woman blessed
Benna, Benni

Beneva
(American) combo of
Ben and Eva; kind
*Benevah, Benna, Benni,
Bennie, Benny, Bineva*

Bening
(Filipino) blessing

Benita
(Latin, Spanish) lovely
Benetta

Benni
(Latin) short for
Benedicta; blessed
Bennie, Binny

Bente
(Latin) blessed

Berdina
(German) bright; robust
*Berd, Berdie, Berdine,
Berdyne, Burdine,
Burdynne, Dina, Dine*

Bergen
(American) pretty
Berg, Bergin

Berget
(Irish) form of Bridget
Bergette

Berit
(Scandinavian) glorious
Beret, Berette

Berkley
(American) smart
*Berkeley, Berkie, Berklie,
Berkly*

Berlynn
(English) combo of
Bertha and Lynn
Berla, Berlinda, Berlyn

Bermuda
(Place name) personable
Bermudoh

Bernadette
(French) form of
Bernadine
Berna, Berneta

Bernadine
(German) brave;
(English) feminine form
of Bernard
*Bernadene, Berni,
Bernie*

Bernice
(Greek) victorious
Berneta, Berni

Berry
(Nature name) tiny;
succulent
Berree, Berrie

Bersaida
(American) sensitive
*Bersaid, Bersaide,
Bersey, Bersy, Sada,
Saida*

Bertha
(German) bright
*Barta, Berta, Berte,
Berthe, Bertie, Bertita,
Berty*

Bertie
(German) bright
Bert, Bertee, Bertey, Berty

Bertina
(German) shining bright; feminine form of masculine Bert

Berule
(Greek) bright; pure
Berue, Berulle

Beryl
(Greek) bright and shining gem
Berlie, Berri, Beryle, Beryn

Bess
(Hebrew) form of Elizabeth
Bessie

Bet
(Hebrew) daughter

Beth
(Hebrew) form of Elizabeth

Betha
(Welsh) devoted to God
Bethah, Bethanne

Bethann
(English); combo of Beth and Ann; devout
B-Anne, Bethan, Beth-ann, Bethanne

Bethany
(Hebrew) God's disciple
Beth, Bethani, Bethania, Bethanie, Betheny, Bethina

Beti
(English) small woman

Betriss
(Welsh) blessed
Betrys

Betsy
(Hebrew) form of Elizabeth
Bet, Betsey, Betsi, Betsie, Betts

Bette
(French) lively; God-loving

Bettina
(Spanish) combo of Beth and Tina
Betina, Betti, Bettine

Betty
(Hebrew) God-loving; form of Elizabeth
Bett, Betti, Bettye

Betula
(Hebrew) dedicated; religious
Bee , Bet, Bett, Betulah

Beulah
(Hebrew) married
Beula, Bew, Bewla

Bev
(English) short for Beverly; friendly

Beverly
(English) beaver stream; friendly
Bev, Beverlee, Beverley, Beverlie, Bevvy, Verly

Bevina
(Irish) vocalist
Beavena, Bev, Beve, Beven, Bevena, Bevy, Bovana

Bevinn
(Irish) royal
Bevan

Bianca
(Italian) white
Beonca, Beyonca, Biancha, Biancia, Bionca, Blanca

Bibi
(Arabic, Latin, French) girl; lively
Bebe

Bijou
(French) saucy
Bejeaux, Bejou, Bejue, Bidge, Bija, Bijie, Bijy

Bik
(Chinese) jade

Bikini
(Place name) fun-loving
Bikinee

Billie
(German) form of
Wilhelmina; (English)
strong-willed
Billa, Billee, Billy, Billye

Billie-Jean
(American) combo of
Billie and Jean
Billie Jean, Billijean

Billie-Jo
(American) combo of
Billie and Jo
Billie Jo, Billyjo

Billie-Sue
(American) combo of
Billie and Sue
Billie Sue, Billysue

Billina
(English) from male
name Bill; kind
*Belli, Bill, Billee, Billie,
Billy*

Billings
(American) bright
*Billey, Billie, Billing, Billy,
Billye, Billyngs, Byllings*

Bina
(Hebrew) perceptive
woman

Binase
(Hebrew) bright
*Beanase, Benace, Bina,
Binah, Binahse*

Bionda
(Italian) black
Beonda, Biondah

Bird
(English)
Birdy

Birdie
(English) bird
Birdee, Birdi

Birgit
(Scandinavian)
spectacular
*Bergette, Berit, Birgetta,
Birgite, Britta, Byrget,
Byrgitt*

Birgitta
(Swedish) excellent
splendor
*Birgette, Brita, Byrgetta,
Byrgitta*

Birte
(Scandinavian) form of
Bridget; powerful
*Berty, Birt, Birtey, Byrt,
Byrtee*

Bishop
(Last name as first
name) loyal
Byshop

Bitsie
(American) small
*Bitsee, Bitzee, Bitzi,
Bytsey*

Bitta
(Scandinavian) variant of
Bridget; excellent
Bit, Bitt, Bittey

Bivona
(African-American) feisty
*BeBe, Biv, Bivon,
Bivonne*

Bjork
(Icelandic) unique
Byork

Blaine
(Irish) thin
Blane, Blayne

Blair
(Scottish) plains-dweller
Blaire

Blaise
(Latin, French)
stammerer
Blaize, Blase, Blaze

Blake
(English) dark

Blakely
(English) dark
*Blakelee, Blakeley,
Blakeli*

Blanca
(Spanish) white
*Blancah, Blonka,
Blonkah*

Blanche
(French) white
*Blanca, Blanch,
Blanchette*

Blanda
(Latin) seductive
Bless
(American) blessed
Blessie
Bleu
(French) blue
Blue
Bliss
(English) blissful girl
Blondie
(American) blonde
Blondee
Blondelle
(French) fair of hair
Blondie
Blossom
(English) flower
Bluebell
(Flower name) pretty
Belle, Blu, Blubel,
Blubell, Blue
Blush
(American) pink-cheeked
Blushe
Bly
(American) soft; sensual
Blye
Blythe
(English) carefree
Blithe, Blyth
Bo
(Chinese) precious girl

Boanah
(American) good
Boana, Bonaa, Bonah,
Bonita
Bobbi
(American) form of
Barbara
Bobbie, Bobby, Bobbye,
Bobi
Bobbiechristine
(American) combo of
Bobbie and Christine
BobbiChris,
Bobbichristine, Bobbie-
Christine
Bobbi-Ann
(American) combo of
Bobbi and Ann
Bobbiann, Bobbyann,
Bobbyanne
Bobbi-Jo
(American) combo of
Bobbi and Jo
Bobbiejo, Bobbijo,
Bobijo
Bobbi-Lee
(American) combo of
Bobbi and Lee
Bobbilee, Bobbylee
Bobby-Kay
(American) combo of
Bobby and Kay
Bobbikay

Bobby-Sue
(American) combo of
Bobby and Sue
Bobbisue, Boby-Sue
Bogdana
(Polish) gift from God
Bogda, Bogna
Bola
(Origin unknown) clever
Bolo
Bona
(Latin, Italian, Polish,
Spanish) good
Bonah, Bonna
Bonda
(Spanish) good
Bona
Bonita
(Spanish) good; pretty
Bona, Bonitah
Bonn
(Place name) satisfied
Bon, Bonne
Bonnevie
(Scandinavian) good life
Bonnie, Bonny
(English, Scottish) pretty
face
Boni, Bonnee, Bonni
Bonnie-Bell
(American) combo of
Bonnie and Belle; lovely
Bonnebell, Bonnebelle,
Bonnibelle

Bootsey
(American) cowgirl
Boots, Bootsie

Bors
(Latin) foreign
Borse

Boston
(American) courteous
Boste, Bosten, Bostin

Boswell
(Last name as first name) intellectual
Boz, Bozwell

Bowdy
(American) outgoing
Bow, Bowdee, Bowdey, Bowdie

Braisly
(American) cautious
Braise, Braislee, Braize, Braze

Brandy
(Dutch) after-dinner drink; fun-loving
Bran, Brande, Brandea, Brandee, Brandeli, Brandi, Brandye, Brandyn, Brani

Brandy-Lynn
(American) combo of Brandy and Lynn
Brandelyn, Brandilynn, Brandlin, Brandy-Lyn

Branka
(Czech) glory
Bran, Branca, Bronca, Bronka

Brayden
(American) humorous
Braden, Brae, Braeden, Bray, Brayd, Braydan, Braydon

Breana
(Irish) form of Briana
Bre-Anna, Breeana

Breann
(Irish) form of Briana
Bre-Ann, Bree, Breean, Breeann

Breck
(Irish) freckled

Bree
(Irish) upbeat
Brea, Brie

Breena
(Irish) glowing
Brena

Breeshonna
(African-American) happy-go-lucky
Bree, Brie, Brieshona

Breezy
(American) easygoing
Breezee, Breezie

Brehea
(American) self-sufficient
Breahay, Brehae, Brehay

Bren
(American) short for Brenda
Breyn

Brenda
(Irish) royal; glowing
Brenna, Brinda, Brindah, Brinna

Brenda-Lee
(American) combo of Brenda and Lee
Brandalee, Brindlee, Brinlee

Brendette
(French) small and royal

Brendie
(American) form of Brenda
Brendee, Brendi

Brendelle
(American) distinctive

Brendolyn
(Invented) combo of Brenda and Madolyn; intelligent
Brend, Brendo, Brendolynn, Brendy

Brenna
(Irish) form of Brenda; dark-haired
Bren, Brenn, Brenie

Brett
(Latin) jolly
Bret, Bretta, Brette

Breyawna
(African-American)
variant of Brianna
Bryawn, Bryawna,
Bryawne

Bria
(Irish) short for Briana;
pure; spirited

Briana
(Irish) virtuous; strong
Breana, Breann, Bria,
Brianna, Briannah, Brie-
Ann, Bryanna

Brianne
(Irish) strong
Briane, Brienne, Bryn

Briar
(French) heather
Brear, Brier

Briar-Rose
(Literature: *Sleeping*
Beauty) princess
Briar, Rose

Brice
(English) quick

Briceidy
(English) precocious
Brice, Bricedi, Briceidee,
Briceidey

Bridey
(Irish) wise
Bredee, Breedee, Bride,
Bryde

Bridget
(Irish) powerful
Birgitt, Bridge,
Bridgette, Bridgey,
Briget, Brigette, Brigid,
Brijette, Brygett

Brie
(French) from Rozay-en-
Brie, a town in France
known for its cheese
Bree, Brielle

Brielle
(Invented) combo of Bri
and Elle
Briell, Bryelle

Briesha
(African-American)
giving
Bri, Brieshe

Brigidine
(Invented) combo of
Brigit and Dine (from
Geraldine)
Brige, Brigid

Bril
(American) strong
Brill

Briley
(Last name as first
name) popular
BeBe, Bri, Brile

Brina
(Latin) short for Sabrina

Brinlee
(American) sweetheart
Brendlie, Brenlee, Brenly

Brionna
(Irish) happy
Breona, Briona

Brinkelle
(American) independent
nature
Binkee, Binky, Brinkee,
Brinkel, Brinkell, Brinkie

Brisa
(Spanish) beloved; In
mythology, the loved
one of Achilles
Breza, Brissa

Brisco
(American) high-energy
woman
Briscoe, Briss, Brissie,
Brissy

Brissellies
(Spanish) happy
Briselle, Briss, Brisse,
Brissel, Brissell, Brissey,
Brissi, Brissies

Britaney
(English) place name
Britanee, Britani,
Briteny, Brittaney,
Brittenie, Britnee,
Britney, Britni

Britt
(Latin) from Britain
Brit

Britta

(Swedish) strong woman
Brita

Brittany

(English) place name; trendy
Briteney, Britni, Brittaney

Bronte

(Literature) romantic
Brontae, Brontay

Bronwyn

(Welsh) white-breasted
Bron, Bronwen, Bronwhen, Bronwynn

Brook

(English) sophisticated
Brooke, Brooky

Brooklyn

(Place name) combo of Brook and Lynn
Brookelyn, Brookelynn, Brooklynn, Brooklynne

Browning

(Literature) romantic

Bruenetta

(French) brown-haired
Bru, Brunetta

Bruneita

(German) brown-haired
Broon, Brune, Bruneite, Brunny

Brunella

(German) intelligent
Brun, Brunela, Brunilla, Brunne

Brunhilda

(German) warrior
Brunhilde, Hilda

Bryanna

(Gaelic) powerful female
Breanna, Brianna, Bryana

Bryanta

(American) form of male name Bryan; strong
Brianta, Bryan, Bryianta

Bryce

(American) happy
Brice

Bryleigh

(English) spinoff of Brittany; jovial
Brilee, Briley, Brily, Brilye, Brylee, Brylie

Bryn

(Welsh) hopeful; climbing a hill
Brenne, Brynnie

Brynn

(Welsh) hopeful
Brenn, Brinn, Brynne

Brynna

(Welsh) optimistic
Brinn, Brinna

Bryonie

(Latin) clinging vine
Breeonee, Brioni, Bryony

Bua

(Vietnamese) fortunate
Boo, Bu

Bubbles

(American) saucy
Bubb

Buffy

(American) plains-dweller
Buffee, Buffey, Buffie

Bukola

(Origin unknown)
Bucola

Bunard

(American) good
Bunerd, Bunn, Bunny

Bunny

(English) little rabbit; bouncy
Bunnee, Bunnie

Burgundy

(French) red wine; unique
Burgandi, Burgandy

Burke

(American) loud
Berk, Burk, Burkie

Burns
(Last name as first name) presumptuous
Bernes, Berns, Burn, Burnee, Burnes, Burney, Burni, Burny

Butter
(American) sweet
Budter

Buzzie
(American) spirited
Buzz, Buzzi

Bwyana
(African-American) smart
Bwya, Bwyanne

Byronae
(American) form of Byron; smart
Byrona, Byronay

Cabriole
(French) adorable
Cabb, Cabby, Cabriolle, Kabriole

Cachay
(African-American) distinctive

Cachet
(French) fetching
Cache, Cachee

Cade
(American) precocious
Kade, Kaid

Cadence
(American) hip
Kadence

Cady
(English) fun-loving
Cadee, Cadey, Cadye, Caidee, Caidy, Kadee, Kady

Cai
(Chinese) wealthy; girlish

Cailin
(American) happy
Cayleen, Caylin, Caylyn, Caylynne

Cairo
(Place name) Egypt's capital; confident
Kairo, Kiero

Cait
(Greek) purest
Cate, Kate

Caitlin
(Irish) virginal
Cailin, Caitleen, Caitlinn, Caitlyn, Catlin, Catlyn, Catlynne

Cala, Calla
(Arabic) strong
Callah

Calandra
(Greek) lark
Calendra, Kalandra

Calantha
(Greek) gorgeous flower
Calanth, Calanthe, Calli

Cale
(Latin) respected
Kale

Caledonia
(Latin) from Scotland; worthy
Kaledonia

Caley
(American) warm
Caleigh, Kaylee

Calhoun
(Last name as first name) surprising

California
(Place name) hip; cool
Callie, Kalifornia, Kallie

Calinda
(American) combo of Cal and Linda
Cal, Calenda, Calli, Callie, Cally, Kalenda, Kalinda

Caliopa
(Greek, Spanish) singing beautifully
Kaliopa

Calista
(Greek) most beautiful
Calysta, Kali, Kalista, Kalli, Kallista

Calla
(Greek) beautiful
Cala, Callie, Cally

Callie
(Greek) beautiful
Caleigh, Callee, Calley, Calli, Cally, Kali, Kallee, Kallie

Calliope
(Greek) muse; poetic
Kalliope

Callison
(American) combo of Calli and Allison; pretty offspring
Cal, Calli, Callice, Callis, Callisen, Callisun

Calypso
(Greek mythology) sea nymph who held Odysseus captive

Cam
(American) short for Cameron
Cami, Camie, Cammie

Cambay
(Place name) saucy
Cambaye, Kambay

Camber
(American) spinoff of Amber; has potential
Cambie, Cambre, Cammy, Kamber

Cambree
(Place name) from Cambria, Wales; ingenious
Cambrie, Cambry, Cambry, Kambree, Kambrie

Camden
(American) glorious face
Cam, Camdon, Cammi, Cammie, Cammy

Cameka
(African-American) form of Tameka/Tamika
Cammey, Cammi, Cammy, Kameka, Kammy

Camellia
(Italian) flower
Camelia, Kamelia

Camelot
(English) elegant
Cam, Cami, Camie, Camy

Cameo
(French) piece of jewelry; singular
Cameoh, Cammie, Kameo

Camera
(Word as name) stunning
Kamera

Camerino
(Spanish) unblemished
Cam, Cammy

Cameron
(Scottish) popular (crooked nose)
Cameran, Camren, Camryn, Kameron, Kamryn

Cami
(French) short for
Camille, Camilla,
Cameron
*Camey, Camie, Cammie,
Cammy*

Camilla
(Latin, Italian) wonderful
Camila, Camillia

Camille
(French) swift runner;
great innocence
*Camila, Cammille,
Cammy, Camylle, Kamille*

Camp
(American) hip
Cam, Campy

Campbell
(Last name as first
name) amazing
*Cam, Cambell, Camey,
Cami, Camie, Camy*

Camrin
(American) variant of
Cameron
Camren, Camryn

Canada
(Place name) decisive
Cann, Kanada

Candace
(Greek) glowing girl
*Candice, Candis, Candys,
Kandace*

Candelara
(Spanish) spiritual
*Cande, Candee,
Candelaria, Candi,
Candy, Lara*

Candida
(Latin) white

Candra
(Latin) she who glows
Candria, Kandra

Candy
(American) short for
Candace
Candee, Candi, Candie

Cannes
(French) place name
Can, Kan

Cantara
(Arabic) bridge
Canta, Kanta, Kantara

Capelta
(American) fanciful
Capeltah, Capp, Cappy

Caplice
(American) spontaneous
*Capleece, Capleese,
Kapleese*

Capri
(Italian) island off coast
of Italy
Caprie, Kapri

Caprice
(Italian) playful;
capricious
*Caprece, Capreese,
Capricia, Caprise*

Capucine
(French) cloak
Cappy

Car
(American) zany
Carr, Kar, Karr

Cara
(Latin, Italian) dear one
Carah, Kara

Caramia
(Italian) my dear
Cara Mia, Cara-Mia

Cardia
(Spanish) giving
Candi, Kardia

Carenleigh
(American) combo of
Caren and Leigh
Caren-Leigh

Carey
(Welsh) by a castle; fond
Caree, Cari, Carrie, Cary

Caridad
(Spanish) giving
Cari

Carina
(Greek, Italian) dearest
*Careena, Carena, Carin,
Carine, Kareena, Karina*

Carissa
(Greek, Italian) beloved
Carisa, Karessa, Karissa

Carita
(Latin) giving; loved
Caritta, Karita

Caritina
(Spanish) combo of Cari and Tina; dearest
Cari, Cartine, Tina

Carla
(German) feminine of Charles, Carl, Carlo
Carlah, Carlia, Karla

Carlee
(German) darling
Carleigh, Carley, Carli, Carly, Karlee, Karley

Carlene
(American) sweet
Carleen

Carlanda
(American) darling
Carlan, Carland, Carlande, Carlee, Carlie, Carly, Karlanda

Carlett
(Spanish) affectionate
Carle, Carlet, Carletta, Carlette, Carley, Carli

Carlin
(Latin, German) winner
Caline, Carlan, Carlen

Carlisle
(Place name) sharp
Carlile, Carrie, Karlisle

Carlisa
(Italian) combo of Carla and Lisa; fond of friends
Carlie, Carlissa, Carly, Carlysa, Karlese, Karlisa

Carlissa
(American) pleasant
Carleeza, Carlisse

Carlotta
(Italian, Spanish) feminine form of Carlo and Carlos; sweetheart
Karlotta

Carly
(German) darling
Carlee, Carley, Carli, Carlie, Karlee

Carma
(Hebrew) short for Carmel; special garden
Car, Carmee, Carmi, Carmie, Karma

Carmel
(Hebrew) place name; garden
Carmela, Carmella, Karmel

Carmela
(Hebrew, Italian) fruitful
Carmalla, Carmel, Carmella, Carmie, Carmilla

Carmen
(Hebrew) crimson
Carma, Carman, Carmela, Carmelinda, Carmita, Carmynne, Chita, Mela, Melita

Carmensita
(Spanish) dear girl
Carma, Carmens, Carmense, Karmence

Carmine
(Italian) sexy
Carmyne, Karmine

Carminia
(Italian) dearest
Carma, Carmine, Carmynea, Karm, Karminia, Karmynea

Carnation
(Latin) flower
Carn, Carna, Carnee, Carney, Carny

Carnethia
(Invented) fragrant
Carnee, Carney, Carnithia, Karnethia

Carnie
(American) happy
Carni, Karni, Karnie

Carody
(American) humorous
*Caridee, Caridey,
Carodee, Carodey,
Carrie, Karodee, Karody*

Carol
(English) feminine;
(French) joyful song;
(German) farming
woman
*Carole, Carroll, Caryl,
Karol, Karrole*

Carolanne
(American) combo of
Carol and Anne
Carolane, Carolann

Carole
(French) a joyous song
Karol, Karole

Carolina
(Italian) feminine
Carrolena, Karolina

Caroline
(German) petite woman
*Caraline, Carilene,
Cariline, Caroleen,
Carolin, Karalyn, Karoline*

Carolyn
(English) womanly
*Carilyn, Carilynn,
Carolyne, Carolynn,
Karolyn*

Caron
(Welsh) giving heart
Carron, Karon

Caronsy
(American) form of
Caron; sweet
*Caronnsie, Caronsi,
Karonsy*

Carrelle
(American) lively
Carrele

Carrie
(French, English) joyful
song
*Carey, Cari, Carri, Carry,
Kari*

Carson
(Nordic) dramatic
*Carse, Carsen, Carsun,
Karrson, Karsen, Karson*

Carylan
(American) combo of
Caryl and An; soft
*Carolann, Caryland,
Carylanna, Karylan*

Caryn
(Danish) form of Karen
*Caren, Carrin, Caryne,
Carynn*

Carys
(Welsh) love

Casey
(Greek, Irish) attentive
female
*Casie, Cassee, Cassey,
Casy, Caysee, Caysie,
Caysy, Kasey*

Cashonya
(African-American)
monied; lively
Kashonya

Casielee
(American) combo of
Casie and Lee; popular
*Caseylee, Casie Lee,
Casielea, Casie-Lee,
Casieleigh*

Casilde
(Spanish) combative
*Casilda, Casill, Cass,
Cassey, Cassie*

Cason
(Greek) seer; spirited
Case, Casey, Kason

Cassandra
(Greek) insightful
*Casandra, Casandria,
Cass, Cassie, Cassondra,
Kassandra*

Cassia
(Greek) spicy; cinnamon

Cassidy
(Irish) clever girl
Casadee, Cass,
Cassidee, Cassidi,
Kassidy

Cassie
(Greek) short for
Cassandra; tricky
Cassey, Cassi

Cassiopeia
(Greek) starry-eyed
Cass, Cassi, Kass,
Kassiopia

Catalina
(Spanish) pure
Catalena, Katalena,
Katalina

Catarina
(Greek, Italian) pure
Katarina

Cather
(Literature) earthy
Kather

Catherine
(Greek, Irish, English)
pure
Cartharine, Cathrine,
Cathryn, Katherine

Cathleen
(Irish) pure
Cathelin, Cathleyn,
Cathlinne, Cathlyn,
Cathy

Cathresha
(African-American) pure;
outspoken
Cathrisha, Cathy,
Kathresha, Resha

Cathryn
(Greek) pure female;
form of Catherine

Cathy
(Greek) pure
Cathee, Cathey, Cathie,
Kathy

Catline
(Irish) form of Caitlin;
virtuous
Cataleen, Catalena,
Catleen, Catlen, Katline

Catrice
(Greek) form of
Catherine; wholesome
Catrece, Catreece,
Catreese, Katreece,
Katrice

Catrina
(Greek) pure
Catreena, Catreene,
Catrene, Katrina

Cavender
(American) emotional
Cav, Cavey, Kav,
Kavender

Cayenne
(Spice name) peppery

Caykee
(American) combo of
Cay and Kee; lively
Caycay, Caykie, Kaykee,
Kee

Cayla
(Hebrew) unblemished
Cailie, Calee, Cayley,
Caylie, Kayla

Cayley
(American) joyful
Caelee, Caeley, Cailey,
Cailie, Caylea, Caylee,
Cayleigh

Caylisa
(American) combo of
Cay and Lisa;
lighthearted
Cayelesa, Cayl, Cay-Lisa,
Caylise, Kayl, Kaylisa

Cayman
(Place name) the
islands; islander spirit
Caman, Caymanne,
Kayman

Cayne
(American) generous
Cain, Kaine

Ceaskarshenna
(African-American)
ostentatious
Ceaskar, Karshenna,
Shenna

Ceci
(Latin) short for Cecilia; dignity
Cecile
(Latin) short for Cecilia; genteel
Cecily
Cecilia
(Latin, Polish) blind; dim-sighted
Cacelia, Cece, Cecelia, Ceil, Celia, Cice, Cicilia, Cilley, Secilia, Sissy
Cedrice
(American) form of male name Cedric; feisty
Ced, Cedrise
Ceil
(Latin) blythe
Ceel, Ciel
Celand
(Latin) heavenward
Cel, Cela, Celanda, Celle
Celebration
(American) word as name; celebrant
Cela, Sela
Celena
(Greek) heavenly; form of Selena
Celeena, Celene
Celery
(Food name) refreshing
Cel, Celeree, Celree, Celry, Sel, Selery, Selry

Celeste
(Latin) gentle and heavenly
Celest, Celestial, Seleste
Celestia
(Latin) heavenly
Celeste, Celestea, Celestiah, Seleste, Selestia
Celestyna
(Polish) heavenly
Cela, Celeste, Celesteenah, Celestinah, Celestyne
Celina
(Greek) loving; form of Celena
Selina, Celena
Celine
(Greek) lovely
Celeen, Celene
Celka
(Latin) celestial
Celk, Celkee, Celkie, Selk, Selka
Celkee
(Latin) form of Celeste; sweet
Celkea, Celkie, Cell, Selkee
Cena
(English) special
Cenna, Sena

Cera
(French) colorful
Cerea
(Greek) thriving
Serea
Ceres
(Latin) joyful
Cerise
(French) cherry red
Cerese, Cerice, Cerrice, Ceryce
Cesary
(Polish) outspoken
Cesarie, Cezary, Ceze
Cesia
(Spanish) celestial
Cesea, Sesia
Chablis
(French) white wine
Chabli
Chacita
(Spanish) lively girl
Chaca, Chacie, Chaseeta, Chaseta
Chadee
(French) goddess
Shadee
Chaemarique
(Invented) combo of Chae and Marique; pretty
Chae, Chaemareek, Marique, Shaymarique

Chafin
(Last name as first name) sure-footed
Chaffin, Shafin

Chai
(Hebrew) life-giving
Chae, Chaeli

Chaka-Khan
(Invented) singer

Chakra
(Sanskrit) energy
Chak, Chaka, Chakara, Chakyra

Chala
(African-American) exuberant
Chalah, Chalee, Chaley, Chalie

Chalette
(American) good taste
Chalett, Challe, Challie, Shalette

Chalice
(French) a goblet; toasting
Chalace, Chalece, Chalyse, Chalyssie

Chaline
(American) smiling
Chacha, Chaleen, Chalene

Chalis
(African-American) sunny disposition
Chal, Chaleese, Chalise

Chalissa
(African-American) optimistic
Chalisa, Chalysa, Chalyssa

Challie
(American) charismatic
Challee, Challi, Chally

Chalondra
(African-American) pretty
Chacha, Chalon, Chalondrah, Cheilonndra, Chelondra

Chalsey
(American) variation of Chelsea
Chalsea, Chalsee, Chalsi, Chalsie, Chalsie

Chambray
(French) fabric; hardy
Chambree

Champagne
(French) wine; luxurious

Chana
(Hindi) moon-like

Chanah
(Hebrew) graceful
Chanach, Channah

Chanal
(American) moon-like

Chanda
(Hindi) moon goddess
Chandi, Chandie, Shanda

Chandelle
(French) candle-lighter
Chandal, Shandalle, Shandel

Chandler
(English) romantic; candle-maker
Chandlee, Shandler

Chandra
(Hindi) of the moon
Chandre, Shandra, Shandre

Chanel
(French) fashionable; designer name
Chan, Chanell, Chanelle, Channel, Shanel, Shanell, Shanelle

Chanelle
(American) stylish
Shanell, Shanelle

Chaney
(English) short for Chandler; cute
Chanie, Chaynee, Chayney

Chanicka
(African-American) loved
Chaneeka, Chani, Chanika, Nicka, Nika, Shanicka

Chanise
(American) adored
Chanese, Shanise

Channing
(Last name as first name) clever
Chanon
(American) shining
Chanen, Chann, Chanun
Chansanique
(African-American) girl singing
Chansan, Chansaneek, Chansani, Chansanike, Shansanique
Chantal
(French) singer of songs
Chandal, Chantale, Chantalle, Chante, Chantee, Chantel, Chantell, Chantelle, Chantile, Chantille, Chawntelle, Shanta, Shantel, Shawntel, Shontelle
Chantee
(American) singer
Chantey, Chanti, Chantie, Shantee, Shantey
Chanti
(American) melodious
Chantee, Chantie
Chantilly
(French) beautiful lace
Chantille, Shantilly

Chantrice
(French) singer of songs
Shantreece, Treece
Chanyce
(American) risk-taker
Chance, Chancie, Chaneese, Chaniece, Chanycey
Chaquanne
(African-American) sassy
Chaq, Chaquann, Shakwan
Charanne
(American) combo of Char and Anne; charitable
Charann, Cherann
Charbonnet
(French) loving and giving
Charbonay, Charbonet, Charbonnay, Sharbonet, Sharbonnet
Charde
(French) wine
Charday, Chardea, Shardae
Chardonnay
(French) white wine
Char, Chardonee, Shardonnay

Charille
(French) variant of Charlotte; feminine; delightful
Char, Chari, Charill, Shar, Sharille
Charis
(Greek) graceful
Charice, Charisse
Charish
(American) cherished
Chareesh
Charisma
(American) charming
Char, Karismah
Charissa
(Greek) giving
Char, Charesa, Charisse, Charissey
Charita
(Spanish) sweet
Cherita
Charity
(Latin) loving; affectionate
Carisa, Charis, Chariti, Sharity
Charla
(French) from Charlotte; feminine
Char
Charlaine
(English) small woman; form of Charlene
Charlane

Charlana
(American) form of
Charlene; feminine
Chalanna

Charlene
(French) petite and
beautiful
*Charla, Charlaine,
Charleen, Sharlene*

Charlesetta
(German) form of
Charles; royal
Charlesette, Charlsetta

Charlesia
(American) form of
Charles; royal; womanly
*Charlese, Charlisce,
Charlise, Charlsie,
Charlsy, Sharlesia*

Charlesey
(American) expansive;
generous
*Charlesee, Charlie,
Charlsie, Charlsy*

Charlianne
(American) combo of
Charlie and Anne
Charlann, Charleyann

Charlie
(American) easygoing
*Charl, Charlee, Charley,
Charli*

Charlize
(American) pretty

Charlotte
(French) little woman
*Carly, Charla, Charle,
Charlott, Charolot*

Charlottie
(French) small
Charlotty

Charlsheah
(American) happy

Charluce
(American) form of
Charles; feminine; royal
Charl, Charla, Charluse

Charm
(Greek) short for
Charmian; charming
*Charma, Charmay,
Sharm*

Charmaine
(Latin) womanly;
(French) singer
*Charma, Charmagne,
Charmane, Charmine,
Charmyn, Sharmaine,
Sharmane, Sharmayne,
Sharmyne*

Charmine
(French) charming
Charmen, Charmin

Charminique
(African-American)
dashing
Charmineek

Charmonique
(African-American)
charming
*Charm, Charmi,
Charmon, Charmoneek,
Charmoni, Charmonik,
Sharmonique*

Charnee
(American) effervescent
Charney, Charnie, Charny

Charneeka
(African-American)
obsessive
Charn, Charnika, Charny

Charnelle
(American) sparkling
*Charn, Charnel, Charnell,
Charney, Sharnell,
Sharnelle*

Charnesa
(African-American)
noticed
Charnessa, Charnessah

Charo
(Spanish) flower
Charro

Charsetta
(American) form of
Charlene; emotional
*Charsee, Charsette,
Charsey, Charsy*

Chartra
(American) classy
Chartrah

Chartres
(French) planner
Chartrys

Charysse
(Greek) graceful girl
Charece, Charese,
Charisse

Chassie
(Latin) form of Chastity;
virtuous
Chass, Chassey, Chassi

Chastity
(Latin) pure woman
Chasta, Chastitie

Chaucer
(English) demure
Chauser, Chawcer,
Chawser

Chava
(Hebrew) life-giving
Chavah, Chave, Hava

Chaviva
(Hebrew) beloved

Chaya
(Jewish) living

Chayan
(Native American)
variant of Cheyenne;
tribe
Chay, Chayanne, Chi,
Shayan, Shy

Chea
(American) witty
Chea, Cheeah

Cheer
(American) joyful

Chekia
(Invented) cheeky
Chekie, Shekia

Cheletha
(African-American)
smiling
Chelethe, Cheley

Chelle
(American) short for
Chelsea; secure
Shell

Chelsea
(Old English) safe harbor
Chelcy, Cheli, Chellsie,
Chelse, Chelsee, Chelsey,
Chelsie, Kelsey, Shelsee

Chenille
(American) soft
Chenile, Chinille

Chenoa
(American) form of
Genoa
Cheney, Cheno

Cher
(French) dear
Sher

Cherelle
(French) dear
Charell, Cherrelle,
Sharelle

Cherie
(French) dear
Cherey, Cheri, Cherice,
Cherree, Cherrie, Cherry

Cherika
(French) form of Cherry;
kind; dear
Chereka, Cherikah

Cherilynn
(American) combo of
Cheryl and Lynn; kind-
hearted
Cheryl-Lynn, Cherylynne,
Sherilyn, Sherilynn,
Sherralin

Cherinne
(American) happy
Charinn, Cherin, Cherry

Cherise
(French) cherry
Cherece, Cherrise

Cherish
(French) precious girl
Charish, Cherishe,
Sherishe

Cherisha
(American) endearing
Cherishah, Cherishuh

Cherita
(Spanish) dearest
Cheritt, Cheritta, Cherrita

Cheritte
(American) held dear
Cher, Cherette, Cheritta

Cherly
(American) form of
Shirley; natural; bright
meadow
Cherlee, Sherly

Cherlyn
(American) combo of
Cher and Lyn; dear one
*Cherlin, Cherlinn,
Cherlynn, Cherlynne*

Cherokee
(Native American) Indian
tribe member

Cherron
(American) graceful
dancer
Cher, Cheron, Cherronne

Cherry
(Latin, French) cherry red
*Cheree, Cherey, Cherrye,
Chery*

Cherrylee
(French, American)
combo of Cherry and
Lee; lively
*Charalee, Charralee,
Cheralee, Cherilea,
Cherilee, Cherileese,
Cher-Lea, Cherry-Lee,
Cherylee, Sharilee,
Sheralea, Sherryleigh*

Cherry-Sue
(American) combo of
Cherry and Sue

Cheryl
(French) beloved
*Charyl, Cherel, Cherelle,
Cheryll*

Chesley
(English) pretty;
meadow
*Ches, Cheslay, Cheslea,
Chesleigh*

Chesna
(Slavic) peace
Ches, Chesnah

Chesney
(English) peacemaker
*Chesnee, Chesni,
Chesnie, Chessnea*

Chesskwana
(African-American)
evoker
*Chesskwan,
Chessquana, Chessy*

Chessteen
(American) needed
*Ches, Chessy, Chesteen,
Chestene*

Chet
(American) vivacious
Chett

Chevy
(American) funny
Chev, Chevee

Cheyenne
(Native American) Indian
tribe; capital of
Wyoming
*Chayanne, Cheyan,
Cheyanna, Cheyene,
Chynne, Shayan,
Shayann, Sheyenne*

Chiara
(Italian) bright and clear
*Cheara, Chiarra, Kiara,
Kiarra*

Chica
(Spanish) girl
Chika

Chick
(American) fun-loving
Chicki, Chickie

Chickadee
(American) cute little girl
*Chicka, Chickady,
Chickee, Chickey, Chicky*

Chikira
(Spanish) dancer
Shakira

Childe
(American) literary
Child

Childers
(Last name as first
name) dignified
*Chelders, Childie,
Chillders, Chylders*

China
(Place name) unique
Chinnah, Chyna, Chynna

Chinadoll
(Invented) fun
China Doll, China-Doll, Chynadoll

Chiquida
(Spanish) form of
Chiquita; small
Chiquide

Chiquita
(Spanish) small girl
Chica, Chick, Chickie, Chikita, Chiquitia, Chiquitta, Shiquita

Chirline
(American) variant of
Charline; sweet
Chirl, Chirlene, Shirl, Shirline

Chivonne
(American) happy
Chevonne, Chivaughan, Chivaughn, Chivon, Chivonn

Chloe
(Greek) flowering
Chloee, Clo, Cloee, Cloey, Khloe, Kloe

Chloris
(Greek) pale-skinned
Cloris, Kloris

Chris
(Greek) form of
Christina; best
Chrissie, Chrissy, Kris

Chrisana
(American) boisterous
Chris, Chrisanah, Crisane

Chrissa
(Greek) form of Christina
Crissa, Cryssa, Krissa

Chrissy
(English) short for
Christina
Chrissie, Krissy

Christa
(German, Greek)
loving
Crista, Krista

Christabelle
(American) combo of
Christa and Belle
Cristabel

Christal
(Latin) form of Crystal
Christall, Christalle, Christel

Christalin
(American) combo of
Christa and Lin
Christalinn, Christalynn

Christanda
(American) smart
Christandah, Christawnda

Christauna
(American) spiritual
Christaun, Christawna, Christown, Christwan

Christen
(Greek) form of
Christina; Christian
Christan, Christin, Cristen, Kristen

Christian
(Greek) Christian

Christiana
(Greek, German)
Christ's follower
Christa, Christianna, Christianne, Christie, Chystyana, Crystianne, Crysty-Ann, Kristiana

Christie
(Greek) short for
Christina
Christi, Kristi, Kristie

Christina
(Greek, Scottish,
German, Irish) the
anointed one
Chris, Chrissie, Christi, Christiana, Chrystina, Crista, Kristina

Christine
(French, English, Latin)
faithful
Christene, Christin, Cristine, Kristine

Christopher
(Greek) devout Christian
Kris, Krissie, Krissy, Krista, Kristofer, Kristopher

Christy
(Scottish) Christian
Christee, Christi, Christie

Chrysanthemum
(American) flower
Chrys, Chrysanthe, Chrysie, Mum

Chrysanthum
(Invented) from flower chrysanthemum; flowering
Chrys, Chrysan, Chrysanth

Chulisa
(Invented) clever
Chully, Ulisa

Ciara
(Irish) brunette
Cearra, Ciarah, Ciarra, Keera, Keerah

Cicely
(Latin) form of Cecilia; clever
Cicelie, Cici, Sicely

Cid
(American) fun
Cyd, Syd

Cidni
(American) jovial
Cidnee, Cidney, Cidnie

Cidrah
(American) unusual
Cid, Ciddie, Ciddy, Cidra

Cieara
(Spanish) dark
CiCi, Ciear, Sieara

Ciera
(Irish) dark
Cíera, Cia, Cieera, Cierra, Cierre

Cilla
(Greek) vivacious
Cika, Sica, Sika

Cille
(American) short for Lucille
Ceele

Cinderella
(French) imaginative; hopeful
Cinda, Cindi, Cindie, Cindy

Cindy
(Greek, Latin) moon goddess;
Cindee, Cindi, Cyndee, Cyndi, Cyndie, Sindee, Syndi, Syndie, Syndy

Cinnamon
(Spice) sweet
Cenamon, Cinna, Cinnammon, Cinnamond, Cinamen, Cynamon

Ciona
(American) steadfast
Cinonah, Cionna, Cyona

Ciprianna
(Italian) from Ciprus; cautious
Cipri, Cipriannah, Cypriana, Cyprianna, Cyprianne, Sipriana, Siprianna

Circe
(Greek) sorceress deity; mysterious
Circee, Cirsey, Cirsie

Ciri
(Latin) regal
Ceree, Ceri, Seree, Siri

Cirila
(Latin) heavenly
Ceri, Cerila, Cerilla, Cerille, Cerine, Ciria, Cirine

Cissy
(American) sweet
Ciss, Cissey, Cissi, Sissi

Citare
(Greek) musical; variant of the Indian lute sitar
Citara, Sitare

Claire
(Latin, French) smart
Clair, Clairee, Claireen, Claireta, Clairy, Clare, Clarette, Clarry, Klair

Clarieca
(Latin) bright
*Claire, Clare, Clari,
Clarieka, Clary, Klarieca,
Klarieka*

Clancey
(American)
devil-may-care
*Clance, Clancee, Clancie,
Clancy*

Clara
(Latin) bright one
Clarie, Clarine, Clary

Clarabelle
(Latin) combo of Clara
and Belle; bright lovely
woman
Claribel

Clarice
(Latin, Italian)
insightful
*Clairece, Claireece,
Clairice, Clarece,
Clareece, Clariece,
Clarise*

Clarissa
(Latin, Greek) smart
and clear-minded
*Claressa, Clarisa,
Clerissa*

Clarity
(American) clear-minded
Clare, Claritee, Claritie

Claudia
(Latin, German, Italian)
persevering
*Claudelle, Claudie,
Claudina, Clodia,
Klaudia*

Claudia-Rose
(American) combo of
Claudia and Rose

Claudette
(French) persevering
*Claude, Claudee,
Claudet, Claudi, Claudie,
Claudy*

Clea
(Invented) short for
Cleanthe and Cleopatra;
famed
Clia, Klea, Klee

Cleanthe
(English) famed
Clea, Klea, Kleanth

Clemence
(Latin) easygoing;
merciful
*Clem, Clemense,
Clements, Clemmie,
Clemmy*

Clementina
(Spanish) kind; forgiving
*Clementyna,
Clymentyna, Klementina*

Clementine
(Latin) gentle;
(German) merciful
*Clemencie, Klementine,
Klementynne*

Cleo
(Greek) short for
Cleopatra

Cleopatra
(Greek) Egyptian queen
Cleo, Clee, Kleeo, Kleo

Clio
(Greek) history muse
Kleeo, Klio

Cloe
(Greek) flourishing
Cloee, Cloey

Cloreen
(American) happy
*Clo, Cloreane, Cloree,
Cloreene, Corean, Klo,
Klorean, Kloreen*

Cloressa
(American) consoling
Cloresse, Kloressa

Clorinda
(Latin) happy
*Cloee, Cloey, Clorinde,
Clorynda, Klorinda*

Clory
(Spanish) smiling
*Clori, Clorie, Kloree,
Klory*

Closetta
(Spanish) secretive
Close, Closette, Klosetta, Klosette

Clotilda
(German) famed fighter
Tilda, Tillie, Tilly

Clotilde
(French) combative

Cloud
(Weather name) light-hearted
Cloudee, Cloudie, Cloudy

Clove
(Spice) distinctive
Klove

Clover
(Botanical) natural
Clove, Kloverr

Clydette
(American) form of Clyde
Clidette, Clydett, Clydie, Klyde, Klydette

Clytie
(Greek) excellent; in love with love
Cly, Clytee, Clytey, Clyty, Klytee, Klytie

Co
(American) jovial
Coco, Ko, Koko

Coby
(American) glad
Cobe, Cobey, Cobie

Coco
(Spanish) coconut
Koko

Cocoa
(Spanish) chocolate; spunky girl

Cody
(English) soft-hearted; pillow
Codi, Codie, Kodie

Coffey
(American) lovely
Cofee, Caufey

Coiya
(American) coquettish
Coyuh, Koya

Cokey
(American) intelligent
Cokie

Colby
(English) enduring
Cobie, Colbi, Kolbee

Cole
(Last name as first name) laughing
Coe, Colie, Kohl

Colemand
(American) adventurer
Colmyand

Colette
(French) spiritual; victorious
Coey, Collette, Kolette

Colina
(American) righteous
Colena, Colin, Colinn

Colisa
(English) delightful
Colissa, Collisa, Collissa

Colleen
(Irish) young girl
Coleen, Colene, Coley, Colleene, Collen, Colli, Kolene, Kolleen

Colley
(English) fearful; worrier
Col, Collie, Kolley

Colola
(African-American) combination of Co and Lola; victor
Co, Cola, Colo

Coloma
(Spanish) calm
Colo, Colom, Colome

Columbine
(Latin) dove; flower

Comfort
(American) comforting; easygoing
Komfort

Comfortyne
(French) comforting
Comfort, Comfortine, Comfurtine, Comfy

Concetta
(Italian) pure female

Conchetta
(Spanish) wholesome
Concheta, Conchette

Conchie
(Latin) conception
Conchee, Conchi, Konchey, Konchie

Conchita
(Spanish) girl of the conception
Chita, Concha, Conchi

Conchiteen
(Spanish) pure
Conchita, Conchitee, Connie

Concordia
(Latin) goddess of peace

Condoleezza
(American) smart
Condeleesa, Condilesa, Condolissa

Coneisha
(African-American) giving
Coneisha, Conisha, Conishah, Conniesha

Conesa
(American) free-flowing nature
Conisa, Connesa, Konesa

Conlee
(American) form of Connelly; radiant
Con, Conlee, Conley, Conlie, Conly, Conly, Connie, Konlee, Konlee, Konlie

Conner
(American) brave
Con, Coner, Coni, Connie, Connor, Conny, Conor

Connie
(Latin, English) short for Constance; constant
Con, Conni, Conny, Konnie

Connie-Kim
(Vietnamese) golden girl
Conni-Kim

Conradina
(German) form of Conrad; brave
Connie, Conradyna, Konnie, Konradina

Conroe
(Place name) small town in Texas
Conn, Connie, Konroe

Conroy
(Last name as first name) stately; literary
Conroi, Konroi, Konroy

Constance
(Latin) loyal
Con, Connie

Constantina
(Italian) loyal; constant
Conn, Connee, Conni, Connie, Conny, Constance, Constanteena, Constantinah

Constanza
(Hebrew) constant
Constanz, Connstanzah

Constanze
(German) unchanging
Con, Connie, Stanzi

Consuelo
(Spanish) comfort-giver
Chelo, Consolata, Consuela

Contessa
(Italian) pretty
Contesa, Contessah, Contesse

Cookie
(American) cute
Cooki

Copeland
(Last name as first
name) good at coping
*Copelan, Copelyn,
Copelynn*

Copper
(American) redhead
Coper

Coppola
(Italian) theatrical
*Copla, Coppi, Coppo,
Coppy, Kopla, Kopola,
Koppola*

Cora
(Greek) maid; giving girl
Corah, Corra, Kora

Coral
(Latin) nature name;
small stone
*Corall, Coraly, Core,
Koral, Koraly*

Coralee
(American) combo of
Cora and Lee
Cora-Lee, Coralie, Koralie

Coralynn
(American) combo of
Cora and Lynn
*Coralene, Coralyn,
Cora-Lyn, Cora-Lynn,
Coralynne, Corline,
Corlynn*

Corazon
(Spanish) heart
Cora, Corrie, Zon, Zonn

Corday
(English) prepared;
heart
*Cord, Cordae, Cordie,
Cordy, Korday*

Cordelia
(Latin) warm-hearted
woman
*Cordi, Cordie, Cordilia,
Kordelia, Kordey, Kordi*

Cordelita
(Latin, Spanish)
heartfelt
*Cordelia, Cordelite,
Cordella*

Cordula
(Latin) heart;
(German) jewel
*Cord, Cordie, Cordoola,
Cordoolah, Cordy*

Corey
(Irish) perky
*Cori, Corree, Corrie,
Korey, Korri, Korrie*

Corgie
(American) funny
Corgi, Korgee, Korgie

Cori
(Greek, Irish) caring
person
Corey, Corri, Corrie, Cory

Corinna
(Greek) young girl
*Corina, Corrinna,
Corryna, Corynna*

Corinne
(Greek) maiden;
(French) protective
*Coreen, Corina, Corine,
Corinna, Corrina, Coryn,
Corynn, Koreene,
Korinne*

Coris
(Greek) singer
Corris, Koris, Korris

Corissa
(Greek) kind-hearted
Korissa

Corky
(American) energetic
*Corkee, Corkey, Corki,
Corkie, Korkee, Korky*

Corliss
(English) open-hearted
*Corless, Corlise, Corly,
Korlis, Korliss*

Corly
(American) energetic
*Corlee, Corli, Corlie,
Korli, Korly*

Corlyn
(American) innovative
*Corlin, Corlinn, Corlynn,
Corlynne, Korlin, Korlyn*

Cormella
(Italian) fiery
*Cormee, Cormela,
Cormelah, Cormellia,
Cormey, Cormie*

Cornae
(Origin unknown)
Coma, Korna, Kornae

Cornelia
(Latin) practical
Carnelia, Corney, Corni

Cornelius
(Latin) realistic
Corneal, Corneelyus, Corney, Corny

Cornesha
(African-American) talkative
Cornee, Corneshah, Cornesia

Corona
(Spanish) crowned; name of a beer
Corone, Coronna, Korona

Correne
(American) musical
Coree, Coreen, Correen, Correna, Korrene, Korene

Corrianna
(American) joyful
Coreanne, Corey, Corianna, Corri, Corriana

Corrinda
(French) girlish
Corri, Corrin, Korin, Korinda

Cortanie
(American) variation on Courtney
Cortanny, Cortany

Cortland
(American) distinctive
Cortlan, Courte, Courtland, Courtlin

Cortlinn
(American) happy
Cortlenn, Cortlin, Cortlyn, Cortlynn

Corvette
(Car model) speedy, dark
Corv, Corva, Corve, Korvette

Cosette
(French) warm
Cossette

Cosima
(Greek, German, Italian) of the universe; in harmony
Coseema, Koseema, Kosima

Cosmee
(Greek) organized
Cos, Cosmi, Cosmie

Cossette
(French) winning
Coss, Cossie, Cossy, Kossee, Kossette

Costner
(American) embraced
Cosner, Cost, Costnar, Costnor, Costnur

Cotcha
(African-American) stylish
Kasha, Katcha, Katshay, Kotsha

Cotrena
(American) form of Katrina; pure
Catreena, Catrina, Catrine, Cotrene, Katrine, Kotrene

Cotton
(American) comforting
Cottie

Countess
(American) blueblood
Contessa

Cournette
(American) form of coronet; regal
Courney, Kournette

Courtney
(English) regal; (French) patient
Cortney, Courtenay, Courteney, Courtnay, Courtnee, Courtny, Kortnee, Kortney

Covin
(American) unpredictable
Covan, Cove, Coven, Covyn

Coy
(American) sly
Coye, Koi, Koy

Coyah
(American) singular
Coya, Coyia

Coyote
(American) wild
Coyo, Kaiote, Kaiotee

Cramer
(American) jolly
Cramar, Cramir, Kramer

Cramisa
(Invented) nice
Cramissa, Kramisa

Cree
(American) wild spirit
Crea, Creeah

Creed
(American) boisterous
Crede, Cree, Kreed

Crescente
(American) impressive
Crescent, Cresent, Cress, Cressie

Cressa
(Greek) delicate (from the name Cressida)
Cresa, Cressah, Cresse, Cress, Kressa

Cressida
(Greek) infidel
Cresida, Cresiduh, Cresside

Cressie
(American) growing; good
Cress, Cressy, Kress, Kressie

Creston
(American) worthy
Crest, Crestan, Creste, Cresten, Crestey, Cresti, Crestie

Cricket
(American) energetic
Kricket

Crimson
(American) deep
Cremsen, Crims, Crimsen, Crimsonn, Crimsun

Criselda
(Spanish) wild
Crisselda

Crishonna
(American) beautiful
Crishona, Crisshone, Crissie, Crissy, Krishona, Krishonna

Crisiant
(Welsh) crystal; clear
Cris, Crissie

Crispy
(Invented) fun-loving; zany
Crispee, Krispy

Crista
(Italian) form of Christina
Krista

Cristin
(Irish) dedicated
Cristen, Crystyn, Kristin, Krystyn

Cristina
(Greek) form of Christina; devout
Christina, Kristina

Cristos
(Greek) dedicated
Criss, Crissie, Christos

Cristy
(English) spiritual
Cristi, Crysti, Krystie, Kristi

Crystal
(Latin) clear; open-minded
Chrystal, Cristal, Cristalle, Crys, Crystelle, Krystal

Crystilis
(Spanish) focused
Chrysilis, Crys, Cryssi, Cryssie, Crystylis

Cullen
(Irish) attractive
Cullan, Cullie, Cullun, Cully

Cumale
(American) open-hearted
Cue, Cuemalie, Cue-maly, Cumahli

Cumthia
(American) open-minded
Cumthea, Cumthee, Cumthi, Cumthie, Cumthy

Cupid
(American) romantic
Cupide

Curine
(American) attractive
Curina, Curinne, Curri, Currin

Curry
(American) languid
Curree, Currey, Curri, Currie

Cursten
(American) form of Kirsten
Curst, Curstee, Curstie, Curstin

Cushaun
(American) elegant
Cooshaun, Cooshawn, Cue, Cushawn, Cushonn, Cushun

Cyan
(American) colorful
Cyanne, Cyenna, Cyun

Cyanetta
(Greek) little blue
Cyan, Cyanette, Syan, Syanette

Cybill
(Latin) prophetess
Cybell, Cybelle, Cybil, Sibyl, Sibyle

Cydell
(American) country girl
Cydee, Cydel, Cydie, Cydile, Cydy

Cydney
(American) perky
Cyd, Cydni, Cydnie

Cylee
(American) darling
Cye, Cyle, Cylea, Cyli, Cylie, Cyly

Cylene
(American) melodious
Cylena, Cyline

Cymbeline
(Greek) Shakespearean play
Beline, Cymba, Cymbe, Cymbie, Cyme, Cymmie, Symbe

Cyn
(Greek) short for Cynthia
Cynnae, Cynnie, Syn

Cynder
(English) having wanderlust
Cindee, Cinder, Cindy, Cyn, Cyndee, Cyndie, Cyndy

Cyntanah
(American) singer
Cintanna, Cyntanna

Cynthia
(Greek, English) moon goddess
Cindy, Cyn, Cyndee, Cyndy, Cynthea, Cynthee, Cynthie

Cyntia
(Greek) variant of Cynthia; smiling goddess
Cyn, Cyntea, Cynthie, Cyntie, Syntia

Cyntrille
(African-American) gossipy
Cynn, Cyntrell, Cyntrelle, Cyntrie

Cypress
(Botanical) swaying
Cypres, Cyprice, Cypriss, Cyprus

Cyra
(American) willing
Cye, Cyrah, Syra

Cyreen
(American) sensual
Cyree, Cyrene, Cyrie

Cyrenian
(American) bewitching
*Cyree, Cyren, Cyrenean,
Cyrey, Siren, Syrenian*

Cyrenna
(American)
straightforward
*Cyrena, Cyrennah,
Cyrinna, Cyryna, Cyrynna*

Cyriece
(American) artistic
*Cyreece, Cyree, Cyreese,
Cyrie*

D'Anna
(Hebrew) special

Dacey
(Irish) a southerner
*Dace, Dacee, Daci,
Dacie, Dacy, Daicie,
Daycee*

Dae
(English) day
Day, Daye

Daelan
(English) aware
*Dael, Daelan, Daelin,
Daely, Dale, Daley,
Daylan, Daylin, Daylind,
Dee*

Daeshonda
(African-American)
combo of Dae and
Shonda
*Daeshanda, Daeshawna,
Daeshondra*

Daffodil
(Botanical) flower
Daffy

Dafnee
(Greek, American) form
of Daphne; pretty
Dafney, Dafnie

Dagmar
(German, Scandinavian)
glorious day
Dag, Dagmarr

Dahlia
(Scandinavian) flower
Dahl, Dollie

Dai
(Welsh, Japanese)
beloved one of great
importance

Daira
(American) outgoing
*D'Aira, Daire, Dairrah,
Darrah, Derrah*

Daisha
(American) sparkling
*D'Aisha, Daish, Daishe,
Dasha, Dashah*

Daisy
(English) flower and
day's eye
*Daisee, Daisi, Daisie,
Daissy, Daizee, Daizi,
Daizy, Dasie, Daysy*

Daisyetta
(American) combo of
Daisy and Etta; spunky;
the day's eye
Daiseyetta, Daizie,
Daiziette, Dasie,
Dazeyetta, Daziette

Daiton
(American) wondrous
Day, Dayten, Dayton

Daja
(American) intuitive
Dajah

Dajanae
(African-American)
persuasive
Daije, Daja, Dajainay,
Dayjanah

Dajon
(American) gifted
D'Jon, Dajo, Dajohn,
Dajonn, Dajonnay,
Dajonne

Dakara
(American) firebrand
Dacara, Dakarah,
Dakarea, Dakarra

Daking
(Asian) friendly

Dakota
(Native American) tribal
name; solid friend
Dacota, Dakohta,
Dakotah, Dakotta

Dalacie
(American) brilliant
Dalaci, Dalacy, Dalasie,
Dalce, Dalci, Dalse

Dalaina
(American) spirited
Dalana, Dalayna,
Delaina, Delaine,
Delayna

Dalaney
(American) hopeful
Dalanee, Dalaynee,
Dalayni

Dale
(English) valley-life
Dalena, Dayle

Daleah
(American) pretty
Dalea

Daley
(Irish) leader
Dailey, Dalea, Daleigh,
Dali, Dalie, Daly

Dalia
(Spanish) flower
Daliah, Dayliah, Doliah,
Dolliah, Dolya

Dalian
(Place name) joy
Dalean

Daliana
(American) joyful spirit
Daliane, Dalianna, Dilial,
Dollianna

Dalice
(American) able
Daleese, Dalleece

Dalila
(African) gentle

Dalin
(American) calm
Dalen, Dalenn, Dalun

Dalita
(American) smooth
Daleta, Daletta, Dalite,
Dalitee, Dalitta

Dallas
(Place name) confident
Dalis, Dalisse, Daliz,
Dallice, Dallis, Dallsyon,
Dallus, Dallys

Dallen
(American) outspoken
Dal, Dalin, Dallin, Dalen

Dallise
(American) gentle
Dalise, Dallece, Dalleece,
Dalleese

Dalondra
(Invented) generous
Dalandra, Dalon,
Dalondrah, Delondra

Dalonna
(Invented) generous
Dalohn, Dalona,
Dalonne

Dalphine
(French) form of Delphine; delicate and svelte
Dal, Dalf, Dalfeen, Dalfene, Dalphene

Dalton
(American) smart
Dallee, Dalli, Dallie, Dallton, Dally, Daltawyn

Daltrey
(American) quiet
Daltree, Daltri, Daltrie

Dalyn
(American) smart
Dalin, Dalinne, Dalynn, Dalynne

Dama
(Hindi) temptress
Dam

Damalla
(Greek) fledgling; young; calf
Damala, Damalas, Damalis, Damall

Damaris
(Greek) calm
Damalis, Damara, Damares, Damaret, Damrez

Damecia
(Invented) sweet
Dameisha, Damesha, Demecia, Demisha, Demeshe

Dami
(Greek) short for Damia; spirited
Damee, Damey, Damie, Damy

Damia
(Greek) spirited
Damiah, Damya, Damyah, Damyen, Damyenne, Damyuh

Damianne
(Greek) one who soothes
Damiana

Damica
(French) open-spirited
Dameeka, Dameka, Damika, Demica

Damita
(Spanish) small woman of nobility
Dama, Damah

Damon
(American) sprightly
Damoane, Damone

Damone
(American) mighty
Dame

Dana
(English) bright gift of God
Daina, Danah, Danna, Dayna, Daynah

Danae
(Greek) bright and pure
Dannae, Danays, Danee

Danala
(English) happy, golden
Dan, Danalla, Danee, Danela, Danney, Danny

Danasha
(African-American) combo of Dana and Tasha; spirited
Anasha, Danas, Danash, Danashah, Daneash, Danesha

Danay
(American) happy
D'Nay, Dánay, Danaye

Dancel
(French) energetic
Dance, Dancell, Dancelle, Dancey, Dancie, Danse, Dansel, Danselle

Dancie
(American) from the word dancer
Dancy

Danelle
(Hebrew) kind-hearted; combo of Dan and Nelle
Danele, Dani, Dannele, Danny

Danelly
(Spanish) form of
Daniel; judged by God
Daneli, Danellie,
Dannelley, Dannelly

Danessa
(American) dainty
Danese, Danesse

Danette
(American) form of
Danielle
Danett

Dangela
(Latin) form of Angela;
angelic
Angee, Angelle, Angie,
Dangelah, Dangelia,
Dangey, Dangi, Dangie

Dani
(Hebrew) short for
Danielle or Danelle
Danee, Danni, Dannie,
Danny

Dania
(Hebrew) short for
Danielle

Daniah
(Hebrew) judged
Dan, Dania, Danny,
Danya

Danica
(Latin, Polish) star of the
morning
Daneeka, Danika,
Dannika

Daniele
(Hebrew, French) form of
Daniel; judged by God
alone
Danelle, Daniell,
Danielle, Danniella,
Danyel

Daniella
(Italian) form of Danielle
Danilla

Danir
(American) fresh
Daner

Danita
(American) combo of
Dan and Anita;
gregarious
Danni, Danny, Denita,
Denny

Danna
(American) cheerful
D'Ana, D'Anna, Dannae,
Danni, Danny

Daphiney
(Greek) form of Daphne;
nymph
Daff, Daph

Daphne
(Greek) pretty nymph
Daphany, Daphiney,
Daphnee, Daphney,
Daphnie, Daphny,
Daphonie, Daphy

Dara
(Hebrew) compassionate
Dahrah, Darah, Darra

Daralice
(Greek) beloved
Dara, Daraleese,
Daraliece

Darby
(Irish) a free woman
Darb, Darbee, Darbi,
Darbie, Darbye

Darcelle
(American) secretive
Darce, Darcel, Darcell,
Darcey

Darci
(Irish) dark
Darce, Darcee, Darcie,
Darcy, Dars, Darsey

Daria
(Greek, Italian) rich
woman of luxury
Dare, Darea, Dareah,
Dari, Darria

Darian
(Anglo-Saxon) precious
Dare, Darien, Darry,
Derian, Derian

Darice
(English) contemporary
Dareese, Darese, Dari,
Dariece, Darri, Darrie,
Darry

Darielle
(French) rich
Darell, Darelle, Dariel,
Darrielle

Darilyn
(American) darling
Darilin, Darilinn,
Darilynn, Derilyn

Darionne
(American)
adventuresome
Dareon, Darion, Darionn,
Darionna

Dariya
(Russian) sweet
Dara, Darya

Darla
(English) short for
Darlene
Darl, Darli, Darlie

Darlee
(English) darling
Darl, Darley, Darli, Darlie

Darlene
(French) darling girl
Darlean, Darleen,
Darlena, Darlin, Darling

Darlie-Lynn
(American) combo of
Darlie and Lynn

Darling
(American) precious
Darline, Darly, Darlyng

Darlonna
(African-American)
darling
Darlona

Darnelle
(Irish) seamstress
Darnel

Daron
(Irish) great woman
Daren, Darun, Daryn

Darrow
(Last name as first
name) cautious
Darro, Darroh

Darryl
(French, English)
beloved
Darel, Darelle, Daril,
Darrell, Darrill, Daryl,
Daryll, Derel, Derrell

Darshelle
(African-American)
confident
Darshel, Darshell

Dart
(English) tenacious
Darte, Dartee, Dartt

Darva
(Invented) sensible
Darv, Darvah, Darvee,
Darvey, Darvi, Darvie

Daryn
(Greek, Irish) gift-giver
Darynn

Dash
(American) fast-moving
Dashee, Dasher, Dashy

Dasha
(Russian) darling
Dashah

Dashanda
(African-American)
loving
Dashan, Dashande

Dashawn
(African-American) brash
Dashawna, Dashay

Dashawntay
(African-American)
careful
Dash, Dashauntay

Dashea
(Hebrew) patient

Dasheena
(African-American)
flashy
Dashea, Dasheana

Dashelle
(African-American)
striking
Dachelle, Dashel,
Dashell, Dashy

Dashika
(African-American)
runner
Dash, Dasheka

Dashilan
(American) solemn
Dashelin, Dashelin,
Dashlinne, Dashlyn,
Dashlynn, Dasialyn

Dasmine
(Invented) sleek
Dasmeen, Dasmin,
Dazmeen, Dazmine

Dassia
(American) pretty
Dasie, Dassea, Dasseah,
Dassee, Dassi, Dassie,
Deassiah

Daureen
(American) darling
Dareen, Daurean,
Daurie, Daury, Dawreen

Daveena
(Scottish) form of David;
loved
Daveen, Davena, Davey,
Davina, Davinna

Davelyn
(Invented) combo of
Dave and Lynn; loved
Davalin, Davalynn,
Davalynne, Dave, Davey,
Davie, Davilynn

Davida
(Hebrew) beloved one
Daveeda, Daveta, Davita

Davina
(Hebrew) believer;
beloved
Daveena, Davene,
Davida, Davita, Devina,
Devinia, Devinya

Davincia
(Spanish) God-loving;
winner
Davince, Davinse, Vincia

Davinique
(African-American)
believer; unique
Davin, Davineek, Vineek

Davis
(American) boyish
Daves

Davisnell
(Invented) vivacious
Daviesnell, DavisNell

Davonne
(African-American)
splashy
Davaughan, Davaughn,
Davion, Daviona, Davon,
Davone, Davonn

Dawa
(Tibetan) girl born on
Monday

Dawanda
(African-American)
righteous
Dawana, Dawand,
Dawanna, Dawauna,
Dawonda, Dawonna,
Dwanda

Dawn
(English) dawn
Daun, Dawna, Dawne

Dawna
(English) eloquence of
dawn
Dauna, Daunda, Dawn,
Dawnah, Dawny

Dawnika
(African-American) dawn
Dawneka, Dawneeka,
Dawnica, Donika

Dawnisha
(African-American)
breath of dawn
Daunisha, Dawnish,
Dawny, Nisa, Nisha

Dawntelle
(African-American)
morning bright
Dawntel, Dawntell,
Dontelle

Dawona
(African-American) smart
Dawonna, Dawonne

Dayana
(American) variant of
Diana; darling
Dayannah, Dyana

Dayanara
(Spanish) form of
Deyanira; forceful;
destructive
*Day, Daya, Dayan,
Dianara, Diannare, Nara*

Daylee
(American) calm;
reserved
*Dailee, Day, Dayley,
Dayly*

Dayna
(English) variant of
Dana; bright gift of God
Daynah

Dayshanay
(African-American) saucy
*Daysh, Dayshanae,
Dayshannay, Dayshie*

Dayshawna
(American) laughing
*Dayshauna, Dayshona,
Dashonah*

Dayshay
(African-American)
lovable
Dashae, Dashay, Dashea

Dayton
(Place name) fast

Daytona
(American) speedy
Dayto, Daytonna

Dayvonne
(African-American)
careful
*Dave, Davey, Davonne,
Dayvaughn*

De
(Chinese) virtuous

Deacon
(Greek) joyful
messenger
*Deak, Deakon, Deecon,
Deke*

Dean
(English) practical
Deanie, Deanni

Deandra
(English) combo of
Deanna and Sandra;
pretty face
Andie, Andra, Dee

Deandralina
(American) combo of
Deandra and Lina; divine
seer
*Deandra-Lina, Deandra
Lina. Deanalina, Lina,
Deandra, Dee, DeeDee*

Deandria
(American) sweetheart
Deandreah, Deandriah

Deanie
(English) form of Dean;
from the valley
Deanee, Deaney, Deani

Deanna
(Latin, English)
divine girl
Deana, Deanne, Dee

Deanne
(Latin) from Diana;
moon goddess
Deann, Dee, Deeann

Dearon
(American) dear one
*Dear, Dearan, Dearen,
Deary*

Dearoven
(American) form of
Dearon
Derovan, Deroven

Debbie
(Hebrew) short for
Deborah
*Deb, Debbee, Debbi,
Debby, Debbye, Debi*

Debbie-Jean
(American) combo of
Debbie and Jean

Debbielou
(American) combo of
Debbie and Lou
Debilou

Debbie-Sue
(American) combo of
Debbi and Sue
Debbisue

Deborah
(Hebrew) prophetess
*Debbie, Deboreh,
Deborrah, Debra*

Debra
(Hebrew) prophetess
Debrah

Debray
(American) form of
Deborah; prophetess
*Dabrae, Deb, Debrae,
Debraye*

Debra-Jean
(American) combo of
Debra and Jean

DeChell
(Invented) combo of De
and Chell; quiet
Dechelle, Dee

Dedra
(American) spirited
*Dee, DeeDee, Deedra,
Deidra, Deirdre*

Dee
(English, Irish) lucky one
*Dedee, DeeDee, Dee-
Dee, Didee*

Deedee
(American) short for D
names; vivacious
*D.D., Dee Dee, DeeDee,
Dee-Dee*

DeErica
(African-American)
audacious
Dee-Erica

Deesha
(American) dancing
*Dedee, Dee, Deesh,
Deeshah, Deisha*

Deidra
(Irish) sparkling
Deedra, Deidre, Dierdra

Deighan
(American) exciting
Daygan, Deigan

Deiondra
(Greek) partier; wine-
loving
*Deandrah, Deann,
Deanndra, Dee, Deean,
Deeann, DeeDee,
Deondra*

Deirdre
(Irish) passionate
*Dedra, Dee, Deedee,
Deedrah, Deerdra,
Deerdre, Didi*

Deishauna
(African-American)
combo of Dei and
Shauna; pious; day of
God
*Dayshauna, Deisha,
Deishaun, Deishaune,
Shauna*

Deissy
(Greek) form of Desma;
sworn; loyal
*Deisi, Deissey, Deissie,
Desma, Desmee,
Desmer, Dessi*

Deitra
(Greek) goddess-like
Deetra

Deja
(French) already seen
D'Ja, Dejah

Deja-Marie
(American) combo of
Deja and Marie
Deja, Dejamarie

Delaine
(American) combo of D
and Elaine; smart
D'Laine, Delane

Delana
(German) protective
*Dalana, Daleena,
Dalena, Deedee*

Delanah
(American) wise
Delana, Dellana, Delano

Delandra
(American) outgoing
Delan, Delande

Delaney
(Irish) bouncy;
enthusiastic
*Dalanie, Delaine,
Delainey, Delane,
DeLayney, Dellie,
Dulaney*

Delcarmen
(Spanish) combo of Del
and Carmen; worldly
*Del, Del Carmen, Del-
Carmen, Delcee, Delcy*

Delcy
(American) friendly
Del, Delcee, Delci

Dele
(American) rash; noble
Del, Dell

Delfina
(Latin, Italian) flowering
Dellfina, Delphina

Delgadina
(Spanish) derivative of
Delgado; slender
Delga, Delgado

Delia
(Greek) lovely; moon
goddess
Deilyuh, Delya, Delyah

Delise
(Latin) delicious
*Del, Delice, Delicia,
Delisa, Delissa*

Delicia
(Latin, Spanish)
delicious; delightful
*Delisa, Delishea, Delisia,
Delysa*

Delilah
(Hebrew) beautiful
temptress
Dalia, Dalila, Delila, Lilah

Delinda
(American) form of
Melinda; pretty
Delin, Delinde, Delynda

Delite
(American) pleasure-
giving
Delight

Dell
(Greek) kind
Del

Della
(Greek) kind
Dee, Del, Dell

Dellana
(Irish) form of Delaney;
vibrant; delight
*Delaine, Delana, Dell,
Dellaina, Dellane,
Dellann*

Dell-Marie
(American) combo of
Dell and Marie; helpful;
gracious
*Dell Marie, Delmaria,
Delmarie*

Delma-Lee
(American) combo of
Delma and Lee;
uncomplicated
Delmalea, Delmalee

Delmee
(American) star
*Del, Delmey, Delmi,
Delmy*

Delmys
(American) incredible
Del, Delmas, Delmis

Delon
(American) musical
Delonn, Delonne

Delores
(Spanish) woman of
sorrowful leaning
Delore, Dolores, Deloris

Delos
(Greek) beautiful brunette; a small Aegean isle; stunning
Delas

Delpha
(Greek) from Delphi, or the flower delphinium; flourishing
Delfa

Delphine
(Latin) swimmer
Delfine, Delphene

Delta
(Greek) door; Greek alphabet letter; (American) land-loving
Del, Dell, Dellta, Delte

Deltrese
(African-American) jubilant
Del, Delltrese, Delt, Delta, Deltreese, Deltrice

Delwyn
(English, Welsh) beautiful friend
Delwen, Delwenne, Delwin

Demetress
(Greek) form of Demetria, corn goddess
Deme, Demetra, Demetres, Demetri, Demetria, Dimi, Tress, Tressie, Tressy

Demetria
(Greek) harvest goddess
Demeteria, Demetra, Demitra

Demi
(French) half
Demie

Dena
(English) laidback; valley
Deena, Denah

Denedra
(American) lively; natural
Den, Dene, Denney

Deneen
(American) from Hebrew Dena; absolved
Denean, Denene

Denes
(English) nature-lover
Denis, Denne, Denny

Denetria
(Greek) from God
Denitria, Denny, Dentria

Denetrice
(African-American) optimistic
Denetrise, Denitrise, Denny

Denise
(French) wine-lover
Danise, Denese, Deniece, Denni, Denny

Denisha
(American) jubilant
Danisha, Deneesha, Deneshea

Denton
(American) Texas town
Dent, Dentun, Denty, Dentyn

Denver
(English) born in a green valley
Denv, Denvie

Denz
(Invented) lively
Dens

Deoniece
(African-American) feminine
Dee, DeeDee, Deo, Deone, Deoneece, Deoneese

Dericka
(American) dancer
D'ericka, Derica, Dericca, Derika

Derie
(Hebrew) form of Derora; dear; bird
Derey, Drora , Drorah

Deronique
(African-American) unique girl
Deron, Deroneek

Derrona
(American) natural
Derona, Derone, Derry

Derry
(Irish) red-haired woman
Deri, Derrie

Desdemona
(Greek) a name from
Greek drama and
Shakespeare's *Othello*;
tragic figure
Des, Desde, Dez

Deshawna
(African-American)
vivacious
*Deshauna, Deshaune,
Deshawnna, Deshona,
Deshonna*

Deshette
(African-American) dishy
Deshett

Deshondra
(African-American)
vivacious
*Deshaundra,
Deshondrah, Deshondria*

Desi
(French) short for
Desiree
Dezi, Dezzie

Desire
(English) desired
Dezire

Desiree
(French) desired
*Des'ree, Desairee,
Desarae, Desaray,
Desaraye, Desaree,
Desarhea, Desary,
Deseri, Desree, Des-Ree,
Dezaray, Deziree, Dezray*

Destin
(American) destiny
Destinn, Destyn

Destina
(Spanish) destiny
Desteena, Desteenah

Destiny
(French) fated
*Destanee, Destanie,
Desteney, Destinay,
Destinee, Destinei,
Destini, Destinyi,
Destnay, Destney,
Destonie, Destony,
Destyni*

Destry
(American) well-fated;
western feel
Destrey, Destri, Destrie

Deterrion
(Latin) form of Detra;
blessed
*Deterr, Deterreyon,
Detra, Detrae*

Detra
(Latin) form of Detta;
blessed
Detraye

Deva
(Hindi) moon goddess;
wielder of power
Devi

Devalca
(Spanish) generous
Deval

Devan
(Irish) poetic
Devana, Devn

Devi
(Hindi) beloved goddess
*Devia, Deviann, Devian,
Devie, Devri*

Devin
(Irish) poetic
Devn, Devyn, Devynne

Devina, Devin
(Irish) divine; creative
*Davena, Devie, Devine,
Devy, Divine*

Devon
(English) place name;
poetic
*Dev, Devaughan,
Devaughn, Devie,
Devonne, Devy*

Devorah
(American) combo of
Devon and Deborah
Devora, Devore

Dew
(American) from the
word dew; fresh
Dewi, Dewie

Dewanna
(African-American) clingy
*D'Wana, Dewana,
Dewanne*

Dexter
(English) spunky;
dexterous
*Dex, Dexee, Dexey,
Dexie, Dext, Dextar,
Dextur, Dexy*

Deyanira
(Spanish) aggressor
*Deyan, Deyann, Dianira,
Nira, Nira*

Dharcia
(American) sparkler
Darch, Darsha, Dharsha

Dharika
(American) sad
Darica, Darika

Dharma
(Hindi) morality; beliefs
Darma, Darmah

Dhazalai
(African)
Dhaze, Dhazie

Dhelal
(Arabic) coy

Dhessie
(American) glowing
*Dhessee, Dhessey,
Dhessi, Dhessy*

Di
(Latin) short for Diane or
Diana
Didi, Dy

Dia
(Greek) shining
Di

Diaelza
(Spanish) divine; pretty
Diael, Dialza, Elza

Diah
(American) pretty
Dia

Diamantina
(Spanish) sparkling
*Diama, Diamante,
Mantina*

Diamond
(Latin) precious
gemstone
*Diamin, Diamon,
Diamonds, Diamun,
Diamyn, Diamynd,
Dyamond*

Diamondah
(African-American)
glowing
Diamonda, Diamonde

Diamondique
(African-American)
sparkling
Diamondik

Diamony
(American) gem
*Diamonee, Diamoney,
Diamoni, Diamonie*

Diana
(Latin) divine woman;
goddess of the hunt and
fertility
*Dee, Di, Diahana,
Diahna, Dianah,
Diannah, Didi, Dihanna,
Dyanna, Dyannah,
Dyhana*

Dianalynn
(American) combo of
Diana and Lynn
*Dianalin, Dianalinne,
Dianalyn*

Diandro
(American) special
*Diandra, Diandrea,
Diandroh*

Diane
(Latin) goddess-like;
divine
*Deedee, Di, Diahann,
Dian, Diann, Dianne,
Didi*

Dianette
(American) combo of Diane and Ette; high-spirited
Di, Diane, Dianett, Didi, Diette, Diyannette, Dyan, Dyanette, Dyanne, Dyenette

Diantha
(Greek) flower; heavenly
Dianth

Diarah
(American) pretty
Dearah, Di, Diara, Diarra, Dierra

Diavonne
(African-American) jovial
Diavone, Diavonna, Diavonni

Dicey
(American) impulsive
Di, Dice, Dicee, Dicy, Dycee, Dycey

Dicia
(American) wild
Desha, Dicy

Diedre
(Irish) variant of Deidre; spunky
Diedra, Diedré

Diesha
(African-American) zany
Diecia, Dieshah, Dieshie, Dieshay

Diggs
(American) tomboyish
Digs, Dyggs

Dihana
(American) natural
Dihanna

Dijonaise
(Invented) condiments; combo of Dijon and mayonnaise
Deejonaise, Dijon, Dijonais, Dijonaze, Naise

Dijonnay
(American) fun-loving
Dijon, Dijonae, Dijonay, Dijonnae, Dijonnaie

Dilan
(American) form of Dylan
Dillan, Dilon

Dillyana
(English) worshipful
Diliann, Dilli, Dillianna, Dilly

Dilynn
(American) variant of Dylan; loving the sea
Di, Dilenn, Dilinn, Dilyn, Lynn

Dima
(American) high-spirited
Deemah, Dema

Dina
(Hebrew, Scottish) right; royal

Dinah
(Hebrew) fair judge
Dina, Dinah, Dinna, Dyna

Dinesha
(American) happy
Dineisha, Dineshe, Diniesha

Dini
(American) joyful
Dinee, Diney, Dinie

Dinora
(Spanish) judged by God
Dina, Dino, Nora

Diona
(Greek) divine woman
Dee, Di, Dion, Dionah, Dionuh

Dioneece
(American) daring
Dee, DeeDee, Deon, Deone, Deonece, Deoneece, Dioniece, Neece, Neecey

Dionicia
(Spanish) vixen
Di, Dione, Dionice, Dionise, Nicia, Nise, Nisee

Dionndra
(American) loving
Diondra, Diondrah, Diondruh

Dionne
(Greek) love goddess
Deona, Dion, Dione,
Dionna

Dionshay
(African-American)
combo of Dion and
Shay; loving
Dionsha, Dionshae,
Dionshaye

Dior
(French) stylish
Diora, Diore

Direll
(American) svelte
Di, Direl, Direlle

Dirisha
(African-American)
outgoing
Di, Diresha, Direshe

Disa
(Scandinavian) goddess

Disha
(American) fine
Dishae, Dishuh

Dishawna
(African-American)
special
Dishana, Dishauna,
Dishawnah, Dishona,
Dishonna

Divina
(American) divine

Divina, Divine
(Italian) divine
Divin, Divina

Divinity
(American) sweet;
devout
Divinitee, Diviniti,
Divinitie

Dix
(French) livewire

Dixann
(American) combo of
Dixie and Ann
Dixan, Dixanne, Dixiana,
Dixieanna

Dixie
(American) southern girl
Dixee, Dixi

D'Nicola
(American) combo of D
and Nicola
D'nicole, Deenicola,
Dnicola

Dnisha
(African-American)
rejoicing
D'Nisha, Dnisa, Dnish,
Dnishay, Dnishe

Dobie
(American) cowgirl
Dobee, Dobey, Dobi

Dodie
(Greek, Hebrew) short
for Dorothy; beloved
woman
Dodi, Dody

Doherty
(American) ambitious
Dhoertey, Dohertee,
Dohertie

Dolcy
(American)
Dolcee, Dolcie, Dolsee

Dolly
(American) effervescent
Doll, Dollee, Dolli

Dolores
(Spanish) woman of
sorrowful leaning
Delores

Dometria
(American) form of
Greek Demetria;
goddess; fruitful
Dome, Dometrea, Domi,
Domini, Domitra

Domini
(Latin) form of Dominick
Dom, Dominee,
Domineke, Dominey,
Dominie, Dominika,
Domino, Dominy

Dominica
(Latin) follower of God
Dominika, Domenika, Domineca, Dom

Dominique
(French) bright; masterful
Dom, Domenique, Domino, Domonik

Dona
(Italian) form of Donna; gracious

Donata
(Italian) celebrating
Donada, Donatah, Donni, Donnie, Donny

Donatella
(Latin, Italian) gift
Don, Donnie, Donny

Donava
(African) jubilant
Donavah

Donika
(African-American) stemming from Donna; home-loving
Donica

Donisha
(African-American) laughing; cozy
Daneesha, Danisha, Doneesha

Donna
(Italian) ladylike and genteel
Dom, Don, Dona, Dondi, Donnie, Donya

Donnata
(Latin) giving
Dona, Donata, Donni

Donnelly
(Italian) lush
Donally, Donelly, Donnell, Donnelli, Donnellie, Donni, Donnie, Donny

Donnis
(American) pleasant; giving
Donnice

Donserena
(American) dancer; giving
Donce, Doncie, Dons, Donse, Donsee, Donser, Donsey

Donyale
(African-American) form of Danielle; kind
Donyelle

Dora
(Greek) gift from God
Dori, Dorie

Dorat
(French) a gift
Doratt, Dorey, Dorie

Doreen
(Greek, Irish) capricious
Dorene, Dorine, Dory

Dorian
(Greek) happy
Dorean, Doreane, Doree, Doriane, Dorri, Dorry

Dorianne
(American) combo of Doris and Ann; sparkly

Dorika
(Greek) God's gift
Doreek, Dorike, Dory

Doris
(Greek) place name; sea-loving; sea nymph mother
Dor, Dorice, Dorise, Doriss, Dory

Dorit
(Greek) God's gift; shy
Dooritt

Dornay
(American) involved
Dorn, Dornae, Dornee, Dorny

Dorren
(Irish) sad-faced
Doren

Dortha
(Greek) God's gift; studious
Dorth, Dorthee, Dorthey, Dorthy

Dory
(French) gilded; gold hair
Dora, Dore, Dorie

Dorthe
(Scandinavian) God's gift

Dorothea
(Greek) open-armed
Dorothia

Dorothy
(Greek) God's gift
Do, Dorathy, Dori, Dorthy

Dossey
(Last name as first) rambunctious
Dosse, Dossi, Dossie, Dossy, Dozze

Dot
(Greek) spunky
Dottee, Dottie, Dotty

Douce
(French) sweet
Doucia, Dulce, Dulci, Dulcie

Dougiana
(American) combo of Dougi and Ana
Dougi

Dove
(Greek) dreamy

Draven
(American) loyal
Dravan, Dravin, Dravine

Draxy
(American) faithful
Drax, Draxee, Draxey, Draxi

Drea
(American) adorable

Dream, Dreama
(American) dreamgirl; misty
Dreamee, Dreamey, Dreami, Dreamie, Dreamy

Dree
(American) softspoken

Dreena
(American) cautious
Dreenah, Drina

Drew
(Greek) woman of valor
Dru, Drue

Drover
(American) surprising
Drovah, Drovar

Dru
(American) bright
Drew, Drue

Druanna
(American) bold
Drewann, Drewanne, Druanah, Druannah

Drucelle
(American) smart
Druce, Drucee, Drucel, Drucell, Drucey, Druci, Drucy

Drusilla
(Latin) strong
Dru, Drucilla

Dryden
(Last name as first name) special
Dydie

Dubethza
(Invented) sad
Dubeth

Duchess
(American) fancy
Duc, Duchesse, Ducy, Dutch, Dutchey, Dutchie, Dutchy

Duffy
(Irish) spunky

Dufvenius
(Swedish) lovely
Duf, Duff

Duhnell
(Hebrew) kind-hearted
Danee, Danny, Nell

Dulce-Maria
(Spanish) sweet Mary
Dulce, Dulcey

Dulcie, Dulcy
(Latin, Spanish) sweet one
Dee, Dulce, Dulcey

Dune
(American) summery
Doone, Dunah, Dunie

Dumia
(Hebrew) quiet
Dumi

Dunesha
(African-American) warm
Dunisha

Dupre
(American) softspoken
Dupray, Duprey

Dusanka
(Slavic) soulful
*Dusan, Dusana, Dusank,
Sanka*

Duscha
(Russian) happy
Dusa

Dusky
(Invented) dreamy

Dusky-Dream
(Invented) dreamy
Duskee-Dream

Dustine, Dustina
(German) go-getter
*Dusteen, Dustene, Dusti,
Dustie, Dusty*

Dusty
(American) southern
*Dustee, Dusti, Dustie,
Dustey*

Dwanda
(American) athletic
*Dwana, Dwayna,
Dwunda*

Dyan
(Latin) form of Diane;
divine
Dian, Dyana, Dyann

Dyandra
(Latin) sleek
*Diandra, Dianndrah,
Dyan, Dyandruh*

Dylan
(Welsh) creative; from
the sea
*Dilann, Dyl, Dylane,
Dylann, Dylanne, Dylen,
Dylin, Dyllan, Dylynn*

Dymond
(American) variant of
diamond
*Dymahn, Dymon,
Dymonn, Dymund*

Dyney
(American) consoling
others
Diney, DiNey, Dy

Dyonne
(American) marvelous
*Dyonn, Dyonna,
Dyonnae*

Dyronisha
(African-American) fine
Dyron

Dyshaunna
(African-American)
dedicated
*Dyshaune, Dyshawn,
Dyshawna*

Dywon
(American) bubbly
*Diwon, Dywan, Dywann,
Dywaughn, Dywonne*

E

Eadrianne
(American) standout
*Eddey, Eddi, Eddy,
Edreiann, Edrian, Edrie*

Earla
(English) leader
*Earlah, Erla, Erlene,
Erletta, Erlette*

Earlean
(Irish) dedicated
Earlene, Earline, Erlenne

Early
(American) bright
*Earlee, Earlie, Earlye,
Erly*

Eartha
(English) earth mother

Easter
(American) born on
Easter; spring-like

Easton
(American) wholesome
*Eastan, Easten, Eeston,
Eastun, Estynn*

Eavan
(Irish) beautiful
Evaughn, Eevonne

Ebba
(English, Scandinavian)
strong
Eb, Eba, Ebbah

Ebban
(American) pretty;
affluent
Ebann, Ebbayn

Ebony
(Greek) hard and dark
*Eb, Ebanie, Ebbeny,
Ebbie, Ebonea, Ebonee,
Eboney, Eboni, Ebonie,
Ebonni*

Ebrel
(Cornish) from the
month April
*Ebby, Ebrelle, Ebrie,
Ebrielle*

Echo
(Greek) smitten
Eko

Ecstasy
(American) joyful
Ecstasey, Ecstasie, Stase

Edaena
(Irish) fiery; energetic
*Ed, Eda, Edae, Edana,
Edanah, Edaneah, Eddi*

Edalene
(German) refined
*Eda, Edalyne, Edeline,
Ediline, Lena, Lene*

Edana
(Irish) flaming energy
Edan, Edanna

Eddi
(English) form of
Edwina; spirited
brunette
Eddie, Eddy

Edel
(German) clever; noble
Edell, Eddi

Eden
(Hebrew) paradise of
delights
Edene, Edyn

Edenathene
(American) combo of
Eden and Athene

Edie
(English) short for Edith;
blessed
Edee, Edy, Eydie

Edith
(English) a blessed girl
who is a gift to mankind
*Edy, Edyth, Edythe,
Eydie*

Edju
(Origin unknown) giving
Eddju

Edlin
(German) noble;
sophisticated
*Eddi, Eddy, Edlan,
Edland, Edlen*

Edmee
(American) spontaneous
*Edmey, Edmi, Edmy,
Edmye*

Edmonda
(English) form of
Edmond; rich
*Edmon, Edmond,
Edmund, Edmunda,
Monda*

Edna
(Hebrew) youthful
Eddie, Ednah, Eydie

Edreanna
(American) merry
*Edrean, Edreana,
Edreanne, Edrianna*

Edrina
(American) old-
fashioned
*Ed, Eddi, Eddrina,
Edrena, Edrinah*

Edsel
(American) plain
Eds, Edsell, Edzel

Edshone
(American) wealthy
Ed, Eds, Edshun

Edwina
(English) prospering
female
*Eddi, Eddy, Edwena,
Edwenna, Edwyna,
Edwynna*

Effemy
(Greek and German)
good singer
*Efemie, Efemy, Effee,
Effemie, Effey, Effie, Effy*

Effie
(Greek) of high morals;
(German) good singer
Effi, Effy

Egan
(American) wholesome
Egen, Egun

Egypt
(Place name) exotic
Egyppt

Egzanth
(Invented) form of
Xanthe; beautiful blonde

Eileen
(Irish) bright and
spirited
*Eilean, Eilee, Eileena,
Eileene, Elene, Ellie*

Eireen
(Scandinavian)
peacemaker
*Eirena, Erene, Ireen,
Irene*

Eires
(Greek) peaceful
Eiress, Eres, Heris

Eirianne
(English) peaceful
Eirian, Eriann

Elaine
(French) dependable girl
*Elane, Elayn, Elayne,
Ellaine*

Elana
(Greek) pretty
Ela, Elanie, Lainie

Elata
(Latin) bright; well-
positioned
*Ela, Elate, Elatt, Elle,
Elota*

Elda
(Italian) protective

Eleacie
(American) forthright
Acey, Elea, Eleasie

Eldee
(American) light
El, Eldah, Elde

Eldora
(Spanish) golden spirit

Eleanor
(Greek) light-hearted
*Elanore, Eleanora,
Eleonore, Ellie, Ellinor,
Ellinore, Lenore*

Electra
(Greek) resilient and
bright
Elec, Elek, Elektra

Elegy
(American) lasting
*Elegee, Eleggee, Elegie,
Eligey*

Elek
    (American) star-like
    Elec, Ellie, Elly
Elena
    (Greek, Russian, Italian,
    Spanish) light and
    bright; beautiful
    *Elana, Eleena, Elene,
    Ilena, Ilene, Lena, Leni,
    Lennie, Lina, Nina*
Eleni
    (Greek) sweet
    Elenee
Eleonore
    (Greek, German) light
    and bright
    Elenore, Elle, Elnore
Eleri
    (Welsh) smooth
    Elere, Eleree
Elettra
    (Latin, Italian) shining
Elfin
    (American) small girl
    *El, Elf, Elfan, Elfee, Elfey,
    Elfie, Elfun, Els*
Elfrida
    (German) peaceful spirit
    *Elfreeda, Elfreyda,
    Elfryda*

Eliana
    (Latin, Greek, Italian)
    sunny
    *Eliane, Elliana, Ellianne,
    Ellie*
Eliane
    (French) cheerful; sunny
Elisa
    (English, Italian) God-
    loving; grace
    *Eleesa, Elesa, Elissa,
    Elisse, Leese, Leesie,
    Lisa*
Elisabet
    (Hebrew, Scandinavian)
    God as her oath
    Bet, Elsa, Else, Elisa
Elisabeth
    (Hebrew, French,
    German) sworn to God
    *Bett, Bettina, Elisa, Elise,
    Els, Elsa, Elsie, Ilsa,
    Ilyse, Liesa, Liese,
    Lisbeth, Lise*
Elise
    (French, English) soft-
    mannered
    *Elice, Elisse, Elle, Ellyse,
    Lisie*
Elisha
    (Greek) God-loving
    *Eleasha, Elicia, Eliesha,
    Ellie, Lisha*

Elite
    (Latina) best
    Elita
Eliza
    (Irish) sworn to God
    Elieza, Elyza
Elizabeth
    (Hebrew) God-directed;
    beauty
    *Beth, Betsy, Elisabeth,
    Elizebeth, Lissie, Liza*
Elke
    (Dutch) distinguished
Elkie
    (Dutch) variant of Elke;
    distinguished
    Elk, Elka
Ella
    (Greek) beautiful and
    fanciful
    Elle, Ellie, Elly
Ella Bleu
    (Invented) combo of Ella
    and Bleu; gorgeous
    daughter of fame
    Ella-Bleu
Ellaina
    (American) sincere
    Elaina, Ellana, Ellanuh
Ellan
    (American) coy
    Elan, Ellane, Ellyn
Elle
    (Scandinavian) woman
    Ele

Ellen
(English) open-minded
El, Elen, Ellie, Ellyn, Elyn
Ellender
(American) decisive
*Elender, Ellander, Elle,
Ellie*
Elletra
(Greek, Italian) shining
Elletrah, Illetrah
Elli
(Scandinavian) aged
Ell, Elle, Ellie
Ellie
(English) candid
Ele, Elie, Elly
Ellyanne
(American) combo of Elly
and Anne
*Elian, Elianne, Ellyann,
Elyann*
Elma
(Turkish) sweet
El
Elmas
(Armenian) diamond-like
Elmaz, Elmes, Elmis
Elnora
(American) sturdy
Ellie, Elnor, Elnorah
Elodia
(Spanish) flowering
Elodi

Eloise
(German) high-spirited
Eluise, Luise
Elora
(American) fresh-faced
Elorah, Flory, Floree
Elpidia
(Spanish) shining
El, Elpey, Elpi, Elpie
Elrica
(German) leader
*Elrick, Elrika, Elrike,
Rica, Rika*
Elsa
(Hebrew, Scandinavian,
German) patient; regal
*Els, Elsah, Elseh, Elsie,
Ellsee*
Elsie
(German) hard-working
Elsee, Elsi
Elsiy
(Spanish) God-loving
*El, Els, Elsa, Elsee, Elsi,
Elsy*
Elspeth
(Scottish)
El, Elle, Els
Elton
(American) spontaneous
Elt, Elten, Eltone, Eltun
Elva
(English) tiny
Elvie, Elvina, Elvah

Elvia
(Latin) sunny
Elvea, Elviah, Elvie
Elvira
(Latin, German) light-
haired and quiet
Elva, Elvie
Elyanna
(American) good friend
*Elyana, Elyannah,
Elyunna*
Elyse
(English) soft-mannered
Elice, Elle, Elysee
Elyssa
(Greek) loving the
ocean; (English) lovely
and happy
*Elisa, Elissa, Elysa,
Illysa, Lyssa*
Elysia
(Latin) joyful
*Elyse, Elysee, Elysha,
Elyshia*
Emalee, Emaline
(German) thoughtful
*Emalea, Emaleigh,
Emaley, Emally, Emaly,
Emmalynn, Emmeline,
Emmelyne*
Emann
(American) softspoken
Eman

Ember
(American)
temperamental
Embere, Embre

Emberatriz
(Spanish) respected
Emb, Ember, Embera,
Emberatrice,
Emberatryce,
Embertrice, Embertrise

Emberli
(American) pretty
Em, Emb, Ember,
Emberlee, Emberley,
Emberly

Eme
(German) short for
Emma; strong
Emee, Emme, Emmee

Eme
(Hawaiian) loved
Em, Emee, Emm,
Emmee, Emmie, Emmy

Emelle
(American) kind
Emell

Emely
(German) go-getter
Emel, Emelee, Emelie

Emena
(Latin) of fortunate birth
Em, Emen, Emene,
Emina, Emine

Emerald
(French) bright as a
gemstone
Em, Emmie

Emestina
(American) form of
Ernestina; competitive
Emee, Emes, Emest, Tina

Emilee
(American) combo of
Emma and Lee

Emilia
(Italian) soft-spirited
Emila

Emily
(German) poised;
(English) competitor
Em, Emalie, Emilee,
Emili, Emilie, Emmi,
Emmie

Emma
(German, Irish) strong
Em, Emmah, Emme,
Emmie, Emmi, Emmot,
Emmy, Emmye, Emott

Emmalee
(American) combo of
Emma and Lee
Em, Emalee, Emliee,
Emma-Lee, Emmali,
Emmie

Emmaline
(French, German) form
of Emily
Em, Emaline, Emalyne,
Emiline, Emmie

Emmanuelle
(Hebrew, French)
believer
Em, Emmi, Emmie,
Emmy

Emmalise
(American) combo of
Emma and Lise; lovely
Emalise, Emmalisa,
Emmelise

Emme
(German) feminine
Em

Emmi
(German) pretty
Emmee, Emmey, Emmy

Emmylou
(American) combo of
Emmy and Lou
Emmilou, Emmi-Lou,
Emylou

Emylinda
(American) combo of
Emy and Linda; happy
and pretty
Emi, Emilind,, Emilynd,
Emy, Emylin, Emylynda

Ena
(Hawaiian) intense
Eana, En, Enna, Ina

Enchantay
(American) enchanting
Enchantee

Endah
(Irish) flighty
Ena, End, Enda

Endia
(American) variant of
India; magical
*Endee, Endey, Endie,
Endy, India, Ndia*

Enedina
(Spanish) praised,
spirited
Dina, Ened

Enid
(Welsh) lively
Eneid

Enore
(English) careful
Enoor, Enora

Enslie
(American) emotional
*Ens, Enslee, Ensley,
Ensly, Enz*

Enya
(Irish) fiery; musician
Enyah, Nya

Epifania
(Spanish) proof
*Epi, Epifaina, Epifanea,
Eppie, Pifanie, Piffy*

Eppy
(Greek) lively, always
"on"
*Ep, Eppee, Eppey, Eppi,
Eps*

Equoia
(African-American) great
equalizer
Ekowya

Eranth
(Greek) spring bloomer
*Erantha, Eranthae,
Eranthe*

Erasema
(Spanish) happy
Eraseme

Ercilia
(American) frank
Erci, Ercilya

Eres
(Greek) goddess of
chaos
Era, Ere, Eris

Erika
(Scandinavian)
honorable; leading
others
*Erica, Ericah, Ericca,
Ericka, Erikka, Eryka*

Erin
(Irish) peace-making
Eran, Erine, Erinne, Eryn

Erina
(American) peaceful
*Era, Erinna, Erinne,
Eryna, Erynne*

Erla
(Irish) playful

Erlind
(Hebrew) from Erlinda;
angelic
Erlinda, Erlinde

Erma
(Latin) wealthy
Erm, Irma

Ermelinda
(Spanish) fresh-faced
*Ermalinda, Ermelind,
Ermelynda*

Ermine
(Latin) rich
Ermeen, Ermie, Ermin

Erna
(English) short for
Ernestine; knowing;
earnest
Emae, Ernea, Ernie

Ernestine
(English) having a
sincere spirit
Ernestina, Ernestyne

Es
(American) short for
Estella
Esa, Essie

Esbelda
(Spanish) black-haired beauty
Es, Esbilda, Ezbelda

Esdey
(American) warm-hearted
Esdee, Esdy, Essdey

Eshah
(African) exuberant
Esha

Eshe
(African) life
Eshay

Eshey
(American) life
Es, Esh, Eshae, Eshay

Esmee
(French) much loved
Esme, Esmie

Esmeralda
(Spanish) emerald; shiny and bright
Es, Esmie, Esmirilda

Esne
(English) happy
Es, Esnee, Esney, Esny, Essie

Esperanza
(Spanish) hopeful
Es, Espe, Esperance

Essence
(American) ingenious
Esence, Essens, Essense

Essie
(English) shining
Es, Essy

Esta
(Hebrew) star
Es, Estah

Estee
(English) brightest
Esti

Estella
(French) star
Es, Estel, Estell, Estelle, Estie, Stell, Stella

Estelle
(French) star
Es, Estel, Estele, Estie

Estevina
(Spanish) adorned; wreathed
Estafania, Este, Estebana, Estefania, Estevan, Estevana

Esthelia
(Spanish) shining
Esthe, Esthel, Esthele, Esthelya

Esther
(Persian, English) shining star
Es, Essie, Ester

Estherita
(Spanish) bright
Estereta

Estime
(French) esteemed
Es

Estrella
(Latin) shining star
Estrell, Estrelle, Estrilla

Eta
(German) short for Henrietta
Etah

Etaney,
(Hebrew) focused
Eta, Etana, Etanah, Etanee

Ethel
(English) class
Ethyl

Ethelene
(American) form of Ethel; noble
Ethe, Etheline

Ethne
(Irish) blueblood
Eth, Ethnee, Ethnie, Ethny

Ethnea
(Irish) kernel; piece of the puzzle
Ethna, Ethnia

Etta
(German, English) short for Henrietta; energetic
Etti, Ettie, Etty

Eudlina
(Slavic) generous; afflent
Eudie, Eudlyna, Udie, Udlina

Eudocia
(Greek) fine
Eude, Eudocea, Eudosia

Eudora
(Greek) cherished

Eugenia
(Greek) regal and polished
Eugeneia, Eugenie, Eugina, Gee, Gina

Eula
(Greek) specific
Eulia

Eulala
(Greek) spoken sweetly
Eulalah

Eulalia
(Greek, Italian) spoken sweetly
Eula, Eulia, Eulie

Eulanda
(American) fair
Eudlande, Eulee, Eulie

Eulee
(Greek)
Eulie, Ulee, Uley

Eunice
(Greek) joyful; winning
Euniece, Eunise

Eupheme
(Greek) well-spoken
Eu, Euphemee, Euphemi, Euphemie

Euphemia
(Greek) respected
Eufemia, Euphie, Uphie

Eurydice
(Greek) adventurous
Euridice

Eustacia
(Greek) industrious
Eustace, Stacey, Stacy

Euvenia
(American) hardworking
Euvene, Euvenea

Eva
(Hebrew, Scandinavian) life
Evah

Evadne
(Greek) pleasing; lucky
Eva, Evad, Evadnee, Evadny

Evaline
(French) form of Evelyn; matter-of-fact
Evalyn, Eveleen

Evalouise
(American) combo of Eva and Louise; witty
Eva-Louise, Evaluise

Eva-Marie
(American) combo of Eva and Marie; generous

Evan
(American) bright; precocious
Evann, Evin

Evana, Evania
(Greek) lovely woman
Eve, Ivana, Ivanna

Evangelina
(Greek) bringing joy
Eva, Evangeline, Eve, Lina

Evania
(Irish) spirited
Ev, Evanea, Eve

Evanthie
(Greek) flowering well
Evanthe, Evanthee, Evanthi

Eve
(French, Hebrew)
Eva, Evie, Evvy

Evelina
(French) lively
Eve, Evelin, Evelinna, Evelyn

Evelina
(Russian) lively
Evalina, Evalinna

Evelyn
(English) optimistic
Aveline, Ev, Evaline, Evalenne, Evline

Ever
(Invented name) cool; vibrant
Ev

Everilde
(Origin unknown) hunter

Evette
(French) dainty
Evett, Ivette

Evonne
(French) form of Yvonne; sensual
Evanne, Eve, Evie, Yvonne

Ewelina
(Polish) life
Eva, Lina

Eydie
(American) endearing
Eidey, Eydee

Eyote
(Native American) great
Eyotee

Ezra
(Hebrew) happy; helpful
Ezrah, Ezruh

Ezza
(American) healthy
Eza

Faba
(Latin) bean; thin
Fabah, Fava

Fabia
(Latin) fabulous; special
Fabiann, Fabianna, Fabianne

Fabienne
(French) farming beans
Fabiola, Fabiole

Fabio
(Latin) fabulous
Fabeeo, Fabeo, Fabeoh

Faillace
(French) delicate beauty
Faill, Faillaise, Faillase, Falace

Faine
(English) happy
Fai, Fainne, Fay, Fayne

Fairlee
(English) lovely
Fair, Fairlea, Fairley, Fairly

Faith
(English) loyal woman
Fay, Fayth

Falesyia
(Hispanic) exotic
Falesyiah, Falisyia

Faline
(Latin, French) lively
Faleen, Falene

Fall
(Season name) changeable
Falle

Fallon
(Irish) fetching; from the ruling class
Falan, Fallen, Fallyn, Falyn

Falsette
(American) fanciful
Falcette

Fanchon
(French) from France
Fan, Fanchee, Fanchie, Fanny, Fran, Frannie, Franny

Fancy
(English) fanciful
Fanci, Fancie

Fane
(American) strict
Fain, Faine

Fanfara
(Last name as first name) fanfare; excitement
Fann, Fanny

Fang
(Chinese) pleasantly scented

Fanny
(Latin) from France; bold; buttocks
Fan, Fani, Fannie

Fantasia
(American) inventive
Fantasha, Fantasiah, Fantasya, Fantazia

Fanteen
(English) clever
Fan, Fannee, Fanney, Fanny, Fantene, Fantine

Faredah
(Arabic) special
Farida

Faris
(American) forgiving
Fair, Farris, Pharis, Pharris

Farrah
(Arabic) beautiful; (English) joyful
Fara, Farah

Farren
(American) fair
Faren, Farin

Farrow
(American) narrow-minded
Farow, Farro

Faryl
(American) inspiring
Farel, Farelle

Fashion
(American) stylish
Fashon, Fashy, Fashyun

Fatima
(Arabic) wise woman; (African) dedicated
Fatema, Fatimah, Fatime

Faulk
(American) respected
Falk

Fauna
(Roman mythology) nature goddess
Faunah, Fawna, Fawnah

Faunee
(Latin) nature-loving
Fauney, Fauneye, Fawnae, Fawni, Fawny

Faustene
(French, American) envied
Fausteen, Faustine, Fausty, Fawsteen

Faustiana
(Spanish) good fortune
Faust, Fausti, Faustia, Faustina

Faustina
(Italian) lucky
Fawsteena, Fostina, Fostynna

Favianna
(Italian) confident
Faviana

Fawn
(French) gentle
Faun, Fawne

Fawna
(French) softspoken
Fawnna, Fawnah, Fawnuh

Faye
(English, French) light-spirited
Fae, Fay, Fey

Fayette
(American) southern
Fayet, Fayett, Fayetta, Fayitte

Fayleen
(American) quiet
Faylene, Fayline, Falyn, Falynn, Faye, Fayla

Fayth
(American) form of Faith; faithful
Faithe, Faythe

Feather
(Native American) svelte
Feathyr

Febe
(Polish, Greek) bright
Febee

February
(Latin) icy
Feb

Felder
(Last name as first
name) bright
Felde, Feldy

Felice
(Latin) happy
Felece, Felise

Felicia
(Latin) joyful
*Faleshia, Falesia, Felecia,
Felisha*

Felicie
(Latin) happy;
(German) fortunate
*Feliccie, Felicee, Felicy,
Felisie*

Felicita
(Spanish) gracious
*Felice, Felicitas, Felicitee,
Felisita*

Felicity
(Latin) happy girl
*Felice, Felicite, Felicitee,
Felisitee*

Felise
(German) joyful
Felis

Femay
(American) classy
Femae

Femi
(African) love-seeking
Femmi

Femise
(African-American)
asking for love
Femeese, Femmis

Fenn
(American) bright
Fen, Fynn

Feo
(Greek) God-given
Fee, Feeo

Feodora
(Greek) God-given girl
Fedora

Fern
(German, English) natural
Ferne

Fernanda
(German) bold
Ferdie, Fernnande

Fernilia
(American) successful
*Fern, Fernelia, Ferny,
Fyrnilia*

Feven
(American) shy
Fevan, Fevun

Fia
(Scandinavian) perky

Fiamma
(Italian) fiery spirit
*Feamma, Fee, Fia, Fiama,
Fiammette, Fifi*

Fidela
(Spanish) loyal
Fidele, Fidella, Fidelle

Fidelia
(Italian) faithful
Fidele

Fidelity
(Latin) loyal
Fidele, Fidelia

Fife
(American) dancing
eyes; musical
Fifer, Fifey, Fyfe

Fifi
(French) jazzy
Fifee

Fifia
(African) Friday's child
FeeFee, Fifeea

Filia
(Greek) devoted
Filea, Feleah, Filiah

Fillis
(Greek) form of Phyllis;
devoted
*Filis, Fill, Fillees, Filly,
Fillys, Fylis*

Finelle
(Irish) fair-faced
*Fee, Finell, Finn, Finny,
Fynelle*

Finesse
(American) smooth
Fin, Finese, Finess

Finn
(Irish) cool

Fion
(Irish) blonde
Fiona
(Irish) fair-haired
Fionna
Fiorella
(Irish) spirited
Fee, Feorella, Rella
Fire
(American) feisty
Firey, Fyre
Flair
(English) stylish
Flaire, Flairey, Flare
Flame
(Invented) sensual
Flanders
(Place name) creative
Fland, Flann
Flannery
(Irish) warm; red-haired
Flann
Flavia
(Latin) light-haired
Flavie
Flax
(Botanical) plant with
blue flowers
Flacks, Flaxx
Fleming
(Last name as first
name) adorable
*Flemma, Flemmie,
Flemming, Flyming*

Flemmi
(Italian) pretty
Flemmy
Fleur
(French) flower
*Fleura, Fleuretta,
Fleurette, Fleuronne*
Flirt
(Invented) flirtatious
Flyrtt
Flo
(American) short for
Florence
Flor
(Spanish) blooming
*Flo, Flora, Floralia,
Florencia, Florencita,
Florens, Florensia,
Flores, Floria, Floriole,
Florita, Florite*
Flora
(Latin, Spanish)
flowering
Floria, Florie
Floramaria
(American) combo of
Flora and Maria; spring;
Mary's flower
Flora Maria, Flora-Maria

Florence
(Latin, Italian) place
name; flourishing and
giving
*Flo, Flora, Florencia,
Florense, Florenze,
Florie, Florina, Flossie*
Florens
(Polish) blooming
Floren
Florent
(French) flowering
*Flor, Floren, Florentine,
Florin*
Florida
(Place name) flowered
Flora, Flory
Florine
(American) blooming
*Flo, Flora, Floren,
Floryne, Florynne*
Florizel
(Literature)
Shakespearean name;
in bloom
Flora, Flori, Florisel
Flower
(American) blossoming
beauty
Flo
Fluffy
(American) fun-loving
Fluff, Fluffi, Fluffie

Flynn
(Irish) red-haired
Flenn, Flinn, Flyn

Fog
(American) dreamy
Fogg, Foggee, Foggy

Fola
(African) honored
Folah

Fonda
(American) risk-taker
Fond

Fondice
(American) fond of
friends
Fondeese, Fondie

Fontaine
(French) fountain-like in
bounty
*Fontane, Fontanna,
Fontanne*

Fontenot
(French) special girl;
fountain of beauty
*Fonny, Fontay, Fonte,
Fonteno*

Ford
(Last name as first
name) confident
Forde

Fortune
(Latin) excellent fate;
prized

Fotine
(Greek) light-hearted
Foty, Fotyne

Fowler
(Last name as first
name) stylish
Fowla, Fowlar, Fowlir

Fran
(Latin) from France;
freewheeling
Frann, Franni, Frannie

France
(Place name) French girl
Frans, Franse

Frances
(Latin) free; of French
origin
*Fanny, Fran, Francey,
Franci, Francie, Franse*

Francesca
(Italian) form of Frances;
open-hearted
*Fran, Francessca,
Franchesca, Frannie*

Franchelle
(French) from France
*Franshell, Franchelle,
Franchey*

Franchesca
(Italian) smiling
*Cheka, Chekkie,
Francheska, Francheska,
Franchessca*

Francine
(French) form of Frances;
beautiful
*Fran, Franceen,
Francene, Francie*

Frankie
(American) a form of
Frances; tomboyish
Franki, Franky

Frannie
(English) friendly
Franni, Franny

Fransabelle
(Latin) beauty from
France
Fransabella, Franzabelle

Frea
(Scandinavian) noble;
hearty
Fray, Freas, Freya

Freddie
(English) short for
Frederica; spunky
Fredi, Freddy

Frederica
(German) peacemaking
*Federica, Fred, Freda,
Freddie, Fritze, Rica*

Free
(American) free; open

Freesia
(Botanical) fragrant
flower

Freida
(German) short for Frederica and Alfreda; graceful
Freda, Frida, Frieda

Frenchie
(French, American) saucy
French, Frenchee, Frenchi, Frenchy

Freya
(Scandinavian) goddess; beautiful
Freja

Frida
(Scandinavian) lovely

Frieda
(German) happy
Freda

Frigg
(Scandinavian) loved one
Frigga

Frigga
(Scandinavian) beloved
Fri, Friga, Frigg

Frond
(Botanical) growing

Frosty
(Name from a song) crisp and cool
Frostie

Frula
(German) hardworking

Fuchsia
(Botanical) blossoming pink
Fuesha

Fructuose
(Latin) bountiful
Fru, Fructuosa, Fruta

Frythe
(English) calm
Frith, Fryth

Fudge
(American) stubborn
Fudgey

Fulvy
(Latin) blonde
Full, Fulvee, Fulvie

Funda
(Turkish)
Fund

Fury
(Latin) raging anger
Furee, Furey, Furie

Fushy
(American) animated; vivid
Fooshy, Fueshy, Fushee

Gable
(German) farming woman
Gabbie, Gabby, Gabe, Gabell, Gabl

Gabor
(French) conflicted
Gaber, Gabi

Gabriela
(Italian, Spanish) God is her strength
Caby, Gabela, Gabi, Gabrela, Gabriella

Gabrielle
(French, Hebrew) strong by faith in God
Gabi, Gabraelle, Gabreelle, Gabreille, Gabríelle, Gabriele, Gabriella, Gabrilla, Gabrille, Gaby, Gaebriell, Gaebrielle, Garbreal

Gadar
(Armenian) perfect girl
Gad, Gadahr, Gaddie, Gaddy

Gaegae
(Greek) from Gaea;
earthy; happy
Gae, Gaege, Gaegie

Gaia
(Greek) goddess of earth
Gaea, Gaya

Gail
(Hebrew) short for
Abigail; energetic
Gaelle, Gale, Gayle

Gaily
(American) fun-loving
Gailai, Galhy

Gaitlynn
(American) hopeful
*Gaitlin, Gaitline,
Gaitlinn, Gaitlyn, Gaytlyn*

Gala
(French, Scandinavian)
joyful celebrant
*Gaila, Gailah, Galaa,
Galuh, Gayla*

Galatea
(Greek) sea nymph in
mythology
Gal, Gala

Galaxy
(American) universal
Gal, Galaxee, Galaxi

Galen
(American) decisive
*Galin, Galine, Galyn,
Gaye, Gaylen*

Galena
(Latin) metal; tough
Galyna, Galynna

Galiana
(German) vaulted
Galiyana, Galli, Galliana

Galina
(Russian) deserving
*Gailina, Gailinna,
Galyna, Galynna*

Galise
(American) joyful
*Galeece, Galeese,
Galice, Galyce*

Galya
(Hebrew) redeemed;
merry
Galia

Garcelle
(French) flowered
Garcel, Garsell, Garselle

Garland
(American) fancy
Garlan, Garlinn, Garlynn

Garlanda
(French) flowered
wreath; pretty girl
*Gar, Garl, Garlynd,
Garlynda*

Garlin
(French) variant of
Garland; decorative;
pretty
Garlyn

Garner
(American) stylesetter
Garnar, Garnir

Garnet
(English) pretty; semi-
precious stone

Garnetta
(French) gemstone;
precious
*Garna, Garnet, Garnie,
Garny*

Garrett
(Last name as first
name) bashful
Garret, Gerrett

Garri
(American) energetic
*Garree, Garrey, Garry,
Garrye*

Garrielle
(American) competent
*Gariele, Garielle,
Garriella*

Garrison
(American) sturdy
*Garisen, Garisun,
Garrisen, Garrisun*

Garrity
(American) smiling
*Garety, Garrety, Garity,
Garritee, Garritie*

Gartha
(American) form of male
name Garth; nature-
loving

Garyn
(American) svelte
Garen, Garin, Garinne, Garun, Garynn, Garynne

Gates
(Last name as first name) careful
Gate

Gauri
(Hindi) golden goddess

Gavin
(American) smart
Gave, Gaven, Gavey, Gavun

Gavion
(American) daring
Gaveon, Gavionne

Gaviotte
(French) graceful
Gaveott, Gaviot, Gaviott

Gavotte
(French) dancer
Gav, Gavott

Gay
(French) jolly
Gae, Gaye

Gayla
(American) planner
Gaila, Gailah, Gala, Gaye, Gaylah, Gayluh

Gaylynn
(American) combo of Gay and Lynn
Gaelen, Gaylene, Gaylyn, Gay-Lynn

Gaynelle
(American) combo of Gay and Nelle
Gaye, Gaynel, Gaynell, Gaynie

Gaynor
(American) precocious
Ganor, Gayner, Gaynorre

Geanna
(American) ostentatious
Geannah, Gianna

Geena
(Italian) form of Gina; statuesque
Gina, Ginah

Gelacia
(Spanish) treasure
Gela, Gelasha, Gelasia

Gelda
(American) gloomy
Geilda, Geldah, Gelduh

Gem
(American) shining
Gemmy, Gim, Jim

Gemesha
(African-American) dramatic
Gemeisha, Gemiesha, Gemme, Gemmy, Gimesha

Gemini
(Greek) twin
Gem, Gemelle, Gemmy

Gemma
(Latin, Italian, French) jewel-like
Gem, Gemmie, Gemmy

Gemmy
(Italian) gem
Gemmee, Gemmi, Gimmy

Gems
(American) shining gem
Gem, Gemmie, Gemmy

Gena
(French) form of Gina; short for Genevieve
Geena, Gen, Genah, Geni, Genia

Genell
(American) form of Janelle
Genill

Genera
(Greek) highborn
Gen, Genere

Generosa
(Spanish) generous
Generosah, Generossa

Genesis
(Latin) fast starter; beginning
Gen, Gena, Geney, Genisis, Jenesis

Geneva
(French) city in Switzerland; flourishing like juniper
Gena, Janeva, Jeneva

Genevieve
(German, French) high-minded
Gen, Gena, Genna, Genavieve, Genovieve

Genica
(American) intelligent
Gen, Genicah, Genicuh, Genika, Gennica, Jen, Jenika, Jennika

Genna
(English) womanly
Gen, Genny, Jenna

Gennelle
(American) combo of Genn and Elle; graceful
Genel, Genelle, Ginelle, Jenele, Jenelle

Gennese
(American) helpful
Gen, Geneece, Geniece, Genny, Ginece, Gineese

Gennifer
(American) form of Jennifer
Genefer, Genephur, Genifer

Genoa
(Italian) playful
Geenoa, Genoah, Jenoa

Genoveva
(American) form of Genevieve; white; light
Genny, Geno

Gentle
(American) kind
Gen, Gentil, Gentille, Gentlle

Gentry
(American) sweet
Gen, Gentree, Gentrie, Jentrie, Jentry

Geoma
(American) outstanding
Gee, GeeGee, Geo, Geomah, Geome, Gigi, Jeoma, Oma, Omah

Geonna
(American) sparkling
Gee, Geionna, Geone, Geonne, Geonnuh

Georgann
(English) bright-eyed
Georganne, Jorgann, Joryann

Georgene
(English) wandering
Georgena, Georgene, Jorgeen, Jorjene

Georgette
(French) lively and little
Jorgette

Georgia
(Greek, English) southern; cordial
Georgi, Georgie, Georgina, Giorgi, Jorga, Jorgia, Jorja

Georgianna
(English) combo of Georgia and Anna; bright-eyed
Georganna, Georgeanna, Jorjeana, Jorgianna

Georgina
(Greek, English) earthy

Geraldine
(German) strong
Geraldyne, Geri, Gerri, Gerry

Geralena
(French) leader
Gera, Geraleen, Geralen, Geralene, Gerre, Gerrilyn, Gerry, Jerrileena, Lena

Germaine
(French) of German origin; important
Germain, Jermaine

Gertrude
(German) beloved
Gerdie, Gerti, Gertie

Gervaise
(French) strong
Gerva, Gervaisa

Gessalin
(American) loving
Gessilin, Gessalyn, Gessalynn, Jessalin, Jessalyn

Gessica
(American) form of Jessica
Gesica, Gesika, Gessika

Gethsemane
(Biblical) peaceful
Geth, Gethse, Gethsemanee, Gethsemaney, Gethsemanie, Gethy

Geynille
(American) womanly
Geynel

Gezelle
(American) lithe
Gezzelle, Gizele, Gizelle

Ghada
(Arabic) graceful
Ghad, Ghadah

Ghadeah
(Arabic) graceful
Gadea, Gadeah

Ghandia
(African) able
Gandia, Ghanda, Ghandee, Ghandy, Gondia, Gondiah

Ghea
(American) confident
Ghia, Jeah, Jeeah

Gherlan
(American) forgiving; joyful
Gerlan, Gherli

Ghita
(Italian) pearl
Gita, Gite

Giacinte
(Italian) hyacinth; flowering
Gia, Giacin, Giacinta

Gianina
(Italian) believer
Gia, Giane, Giannina, Gianyna, Janeena, Janina, Jeanina

Gianna
(Italian) forgiving
Geonna, Giana, Gianne, Gianne, Gianni, Giannie, Gianny, Ginny

Gianne
(Italian) combo of Gi and Anne; divine
Gia, Gian, Giann, Gigi

Giannelle
(American) hearty
Geanelle, Gianella, Gianelle, Gianne

Giannesha
(African-American) friendly
Geannesha, Gianesha, Giannesh, Gianneshah, Gianneshuh

Giara
(Italian) sensual
Gee, Geara, Gia, Giarah

Gidget
(American) cute
Gidge, Gidgett, Gidgette, Gydget

Gift
(American) blessed
Gifte, Gyft

Gigi
(French) small, spunky
Geegee, Giggi

Gilberta
(German) smart
Bertie, Gill

Gilda
(English) gold-encrusted
Gildi, Gildie, Gill

Gilleese
(American) funny
Gill, Gillee, Gilleece, Gillie, Gilly

Gillen
(American) humorous
Gill, Gilly, Gillyn, Gyllen

Gilli
(American) joyful
Gill, Gillee, Gilly

Gillian
(Latin) youthful
Gila, Gili, Gilian, Giliana, Gilliana, Gilliane, Gillie, Gilly, Jillian

Gillis
(Last name as first name) conservative
Gillice, Gillis, Gilise, Gylis, Gyllis

Gilma
(American) form of Wilma; fortified
Gee, Gilly

Gilmore
(Last name as first name) striking
Gilmoor, Gill, Gillmore, Gylmore

Gina
(Italian) well-born
Geena, Gin, Ginah, Ginny, Jenah

Ginacarol
(American) combo of Gina and Carol
Gina-Carol, Gina-Carrol, Gyna-Carole

Ginamarie
(Italian) combo of Gina and Marie
Gina-Marie, Ginamaria

Ginane
(French) well-born
Gigi, Gina, Gine, Jeanan, Jeanine

Ginger
(Latin) spicy
Gin, Ginny, Jinger

Ginnifer
(American) form of Jennifer
Gini, Ginifer, Giniferr, Ginifir, Ginn

Gioconda
(Italian) pleasing
Gio, Giocona

Giono
(Last name as first name) delight; friendly
Gio, Gionna, Gionno

Giorgio
(Italian) form of George; earthy; vivacious
Giorgi, Giorgie, Jorgio

Giovanna
(Italian) gracious believer; great entertainer
Geo, Geovanna, Gio, Giovahna, Giovana

Giritha
(Sri Lankan) melodic
Giri, Girith

Gisbelle
(American) lovely girl
Gisbel

Giselle
(German) naïve;
(French) devoted friend
Gis, Gisel, Gisela, Gisele, Gissel, Gissell, Gissella, Gisselle, Gissie, Jizele

Gita
(Sanskrit) song
Geta, Gete, Git, Gitah

Gitele
(Hebrew) good
Gitel

Gitika
(Sanskrit) little singer
Getika, Gita, Giti, Gitikah

Givonnah
(Italian) loyal; believer
Gevonna, Gevonnuh, Givonn, Givonna, Givonne, Jevonah, Jevonna, Jivonnah, Juvona

Gizela
(Polish) dedicated
Giz, Gizele, Gizzy

Gizmo
(American) tricky
Gis, Gismo, Giz,

Gladiola
(Botanical) blooming; flower
Glad, Gladdee, Gladdy

Gladys
(Welsh) flower; princess
Glad, Gladice, Gladise, Gladdie

Glafira
(Spanish) giving
Glafee, Glafera, Glafi

Gleam
(American) bright girl
Glee, Gleem

Glenda
(Welsh) bright; good
Glinda, Glynda, Glynn, Glynnie

Glenna
(Irish) form of Glenda; fair
Glenn

Glenna
(Irish) valley-living
Glena, Glenah, Glenuh, Glyn, Glynna

Glennesha
(African-American) special
Glenesha, Gleneshuh, Gleniesha, Glenn, Glenneshah, Glenny, Glinnesha

Glennice
(American) topnotch
Glenis, Glennis, Glenys, Glenysse, Glynnece, Glynnice

Gloria
(Latin) glorious
Glorea, Glorey, Glori, Gloriah, Glorrie, Glory

Glorianne
(American) combo of Gloria and Anne
Gloriann, Glori-Ann, Glorianna, Gloryann, Glory-Anne

Glorielle
(American) generous
Gloriel, Gloriele, Glory, Gloree, Glori

Gloris
(American) glorious
Gloeeca, Glores, Gloresa, Glorisa, Glorus, Gloryssa

Glory
(Latin) shining
Gloree, Glori, Glorie

Gloss
(American) showy
Glosse, Glossee, Glossie, Glossy

Glynisha
(African-American) vibrant
Glynesh, Glynn, Glynnecia, Glynnesha, Glynnie, Glynnisha

Glynnis
(Welsh) vivacious; glen
Glenice, Glenis, Glennis, Glinice, Glinnis, Glynn, Glynnie, Glynny

Goala
(American) goal-oriented
Go, GoGo, Gola

Goddess
(American) gorgeous
Godess, Goddesse

Godiva
(English) God's gift; brazen
Godeva, Godivah

Golda
(English) golden
Goldi, Goldie

Golden
(American) shining
Goldene, Goldon, Goldun, Goldy

Goldie
(English) bright and golden girl; form of Yiddish Golda
Goldi, Goldy

Goliad
(Spanish) goal-oriented
Goleade, Goliade

Goneril
(Literature)
Shakespearean name in
King Lear
Gonarell, Gonarille,
Gonereal

Grable
(American) handsome
woman
Gray, Graybell

Grace
(Latin) graceful
Graci, Gracie, Gracy,
Gray, Grayce

Graceann
(American) girl of grace
Gracean, Grace-Ann,
Graceanna, Graceanne,
Gracee, Gracy

Gracie
(Latin) graceful
Graci, Gracy, Graecie,
Gray

Graciela
(Spanish) pleasant; full
of grace
Chita, Gracee, Gracella,
Gracey, Gracie, Graciella,
Gracilla, Grasiela,
Graziela

Graham
(American) sweet
Graehm, Grayhm

Grania
(Irish) love
Grainee, Graini

Gratia
(Scandinavian) beautiful
girl
Gart, Gert, Gertie,
Grasha, Gratea, Gratie

Gratia
(Scandinavian) graceful;
gracious
Grateah

Gray
(Last name as first
name) quiet
Graye, Grey

Grayson
(Last name as first) child
of quiet one
Graison, Grasen,
Greyson

Grazie
(Italian) graceful;
pleasant
Grasie, Grazee, Grazy

Grazyna
(Polish) graceful;
pleasant

Gregory
(American) scholarly
Gregoree, Gregge,
Greggy, Gregoria,
Gregorie

Greshawn
(African-American) lively
Greeshawn, Greshaun,
Greshawna, Greshonn,
Greshun

Gresia
(American) compelling
Grecia, Grasea, Graysea,
Grayshea

Greta
(German) a pearl
Gretah, Grete, Gretie,
Grette, Grytta

Gretchen
(German) a pearl
Gretch, Gretchin,
Gretchun, Grethyn

Gretel
(German) pearl; fanciful
Gretal, Grettel, Gretell,
Gretelle

Greyland
(American) focused
Grey, Greylin, Greylyn,
Greylynne

Griffie
(Welsh) royal
Griff, Griffee, Griffey,
Griffi, Gryffie

Griffin
(Welsh) royal
Griff

Griselda
(German) patient
Grezelda, Grisel, Grissy, Grizel, Grizelda, Grizzie

Grisham
(Last name as first name) ambitious
Grish

Grindelle
(American) livewire
Dell, Delle, Grenn, Grin, Grindee, Grindell, Grindy, Renny

Griselia
(Spanish) gray; patient
Grise, Grisele, Grissy, Seley, Selia

Grizel
(Spanish) longsuffering
Griz, Grizelda, Grizelle, Grizzy

Guadalupe
(Spanish) patron saint; easygoing
Lupe, Lupeta, Lupita

Gubby
(Irish) cuddly
Gub, Gubee, Gubbie

Gudrun
(Scandinavian) close friend; (German) contentious
Gudren, Gudrenne, Gudrin, Gudrinne

Guinevere
(Welsh) queen; white
Guin, Gwen

Gunilla
(Scandinavian) warlike
Gun, Gunn

Gunun
(German) lively
Gunan, Gunen

Gurlene
(American) smart
Gurl, Gurleen, Gurleene, Gurline

Gurshawn
(American) talkative
Gurdie, Gurshauna, Gurshaune, Gurshawna, Gurty

Gussie
(Latin) short for Augusta; industrious
Gus, Gussy, Gustie

Gusta
(German) from Gustava; watchful
Gussy, Gusta, Gustana, Gusty

Guy
(French) guiding; assertive
Guye

Guylaine
(American) combo of Guy and Laine; haughty
Guylane, Gylane

Guylynn
(American) combo of Guy and Lynn; tough-minded
Guylinne, Guylyn, Guylyne

Gwen
(Welsh) short for Gwendolyn; happy
Gwyn, Gweni, Gwenna

Gwendolyn
(Welsh) mystery goddess; bright
Gwenda, Gwendalinne, Gwendalyn, Gwendelynn, Gwendolen, Gwendolin, Gwendoline, Gwendolynn, Gwennie, Gywnne

Gwenless
(Invented) fair
Gwen, Gwenles, Gwenny

Gwenora
(American) combo of Gwen and Nora; playful; fair-skinned
Guinn, Guinna, Guinnora, Guinnoray, Guinore, Gwen, Gwena, Gwenda, Gwendah, Gwenee, Gwenna, Gwennie, Gwennora, Gwenny, Gwenorah, Gwenore, Nora, Nore, Norra

Gwyn
    (Welsh) short for
    Gwyneth; happy
    Gwenn, Gwinn, Gwynne
Gwyneth
    (Welsh) blessed
    *Gwennie, Gwinith,
    Gwynith, Gwynne,
    Gwynneth, Win, Winnie*
Gylla
    (Spanish) from
    Guillermo; determined
    Guilla, Gye, Gyla, Jilla
Gynette
    (American) form of
    Jeannette; believer
    *Gyn, Gynett, Gynnee,
    Gynnie*
Gypsy
    (English) adventurer
    Gippie, Gipsie, Gypsie
Gyselle
    (German) variant of
    Giselle; naïve
    Gysel, Gysele
Gythae
    (English) feisty
    Gith, Gyth, Gythay

Ha
    (Vietnamese) happy
Habiba
    (Arabic) well-loved
    Habibah
Hadassah
    (Hebrew) form of Esther;
    myrtle; love
    *Hadasah, Hadassa,
    Haddasah, Haddee,
    Haddi, Haddy*
Hadil
    (Arabic) cooing
Hadlee
    (English) girl in heather
    *Hadlea, Hadley, Hadli,
    Hadly*
Hady
    (Greek) soulful
    *Haddie, Hadee, Hadie,
    Haidee, Haidie*
Hadyn
    (American) smart
    Haden
Haelee
    (English) form of Hailey

Hagar
    (Hebrew) stranger
    Haggar, Hager, Hagur
Hagir
    (Arabic) wanderer
    Hajar
Hailey
    (English) natural; hay
    meadow
    *Hailea, Hailee, Hailie,
    Halee, Haley, Hallie*
Halcyone
    (Greek) calm
    Halceonne, Halcyon
Haletta
    (Greek) little country girl
    from the meadow
    *Hale, Halette, Hallee,
    Halletta, Halley, Hallie,
    Hally, Letta, Lettie, Letty*
Haleyanne
    (American) combo of
    Haley and Anne
    *Haleyana, Haleyanna,
    Haley-Ann*
Halima
    (Arabic) gentle
Hall
    (Last name as first
    name) distinguished
    Haul
Hallie
    (German) high-spirited
    *Halle, Hallee, Haleigh,
    Hali, Halie, Hally, Hallye*

Halsey
(American) playful
Halcie, Halsee, Halsie

Halston
(American) stylish
Hall, Halls, Halsten

Halzey
(American) leader
*Hals, Halsee, Halsi,
Halsy, Halze, Halzee*

Hameedah
(Arabic) grateful

Hamilton
(American) wishful
*Hamil, Hamilten,
Hamiltun, Hamma,
Hamme*

Hanna
(Polish) grace

Hannah
(Hebrew) merciful; God-
blessed; a sweet Biblical
name
*Hanae, Hanah, Hanan,
Hannaa, Hanne, Hanni*

Hannette
(American) form of
Jannette; graceful
Hann, Hanett, Hannett

Hansa
(Indian) swan-like
*Hans, Hansah, Hansey,
Hanz*

Happy
(English) joyful
Hap, Happee, Happi

Harla
(English) country girl
from the fields
*Harlah, Harlea, Harlee,
Harlen, Harlie, Harlun*

Harlan
(English) athletic
Harlen, Harlon, Harlun

Harlequine
(Invented) romantic
Harlequinne, Harley

Harley
(English) wild thing
*Harlea, Harlee, Harleey,
Harli, Harlie, Harly*

Harlinne
(American) vivacious
*Harleen, Harleene,
Harline, Harly*

Harlow
(American) brash
Harlo, Harly

Harmon
(Last name as first
name) attuned
*Harmen, Harmone,
Harmun, Harmyn*

Harmony
(Latin) in synchrony
*Harmonee, Harmoni,
Harmonie*

Harper
(English) musician;
writer
Harp

Harrell
(American) leader
*Harell, Harill, Haryl,
Harryl*

Harriet
(French) homebody
*Harri, Harrie, Harriett,
Harriette, Hattie*

Hart
(American) romantic
*Harte, Hartee, Hartie,
Harty, Heart*

Hasina
(African) beauty

Hattie
(English) home-loving
Hatti, Hatty, Hettie, Hetty

Haute
(French, American)
stylish
Hautie

Hava
(Hebrew) life; lively
Chaba, Chaya, Haya

Havana
(Cuban) loyal
*Havanah, Havane,
Havanna, Havvanah,
Havanuh*

Haven
(American) safe place; open
Havin, Havun

Haviland
(American) lively; talented
Havilan, Havilynd

Hawkins
(American) wily
Hawk, Hawkens, Hawkey, Hawkuns

Hawlee
(American) negotiator
Hawlea, Hawleigh, Hawlie, Hawley, Hawly

Haydee
(American) capable
Hady, Hadye, Haydie

Haydon
(American) knowing
Hayden, Hadyn

Hayfa
(Arabic) slim

Hayley
(English) natural; hay meadow
Hailey, Haley, Haylee, Haylie

Hayleyann
(American) combo of Hayley and Ann
Haleyan, Haylee-Ann, Hayley-Ann, Hayli-Ann

Haze
(American) word as a name; spontaneous
Haise, Hay, Hays, Hazee, Hazey, Hazy

Hazel
(English) powerful
Hazell, Hazelle, Hazie, Hazyl, Hazzell

Heart
(American) romantic
Hart, Hearte

Heath
(English) open; healthy
Heathe

Heather
(Scottish) flowering
Heathar, Heathor, Heathur

Heaven
(English) happy and beautiful
Heavyn, Hevin

Heavenly
(American) spiritual
Heaven, Heavenlee, Heavenley, Heavynlie, Hevin

Hedda
(German) capricious; warring
Heda, Heddie, Hedi, Hedy, Hetta

Hedy
(German) mercurial
Hedi

Hedy-Marie
(German) capricious

Heidi
(German) noble; watchful; perky
Heide, Heidee, Heidie, Heidy, Hidi

Heidirae
(American) combo of Heidi and Rae
Heidi-Rae, Heidiray

Heija
(Korean) bright
Hia, Hya

Helaine
(French) ray of light; gorgeous
Helainne, Helle, Helyna, Hellyn

Helanna
(Greek) lovely
Helahna, Helana, Helani, Heley, Hella

Helen
(Greek) beautiful and light
Hela, Hele, Helena, Helyn, Lena, Lenore

Helena
(Greek) beautiful;
ingenious
*Helana, Helāyna,
Heleana, Helene,
Hellena, Helyena, Lena*

Helene
(French) form of Helen;
pretty but contentious
Helaine, Heleen, Heline

Helenore
(American) combo of
Helen and Lenore; light;
darling
*Hele, Helen, Helenoor,
Helenor, Helia, Helie,
Hellena, Lena, Lennore,
Lenora, Lenore, Lenory,
Lina, Nora, Norey, Norie*

Helga
(Anglo-Saxon) pious
Helg

Helia
(Greek) sun
Heleah, Helya, Helyah

Helie
(Greek) sunny
Heley, Heli

Helina
(Greek) delightful
*Helinah, Helinna,
Helinnuh*

Helki
(Native American) tender
Helkie, Helky

Heloise
(German) hearty
*Hale, Haley, Heley,
Heloese, Heloyse*

Hender
(American) embraced
Hendere

Henley
(American) sociable
*Hendlee, Hendly, Henli,
Henlie, Hinlie, Hynlie*

Henna
(Hindi, Arabic) plant that
releases colorful dye
*Hena, Hennah, Hennuh,
Henny*

Henrietta
(English, German)
home-ruler
*Harriet, Hattie, Henny,
Hetta, Hettie*

Hensley
(American) ambitious
Henslee, Henslie, Hensly

Hera
(Greek) wife of Zeus;
radiant

Herendira
(Invented) tender and
dear
Heren

Herise
(Invented) warm
Heree, Hereese, Herice

Herleen
(American) quiet
*Herlee, Herlene,
Hurleen, Herley, Herline,
Herly*

Hermilla
(Spanish) fighter
Herm, Hermila, Hermille

Hermione
(Greek) sensual
Hermina, Hermine

Hermosa
(Spanish) beautiful
Ermosa

Hersala
(Spanish) lithe and
lovely
*Hers, Hersila, Hersilia,
Hersy*

Hest
(Greek) star-like; variant
of Hester
Hessie, Hesta, Hetty

Hester
(American) literary
Hestar, Hesther

Hester-Mae
(American) combo of
Hester and Mae; star
Hester May, Hestermae

Hetta
(German)
*Hedda, Heta, Hettie,
Hetty*

Heven
(American) pretty
*Hevan, Hevin, Hevon,
Hevun, Hevven*

Heyzell
(American) form of
Hazel; tree; homebody
*Hayzale, Heyzel,
Heyzelle*

Hiah
(Korean) form of Heija;
bright
Hia, Hy, Hya, Hye

Hiatt
(English) form of Hyatt;
splendid
Hi, Hye

Hicks
(Last name as first
name) saucy
Hicksee, Hicksie

Hidee
(American) form of
Heidi; wry-humored
*Hidey, Hidie, Hidy,
Hydee, Hydeey*

Hilaria
(Latin, Polish)
merrymaker
*Hilarea, Hilareeah,
Hilariah*

Hilary
(Latin) cheerful and
outgoing
*Hilaire, Hilaree, Hilari,
Hilaria, Hillarree, Hillary,
Hillerie, Hillery*

Hilda
(German) practical;
(Scandinavian) fighter
Hildi, Hildie, Hildy

Hildegard
(German, Scandinavian)
steadfast protector
*Hilda, Hildagarde,
Hildegarde, Hildred,
Hillie*

Hilton
(American) wealthy
*Hillie, Hilltawn, Hillton,
Hilly*

Himalaya
(Place name) upwardly
mobile
Hima

Hinton
(American) affluent
*Hintan, Hinten, Hintun,
Hynton*

Hodge
(Last name as first
name) confident
Hodj

Holden
(English) willing
Holdan, Holdun

Holder
(English) beautiful voice
Holdar, Holdur

Holiday
(American) jazzy
*Holidae, Holidaye,
Holladay, Holliday, Holly*

Holine
(American) special
*Hauline, Holinn, Holli,
Holyne*

Holland
(Dutch) place name;
expressive
Hollan, Hollyn, Holyn

Hollis
(English) smart; girl by
the holly
Hollice, Hollyce

Hollisha
(English) ingenious;
Christmas-born; holly
*Holicha, Hollice,
Hollichia, Hollise*

Holly
(Anglo-Saxon)
Christmas-born; holly
tree
*Hollee, Holleigh, Holley,
Holli, Hollye*

Holsey
(American) laidback
Holsee, Holsie

Holton
(American) whimsical
Holt, Holten, Holtun

Holyn
(American) fresh-faced
*Holan, Holen, Holland,
Hollee, Hollen, Holley,
Hollie, Holly, Hollyn,
Hollyn*

Homer
(American) tomboyish
*Homar, Home, Homera,
Homie, Homir, Homma*

Honesty
(American) truthful
*Honeste, Honestee,
Honesti, Honestie,
Honestye*

Honey
(Latin) sweet-hearted
Honie, Hunnie

Honor
(Latin) ethical
Honer, Honora, Honour

Honora
(Latin) honorable
*Honorah, Honoree,
Honoria, Honoura*

Honorata
(Polish) respected
woman

Honoria
(Spanish) of high
integrity; a saint
Honoreah

Honorina
(Spanish) honored
*Honor, Honora,
Honoryna*

Hope
(Anglo-Saxon) optimistic

Hopkins
(American) perky
Hopkin

Hortencia
(Spanish) green thumb
*Hartencia, Hartense,
Hartensia, Hortence,
Hortense, Hortensia*

Hortense
(Latin) caretaking the
garden
*Hortence, Hortensia,
Hortinse*

Houston
(Place name) southern
Houst, Houstie, Huston

Hud
(American) tomboyish
Hudd

Huda
(Arabic) the right way
Hoda

Hudson
(English) explorer;
adventuresome
Hud, Huds

Hueline
(German) smart
*Hue, Huee, Huel, Huela,
Huelene, Huelette,
Huelyne, Huey, Hughee,
Hughie*

Huella
(American) joyous
Huela, Huelle

Hulda
(Scandinavian)
sweetheart

Hun
(American) short for
Hunny
Hon

Hunter
(English) searching;
jubilant
*Hun, Huner, Hunner,
Hunt, Huntar, Huntter*

Hurley
(English) fit
Hurlee, Hurlie, Hurly

Hutton
(English) right
Hutten, Huttun

Huxlee
(American) creative
*Hux, Huxleigh, Huxley,
Huxly*

Hyacinth
(Greek) flower
Hy, Hycinth, Hyacinthe
Hyde
(American) tough-willed
Hide, Hydie
Hydie
(American) spirited
Hidi, Hydee, Hydey, Hydi

Iana
(Greek) flowering; from the flower name Iantha
Iann
Ida
(German) kind;
(English) industrious
Idah, Iduh
Idahlia
(Greek) sweet
Idali, Idalia
Idalia
(Italian) sweet
Idarah
(American) social
Idara, Idare, Idareah
Idelle
(Celtic) generous
Idele
Idetta
(German) serious worker
Ideta, Idettah, Idette
Idil
(Latin) pleasant
Idee, Idey, Idi, Idie, Idyll

Idolina
(American) idolizes
Idol, Idolena
Iduvina
(Spanish) dedicated
Iduvine, Iduvynna, Vina
Ieesh
(Arabic) feminine
Ieasha, Ieesha, Iesha, Yesha
Ihab
(Arabic) gift
Ikea
(Scandinavian) smooth
Ikee, Ikeah, Ikie
Ikeida
(Invented) spontaneous
Ikae, Ikay
Ilamay
(French) sweet; from an island
Ila May, Ilamae, Ila-May, Ilamaye
Ilana
(Hebrew) tree; gorgeous
Elana, Ilaina, Ilane, Ilani, Illana, Lainie, Lanie
Ileannah
(American) soaring
Ileanna, Iliana, Ilianna, Illeana
Ilene
(American) svelte
Ileen, Ilenia

Ilena
(Greek) regal
Ileena, Ilina

Iliana
(Greek) woman of Troy
Ileanai, Illeana

Ilsa
(Scottish) glowing
Elyssa, Illisa, Illysa, Ilsah, Lissie

Ima
(German) affluent;
(Japanese) current
Imah

Imaine
(Arabic) form of Iman;
exotic; believer
Imain, Iman, Imane

Iman
(Arabic, African)
living in the present
Imen

Imelda
(German) contentious
Imalda

Imogen
(Celtic, Latin) girl who
resembles her mother
Emogen, Imogene

Ina
(Latin) small
Inah

Inca
(Indian) adventurer
Incah

India
(Place name) woman of
India
*Indeah, Indee, Indie,
Indy, Indya*

Indiana
(Place name) salt-of-the-
earth
Inda, India, Indianna

Indiece
(American) capable
Indeece, Indeese

Indigo
(Latin) eyes of deep blue
Indego, Indigoh

Indira
(Hindi) ethereal; god of
heaven and
thunderstorms
Indra

Indra
(Hindi) goddess of
thunder and rain;
powerful
Indee, Indi, Indira, Indre

Indray
(American) outspoken
Indrae, Indee, Indree

Ineesha
(African-American)
sparkling
Inesha, Ineshah, Inisha

Ines
(Spanish) chaste
Inez, Innez, Ynez

Inessa
(Russian) pure
Inesa, Nessa

Inez
(Spanish) lovely
Ines

Infinity
(American) lasting
*Infinitee, Infinitey,
Infiniti, Infinitie*

Inge
(Scandinavian) fertile
Inga

Ingrad
(American) variant of
Ingrid; beauty
Inger, Ingr

Ingrid
(Scandinavian) beautiful
Inga, Inge, Inger, Ingred

Iniguez
(Spanish) good
Ina, Ini, Niqui

Innocence
(American) pure
*Innoce, Innocents,
Inocence, Inocencia,
Inocents*

Integrity
(American) truthful
Integritee, Integritie

Iola
(Greek) dawn
Iole

Iona
(Greek, Scottish)
place name
Ione, Ionia

Ira
(Hebrew) contented;
watchful
Irah

Ireland
(Irish) place name;
vibrant
Irelan, Irelande, Irelyn, Irelynn

Irina
(Greek, Russian)
comforting
Ireena, Irena, Irenah, Irene, Irenia, Irenya

Irene
(Greek) peace-loving;
goddess of peace
Irine

Irina
(Russian) soother
Irena, Iryna, Rina

Iris
(Greek) bright; goddess
of the rainbow

Irma
(Latin) realistic
Irmah

Irodell
(Invented) peaceful
Irodel, Irodelle

Isa
(Spanish) dark-eyed
Isah

Isabel
(Spanish) God-loving
Isabela, Isabella, Isabelle, Issie, Iza

Isabella
(Spanish, Italian)
dedicated to God
Isabela, Izabella

Isadora
(Greek) beautiful; gift of
Isis; fertile
Dora, Dory, Isidora

Isairis
(Spanish) lively
Isa, Isaire

Isela
(American) giving
Iselah

Isis
(Egyptian) goddess
supreme of moon and
fertility

Ismene
(French) from the name
Esme; respected
Isme, Ismyne

Isolde
(Welsh) beautiful
Isolda

Itica
(Spanish) eloquent
Itaca, Iticah

Itzel
(Spanish) from Isabella;
God-loving
Itz

Itzy
(American) lively
Itsee, Itzee, Itzie

Iva
(Slavic) dedicated
Ivah

Ivanna
(Russian) gracious gift
from God
Iva, Ivana, Ivanka, Ivie, Ivy

Ivelisa
(American) combo of Ivy
and Lisa
Ivalisa, Ivelise, Ivelisee, Ivelissa, Ivelyse

Ivette
(French) clever and
athletic
Ivet, Ivett

Ivey
(English, American)
easygoing
Ivee, Ivie, Ivy

Iviannah
(American) adorned
Iviana, Ivianna, Ivie, Ivy

Ivisse
(American) graceful
Ivice, Iviece, Ivis, Ivise

Ivon
(Spanish) light
Ivonie, Ivonne

Ivona
(Slavic) gift
Ivonah, Ivone, Ivonne

Ivonne
(French) athlete
Ivonn

Ivory
(Latin) white
Ivoree, Ivori, Ivorie

Ivy
(English) growing
Iv, Ivee, Ivey, Ivie

Iwona
(Polish) archer; athletic;
gift
Iwonna

Izabella
(American) variant of
Isabella
*Iza, Izabela, Izabelle,
Izabell*

Izanne
(American) calming
*Iza, Izan, Izann, Izanna,
Ize*

Izolde
(Greek) philosophical
Izo, Izolade, Izold

Izzy
(American) zany
Izzee, Izzie

Jacey
(Greek) sparkling
*J.C., Jacee, Jaci, Jacie,
Jacy*

Jacinda
(Greek) attractive girl
Jacey, Jaci

Jacinta
(Spanish) flowering;
sweet

Jacinta
(Spanish) hyacinth
*Jace, Jacee, Jacey,
Jacinda, Jacinna,
Jacintae, Jacinth,
Jacinthia, Jacy, Jacynth*

Jackie
(French) short for
Jacqueline
Jackee, Jacki, Jacky, Jaki

Jackson
(Last name as first
name) swaggering
Jacksen, Jaksin, Jakson

Jaclyn
(French) form of Jacqueline
Jacalyn, Jackalene, Jackalin, Jackalyn, Jackeline, Jackolynne

Jacobi
(Hebrew) stand-in
Cobie, Coby

Jacqueline
(French) little Jacquie; small replacement
Jacki, Jackie, Jacklin, Jacklyn, Jaclyn, Jacqualyn, Jacquel, Jacquelyn, Jacquelynn, Jacqui, Jacquie, Jakie, Jakline, Jaklinn, Jaklynn, Jaqueline, Jaquie

Jacquet
(Invented) form of Jacquelyn
Jackett, Jackwet, Jacquee, Jacquie, Jakkett

Jacqui
(French) short for Jacquline
Jacque, Jacquie, Jakki, Jaki, Jaquay

Jada
(Spanish) personable; precious
Jadah

Jade
(Spanish) green gemstone; courageous; adoring

Jaden
(African-American) exotic
Jadi, Jadie, Jadin, Jadyn, Jaeden, Jaiden

Jadwiga
(Polish) religious
Jad, Jadwig, Wiga

Jae
(Latin) small; jaybird
Jay, Jayjay

Jael
(Hebrew) high-climbing
Jaeli

Jaela
(Hebrew) bright
Jael, Jaell, Jayla

Jaelyn
(African-American) ambitious
Jaela, Jaelynne, Jala, Jalyn, Jaylyn

Jaenesha
(African-American) spirited
Jacey, Jae, Jaeneisha, Jaeniesha, Janesha, Jaynesha, Nesha

Jaffa
(Hebrew) lovely

Jagan
(American) form of Jadan; wholesome
Jag, Jagann, Jagen, Jagun

Jagger
(English) cutter
Jaeger, Jag, Jager

Jaguar
(American) runner
Jag, Jaggy, Jagwar, Jagwor

Jahnny
(American) form of Johnny
Jahnae, Jahnay, Jahnie, Jahnnee, Jahnney, Jahnnie, Jahny

Jaidan
(American) golden child
Jaedan, Jai, Jaide, Jaidee, Jaidi, Jaidon, Jaidun, Jaidy, Jaidyn, Jaydan, Jaydyn

Jaime
(French) girl who loves; I love
Jaeme, Jaemee, Jaimee, Jaimi, Jaimie, Jaimy, Jamie, Jaymee

Jaime-Day
(American) loving

Jakisha
(African-American)
favored
Jakishe

Jaleesa
(African-American)
combo of Ja and Leesa
Gilleesa, Jalesa, Jilleesa

Jalene
(American) combo of
Jane and Lene; pretty
*Jaleen, Jaline, Jalinn,
Jalyn, Jalyne, Jalynn,
Jlayna*

Jalisa
(American) combo of Jay
and Lisa
*Gillisa, Jalise, Jaylisa,
Jelisa*

Jalit
(American) sparkling
Jal, Jalitt, Jalitte, Jallit

Jamaica
(Place name) Caribbean
island
*Jama, Jamaika, Jamaka,
Jamake, Jamana, Jamea,
Jamiqua*

Jamais
(French) ever
Jamay, Jamaye

Jamalita
(Invented) form of
James; little Jama
Jama

Jamar
(African-American)
strong
*Jam, Jamara, Jamareah,
Jamaree, Jamarr,
Jamarra, Jammy*

Jamashia
(African-American)
soulful
Jamash, Jamashea

Jameah
(African-American) bold
Jamea, Jameea, Jamiah

Jamecka
(African-American)
studious
*Jamecca, Jameeka,
Jameka, Jameke,
Jamekka, Jamie, Jamiea,
Jamieka*

Jamesetta
(American) form of
James
Jamesette

Jamesha
(African-American)
outgoing
*Jamece, Jamecia,
Jameciah, Jameisha,
James, Jamie, Jamisha,
Jay*

Jamiann
(American) combo of
Jami and Ann
*Jami, Jamia, Jami-Ann,
Jamian, Jamiane*

Jamie
(Hebrew) supplants; fun-
loving
*Jami, Jamee, James,
Jaymee*

Jamielyn
(American) combo of
Jamie and Lyn; pretty
*Jameelyn, Jamelinn,
James, Jamie,
Jamie-Lynn, Jamilin,
Jami-Lyn*

Jamika
(African-American)
buoyant
*Jameeka, Jamey, Jamica,
Jamicka, Jamie*

Jamila
(Arabic) beautiful female
*Jam, Jameela, Jami,
Jamie, Jamil, Jamilah,
Jamile, Jamilla, Jamille,
Jamilya, Jammell,
Jammie*

Jan
(English) short for Janet
or Janice; cute
Jani, Jannie, Janny

Jana
(Slavic, Scandinavian) gracious
Janna, Janne

Janae
(American) giving
Janea, Jannay, Jennae, Jannah, Jennay

Janaleigh
(American) combo of Jana and Leigh; friendly
Jana, Janalea, Janalee, Janalee, Jana-Lee, Jana-Leigh, Janlee, Jannalee, LeeLee, Leigh

Janalyn
(American) giving
Jan, Janalynn, Janelyn, Janilyn, Jannalyn, Jannnie, Janny

Janan
(Arabic) soulful
Jananee, Janann, Jannani

Janara
(American) generous
Janarah, Janerah, Janira, Janirah

Janay
(American) forgiving
Janae, Janah, Janai

Jancy
(American) risk-taker
Jan, Jance, Jancee, Jancey, Janci, Jancie, Janny

Jandy
(American) fun
Jandee, Jandey, Jandi

Jane
(Hebrew) believer in a gracious God
Jaine, Janelle, Janene, Janeth, Janett, Janetta, Janey, Janica, Janie, Jannie, Jayne, Jaynie

Janeana
(American) sweet
Janea, Janean, Janeanah, Janine

Janene
(American) form of Jane
Janeen, Jenean, Janine, Jenine

Janella
(American) combo of Jan and Ella; sporty
Jan, Janela, Janelle, Janny

Janelle
(French) exuberant
J'Nel, J'nell, Janel, Janell, Jannel, Jenelle, Nell

Janessa
(American) forgiving
Janessah, Janie, Janyssa

Janet
(English) small; forgiving
Janett, Janetta, Janette, Jannet, Jannett, Janot, Jessie, Jinett, Johnette, Jonetta, Jonette

Janeth
(American) fascinating
Janith

Janice
(Hebrew) knowing God's grace
Genese, Janece, Janeese

Janie
(English) form of Jane
Janey, Jani, Jany

Janiece
(American) devout; enthusiastic
Janece, Janecia, Janeese, Janese, Janesea, Janesse, Janneece, Jeneece, Jeneese

Janiecia
(African-American) sporty
Janesha, Janeisha, Janeshah, Janisha, Jan, Jannes, Jannesa

Janika
(Scandinavian) believer in a gracious God
Janica, Janicah, Janik, Jannike, Janikka

Janine
(American) kind
Janean, Janeen, Janene,
Janey, Janie

Janis
(English) form of Jane
Jenice, Jenis, Janise

Janjan
(Last name as first)
sweet; believer
Jan Jan, Jange, Janja,
Jan-Jan, Janje, Janni,
Jannie, Janny

Janke
(Scandinavian) believer
in God
Jankee, Jankey, Jankie

Jan-Marie
(American) combo of Jan
and Marie; believer
Jan Marie, Janmarie,
Jannemarie

Janna
(Hebrew) short for
Johana; forgiving

Jannette
(American) lovely
Jan, Janette, Jannett,
Jannie, Janny

Jannie
(English) form of Jane
and Jan
Janney, Janny, Jannye

Jansen
(Scandinavian) smooth
Jan, Jannsen, Jans,
Jansie, Janson, Jansun,
Jansy

Jaqueline
(French) form of
Jacquelyn
Jaqlinn, Jaqlyn, Jaqlynn,
Jaqua, Jaquaeline,
Jaqualine, Jaqualyn,
Jaquelina, Jaquelyn,
Jaquelynne, Jaquie,
Jaqulene

Jaquonna
(African-American)
spoiled
Jakwona, Jakwonda,
Jakwonna, Jaqui, Jaquie,
Jaquon, Jaquona,
Jaquonne

Jardana
(American) gardener
Jardana, Jarde, Jardee,
Jardy

Jarene
(American) bright
Jare, Jaree, Jareen, Jaren,
Jareni, Jarine, Jarry,
Jaryne, Jerry

Jarone
(American) optimistic
Jaron, Jaroyne, Jerone,
Jurone

Jarren
(American) lovable
Jaren, Jarran, Jarre

Jasalin
(American) devoted
Jasalinne, Jasalyn,
Jasalynn, Jaselyn,
Jasleen, Jaslene, Jass,
Jassalyn, Jassy, Jazz,
Jazzy

Jasmine
(Persian, Spanish)
fragrant; sweet
Jas'mine, Jasamine,
Jasime, Jasimen, Jasimin,
Jasimine, Jasmaine,
Jasman, Jasme, Jasmie,
Jasmina, Jasminah,
Jasminen, Jasminne,
Jasmon, Jasmond,
Jasmone, Jasmyn,
Jasmynn, Jasmynne,
Jazie, Jazmaine, Jazman,
Jazmeen, Jazmein,
Jazmen, Jazmin, Jazmine,
Jazmon, Jazmond,
Jazmyn, Jazmyne, Jazs,
Jazsmen, Jazz, Jazza,
Jazzamine, Jazzee, Jazzi,
Jazzmeen, Jazzmin,
Jazz-Mine, Jazzmun,
Jazzy

Jasna
(American) talented
Jas, Jazna, Jazz

Ja-Tawn
(African-American) tawny
J'Tawn, Ja Tawn, Jatawn

Jatsue
(Spanish) lively
Jat, Jatsey

Jaya
(Hindi) winning
Jaia, Jay, Jayah

Jayci
(American) vivacious
Jaycee, Jaycie

Jaydee
(American) combo of Jay and Dee; perky
Jadee, Jayde, Jayda, Jayd, Jaydia, Jaydn, Jayia

Jayden
(American) enthusiastic
Jaden, Jay, Jaydeen, Jaydon, Jaydyn, Jaye

Jaydie
(American) lively
Jadie, Jady, Jay-Dee, Jaydeye, Jaydie

Jaydra
(Spanish) treasured jewel; jade
Jadra, Jay, Jaydrah

Jaye
(Latin) small as a jaybird
Jae, Jay

Jayla
(American) smiling
Jaila, Jaylah, Jayle, Jaylee

Jaylo
(American) combo of Jennifer and Lopez; charismatic
J. Lo, Jalo, Jayjay, Jaylla, Jaylon, J-Lo

Jayme
(English)
Jami, Jamie, Jaymee, Jaymi, Jaymie

Jayne
(Hindi, American) winning
Jane, Janey, Jani, Jaynee, Jayni, Jaynie

Jaynell
(American) combo of Jay and Nell; southern belle
Janell, Janelle, Jaynel, Jaynelle, Jeanel, Jeanell, Jeanelle, Jeanelly

Jazz
(American) short for Jasmine; flowering; high-spirited
Jas, Jassie, Jaz, Jazzi, Jazzie, Jazzle, Jazzy

Jazzell
(American) spontaneous
Jazel, Jazell, Jazz, Jazzee, Jazzie

Jazzlyn
(American) combo of Jazz and Lyn
Jaz, Jazilyn, Jazlin, Jazlinn, Jazlinne, Jazlyn, Jazlynn, Jazlynne

Jean
(Scottish) God-loving and gracious
Jeana, Jeanie, Jeanne, Jeannie, Jeanny, Jena, Jenay, Jenna

Jeanetta
(American) smallish imp
Janetta, Jeannet, Jeannette, Jeanney, Jen, Jenett, Jennita

Jeanette
(French) lively
Janette, Jeannete, Jeanett

Jeanie
(Scottish) devout; outspoken
Jeannie, Jeanny

Jeanine
(Scottish) peace-loving
Jeanene, Jenine

Jeanisha
(African-American) pretty
Jean, Jeaneesh, Jeanise, Jeanna, Jeannie, Jenisha

Jearlean
(American) vibrant
Jearlee, Jearlene, Jearley, Jearli, Jearline, Jearly, Jerline

Jecelyn
(Invented) form of
Jocelyn; innovative
Jece, Jecee, Jeselyn, Jess

Jeffrey
(German) peaceful;
sparkling personality
Jef, Jeff, Jeffa, Jefferi, Jeffery, Jeffie, Jeffre, Jeffrie, Jeffy, Jefry

Jelane
(Russian) light heart
Jelaina, Jelaine, Jelanne, Jilane, Julane

Jelani
(American) pretty sky
Jelaney, Jelani, Jelanie, Jelainy, Jelanni

Jemima
(Hebrew) dove-like
Jem, Jemi, Jemimah, Jemm, Jemmi, Jemmy, Jemora

Jemine
(American) treasured
Jem, Jemmy, Jemyne

Jemma
(Hebrew, English)
nickname for Jemima;
peaceful
Jem

Jems
(American) form of
Gems; treasured
Gemas, Jemma, Jemmey, Jemmi, Jemmy

Jena
(Arabic); small
Jenaa, Jenaeh, Jenah, Jenai, Jenna

Jencynn
(American) combo of Jen
and Cynn; sweetheart
Jencin, Jen-Cynn, Jensynn

Jenell
(American) combo of
Jenny and Nell
Janele, Jen, Jenaile, Jenalle, Jenel, Jenella, Jennelle, Jenny

Jenifer
(Welsh) beautiful; fair
Gennefer, Gennifer, Ginnifur, Ginnipher, Jay, Jenefer, Jenifer, Jenjen, Jenna, Jenni, Jennifer, Jenny

Jenilynn
(American) combo of
Jenny and Lynn; precious
Jennalyn, Jennilin, Jennilinn, Jennilyn, Jenny-Lynn, Jennylynn

Jenna
(Scottish, English)
sweet
Jena, Jynna

Jennifer
(Welsh, English)
fair-haired; beautiful
perfection
Gennefur, Jen, Jenife, Jeniferr, Jenn, Jenna, Jennae, Jennafer, Jennefer, Jenni, Jennipher, Jenniphur, Jenny, Jennyfer, Jennypher

Jennings
(Last name as first
name) pretty
Jen, Jenny

Jennis
(American) white;
patient
J, Jay, Jen, Jenace, Jenice, Jenis, Jenn, Jennice

Jennison
(American) variant of
Jennifer; darling
Gennison, Jenison, Jennisyn, Jenson

Jenny
(Scottish, English) short for Jennifer; blessed; sweetheart
Jen, Jenae, Jeni, Jenjen, Jenni, Jennie, Jennye

Jenteale
(American) combo of Jen and Teale; blue-eyed and pretty
Jen, Jenny, Jenteal, Jentelle, Jyn, Jynteale, Teal, Teale

Jenvie
(American) lovely
Jennvey, Jenvee, Jenvy

Jenz
(Scandinavian) form of male name Johannes; believer in God
Jen, Jens

Jeri
(American) hopeful
Geri, Jere, Jerhie, Jerree, Jerri, Jerry, Jerrye

Jeridean
(American) combo of Jeri and Dean; leader; musical
Geridean, Jerdean, Jeri Dean, Jeri-Dean, Jerridean, Jerrydean

Jerikah
(American) sparkling
Jereca, Jerecka, Jeree, Jeri, Jerica, Jerik, Jeriko, Jerrica, Jerry

Jerilyn
(American) combo of Jeri and Lynn
Jeralyn, Jeralynn, Jerrilin, Jerrilyn

Jerin
(American) daring
Jere, Jeren, Jeron, Jerinn, Jerun

Jermaine
(French) form of Germaine
Germaine, Jermane, Jermanee, Jermani, Jermany, Jermayne

Jerrett
(American) spirited
Jerett, Jeriette, Jerre, Jerret, Jerrette, Jerrie, Jerry

Jerrica
(American) free spirit
Jerrika

Jesenia
(Spanish) witty
Jesene, Jess, Jessenia, Jessie, Jessie, Jisenia, Yesenia

Jessa
(American) spontaneous
Jessah

Jessalyn
(American) combo of Jessica and Lynn; exciting
Jesalyn, Jesilyn, Jeslin, Jeslyn, Jessaline, Jessie, Jesslin

Jessamine
(French) form of Jasmine; sassy
Jesamyn, Jess, Jessamin, Jessie, Jessmine

Jesse
(Hebrew) friendly
Jesie, Jessey, Jessi, Jessy

Jessica
(Hebrew) rich
Jesica, Jess, Jessa, Jessie, Jessika, Jessy, Jezika

Jessie
(Scottish) casual
Jesey, Jess, Jessee, Jessi, Jessye

Jessie-Mae
(American) combo of Jessie and Mae; country girl
Jessee-May, Jessemay, Jessie Mae, Jessie May, Jessiemae, Jessmae

Jesusita
(Spanish) little Jesus
Jett
(American) high-flying
Jettie, Jetty
Jette
(German, Scandinavian)
lovely gem
*Jet, Jeta, Jetia, Jetta,
Jette, Jettee, Jettie*
Jeudi
(French) born on
Thursday
Jeune-Fille
(French) young girl
Jevae
(Spanish) desired
Jevaie, Jevay
Jevonne
(African-American) kind
*Jev, Jevaughan,
Jevaughn, Jevie, Jevon,
Jevona, Jevonn, Jevvy*
Jewel
(French) pretty
*Jeul, Jewelia, Jewelie,
Jewell, Jewelle, Jewels,
Jule*
Jewellene
(American) combo of
Jewel and Lene;
treasured
*Jewelene, Jeweline,
Jewels, Julene*

Jezebel
(Hebrew) wanton
woman
*Jessebelle, Jez, Jeze,
Jezebell, Jezel, Jezell,
Jezybel, Jezzie*
Jezenya
(American) flowering
Jesenya, Jeze, Jezey
Jhamesha
(African-American)
lovely; soft
Jamesha, Jmesha
Jilan
(American) mover
*Jilyn, Jillan, Jillyn, Jylan,
Jylann*
Jill
(English) short for Jillian;
high-energy and
youthful
Jil, Jilee, Jilli, Jillie, Jilly
Jilleen
(American) energetic
*Jil, Jileen, Jilene, Jiline,
Jill, Jillain, Jilline, Jlynn*
Jillian
(Latin) youthful
*Giliana, Jill, Jillaine,
Jillana, Jillena, Jilliane,
Jilliann, Jillie, Jillion,
Jillione, Jilly, Jilyan*
Jimmi
(American)
Jim, Jimi, Jimice, Jayjay

Jin
(Chinese) golden; gem
Jinn, Jinny
Jinger
(American) form of
Ginger; go-getter
Jin, Jinge
Jinkie
(American) bouncy
Jinkee, Jynki, Jinky
Jinny
(Scottish) form of Jenny
Jinna, Jinney
Jinx
(Latin) spell
*Jin, Jinks, Jinxie, Jinxy,
Jynx*
Jinxia
(Latin) form of Jinx;
spellbinder
Jinx, Jynx, Jynxia
Jnae
(American) darling
J'Nay, Jenae, Jnay, Jnaye
J'Netta
(American) form of
Jeanetta; sweetness
*J'netta, J'Nette, Janetta,
Janny*
J-Nyl
(American) flirtatious
Jo
(American) short for
Josephine; spunky
Joey, Jojo

Jo-Allene
(American) combo of Jo and Allene; effervescent
Jo Allene, Joallene, Joallie, Joeallene, Joealli, Jolene

Joan
(Hebrew) heroine; God-loving
Joane, Joane, Joani, Joanie, Joanni, Joannie, Jonie

Joana
(Hebrew) kind
Joanah, Joanna, Joannah, Jonah

Joanie
(Hebrew) kind
Joanney, Joanni, Joannie, Joanny, Joany, Joni

Jo-Ann
(French) believer; gregarious
Joahnn, JoAn, JoAnn, Joann, Joanna, Joanne, Jo-Anne, Joannie

Joanna
(English) kind
Jo, Joeanna, Johannah, Josie

Joanne
(English) form of Joan; excellent friend
JoAnn, Joann, Jo-Ann, JoAnne, Joeanne

Joannie
(Hebrew) forgiving
Joani, Joany, Joanney, Joanni

Jobelle
(American) combo of Jo and Belle; beautiful
Jobel, Jobell, Jobi, Jobie, Joebel

Jobeth
(American) combo of Jo and Beth; vivacious
Beth, Bethie, Jo, Jobee, Jobie

Jobi
(Hebrew) misunderstood; inventive
Jobee, Jobey, Jobie, Joby

Jo-Carol
(American) combo of Jo and Carol; lively
Jo Carol, Jocarol, Jocarole

Jocelyn
(Latin) joyful
Jocelie, Jocelin, Jocelyne, Jocelynn, Joci, Joclyn, Joclynn, Jocylan, Jocylen, Joycelyn

Joci
(Latin) happy
Jocee, Jocey, Jocie, Jocy, Josi

Jocklyn
(American) combo of Jock and Lyn; athletic
Jock, Joklyn

Jodase
(American) brilliant
Jo, Jodace, Jodasse, Jodie, Jody

Jo-Dee
(American) combo of Jo and Dee
Jo Dee, Jodee, Joedee

Jodee-Marie
(American) combo of Jodee and Marie
Jodeemarie, Jodymarie

Jodelle
(American) combo of Jo and Delle
Jodel, Jodell, Jodie, Jody

Jodie
(American) happy girl
Jo, Jodee, Jodey, Jodi, Jody

Joedy
(American) jolly
Joedey, Joedi, Joedie

Joe-Leigh
(American) combo of Joe and Leigh; happy
Joe Leigh, Joel, Joelea, Joesey, Jolee, Joleigh, Jolie, Jollee, Jose, Joze

Joelle
(Hebrew) willing
Jo, Joel, Joele, Joeleen, Joell, Joella, Joelle, Joelly

Joely
(Hebrew) believer; lively
Jo, Joe, Joey

Joelly
(American) kindhearted
Joelee, Joeli, Joely

Joetta
(American) combo of Jo and Etta; creative
Jo, Joe, Joettah, Joette

Joey
(American) easygoing
Joe, Joeye

Joezee
(American) form of Josey; attractive
Jo, Joe, Joes, Joezey, Joezy

Johanna
(German) believer in a gracious God
Johana, Johanah, Johanna, Jonna

Johnay
(American) steadfast
Johnae, Jonay, Jonaye, Jonnay

Johnica
(American) form of John; believer in a gracious God
Jonica

Johnna
(American) upright
Jahna, John, Johna, Johnae, Jonna, Jonnie

Johnnell
(American) happy
Johnelle, Jonell, Jonnel

Johnnetta
(American) joyful
Johneta, Johnete, Johnetta, Johnette, Jonetta, Jonette, Jonietta

Johnnisha
(African-American) steady
Johnisha, Johnnita, Johnny, Jonnisha

Johnson
(Last name as first name) confident
Johns

Johntell
(African-American) sweet
Johna, Johntal, Johntel, Johntelle, Jontell

Joi
(Latin) joyful
Joicy, Joie, Jojo, Joy

Jo-Kiesha
(African-American) vibrant
Joekiesha

Jolanda
(Latin, Italian) violet; pretty flower
Jolana, Jolande, Jolane

Jolene
(American) jolly
Jo, Joeleane, Joeleen, Joelene, Joelynn, Joleen, Joleene, Jolen, Jolena, Joley, Jolie, Joline, Jolyn, Jolynn

Joletta
(American) happy-go-lucky
Jaletta, Jolette, Joley, Joli, Jolie, Jolitta

Jolie
(French) pretty
Jo, Jolee, Joli, Jollee

Jolienne
(American) pretty
Joliane, Jolianne, Jolien, Jolina, Joline

Jolisa
(American) combo of Jo and Lisa; cheerful
Joelisa, Joli, Jo-Lisa, Jolise, Lisa

Jolyane
(American) sweetheart
Joliane, Jollyane, Jolyan, Jolyann, Jolyanne

Jolynn
(American) combo of Jo and Lynn
Jo, Jolene, Jolynda, Jolyne

Jonelle
(American) combo of Joan and Elle
Jo, Johnel, Jonel, Jonell, Jonnell, Jynel

Jones
(American) saucy

Joni
(American) short for Joan
Joanie, Jonie, Jony

Jonice
(American) casual
Joneece, Joneese, Jonni, Jonise

Jonita
(Hebrew) pretty little one
Janita, Jonite

Jonquill
(American) flower
Jonn, Jonque, Jonquie, Jonquil, Jonquille

Jontelle
(American) musical
Jahntelle, Jontel, Jontlyl

Jorah
(Hebrew) fresh as rain
Jora

Jo-Rain
(American) combo of Jo and Rain; zany
Jo Rain, Jorain, JoRaine

Jordan
(Hebrew) excellent descendant
Johrdon, Jordaine, Jordane, Jorden, Jordenne, Jordeyn, Jordi, Jordie, Jordin, Jordon, Jordyn, Jordynne, Joudane, Jourdan

Jordana
(Hebrew) smart
Giordanna, Jordann, Jordanna, Jordannuh, Jordona, Jordonna, Jourdanna

Jordy
(American) quick
Jordee, Jordey, Jordi, Jordie, Jorey

Jorgina
(Spanish) nurturing
Jorge, Jorgine, Jorgy, Jorgie, Jorgi, Georgina, Georgeena

Jorie
(Hebrew) short for Jordan
Joree, Jorey, Jorhee, Jorhie, Jori, Jorre, Jorrey, Jorri, Jory

Jorja
(American) smart
Georgia, Jorge, Jorgia, Jorgie, Jorgy

Josefat
(Spanish) form of Joseph; gracious
Fata, Fina, Josef, Josefa, Josefana, Josefenna, Josefita, Joseva, Josey, Josie

Josefina
(Hebrew) fertile
Jose, Josephina, Josey, Josie

Joselyn
(German) pretty
Joseline, Josey, Joslyn, Josselen, Josseline, Josselyne, Josslyn, Josslynn, Josylynn

Josephine
(French) blessed
Fena, Jo, Joes, Josefina, Josephene, Josie, Jozaphine

Josette
(French) little Josephine

Josey
(Hebrew, American) saucy
Josee, Josi, Josie, Jozie

Josiann
(American) combo of Josey and Ann; prettiest one
Josann, Josiane, Josianne, Joseyann

Josie-Mae
(American) combo of Josie and Mae
Josee-Mae, Josiemae

Joslyn
(Latin) jocular
Joclyn, Joslene, Joslinn, Josslin, Josslyn, Josslynn

Jostin
(American) adorable
Josten, Jostun, Josty, Jostyn

Jour
(French) day

Jovannah
(Latin) regal
Jouvanna, Jovanee, Jovani, Jovanna, Jovanne, Jovannie

Jovita
(Latin) glad
Joveeta

Jovonne
(American) combo of Jo and Yvonne; queenly
Javonne, Jovaughn, Jovon, Jovonnie

Jovita
(Latin) happy
Joveeda, Jovetta, Jovi, Jovie, Jo-Vita, Jovy

Jowannah
(American) happy
Jowanna, Jowanne, Jowonna

Joy
(Latin) joyful
Joi, Joie, Joya, Joye

Joyce
(Latin) joyous
Joice, Joy, Joyci, Joycie

Joyleen
(American) combo of Joy and Eileen; happy lady
Joyleena, Joylene, Joyline

Joyous
(American) joyful
Joy, Joyus

Joyslyn
(American) form of Jocelyn; cheery
Joycelyn, Joyslin, Joyslinn

Juanisha
(African-American) delightful
Juanesha, Juaneshia, Juannisha

Juanita
(Spanish) believer in a gracious God; forgiving
Juan, Juana, Juaneta, Juanika, Juanna, Juanne, Juannie, Juanny, Wanita

Jubelka
(African-American) jubilant
Jube, Jubi, Jubie

Jubilee
(Hebrew) jubilant
Jubalie

Jubini
(American) grateful; jubilant
Jubi, Jubine

Jucinda
(American) relishing life
Jucin, Jucindah, Jucinde

Judalon
(Hebrew) merry
Judalonn, Juddalone, Judelon

Jude
(French) confident
Judea, Judee, Judde

Judit
(Hebrew) Jewish
Jude, Judi, Juditt

Judith
(Hebrew) woman worthy
of praise
*Jude, Judi, Judie, Juditha,
Judy, Judyth, Judythe*

Judy
(Hebrew) short for Judith
*Judi, Judie, Joodie,
Judye, Jude*

Juel
(American) dependable
*Jewel, Juelle, Juels, Jule,
Juile*

Juirl
(American) careful
Ju, Juirll

Juleen
(American) sensual
Jule, Julene, Jules

Jules
(American) brooding
Jewels, Juels

Julia
(Latin) forever young
Jula, Julina, Julya

Julian
(Latin) effervescent
*Jewelian, Julean, Juliann,
Julien, Juliene, Julienn,
Julyun*

Juliana
(Italian, German,
Spanish) youthful
*Juleanna, Julianna,
Juliannah, Julie-Anna,
Jullyana*

Julianne
(American) combo of
Julie and Anne
Juleann, Jules, Julieann

Julie
(English) young and
vocal
*Juel, Jule, Juli, Juliene,
Julye*

Juliet
(Italian) loving

Juliette
(French) romantic
Julie, Jules, Juliet, Julietta

Julimarie
(American) combo of Juli
and Marie; young;
alluring
*Joolimarie, Julie Marie,
Juliemarie, Julie-Marie*

Julissa
(Latin) universally loved
*Jula, Julessa, Julisa,
Julisha*

Julita
(Spanish) adorable;
young
Juli, Julitte

Juluette
(American) adorable;
young
*Jule, Jules, Julett, Julette,
Julie, Julu, Julue, Juluett,
Julu-Ette, LuLu*

July
(Latin) month; warm

Jumoke
(African) most popular

June
(Latin) born in June
*Juneth, Junie, Junieth,
Juney, Juny*

Junieth
(Latin) from the month
June; heavenly
*Juney, Juni, Junie,
Juniethe*

Juno
(Latin) queenly
Juna, June

Juqwanza
(African-American)
bouncy
*Jukwanza, Juqwann,
Qwanza*

Justice
(Latin) fair-minded
Just, Justise, Justy

Justika
(American) dancing-girl
*Justeeka, Justica, Justie,
Justy*

Justina
(Latin) honest
Justeena, Justena

Justine
(Italian, Latin) fair-minded
Justa, Juste, Justean, Justeen, Justena, Justene, Justi, Justie, Justina, Justinna, Justyne, Justynn, Justynne, Juzteen

Jutta
(American) ebullient
Juta

Juvelia
(Spanish) young
Juvee, Juvelle, Juvelya, Juvie, Juvilia, Velia, Velya

Juwanne
(African-American) lively
Juwan, Juwann, Juwanna, Juwon, Jwanna, Jwanne

Kacey
(Irish) daring
Casey, Casie, K.C., K.Cee, Kace, Kacee, Kaci, Kacy, Kasey, Kasie, Kaycee, Kaycie, Kaysie

Kachina
(Native American) sacred dancer; doll-like
Cachina, Kachena, Kachine

Kacondra
(African-American) bold
Condra, Connie, Conny, Kacon, Kacond, Kaecondra, Kakondra, Kaycondra

Kaden
(American) charismatic
Caden, Kadenn

Kadie
(American) virtuous
Kadee

Kady
(English) sassy
Cady, K.D., Kadee, Kadie, Kaydie, Kaydy

Kaelin
(Irish) pure; impetuous
Kaelan, Kaelen, Kaelinn, Kaelyn, Kaelynn, Kaelynne, Kaylin

Kaelynn
(American) combo of Kae and Lynn; beloved
Kaelin, Kailyn, Kay-Lynn

Kai
(Hawaiian, African) attractive
Kaia

Kailah
(Greek) virtuous
Kail, Kala, Kalae, Kalah

Kailey
(American) spunky
Kalee, Kaili, Kailie, Kaylee, Kaylei

Kaitlin
(Irish) pure-hearted
Caitlin, Kaitlan, Kaitland, Kaitlinn, Kaitlynn, Kalyn

Kalani
(Hawaiian) leader
Kalauni, Kaloni, Kaylanie

Kaleigh
(Sanskrit) energetic; dark
Kalea

Kalet
(French) beautiful energy
Kalay, Kalaye

Kali
(Greek) beauty
Kalli

Kalidas
(Greek) most beautiful
Kaleedus, Kali

Kalila
(Arabic) sweet; lovable
Kaililah, Kaleah, Kalela, Kay, Kaykay, Kaylee, Kyle

Kalisa
(American) combo of Kay and Lisa; pretty and loving
Caylisa, Kaleesa, Kalisha Kalyssa, Kaylisa, Kaykay

Kallan
(American) loving
Kall, Kallen, Kallun

Kallie
(Greek) beautiful
Callie, Kalley, Kali, Kalie, Kally

Kalliope
(Greek) beautiful voice
Calli, Calliope, Kalli

Kallista
(Greek) pretty; bright-eyed
Callista, Kalesta, Kalista, Kalysta

Kalyn
(Arabic) loved
Calynn, Calynne, Kaelyn, Kaelynn, Kalen, Kalin, Kalinn, Kallyn

Kami
(Japanese) perfect aura
Cami

Kamilia
(Polish) pure

Kama
(Sanskrit) beloved; Hindu god of love
Kam, Kamie

Kamala
(American) interesting
Camala, Kam, Kamali, Kamilla, Kammy

Kamea
(Hawaiian) precious darling
Cammi, Kam, Kammie

Kamela
(Italian) form of Camilla; wonderful
Kam, Kamila, Kammy

Kameron
(American) spiritual
Cam, Cameron, Cami, Cammie, Kamreen, Kamrin

Kami
(Italian) spiritual little one
Cami, Cammie, Cammy, Kammie, Kammy

Kamilah
(North African) perfect

Kamilia
(Polish) perfect character
Kam, Kamila, Kammy, Milla

Kamyra
(American) light
Kamera

Kandace
(Greek) charming; glowing
Candace, Kandace, Kandi, Kandice, Kandy

Kandi
(American) short for Kandace
Candi, Kandie, Kandy

Kandra
(American) light
Candra

Kaneesha
(American) dark-skinned
Caneesha, Kaneesh, Kaneice, Kaneisha, Kanesha, Kaneshia, Kaney, Kanish, Nesha

Kanesha
(African-American)
spontaneous
*Kaneesha, Kaneeshia,
Kaneisha, Kanisha,
Kannesha*

Kansas
(Place name) practical
Kanny

Kaprece
(American) capricious
*Caprice, Kapp, Kappy,
Kapreece, Kapri, Kaprise,
Kapryce, Karpreese*

Kara
(Danish, Greek) dearest
*Cara, Kar, Karah, Kari,
Karie*

Karalenae
(American) combo of
Kara and Lenae
Kara-Lenae, Karalenay

Karbie
(American) energetic
Karbi, Karby

Karelle
(French) joyful singer
Carel, Carelle, Karel

Karen
(Greek, Irish) pure-
hearted
*Caren, Caryn, Kare,
Kareen, Karenna, Karin,
Karina, Karron, Karyn,
Keren*

Karenz
(English) from Kerenza;
sweet girl
*Karence, Karens,
Karense*

Kari
(Scandinavian) pure
Cari, Karri, Karrie, Karry

Karian
(American) daring
Kerian

Karianne
(American) combo of
Kari and Anne
*Kariane, Kariann,
Kari-Ann, Karianna,
Kerianne*

Karilynne
(American) combo of
Kari and Lynne
*Cariliynn, Kariline,
Karylynn*

Karima
(Arabic) giving
Karimah

Karin
(Scandinavian) kind-
hearted
Karen, Karine, Karinne

Karina
(Russian) best of heart;
(Latin) even
*Kare, Karinda, Karine,
Karinna, Karrie, Karrina,
Karyna*

Karise
(Greek) graceful woman
Karis, Karisse, Karyce

Karissa
(Greek) longsuffering
Carissa, Karessa, Karisa

Karizma
(African) hopeful
Karisma

Karla
(German) bright-eyed;
feminine form of
Carl/Karl
Carla, Karlie

Karla-Faye
(American) combo of
Karla and Faye

Karleen
(American) combo of
Karla and Arleen; witty
Karlene, Karline, Karly

Karly
(Latin, American)
strong-voiced
*Carly, Karlee, Karlie,
Karlye*

Karma
(Hindi) destined for
good things
Karm, Karmie, Karmy

Karmel
(Hebrew)
*Carmel, Karmela,
Karmelle*

Karmen
(Hebrew) loving songs
*Carmen, Karmin,
Karmine*

Karnesha
(American) spicy
*Carnesha, Karnisha,
Karny*

Karolanne
(American) combo of
Karol and Anne
*Karol, Karolan, Karolane,
Karolann, Karolen*

Karolina
(Polish) form of Charles
Karo

Karoline
(German) form of Karl
*Kare, Karola, Karolah,
Karolina, Lina*

Karolyn
(American) friendly
*Carolyn, Kara, Karal,
Karalyn, Karilynne,
Karolynn*

Karrington
(Last name as first
name) admired
Carrington, Kare, Karring

Karyn
(American) sweet
Caren, Karen

Kasey
(American) spirited
*Casey, Kacey, Kasie,
Kaysie*

Kashmir
(Sanskrit) place name
*Cahmere, Cashmir, Kash,
Kashmere*

Kashonda
(African-American)
dramatic
*Kashanda, Kashawnda
Koshonda*

Kashondra
(African-American)
bright
*Kachanne, Kachaundra,
Kachee, Kashandra,
Kashawndra, Kashee,
Kashon, Kashondrah,
Kashondre, Kashun*

Kasi
(American) form of
Cassie; seer
Kass, Kassi, Kassie

Kassandra
(Greek) capricious
*Cassandra, Kass,
Kasandra, Kassandrah,
Kassie*

Kassidy
(Irish) clever
*Cassidy, Cassir, Kasadee,
Kass, Kassie, Kassy,
Kassydi*

Kassie
(American) clever
Kassee, Kassi, Kassy

Kat
(American) outrageous
Cat

Katarina
(Greek) pure
*Katareena, Katarena,
Katarinna, Kataryna,
Katerina, Katryna*

Katarzyna
(Origin unknown)
creative
Katarzina

Katchen
(Greek) virtuous
Kat, Katshen

Katchi

(American) sassy
Catshy, Cotchy, Kat, Kata, Katchie, Kati, Katshi, Katshie, Katshy, Katty, Kotchee, Kotchi, Kotchie

Kate

(Greek, Irish) pure-hearted
Katie, Katy, Kay-Kay

Katelyn

(Irish) pure-hearted
Caitlin, Kaitlin, Kaitlynne, Kat, Katelin, Katelynn, Kate-Lynn, Katline, Katy

Katera

(Origin unknown) celebrant
Katara, Katura

Katharine

(Greek) powerful; pure
Kat, Katharin, Katherin, Katherine, Kathy, Kathyrn, Kaykay

Kathlaya

(American) fashionable

Kathleen

(Irish) brilliant; unflawed
Cathleen, Kathlene, Kathlynn, Kathlyn, Kathie, Kathy

Kathryn

(English) powerful and pure
Kathreena, Kathren, Kathrene, Kathrin, Kathrine, Kathryne

Kathy

(English) pure; (Irish) spunky
Cathy, Kath, Kathe, Kathee, Kathi, Kathie

Katia

(French) stylish
Kateeya, Kati, Katya

Katie

(English) lively
Kat, Katy, Kay, Kaykay, Kate, Kaytie

Katina

(American) form of Katrina; virtuous
Kat, Kateen, Kateena

Katlynn

(Greek) pure
Kat, Katlinn, Katlyn

Katrice

(American) graceful
Katreese, Katrese, Katrie, Katrisse, Katry

Katrina

(German) melodious
Catrina, Katreena, Kay

Katrine

(German, Polish) pure
Catrene, Kati, Katrene, Katrinna, Kati

Katy

(English) lively
Cady, Katie, Kattee, Kattie, Kaytee

Kavinli

(American) form of Kevin; eager
Cavin, Kaven, Kavin, Kavinlee, Kavinley, Kavinly

Kavita

(Hindi) poem
Kaveta, Kavitah

Kay

(Greek, Latin) fun-loving
Cay, Caye, Kaye, Kaykay

Kaycie

(American) merrymaker
CayCee, K.C., Kaycee, Kayci, Kaysie

Kayla

(Hebrew, Arabic) sweet
Cala, Cayla, Kala, Kaela, Kaila, Kaylah, Keyla

Kaylee

(American) open
Cayley, Kaelie, Kaylea, Kaylie, Kayleigh

Kayleen
(Hebrew) sweet; combo of Kay and Eileen
Kaileen, Kalene, Kay, Kaylean, Kayleene, Kaykay

Kaylin
(American) combo of Kay and Lynn
Kaylan, Kaylen, Kaylynn

Kaylinda
(American) combo of Kae and Linda
Kaelinda, Kaelynda, Kay-Linda

Kaylon
(American) form of Caylin; outgoing
Kay, Kaylen, Kaylun

Kaylon
(Hebrew) crowned
Kaylan, Kayln, Kaylond, Kaylon, Kalonn

Keane
(American) keen
Kanee, Keanie, Keany, Keen

Keanna
(American) curious
Keana, Keannah

Kearney
(Irish) winning
Kearne, Kearni, KeKe, Kerney

Keekee
(American) dancing
Keakea, KeeKee, Kee-Kee

Keeley
(Irish) noisy
Keely, Keylee

Keenan
(Irish) small
Keanan, Keen, Keeny

Kehohtee
(Invented) alternate spelling for Quixote

Keidra
(American) form of Kendra; aware
Kedra, Keydra

Keilani
(Hawaiian) graceful leader
Kei, Lani, Lanie

Keira
(Irish) dark-skinned
Keera, Kera

Keisha
(American) dark-eyed
Keesha, Keeshah, Keysha

Keishla
(American) dark

Kelila
(Hebrew) regal woman
Kelylah

Keller
(Irish) daring
Kellers

Kelley
(Irish) brave
Keli, Kellie, Kelly, Kellye

Kelsey
(Scottish) opinionated
Kelcie, Kelsi, Kelsie

Kember
(American) zany
Kem, Kemmie, Kimber

Kemella
(American) self-assured
Kemele, Kemellah, Kemelle

Kendall
(English) quiet
Kendahl, Kendelle, Kendie, Kendylle

Kendra
(American) ingenious
Ken, Kendrah, Kennie, Kindra, Kyndra

Keneisha
(American) combo of Ken and Aisha
Kaneesha, Kenesha, Kenisha, Kennie, Kaykay

Kenia
(African) giving (from the place name Kenya)
Ken, Keneah

Kenna
(English) brilliant
Kennah, Kynna

Kennae
(Irish) form of Ken;
attractive
Kenae, Kenah

Kennedy
(Irish) formidable
Kennedie, Kenny

Kensington
(English) brash
Kensingtyn

Kentucky
(American) place name
Kentuckie

Kenya
(African) place name

Kenyatta
(African)

Kenzie
(Scottish) pretty
Kensey, Kinsey

Keoshawn
(African-American)
clever
Keosh, Keoshaun

Kerdonna
(African-American)
loquacious
*Donna, Kerdy, Kirdonna,
Kyrdonna*

Kerra
(American) bright
Cara, Carrah, Kara, Kerrah

Kerry
(Irish) dark-haired
Carrie, Kari, Keri, Kerrie

Kerthia
(American) giving
*Kerth, Kerthea, Kerthi,
Kerthy*

Kesha
(American) laughing
Kecia, Kesa, Keshah

Keshon
(African-American)
happy
*Keshann, Keshaun,
Keshonn, Keshun,
Keshawn*

Keshondra
(African-American) joy-
filled
*Keshaundra,
Keshondrah, Keshundra,
Keshundrea, Keshundria,
Keshy*

Keshonna
(African-American)
happy
*Keshanna, Keshauna,
Keshaunna, Keshawna,
Keshona, Keshonna*

Keturah
(African) longsuffering

Kevine
(Irish) lively
Kevynne

Keydy
(American) knowing
Keydee, Keydi, Keydie

Keyonna
(African-American)
energetic

Keyshawn
(American) lively
*Keyshan, Keyshann,
Keyshaun, Keyshaunna,
Keyshon, Keyshona,
Keshonna, Keykey, Kiki*

Khadijah
(Arabic)

Khai
(American) unusual
Ki, Kie

Khaki
(American) personality-
plus
*Kakee, Kaki, Kakie,
Khakee, Khakie*

Khali
(Origin unknown) lively
*Khalee, Khalie, Koli,
Kollie*

Khiana
(American) different
*Kheana, Khianah,
Khianna, Ki, Kianah,
Kianna, Kiannah*

Kia
(American) short for
Kiana
Keeah, Kiah

Kiana
(American) graceful
Kianna, Kiannah

Kiara
(Irish) dark-skinned
Chiara, Chiarra, Keearah

Kibibi
(African) small girl

Kidre
(American) loyal
Kidrea, Kidrey, Kidri

Kienalle
(American) light
Kieana, Kienall, Kieny

Kienna
(Origin unknown) brash
Kiennah, Kienne

Kiera
(Irish) dark-skinned
Keara, Keera, Kierra

Kiersten
(Greek) blessed
*Kerston, Kierstin,
Kierstn, Kierstynn, Kirst,
Kirsten, Kirstie, Kirstin,
Kirsty*

Kiki
(Spanish, American)
vivacious
Keiki, Ki, Kiekie, Kikee

Kiko
(Japanese) lively
Kiki, Kikoh

Kiley
(Irish) pretty
*Kilea, Kilee, Kili, Kylee,
Kylie*

Kim
(English, Vietnamese)
*Kimey, Kimmi, Kimmy,
Kym*

Kimberlin
(American) combo of
Kimberly and Lin
*Kimberlinn, Kimberlyn,
Kimberlynn*

Kimberly
(English) leader
*Kim, Kimber-Lea,
Kimberlee, Kimberleigh,
Kimberley, Kimberli,
Kimberlie, Kimmy,
Kymberly, Kimmie*

Kimbrell
(African-American)
smiling
*Kim, Kimbree, Kimbrel,
Kimbrele, Kimby, Kimmy*

Kimeo
(American) form of Kim;
happy
Kim, Kime, Kimi

Kimetha
(American) form of Kim;
happy
Kimeth

Kimi
(Japanese) spiritual

Kimone
(Origin unknown) darling
Kimonne, Kymone

Kineisha
(American) form of
Keneisha
*Keneesha, Keneisha,
Kineasha, Kinesha,
Kineshia, Kiness,
Kinisha, Kinnisha, Kinny*

Kinsey
(English) child
Kensey, Kinsey

Kintra
(American) joyous
Kentra, Kint, Kintrey

Kipling
(Last name as first
name) energetic
Kiplin

Kira
(Russian) sunny; light-
hearted
Kera

Kiran
(Irish) pretty
Kiara, Kiaran, Kira, Kiri

Kirby
(Anglo-Saxon) right
Kirbee, Kirbey, Kirbie

Kirsten
(Scandinavian, Greek)
spiritual
*Karsten, Kirstene,
Kirstin, Kirston, Krystene*

Kirstie
(Scandinavian)
effervescent
Kerstie, Kirstee, Kirsty

Kisha
(Russian) ingenious
Keshah

Kismet
(Hindi) destiny; fate
Kismete, Kismett

Kissa
(African) a baby born
after twins

Kit
(American) strong
Kitt

Kithos
(Greek) worthy

Kitty
(Greek, American) flirty
Kit, Kitti, Kittie

Kiva
(Origin unknown) bright
Keva

Kiwa
(Origin unknown) lively
Kiewah, Kiwah

Kiya
(Australian) from the
name Kylie; always
returning; pretty girl
Kya

Kizzie
(African) energetic
*Kissee, Kissie, Kiz,
Kizzee, Kizzi, Kizzy*

Klarissa
(German) bright-minded
Clarissa, Klarisa, Klarise

Klarybel
(Polish) beauty
Klaribel, Klaribelle

Klea
(American) bold
*Clea, Kleah, Kleea,
Kleeah*

Kleta
(Greek) form of
Cleopatra; noble-born;
temptress
Cleta

Kobi
(American) California girl
Cobi, Kobe

Kogan
(Last name as first) self-
assured
*Kogann, Kogen, Kogey,
Kogi*

Konstance
(Latin) loyal
*Constance, Kon, Konnie,
Konstanze*

Kora
(Greek) practical
Cora, Koko, Korey, Kori

Kori
(Greek) little girl;
popular
*Cori, Corrie, Koree,
Korey, Kory*

Korina
(Greek) strong-willed;
(German) small girl
*Corinna, Koreena,
Korena, Korinna, Koryna*

Kornelia
(Latin) straight-laced
*Cornelia, Korney, Korni,
Kornie*

Kortney
(American, French)
dignified
*Courtney, Kortnee,
Kortni, Kourtney,
Kourtnie*

Koshatta
(Native American) form
of Coushatta; diligent
*Coushatta, Kosha,
Koshat, Koshatte,
Koshee, Koshi, Koshie,
Koushatta*

Krenie
(American) capable
Kren, Kreni, Krenn, Krennie, Kreny

Kris
(American) short for Kristina
Kaykay, Krissie, Krissy

Krishen
(American) talkative
Crishen, Kris, Krish, Krishon

Krissy
(American) friendly
Kris, Krisie, Krissey, Krissi

Krista
(German) short for Christina
Khrista, Krysta

Kristalee
(American) combo of Krista and Lee
Kristalea, Krista-Lee, Kristaleigh

Kristen
(Greek) Christ's follower; (German) bright-eyed
Christen, Cristen, Kristin

Kristian
(Greek) Christian woman
Kristiana, Kristianne, Kristyanna

Kristie
(American) saucy
Christi, Christy, Kristi

Kristin
(Scandinavian) high-energy
Kristen, Kristyne

Kristina
(Greek) anointed; (Scandinavian) Christ's follower
Christina, Krista, Kristie, Krysteena, Tina

Kristine
(Swedish) Christ's follower
Christine, Kristee, Kristene, Kristi, Kristy

Kristy
(American) short for Kristine
Kristi, Kristie

Krysta
(Polish) clear
Chrsta, Krista

Krystal
(American) clear and brilliant
Crystal, Crystalle, Kristel, Krys, Krystelle, Krystie, Krystylle

Krystyna
(Polish) Christian

Kurrsten
(Scandinavian, Greek) form of Kirsten; spiritual
Kurrst, Kurst, Kurstie

Kyla
(Irish) pretty
Kiela, Kila, Ky

Kyle
(Irish) pretty
Kylee, Kylie, Kyll

Kylee
(Australian, Irish) pretty
Kielie, Kiely, Kiley, Kye, Kyky, Kyleigh, Kylie

Kylene
(American) cute
Kyline

Kylynne
(American) fashionable
Kilenne, Kilynn, Kyly

Kym
(American) favorite
Kim, Kymm, Kymmi, Kymmie, Kymy

Kynthia
(Greek) goddess of the moon
Cinthia, Cynthia

Kyra
(Greek) feminine
Kira, Kyrah, Kyrie, Kyry

Kyria
(Greek) form of Kyra; ladylike
Kyrea, Kyree, Kyrie, Kyry

Labe
(American) slow-moving
Labie

Lace
(American) delicate
Lacee, Lacey, Laci, Lacie, Lase

Lacey
(Greek) cheery
Lacee, Laci, Lacie, Lacy

Lachelle
(African-American) sweetheart
Lachel, Lachell, Laschell, Lashelle

Lacole
(American) sly
Lucole

Lacreta
(Spanish) form of Lacretia; efficient
Lacrete, LaLa

Lacretia
(Latin) efficient
Lacracia, Lacrecia, Lacrisha, Lacy

LaDaune
(African-American) the dawn
Ladaune, LaDawn

Ladda
(American) open
Lada

Ladonna
(American) combo of La and Donna; beautiful
Ladona, LaDonna

Lady
(American) feminine
Ladee, Ladie

Ladrenda
(African-American) cagy
Ladee, Ladey, Ladren, Ladrende, Lady

Lafonde
(American) combo of La and Fonde; fond

Laguna
(Place name) Laguna Beach, California; water-loving
Lagunah

Laila
(Scandinavian) dark beauty
Layla, Laylah, Leila

Lainil
(American) soft-hearted
Lainie, Lanel, Lanelle

Lajean
(French) soothing; steadfast
L'Jean, LaJean, Lajeanne

LaJuana
(American) combo of La and Juana
Lajuana, Lala, Lawanna

Lake
(Astrology) graceful dancer

Lakela
(Hawaiian) feminine
Lakla

Lakesha
(African-American) favored
Keishia, Lakaisha, Lakeesha, Lakeisha, Lakeishah, Lakezia, Lakisha

Lalaney
(American) form of Hawaiian name Leilani; celestial
Lala, Lalanee, Lalani

Laleema
(Spanish) devoted
Lalema, Lalima

Lalita
(Sanskrit) charmer
Lai, Lala, Lali, Lalitah, Lalite, Lalitte

Lalya
(Latin) eloquent
Lalia, Lall, Lalyah

Lamarian
(American) conflicted
Lamare, Lamarean

Lamia
(Egyptian) calm
Lami

Lamika
(African-American) variant of Tamika; calm

L'Amour
(French) love
Amor, Amour, Lamore, Lamour, Lamoura

Lana
(Latin) pretty peacemaker
Lan, Lanna, Lanny

Land
(American) word as name; confident
Landd

Landa
(American) blonde beauty
Landah

Landry
(American) leader
Landa, Landree

Landy
(American) confident
Land, Landee, Landey, Landi

Lane
(Last name as first name) precocious
Laine, Lainey, Laney, Lanie, Layne, Laynie

Lanee
(Asian) graceful

Lanette
(American) healthy
La-Net, LaNett, LaNette

Langley
(American) special
Langlee, Langli, Langlie, Langly

Lani
(Hawaiian) short for Leilani
Lannie

Lansing
(Place name) hopeful
Lanseng

Laquanna
(African-American) outspoken
Kwanna, LaQuanna, LaQwana, Quanna

Laquita
(American)
Laqueta, Laquetta

Lara
(Russian) lovely

Laraine
(Latin) pretty
Lareine, Larene, Loraine

Larby
(American) form of
Darby; pretty
Larbee, Larbey, Larbi,
Larbie

Larhonda
(African-American)
combo of La and
Rhonda; flashy
LaRhonda, Laronda

Larinda
(American) smart
Lare, Larin, Larine,
Lorinda

Larissa
(Latin) giving cheer
Laressa, Larisse, Laryssa

Lark
(American) pretty
Larke

Larkin
(American) pretty
Larken, Larkun

Larrie
(American) tomboyish
Larry

LaRue
(American) combo of La
and Rue
Laroo, Larue

Lasha
(Spanish) forlorn
Lash, Lass

Lashanda
(American) brassy
Lala, Lasha, LaShanda,
LaShounda

Lashauna
(American) happy
Lashona, Leshauna,
Lashawna

LaShea
(American) sparkling
Lashay, La-Shea, Lashea

Lashoun
(African-American)
content
Lashaun, Lashawn,
Lashown

Lassie
(American) lass
Lass

Latanya
(African-American)

Latasha
(American)
Latacha, LaTasha,
Latayshah

LaTeasa
(Spanish) tease
Latea, Lateasa, LaTease,
LaTeese

Lateefah
(Arabic, African, Hebrew)
kind queen
Lateefa, Latifa, Latifah,
Lotifah, Tifa, Tifah

Latesha
(Latin, American)
joyful
Lateesha, Lateisha,
Lateshah, Laticia,
Latisha

Latifah
(Muslim) gentle
Lateefa, Latifa, Latiffe,
Latifuh

Lathenia
(American) verbose
Lathene, Lathey

Latisehsha
(African-American)
happy; talkative
Lati, Latise, Latiseh,
Latisha

Latonia
(African-American) rich
Latone, Latonea

Latosha
(African-American)
happy

Latoya
(American) combo of La
and Toya
LaToya, Lata, Toy, Toya

Latreece
(American) go-getter
Latreese, Latrice, Letrice,
Lettie, Letty

Latrelle
(American) laughing
*Lettie, Letrel, Letrelle,
Litrelle*

Latrice
(Latin) noble
Latreece, Latreese

Latricia
(American) happy
*Latrecia, Latreesha,
Latrisha, Latrishah*

Latrisha
(African-American)
prissy
Latrishe

Laura
(Latin) laurel-crowned
and joyous
Lara, Lora

Laurann
(American) combo of
Laura and Ann
*Lauran, Laurana,
Lauranna, Lauranne*

Lauralee
(American) combo of
Laura and Lee
*Laura-Lee, Loralea,
Loralee, Lorilee*

Laureen
(American) old-
fashioned
Laurie, Laurine, Loreen

Laurel
(American) flourishing
Laurell, Lorel, Lorell

Laurel
(Latin) graceful
*Laural, Laurell, Laurella,
Laurelle, Lorel, Lorella,
Lourelle*

Lauren
(English, American)
flowing
*Laren, Lauryn, Laryn,
Loren*

Laurent
(French) graceful
Lorent, Laurente

Lauretta
(American) graceful
*Laureta, Laurettah,
Lauritta, Lauritte, Loretta*

Laurette
(American) from Laura;
graceful
*Etta, Ette, Laure, Laurett,
Lorette*

Laurie
(English) careful
Lari, Lauri, Lori

Lauriann
(American) combo of
Laurie and Ann
Laurian, Laurianne

Lavena
(French, Latin)
purest woman
Lavi, Lavie, Lavina

Laverne
(Latin) breath of spring
*Lavern, Lavirne, Verna,
Verne*

Lavette
(Latin) pure; natural
*Laveda, Lavede, Lavete,
Lavett*

Lavita
(American) charmer
Laveta, Lavitta, Lavitte

Lavinia
(Greek) ladylike
Lavenia

Lavonne
(American) combo of La
and Yvonne
*Lavaughan, Lavaughn,
Lavon, Lavone, Lavonn,
Lavonna, Lavonnah*

Lawanda
(American) sassy
LaWanda, Lawonda

Layce
(American) spunky

Layla
(Arabic) dark
*Laela, Laila, Lala, Laya,
Laylah, Laylie, Leila*

Layne
(French)
Laine, Lainee, Lainey

Lea
(Hawaiian) goddess-like

Leaf
(Botanical) hip

Leah
(Hebrew) tired and
burdened
Lea, Lee, Leeah, Leia, Lia

Leala
(French) steadfast

Leandra
(Greek) commanding as
a lioness
*Leandrea, Leanndra,
Leeandra, Leedie*

Leanna
(English) leaning
Leana, Leelee, Liana

Leanne
(English) sweet
*Lean, Leann, Lee, Leelee,
Lianne*

Leanore
(English, Greek) stately
Lanore

Leatrice
(American) charming
Leatrise

Lecia
(Latin) short for Leticia
*Leecia, Leesha, Lesha,
Lesia*

Leda
(Greek) feminine
Ledah, Lida, Lita

Lee
(English, American,
Chinese) light-footed
Lea, Leelee, Leigh

Leeanne
(English) combo of Lee
and Anne
*Lean, Leann, Lee Ann,
Lee-Ann, Leianne*

Leeannette
(Greek) form of Leandra;
lionine
*Leann, Lee Annette,
Leeanett, Lee-Annette,
Leiandra*

Leelee
(American, Slavic) short
for Leanne, Lena, Lisa,
Leona
Lee-Lee, Lele, Lelee

Leeline
(American) combo of Lee
and Line; pastural; loyal
*Lee, Leela, LeeLee,
Leelene*

Leeo
(American) sunny
Leo

Leeza
(American) gorgeous
Leesa, Leeze, Liza, Lize

Legend
(American) memorable
Legen, Legende, Legund

Legia
(Spanish) bright
Legea

Lei
(Hawaiian) short for
Leilani
Leilei

Léi
(Chinese) open; truthful

Leigh
(English) light-footed
Lee, Leelee

Leila
(Arabic) beauty of the
night
Layla, Leela, Lelah, Leyla

Leilani
(Hawaiian) heavenly girl
Lanie

Lejoi
(French) joy
Joy, Lejoy

Leland
(American) special
Lelan, Lelande

Lelia
(Greek) articulate
Lee, Leelee

Lena
(Latin) siren
Lina

Lenesha
(African-American) smiling
Leneisha, Lenisha, Lenni, Lennie, Neshie

Lenice
(American) delightful
Lenisa, Lenise

Lenita
(Latin) gentle spirit
Leneeta, Leneta, Lineta

Lenoa
(Greek) form of Lenore; light
Len, Lenor, Lenora

Leola
(Latin) fierce; lionine
Lee, Leo, Leole

Leona
(Greek, American) brave-hearted
Liona

Leondrea
(Greek) strong
Leondreah, Leondria

Leonie
(Latin) lion-like; fierce
Leonee, Leoni, Leoney, Leony

Leonore
(Greek)
Lenore, Leonor

Leonsio
(Spanish) form of male name Leon; fierce
Leo, Leonsee, Leonsi

Leopoldina
(Invented) form of Leopold; brave
Dina, Leo, Leopolde, Leopoldyna

Leora
(Greek) light-hearted
Liora, Leorah

Lera
(Russian)
Lerae, Lerie, Lira

Leretta
(American) form of Loretta
Lere, Lerie, Loretta

Lesley
(Scottish) strong-willed
Les, Lesle, Lesli, Leslie, Leslye, Lezlie

Letha
(Greek) ladylike
Litha

Leticia
(Latin, Spanish) joyful woman
Letecia, Letisha, Letitia, Lettie, Letty

Letichel
(American) happy; important
Chel, Chelle, Leti, Letichell, Letishell, Lettichelle, Lettychel

Letsey
(American) form of Letty; glad
Letsee, Letsy

Lettie
(Latin, Spanish) happy
Lettee, Letti, Letty, Lettye

Levana
(Hebrew) fair
Lev, Liv, Livana

Levitt
(American) straight-forward
Levit

Levity
(American) humorous

Levora
(American) home-loving
Levorah, Levore, Livee, Livie, Livora, Livore

Lexa
(American) effervescent
Lex, Lexah

Lexi
(Greek) helpful; sparkling
Lex, Lexie, Lexsey, Lexsie, Lexy

Lexine
(Scottish) helper
Lexus
(American) rich
Lexi, Lexorus, Lexsis,
Lexuss, Lexxus
Lexy
(Scottish) helper
Lezena
(American) smiling
Lezene, Lezina, Lyzena
Li
(Chinese) plum
Lia
(Greek, Russian, Italian)
singular
Li, Liah
Lian
(Latin, Chinese)
graceful
Leane, Leanne, Liane
Liana
(Greek) flowering;
complicated
Leanna, Lee, Liane
Libby
(Hebrew) short for
Elizabeth; bubbly
Lib, Libbi, Libbie
Liber
(American) from the
word liberty; free
Lib, Libby, Lyber

Liberty
(Latin) free and open
Lib, Libbie
Librada
(Spanish) free
Libra, Libradah
Lichelle
(American) combo of Li
and Chelle
Leshel, Leshelle, Licha,
Lili
Licia
(Greek) outdoorsy
Lisha
Lida
(Greek) beloved girl
Leedah, Lyda
Lidia
(Greek) pleasant spirit
Lydia
Liesel
(German) pretty
Leesel, Leezel
Light
(American) light-hearted
Li, Lite
Ligia
(Greek) talented
musician
Ligea, Lygia, Lygy
Likiana
(Invented) likeable
Like, Likia

Lila
(American) short for
Delilah, form of Leila;
(Arabic) playful
Lilah, Lyla, Lylah
Lila-Lynn
(American) combo of Lila
and Lynn; night-loving;
delight
Lilalinn, Lilalyn, Lilalynn,
Lilalynne
Lilac
(American) flowery
Lila
Lilakay
(American) combo of Lila
and Kay
Lilaka, Lilakae, Lila-Kay,
Lilakaye, Lylakay
Lileah
(Latin) lily-like
Lili, Liliah, Lill, Lily, Lilya
Lilette
(Latin) little lily; delicate
Lill, Lillette, Lillith, Lilly,
Lilly
Lilia
(American) flowing
Lileah, Lyleah, Lylia
Liliana
(Italian) pretty
Lilianah, Lylianah

Liliash
(Spanish) lily; innocent
Lil, Lileah, Liliosa, Lilya, Lyliase, Lylish

Lilith
(Arabic) nocturnal
Lill, Lilli, Lillie, Lilly, Lilyth, Lilythe

Lillian
(Latin) pretty as a lily
Lileane, Lilian, Liliane, Lill, Lillie, Lillyan, Lillyann, Lilyanne, Liyan

Lillibeth
(American) combo of Lilli and Beth; flower; lovely girl
Lilibeth, Lillibethe, Lilybeth

Lily
(Latin, Chinese) elegant
Lil, Lili, Lilie

Lin
(English, Chinese) beautiful
Linn, Lynn

Lina
(Greek, Latin, Scottish) light of spirit; lake calm
Lena, Lin, Linah, Lynn

Linda
(Spanish) pretty girl
Lind, Lindy, Lynda

Linden
(American) harmonious
Lindan, Lindun, Lynden, Lynnden

Lindsay
(English, Scottish) calming; bright and shining
Lindsee, Lindsey, Lindsi, Lindz, Lyndsie, Lyndzee, Lynz

Lindse
(Spanish) form of Lindsey; enthusiastic
Linds, Lindz, Lindze, Lyndzy

Lindy
(American) music-lover
Lind, Lindee, Lindi, Lindie, Linney, Linnie, Linse, Linz, Linze

Linette
(French, English, American) graceful and airy
Lanette, Linnet, Lynette

Lin-Lin
(Chinese) beauty of a tinkling bell
Lin, Lin Lin

Ling
(Chinese) delicate

Linnea
(Swedish) statuesque
Lin, Linayah, Linea, Linnay, Linny, Lynnea

Linsey
(English) bright spirit
Linsie, Linsy, Linzi, Linzie

Linzetta
(American) form of Linzey; pretty
Linze, Linzette, Linzey

Lisa
(Hebrew, American) dedicated and spiritual
Lee, Leelee, Leesa, Leesah, Leeza, Leisa, Lesa, Lysa

Lisamarie
(American) combo of Lisa and Marie
Lisamaree, Lisa-Marie, Lise-Marie, Lis-Maree

Lisarae
(American) combo of Lisa and Rae
Lisa-Rae, Lisa-Ray, Lisaray

Lisbeth
(Hebrew) short for Elizabeth

Lise
(German) form of Lisa; solemn
Lesa

Lisette
(French) little Elizabeth
Lise, Lisete, Lissette, Liz
Lisha
(Hebrew) short for
Elisha; dark
Lish, Lishie
Lissa
(Greek) sweet
Lyssa
Lisseth
(Hebrew) form of
Elizabeth; devout
*Liseta, Liseth, Lisette,
Lisith, Liss, Lisse, Lissi*
Lissie
(American) short for
Elise; flowery
Lis, Lissi, Lissey, Lissy
Lita
(Latin) short for
Carmelita; life-giving
Leta
Liv
(Latin, Scandinavian)
lively
Leev
Livia
(Hebrew) lively
Levia, Livya
Livona
(Hebrew) vibrant
Levona, Liv, Livvie, Livvy

Liz
(English) short for
Elizabeth; excitable
*Lis, Lissy, Lizy, Lizzi,
Lizzie*
Liza
(American) smiling
*Leeza, Liz, Lizah, Lizzie,
Lizzy, Lyza*
Lizbeth
(American) combo of Liz
and Beth; devout
Liz Beth, Liz-Beth, Lizeth
Lizeth
(Hebrew) ebullient
Liseth, Lizethe
Lizette
(Hebrew) lively
Lizet, Lizett
Lizibeth
(American) combo of Lizi
and Beth
*Lizabeth, Liza-Beth,
Lizzie, Lizziebeth*
Lizzie
(American) devout
*Liz, Liza, Lizae, Lizette,
Lizzee, Lizzey, Lizzi, Lizzy*
Lo
(American) spunky
Loe
Loanna
(American) combo of Lo
and Anna; loving
Lo, Loann, Loanne, LoLo

Logan
(English) climbing
Lo, Logun
Loibeth
(American) combo of Loy
and Beth; popular
*Beth, Loi, Loy Beth, Loy,
Loybeth, Loy-Beth*
Loicy
(American) delightful
*Loice, Loisee, Loisey,
Loisi, Loy, Loyce, Loycy,
Loyse, Loysie*
Lois
(Greek) good
Lo, Loes
Lojean
(American) combo of Lo
and Jean; bravehearted
Lojeanne
Lola
(Spanish) pensive
Lo, Lolah, Lolita
Loleen
(American) jubilant
Lolene
Lolita
(Spanish) sad
Lo, Lola, Loleta, Lita
Lomita
(Spanish) good
Londa
(American) shy
Londah, Londe, Londy

London
(Place name) calming
*Londen, Londun, Londy,
Loney, Lony*

Loni
(American) beauty
*Loney, Lonie, Lonnie,
Loney*

Lonnette
(American) pretty
*Lonett, Lonette, Lonnie,
Lonn*

Lora
(Latin) regal
*Laura, Lorah, Lorea,
Loria*

Loranden
(American) ingenious
*Lorandyn, Lorannden,
Luranden*

Lorelei
(German) siren
Loralee, Lorilie, LoraLee

Lorelle
(American) lovely
*Lore, Loreee, Lorel,
Lorey, Lori, Lorie, Lorille,
Lorel, Lorille*

Loren
(American) form of
Lauren; picture-perfect
*Lorren, Lorri, Lorrie,
Lorron, Lorryn, Lory,
Loryn, Lourie*

Lorena
(English) photogenic
*Loreen, Lorene, Lorrie,
Lorrine*

Loretta
(English) large-eyed
beauty
Lauretta

Lori
(Latin) laurel-crowned
and nature-loving
Laurie, Loree, Lorie, Lory

Lorinda
(American) combo of
Lori and Linda;
gregarious
*Larinda, Lorenda, Lori,
Lorie*

Loris
(Greek, Latin) fun-loving
Lorice, Lauris

Lorna
(Latin) laurel-crowned;
natural
Lorenah

Lorraine
(Latin, French)
sad-eyed
*Laraine, Lauraine,
Lorain, Loraine, Lorrie,
Lors*

Lotis
(Greek) flower
Lottie, Lotty, Lotus

Lotta
(Swedish) sweet

Lottie
(American)
old-fashioned
Lottee, Lotti, Lotty

Lotus
(Greek) flowery
Lolo, Lotie

Lou
(American) short for
Louise
Loulou, Lu

Louisa
(English) patient
*Lou, Loulou, Luisa,
Luizza*

Louise
(German) hardworking
and brave
Lolah, Lou, Loulou, Luise

Lourdes
(French) girl from
Lourdes, France;
hallowed
Lourd, Lordes, Lordez

Lordyn
(American) enchanting
*Lorden, Lordin, Lordine,
Lordun, Lordynn*

Love
(English, American)
loving
Lovey, Lovi, Luv

Loveada
(Spanish) loving
Lova, Lovada

Loveanna
(American) combo of
Love and Anna; loving
*Lovanna, Love-Anna,
Loveanne, Luvana,
Luvanna*

Lovella
(Native American) soft
spirit
Lovela

Lovely
(American) loving
*Lovelee, Loveley, Loveli,
Lovey*

Lovie
(American) warm
Lovee, Lovey, Lovi, Lovy

Lovina
(American) warm
*Lovena, Lovey, Lovinah,
Lovinnah*

Lowell
(American) lovely
Lowel

Loyalty
(American) loyal
Loyaltie

Luann
(Hebrew) combo of Lou
and Ann; happy girl
*Lou, Louann, Louanne,
Loulou, Luan, Luanne*

Luberda
(Spanish) light; dear
Luberdia

Luca
(Spanish) light
Luka

Luceil
(French) light; lucky
Luce, Lucee, Lucy

Lucero
(Italian) light-hearted
Lucee, Lucey, Lucy

Lucia
(Italian, Greek, Spanish)
light; lucky in love
*Chia, Luceah, Lucey,
Lucey, Luci*

Luciana
(Italian) fortunate
*Louciana, Luceana,
Lucianah*

Lucie
(French, American)
lucky girl
Lucy

Lucienne
(French) lucky
*Lucianne, Lucienn,
Lucy-Ann*

Lucille
(English) bright-eyed
Lucie, Lucile, Lucy

Lucina
(American) happy
*Lucena, Lucie, Lucinah,
Lucy, Lucyna*

Lucinda
(Latin) prissy
*Cinda, Cindie, Lu,
Luceenda, Lucynda, Lulu*

Lucja
(Polish) light
Luscia

Luckette
(Invented) lucky
Luckett

Lucretia
(Latin) wealthy woman
*Lu, Lucrecia, Lucreesha,
Lucritia*

Lucy
(Latin, Scottish,
Spanish) light-hearted
*Lu, Luca, Luce, Luci,
Lucie*

Lucyann
(American) combo of
Lucy and Ann
*Luce, Luciana, Luciann,
Lucianne, Lucy, Lucyan,
Lucy-Ann, Lucyanne*

Lucylynn
(American) combo of
Lucy and Lynn;
light-hearted
*Lucilyn, Lucylin, Lucy-
Lynn*

Ludivina
(Slavic) loved
Ludmilla
(Slavic) beloved one
*Lu, Ludie, Ludmila,
Ludmylla, Lule, Lulu*
Lue-Ella
(English) combo of Lue
and Ella; tough;
assertive
Louel, Luella, Luelle
Luella
(German) conniving
*Loella, Louella, Lu, Lula,
Lulah, Lulu*
Luenetter
(American) egotistical
Lou, Lu, Luene, Luenette
Luisa
(Spanish) smiling
Louisa
Luisana
(Place name) form of
Louisiana; combative
*Luisanna, Luisanne,
Luisiana*
Luke
(American) bouncy
Luc, Luka, Lukey, Lukie
Lula
(German)
all-encompassing
Lulu

Lulani
(Polynesian) heavensent
Lula, Lani, Lanie
Lulu
(German, English) kind
Lou, Loulou, Lu, Lulie
Lulubell
(American) combo of
Lulu and Bell; well-
known
*Bell, Bella, Belle, Lulu,
Lulubel, Lulu-Bell,
Lulubelle*
Luna
(Latin) moonstruck
Loona
Lund
(German) genius
Lun, Lunde, Lundy
Lundyn
(American) different
Lundan, Lunden, Lundon
Lupe
(Spanish) enthusiastic
*Loopy, Loopey, Lupeta,
Lupey, Lupie, Lupita*
Luquitha
(African-American) fond
Luquetha, Luquith
Lura
(American) loquacious
Loora, Lur, Lurah, Lurie

Lurajane
(American) combo of
Lura and Jane; cuddly
little one
*Janie, Loorajane,
Lura-Jane, Luri, Lurijane*
Lurissa
(American) beguiling
*Luresa, Luressa, Luris,
Lurisa, Lurissah, Lurly*
Lurlene
(German) tempting;
(Scandinavian) bold
*Lura, Lurleen, Lurlie,
Lurline*
Luvelle
(American) light
*Luvee, Luvell, Luvey,
Luvy*
Luvy
(American) spontaneous
Lovey, Luv
Lux
(Latin) light
Luxe, Luxee, Luxi, Luxy
Luz
(Spanish) light-hearted
Lusa, Luzana, Luzi
Luzille
(Spanish) light
Luz, Luzell
Lyanne
(Greek) melodious
*Liann, Lianne, Lyan,
Lyana, Lyaneth, Lyann*

Lyawonda
(African-American)
friend
Lyawunda, Lywanda,
Lywonda

Lydia
(Greek) musical;
unusual
Lidia, Lidya, Lydie, Lydy

Lyla
(French) island girl
Lila, Lilah, Lile

Lyle
(English) strident
Lile

Lymekia
(Greek) form of Lydia;
royal
Lymekea

Lynda
(Spanish) beautiful
Linda, Lindi, Lynde,
Lyndie, Lynn

Lyndsay
(Scottish) bright and
shining
Lindsay, Lindsey

Lynelle
(English) pretty girl;
bright as sunshine
Linelle, Lynel, Lynie, Lynn

Lynette
(French) small and fresh
Lyn, Lynet, Lynnet,
Lynette, Lynnie

Lynn
(English) fresh as spring
water
Lin, Linn, Linnie, Lyn,
Lynne

Lynsey
(American) form of
Lindsay
Linzie, Lyndsey, Lynze,
Lynzy

Lyra
(Greek) musical
Lyre

Lyric
(Greek) musical
Lyrec

Lysa
(Hebrew) God-loving
Leesa, Lisa

Lysandra
(Greek) liberator; she
frees others
Lyse, Lysie

Lysanne
(Greek) helpful
Lysann

Lysett
(American) pretty little
one
Lyse, Lysette

Lyssan
(Greek) form of
Alexandra; supportive
Liss, Lissan, Lissana,
Lissandra, Lyss

Lytanisha
(African-American)
scintillating
Litanisha, Lyta, Lytanis,
Lytanish, Lytanishia,
Nisa, Nisha

Mab
(Literature) Shakespearean queen of fairies

Mabel
(Latin) well-loved
Mabbel, Mable, Maybel, Maybie

Macallister
(Irish) confident

Macarena
(Spanish) name of a dance; blessed
Macarene, Macaria, Macarria, Rena

Macaria
(Spanish) blessed
Maca, Macarea, Macarie, Maka

Macey
(American) upbeat; happy
Mace, Macie, Macy

Mackenzie
(Irish) leader
Mac, Mackenzy, Mackie, Mackinsey, Mckenzie, McKinsey, McKinzie

Mada
(American) helpful
Madah, Maida

Madalyn
(Greek) high goals
Madelyn

Madchen
(Actress name) resourceful
Madchan, Madchin, Maddchen

Maddie
(English) form of Madeline
Mad, Maddi, Maddy, Mady

Maddox
(English) giving
Maddax, Maddee, Maddey, Maddie, Maddux, Maddy

Madelcarmen
(American) combo of Madel and Carmen; old-fashioned
Madel-Carmen, Madlecarmen

Madeleine
(French) high-minded
Madelon

Madeline
(Greek) strength-giving
Madaleine, Maddie, Maddy, Madelene, Madi

Madelyn
(Greek) strong woman
Madalyn, Madlynne, Madolyn

Madge
(Greek, American) spunky
Madgie, Madg

Madina
(Greek) form of Madeline; happy
Mada, Maddelina, Maddi, Maddy, Madele, Madena, Madlin

Madison
(English) good-hearted
Maddie, Maddison, Maddy, Madisen, Madysin

Madonna
(Latin) my lady; spirited

Madrina
(Spanish) godmother
Madra, Madreena, Madrine

Madrona
(Spanish) mother; maternal
Madrena

Mae
(English) bright flower
May

Maegan
(Irish) a gem of a woman
Megan

MaElena
(Spanish) light
Elena, Lena

Maeve
(Irish) queen
Mave

Maezelma
(American) combo of
Mae and Zelma;
practical
*Mae Zelma, Maez, Mae-
Zelma, Maezie,
Mayzelma*

Magan
(Greek) heavy-hearted
Mag, Magen, Maggie

Magda
(Scandinavian) believer
Mag, Maggie

Magdalene
(Greek, Scandinavian)
spiritual
*Mag, Magda,
Magdalena, Magdaline,
Magdalyn, Magdelin,
Maggie*

Maggie
(Greek, English, Irish)
priceless pearl
Mag, Maggee, Maggi

Magina
(Russian) hard-working
Mageena, Maginah

Magnolia
(Botanical) flower;
(Latin) flowering and
flourishing
*Mag, Maggi, Maggie,
Maggy, Magnole, Nolie,*

Magryta
(Slavic) desired

Mahal
(Filipino) loving woman
Mah, Maha

Mahala
(Hebrew, Native
American) tender female
*Mah, Mahalah, Mahalia,
Mahla, Mahlie*

Mahogany
(Spanish) rich as wood
Mahagonie, Mahogony

Mahoney
(American) high energy
*Mahhony, Mahonay,
Mahonie, Mahony*

Mai
(Scandinavian, Japanese)
treasure; flower; singular
Mae, May

Maia
(Greek) fertile; earth
goddess
Maya, Mya

Maida
(Greek) shy girl
*Mady, Maidie, May,
Mayda*

Maidie
(Scottish) maiden; virgin
*Maidee, Maydee,
Maydie*

Maira
(Hebrew) bitter; saved
Mara, Marah

Maired
(Irish) pearl; treasured
Mairead, Mared

Maisie
(Scottish) treasure
Maisee, Maizie, Mazee

Maja
(Scandinavian) fertile

Majidah
(Arabic)

Makala
(Hawaiian) natural
outdoors
Makal, Makie

Makayla
(American) magical
*Makaila, Makala,
Michaela, Mikaela,
Mikayla, Mikaylah*

Makyll
(American) innovative
Makell

Makynna
(American) friendly
Makenna, Makinna

Malak
(Arabic) angelic

Malay
(Place name) softspoken
Malae

Malaya
(Filipino) free and open
Malea

Malha
(Hebrew) queenlike and regal

Mali
(Thai) flowering beauty
Malee, Maley, Mali, Malley, Mallie

Malia
(Hawaiian) thoughtful
Maylia

Maliaval
(Hawaiian) peaceful

Malika
(Hungarian) hardworking and punctual
Maleeka

Malin
(Native American) comfort-giver
Malen, Maline, Mallie

Malinda
(Greek, American)
Melinda

Malissa
(American, Greek) combo of May and Melissa; sweet
Melissa

Mallika
(Indian) watchful; tending the garden
Malika

Mallory
(French, German, American) tough-minded; spunky
Mal, Mallari, Mallery, Mallie, Mallori, Mallorie, Malorie

Malu
(Hawaiian) peaceful
Maloo

Malvina
(Scottish) romantic
Malv, Malva, Malvie, Melvina

Mancie
(American) hopeful
Manci, Mansey, Mansie

Manda
(American) short for Amanda; beloved
Amand, Mandee, Mandi, Mandy

Mandy
(Latin) lovable
Manda, Mandee, Mandi, Mandie

Mandymay
(American) combo of Mandy and May
Mandeemae, Mandimae, Mandimay, Mandymae

Mane
(American) top
Main, Manie

Manee
(Korean) peace giving
Mani, Manie

Manon
(French) exciting

Mantill
(American) guarded
Mant, Mantell, Mantie

Manzie
(American) musical
Mansie, Manzey, Manzi

Manzie
(Native American) flower
Mansi

Mara
(Greek) thoughtful believer
Marah, Marra

Marajayne
(American) combo of Mara and Jayne; lively
Mara Jayne, Marajane, Mara-Jayne, Maryjayne

Maranda
(Latin) wonderful
Marandah, Miranda
Marbella
(Spanish) pretty
Marb, Marbela, Marbelle
Marbury
(American) substantial
Mar, Marbary
Marcella
(Latin) combative
Marce, Marcela, Marci,
Marcie, Marse, Marsella
Marcelline
(French) pretty
Marceline, Marcelyne,
Marcie, Marcy, Marcyline
Marcellita
(Spanish) desired, feisty
Marcel, Marcelita,
Marcelite, Marcelle,
Marcelli, Marcey, Marci
Marcena
(Latin, American)
spirited
Marce, Marceen,
Marcene, Marcie
Marcia
(Latin, American)
combative
Marcie, Marsha
Marcie
(English) chummy
Marci, Marcy, Marsi,
Marsie

Marcilyn
(American) combo of
Marci and Lyn; physical
Marce, Marcie-Lyn,
Marci-Lyn, Marclinne,
Marclyn, Marcy, Mars,
Marse, Marslin, Marslyn
Marcine
(American) bright
Marceen, Marceene
Marcy
(English, American)
opinionated
Marci, Marsie, Marsy
Mardonia
(American) approving
Mardee, Mardi,
Mardone, Mardonne,
Mardy
Mare
(American) living by the
ocean
Maren
(American) ocean-lover
Marin, Marren, Marrin
Marg
(American) tenacious
Mar

Margaret
(Greek, Scottish,
English) treasured pearl;
pure-spirited
Mag, Maggie, Marg,
Margerite, Margie,
Margo, Margret, Meg,
Meggie
Margarita
(Italian, Spanish)
winning
Marg, Margarit,
Margarite, Margie,
Margrita, Marguerita
Margarite
(Greek, German)
pearl
Gretal, Marga, Margit,
Margot
Marge
(English, American)
short for Marjorie;
easygoing
Marg, Margie
Margherita
(Italian, Greek)
treasured pearl
Marg
Margia
(American) form of
Margie; friendly
Marge, Margea, Margy
Margie
(English) friendly
Margey, Margy, Marjie

Margina
(American) centered
Margot
(French) lively
Margaux, Margo
Marguerite
(French) stuffy
Maggie, Marg,
Margerite, Margie,
Margina, Margurite
Maria
(Latin, French, German,
Italian, Polish, Spanish)
desired child
Maja, Malita, Mareea,
Marica, Marike,
Marucha, Mezi, Mitzi
Mariah
(Hebrew) sorrowful
singer
Marayah, Mariahe,
Marriah, Meriah, Moriah
Marializa
(Spanish) combo of
Maria and Liza; desired
Liza, Maria Liza, Maria,
Maria-Liza, Mariliza
Marialourdes
(Spanish) combo of
Maria and Lourdes;
sweet
Maria Lourdes,
Maria-Lourdes

Mariamne
(French) form of Miriam;
sea of sadness
Mariam, Marianne
Marian
(English) thoughtful
Mariane, Marianne,
Maryann, Maryanne
Mariana
(Spanish) quiet girl
Maryanna
Marianella
(French) combo of
Marian and Ella; girl of
the sea
Ella, Marian, Mariane
Mariangela
(American) combo of
Mary and Angela;
angelic
Mary Angela,
Mary-Angela,
Mariangelle
Maria-Teresa
(Spanish) combo of
Maria and Teresa;
desired
Maria Teresa,
Mariateresa,
Maria-Terese,
Maria-Theresa

Maribel
(French, English,
American) combo of
Mary and Belle
EmBee, Marabel,
Maribela, Merrybelle
Maribeth
(American) combo of
Mari and Beth
Mary Beth Mary-Beth,
Marybeth
Marie
(French) form of Mary;
dignified and spiritual
Maree
Mariel
(German) spiritual
Mari, Mariele, Marielle
Marielena
(Spanish) combo of
Marie and Lena; desired
Mari, Mari-Elena, Marie-
Lena, Maryelenna
Mariellen
(American) combo of
Mari and Ellen; dancer
Mare, Marelle, Mariella,
Maryellen, MaryEllen
Mariene
(Spanish) devout
Mari, Marienne
Marietta
(French) combo of Mary
and Etta; spright spirit
Marieta

Marigold
(Botanical) sunny
Maragold, Marigole, Marrigold

Marihelen
(American) combo of Mary and Helen; steadfast friend
Marihelene, MaryHelen

Marika
(Slavic, American) thoughtful and brooding
Marica, Merica, Merika, Merk, Merkie

Marikaitlynn
(American) combo of Mari and Kaitlynn; desired
Kait, Kaiti, Mari, Marreekaitlyn, Mary Kaitlynn, Mary-Kaitlynn

Marilee
(American) combo of Mary and Lee; dancing
Marylee, Merilee, Merrilee

Marilou
(American) combo of Mary and Lou; jubilant
Marilu, Marrilou, Marylou, Marylu

Marilyn
(Hebrew) fond-spirited
Maralynne, Mare, Mariline, Marrie, Marrilyn, Marylyn, Merilyn, Merrilyn

Marin
(Latin) sea-loving
Mare, Maren

Marina
(Latin) lover of the ocean
Marena, Marina

Marinella
(French) combo of Marin and Ella; soft
Ella, Marin, Mari-Nella, Marin-Ella, Nella

Marion
(French) form of Mary; delicate spirit
Mare, Marrion, Mary, Maryian

Mariposa
(Spanish) kind
Mari, Mariposah

Mariquita
(Spanish) form of Margaret; party-loving
Marikita, Marrikita, Marriquita

Maris
(Latin) sea-loving
Mere, Marice, Meris, Marys

Marisa
(Latin) sea-loving; (Spanish) combo of Maria and Luisa
Marce, Maressa, Marissa, Marisse, Mariza Marsie, Marysa, Merisa

Marisela
(Spanish) hearty
Marisella, Marysela

Mariska
(American) endearing
Mareska, Marisca, Mariskah

Marisol
(Spanish) stunning
Mare, Mari, Marizol, Marrisol, Marzol, Merizol

Maritza
(Place name) St. Moritz, Switzerland

Marixbel
(Spanish) pretty
Marix

Marjie
(Scottish) short for Marjorie
Marji, Marjy

Marjorie
(Greek, English, Scottish) bittersweet; pert
Marg, Marge, Margerie, Margery, Margorie, Marjie, Marjori

Marky
(American) mischievous
Marki, Markie
Marla
(German) believer;
easygoing
Marlah, Marlla
Marlaina
(American) form of
Marlene; dramatic
Marlaine, Marlane
Marlana
(Hebrew, Greek)
vamp
Marlanna
Marleal
(American) form of
Mary; desired
Marle, Marleel, Marly
Marlee
(Greek) guarded
Marley, Marlie
Marlen
(American) desired
Marl, Marla, Marlin
Marlena
(German) pretty;
bittersweet
*Marla, Marlaina,
Marlina, Marlynne,
Marnie*

Marlene
(Greek) high-minded;
attractive; (English)
adorned
*Marlean, Marlee,
Marleen, Marleene,
Marley, Marline, Marly*
Marley
(English) form of
Marlene
*Mar, Marlee, Marlie,
Marly*
Marlis
(German) combo of
Maria and Elisabeth;
religious
Marl, Marlice
Marlise
(English) considerate
Marlice, Marlis, Marlys
Marlo
(American) vivacious
Marloe, Marloh
Marlycia
(Spanish) desired
Lycia, Marly, Marlysia
Marnie
(Hebrew) storyteller
*Marn, Marnee, Marni,
Marny*
Marnita
(American) worrier
*Marneta, Marni, Marnite,
Marnitta, Marny*

Marolyn
(Invented) form of
Marilyn; desired;
precious
*Maro, Marolin,
Marolinne*
Maromisa
(Japanese) warm; combo
of Maro and Misa
Maromissa
Marquise
(French) noble-spirited
*Markeese, Marquees,
Marquisa, Mars*
Marquisha
(African-American) form
of Marquise
Marquish
Marquita
(Spanish) happy girl
*Marqueda, Marquitta,
Marrie*
Marrie
(American) variant of
Mary; desired
Marry
Marsala
(Italian) of Marseille,
Italy; rambunctious
Marse, Marsela, Marsie
Marsha
(Latin) light-haired;
combative
Marcia, Mars, Marsie

Marshay
(American) exuberant
Marshae, Marshaya

Marta
(Danish) treasure
Mart, Marte, Marty, Merta

Marterrell
(American) changeable
Marte, Marterill, Martrell

Martha
(Aramaic) lady
Marta, Marth, Marti, Marty, Mattie

Marti
(English) short for Martha; dreamy
Martie, Marty

Martina
(Latin, German) combative
Marteena, Martene, Marti, Martinna, Martyna, Tina

Martivanio
(Italian) form of Martina; feisty; fighter
Mart, Marti, Tivanio

Martonette
(American) form of male name Martin; feisty little girl
Martanette, Martinette, Martonett

Marusya
(Slavic) soft-hearted

Marvella
(French) marvelous woman
Marva, Marvelle, Marvie, Mavela

Mary
(Hebrew) bitter; in the Bible, the mother of Jesus
Maire, Mara, Mare, Maree, Mari, Marie, Mariel, Marlo, Marye, Merree, Merry, Mitzie

Marya
(Arabic) white and bright
Marja

Maryalice
(American) combo of Mary and Alice; friendly
Marialice, Maryalyce

Maryann
(English, American) combo of Mary and Ann; special
Marianne, Maryan

Mary-Catherine
(American) combo of Mary and Catherine; outgoing
Maricatherine, Marycatherine, Mary-Kathryn

Mary-Elizabeth
(American) combo of Mary and Elizabeth; kind
Marielizabeth, Mary Elizabeth, Maryelizabeth

Marykate
(American) combo of May and Kate; splendid
Marikate, Mary-Kate

Marykay
(American) combo of Mary and Kay; adorned
Marikay, Marrikae

Maryke
(Dutch) kind; desired
Mairek, Marika, Maryk, Maryky

Mary-Lou
(American) combo of Mary and Lou; athletic
Mary Lou, Marylou

Mary-Marg
(American) dramatic
Marimarg

Mary-Margaret
(American) combo of Mary and Margaret; dramatic, kind
Marimargaret, Mary Margaret, Marymarg, Marymargret

Marypat
(American) combo of Mary and Pat; easygoing
Mary-Pat, Mary Pat

Marysue
(American) combo of Mary and Sue; country girl
MariSue, Merrysue, Mersue

Masha
(Russian) child who was desired

Mashonda
(African-American) believer
Masho, Mashonde

Mason
(French) diligent; reliable

Massey
(German) confident
Massi, Massie

Massiel
(American) giving
Masie, Masiel, Massey, Massielle

Massim
(Latin) great
Massima, Maxim, Maxima

Matia
(Hebrew) a God-given gift
Matea, Mattea, Mattie

Matilda
(German) powerful fighter
Mat, Mathilda, Mattie, Tilda, Tillie, Tilly

Mattie
(English) most honored
Matt, Matte, Matti, Matty

Matylda
(Polish) strong fighter
Matyld

Maude
(English) old-fashioned
Maud, Maudie

Maudeen
(American) countrified
Maudie, Mawdeen, Mawdine

Maudisa
(African) sweet
Maudesa, Maudesah

Mauna
(American) attractive
Maune, Mawna, Mon

Maura
(Latin, Irish) dark
Moira, Maurie

Maureen
(Irish, French) night-loving
Maura, Maurene, Maurine, Moreen, Morene

Maurelle
(French) petite
Maure, Maurie, Maurielle

Maurise
(French) dark
Morise, Maurice

Mauve
(French) gentle
Mauvey, Mauvie

Mavis
(French) singing bird
Mauvis, Mav, Mave

Maxeeme
(Latin) form of Maxime; maximum

Maxie
(Latin) fine
Maxee, Maxey, Maxy

Maxime
(Latin) maximum
Maxey, Maxi, Maxim

Maxine
(Latin) greatest of all
Max, Maxeen, Maxene, Maxie, Maxy

May
(Old English) bright flower
Mae, Maye

Maya
(Latin, Hindi, Mayan) creative; mystical
Maia, Maiya, Mayah, Mya, Myah, Mye

Maybelle
(American) combo of May and Belle; lovely May
Mabelle, Maebelle, Maybell, May-Belle

Maybelline
(Latin)
Mabie, May, Maybeline, Maybie, Maybleene

Mayella
(American) combo of May and Ella; jolly
Ella, Maella, May, Mayela, Mayell, Mella

Mayghaen
(American) fortunate

Mayim
(Origin unknown) special
Mayum

Maykaylee
(American) ingenious
Maykayli, Maykaylie, Maykayly

Mayo
(Irish) place name; vibrant
Mayoh

Mayra
(Spanish) flourishing; creative
Mayrah

Mayrant
(Spanish) industrious
Maya, Mayrynt

Mazel
(American) form of Hazel; shining
Masel, Mazil

Mazel
(Hebrew) lucky girl
Mazal

Mazie
(Scottish) form of Maisie

McCanna
(American) ebullient
Maccanna, McCannah

McCauley
(Irish) feisty
Mac, McCauly, McCawlie

McCay
(Irish) creative
Mackaylee, McCaylee

McCormick
(Irish) last name as first name
MacCormack, Mackey

McGown
(Irish) sensible
Mac, MacGowen, Mackie, McGowen

McKenna
(American) able
Mackenna, Makenna

McKenzie
(Scottish) form of Mackenzie
Mackie, McKinzie, Mickey

McMurtry
(Irish) last name as first name
Mac, McMurt

Mead
(Greek) honey-wine-loving
Meade

Meadow
(English) place name; calm
Meadoh

Meagan
(Irish) joyous; precious
Maegan, Meaghan, Meegan, Meg, Meganne, Meggie, Meggye, Meghan

Meashley
(American) charmer
Meash, Meashlee

Meatah
(American) athletic
Mea, Mia, Miata (car), Miatah

Medalle
(American) pretty
Medahl, Medoll

Medardo
(Spanish) pretty

Medea
(Greek) ruling; cruel
Medeia

Meg
(Greek) able; lovable
Megs

Megan
(Irish) precious, joyful
*Meagan, Meaghen,
Meggi, Meghan,
Meghann*

Meggie
(Greek) best
Meggey, Meggi, Meggy

Mel
(Greek) sporty
Mell

Melana
(Greek) giving; dark

Melancon
(French) dark beauty;
sweet
*Mel, Melance, Melaney,
Melanie, Melanse,
Melanson, Melonce,
Melonceson*

Melania
(Italian) giving;
philanthropic
Mel, Melly

Melanie
(Greek) dark; sweet
Melanee

Melantha
(Greek) dark-skinned;
sweet
Melanthah

Melba
(Australian) talented;
light-hearted
Melbah

Melia
(German) dedicated
Meelia, Melyah

Melina
(Greek) honey; sweet
Melena, Melinah

Melinda
(Latin) honey;
sweetheart
*Linda, Linnie, Linny,
Lynda, Mellie, Melynda,
Milinda, Mylinde*

Melissa
(Greek) a honey
*Melisa, Melyssa,
Melyssuh*

Melody
(Greek) song; musical
*Mel, Mellie, Melodee,
Melodey, Melodie*

Meloney
(American) form of
Melanie; dark and sweet
Mel, Melone, Meloni

Melora
(Latin) good
*Meliora, Melorah,
Melourah*

Melrose
(Place name) sweet girl
Mellrose, Melrosie

Melvia
(American) leader; dark
Mel, Mell, Melvea

Mena
(Egyptian) pretty
Meenah, Menah

Meosha
(African-American)
talented
*Meeosha, Meoshe,
Miosha*

Merary
(American) merry
*Marary, Meraree,
Merarie*

Mercedes
(Spanish) merciful;
rewarded
*Mercedez, Mercides,
Mersadez, Mersaydes*

Mercy
(English) forgiving
*Merce, Mercee, Mercey,
Merci, Mercie*

Meredith
(Welsh) protector
Mer, Meredithe, Meredyth, Merridith, Merry

Meri
(Irish) by the sea
Merrie

Meridian
(American) perfect posture
Meredian, Meridiane

Merie
(French) secretive; blackbird
Mer, Meri, Myrie

Meriel
(Irish) girl who shines like the sea
Meri, Merial, Merri, Merriyl, Merry

Merilyn
(English, American) combo of Merry and Lynn
Marilyn, Mer, Meralyn, Merelyn, Meri, Merill, Merilynn, Merilynne, Merri, Merrill, Merrylyn

Merissa
(Latin) ocean-loving
Merisa, Meryssa

Merit
(American) deserving
Merite, Meritte, Mirit

Merribeth
(English) cheerful
Merri-Beth, Merrybeth

Merrilee
(American) combo of Merri and Lee; happy
Marilee, Merilee, Merrylee, Merry-Lee

Merry
(English) cheerful
Mer, Merie, Merri, Merrie

Merryjane
(English) combo of Merry and Jane; happy
Merijane, Merrijane, Merrijayne, Merryjaine, Merryjayne

Mersaydes
(Invented) variant of Mercedes
Mercy, Mersa, Mersy

Mersey
(Place name)
Merce, Merse

Mersia
(Hebrew) variant of Mersera; princess
Mercy, Mers, Mersea, Mersy

Meryl
(German) well-known; (Irish) shining sea
Mer, Merel, Merri, Merrill, Merryl, Meryll

Mesa
(Place name) earthy
Mase, Maysa, Mesah

Mi
(Chinese) obsessive
My, Mye

Mia
(Scandinavian, Italian) blessed; girl of mine
Me, Mea, Meah, Meya

Miaka
(Japanese) influential

Miana
(American) combo of Mi and Ana
Mianna

Micah
(Hebrew) religious
Mica, Mika, My, Myca

Michaela
(Hebrew) God-loving
Meeca, Micaela, Michael, Michal, Michala, Michalla, Mikala

Michaelannette
(American) combo of Michael and Annette; spirited
Annette, Michelannet

Michaele
(Hebrew) loving God

Michele
(Italian, French, American) God-loving
Machele, Machelle, Mechele, Mia, Michell, Michelle, Mish, Mishelle

Michelin
(American) lovable
Michalynn, Mish, Mishelin

Micheline
(French) form of Michele; delightful
Mishelinne

Micki
(American) quirky
Mick, Mickee, Mickey, Micky, Miki, Mycki

Mickley
(American) form of Mickey; fun-loving
Mick, Mickaella, Micklee, Mickley, Mickli, Miklea, Miklee, Mikleigh, Mikley, Myk, Mykkie

Micole
(American) combo of Micha and Nicole; happy-go-lucky girl
Macole, Micolle

Mid
(American) middle child
Middi, Middy

Migon
(American) precious
Mignonne, Migonette, Migonn, Migonne

Mignon
(French) cute
Migonette, Mim, Mimi, Minyon, Minyonne

Miguelinda
(Spanish) combo of Miguel and Linda; strong-willed beauty
Miguel-Linda, Miguelynda

Mika
(Hebrew) wise and pious
Micah, Mikah, Mikie

Mikaela
(Hebrew) God-loving
Mik, Mikayla, Mike, Mikhaila, Miki

Mila
(Russian, Italian) short for Camilla; dearest
Milah, Milla, Millah, Mimi

Milagros
(Spanish) miracle
Mila, Milagro

Milantia
(Panamanian) calm
Mila

Mildred
(English) gentle
Mil, Mildread, Mildrid, Millie, Milly

Milena
(Greek) loving girl
Mela, Mili, Milina

Miliani
(Hawaiian) one who caresses
Mil, Mila

Milissa
(Greek) softspoken
Melissa, Missy

Milla
(Polish) gentle; pure
Mila, Millah

Millay
(Literature) soft

Millicent
(Greek, German) soft-hearted
Melicent, Melly, Millie, Millisent, Milly, Missy

Millie
(English) short for Mildred and Millicent
Mil, Mili, Milly

Mimi
(French) short for Camilla; willful
Meemee, Mim, Mims, Mimsie

Min
(Chinese) sensitive; soft-hearted

Mina
(German, Polish) resolute
protector; willful
Mena, Min, Minah

Mindy
(Greek) short for
Melinda; breezy
*Mindee, Mindi, Mindie,
Myndee*

Minerva
(Latin, Greek) bright;
strong
*Menerva, Min, Minnie,
Myn*

Minette
(French) loyal woman
Min, Minnette, Minnie

Ming
(Chinese) shiny; hope of
tomorrow

Minhtu
(Asian) light and clear

Mini
(Scandinavian) mine

Miniver
(English) assertive
*Meniver, Minever,
Miniverr*

Minna
(German) sturdy
Mina, Minnie

Minnie
(German) short for
Minerva
Mini, Minni, Minny

Mira
(Latin, Spanish)
wonderful girl
Meara, Mirror

Mirabel
(Latin) marvelous;
beautiful reflection
*Marabelle, Mira,
Mirabell, Mirabelle*

Mirabella
(Italian) marvelous
Mira, Mirabellah

Miraclair
(Latin) combo of Mira
and Clair; wonderful;
gentle
*Mira-Clair, Miraclaire,
Miraclare*

Miracle
(American) miracle baby
*Merry, Mira, Mirakle,
Mirry*

Miranda
(Latin) unique and
amazing
*Maranda, Meranda,
Mira, Mirrie, Myranda*

Mirella
(Spanish) wonderful
*Mira, Mirel, Mirell,
Mirelle*

Mireya
(Hebrew) form of
Miriam; melancholy

Mireyli
(Spanish) wondrous;
admirable
Mire, Mirey

Miriam
(Hebrew) living with
sadness
*Mariam, Maryam,
Meriam, Miri, Miriame,
Mirriam, Mitzi*

Mirka
(Polish) glorious
Mira, Mirk

Mirtha
(Greek) burdened
*Meert, Meerta, Mirt,
Mirta*

Mischanna
(Hebrew) form of
Miriam; desired
*Misch, Mischana, Mish,
Mishanna, Mishke*

Mishelene
(French) form of
Micheline; pretty;
believer
Mish, Misha, Mishlene

Missy
(English) short for
Melissa
Miss, Missi, Missie

Misty
(English) dreamy
*Miss, Missy, Mistee,
Misti, Mistie, Mysti*

Mitten
(American) cuddly
Mitt, Mittun, Mitty

Mittie
(American) short for
Matilda and Mitten;
darling
*Mittee, Mittey, Mitti,
Myttie*

Mitzi
(German) dancer
*Mitsee, Mitzee, Mitzie,
Mitzy*

Miya
(Japanese) peaceful as a
temple
Miyah

Mobley
(Last name as first
name) beauty queen
*Moblee, Mobli, Moblie,
Mobly*

Mocha
(Arabic) coffee with
chocolate
Mo, Moka, Mokka

Modesty
(Latin) modest
Modesti, Modestie

Moeshea
(African-American)
talented
*Moesha, Moeshia,
Mosha*

Moira
(English, Irish) pure;
great one
*Maura, Moir, Moirah,
Moire, Moyrah*

Mokysha
(African-American)
dramatic
*Kisha, Kysha, Mokesha,
Mokey*

Moll
(Literature) Moll
Flanders; outgoing
Molly

Molly
(Irish) jovial
*Moli, Moll, Molley,
Mollie*

Momo
(Japanese) peaches

Mona
(Greek) short for
Ramona; shining-
cheeked
Monah, Mone

Moneek
(Invented) form of
Monique; saucy; advisor
Moneeke

Monet
(French) artistic
Mon, Monae, Monay

Monica
(Greek) seeking
company of others
*Mon, Mona, Monicka,
Monika, Monike,
Monique*

Monical
(American) combo of
Monica and L; lively
*Monecal, Moni, Monicle,
Monikal*

Monika
(Polish) advisor

Monique
(French) saucy; advisor
*Mon, Mone, Monee,
Moni*

Monserrat
(Latin) tall
Monserat

Montana
(Place name) mountain
of strength
*Montayna, Montie,
Monty*

Montenia
(Spanish) climber
*Monte, Montenea,
Montynia*

Monya
(American) confident
Mon, Monyeh

Moon
(American) dreamy
Monnie, Moone,
Moonee, Mooney,
Moonny, Moonnye

Moon Unit
(Invented) universal
appeal
Moon-Unit

Mor
(Irish) sweet

Mora
(Spanish) sweet as a
blueberry

Morag
(Scottish) goddess
Morrag

Moraima
(Spanish) forgiving
Mora, Morama

More
(American) bonus
Moore, Morie

Morgan
(Welsh) girl on the
seashore
Mor, Morey, Morgane,
Morgannna, Morgen

Moriah
(French) dark girl;
(Hebrew) God-taught
Mareyeh, Mariah,
Moorea, More, Morie,
Morria

Morine
(American) form of
Maureen; fond of night
Morri

Moritza
(Place name) St. Moritz,
Switzerland; playful

Morla
(American) form of
Marla; easygoing
Morley, Morly

Morven
(American) magical
Morvee, Morvey, Morvi

Morwyn
(Welsh) maiden
Morwen, Morwenn,
Morwynn, Morwynna

Moselle
(Hebrew) uplifted
Mose, Mozelle, Mozie

Moya
(Scandinavian) mother
Moy

Mudiva
(Slavic)
Mudeva

Murdina
(Slavic) dark spirit
Murdi, Murdine

Muriel
(Celtic) shining
Meriel, Mur, Murial,
Muriele, Murielle

Murphy
(Irish) spirited
Murphee, Murphey,
Murphi

Murray
(Last name as first
name) brisk
Muray, Murraye

Musique
(French) musical
Museek, Museke, Musik

Mussie
(American) musical
Muss, Mussi, Mussy

Myeshia
(African-American)
giving
Meyeshia, Mye, Myesha

Mykala
(Scandinavian) giving
Mykaela, Mykela, Mykie

Mykelle
(American) generous
Mykell

Myla
(English) forgiving
Miela, Mylah

Mylene
(Greek) dark-skinned girl
Myleen

Mylie
(German) forgiving
Miley, Mylee, Myli

Mynola
(Invented) smart
Minola, Monoa, Mynolla, Mynolle

Myra
(Latin) fragrant
Myrah

Myrischa
(African-American) fragrant doll
Myresha, Myri, Myrish, Myrisha, Rischa

Myrka,
(Slavic) great
Mirk, Mirka, Myrk

Myrka
(Spanish) rambunctious
Merka, Mirka, Myrkah

Myrna
(Irish) loved
Merna, Mirna, Murna

Myrtle
(Greek) loving
Mertle, Mirtle, Myrt, Myrtie

Mysha
(Russian) form of Misha; protective
Mischa, Mish, Misha, Mysh

Mysta
(Invented) mysterious
Mista, Mystah

Mystique
(French) intriguing woman
Mistie, Mistik, Mistique, Misty, Mystica

N

Naama
(Hebrew) sweet
Naamah, Naamit

Naamah
(Biblical) sweet
Nanay, Nayamah, Naynay

Naava
(Hebrew) delightful girl
Naavah, N'Ava

Nada
(Arabic) morning dew; giving

Nadelie
(American) form of Natalie; Christmas-born beauty
Nadey

Nadeline
(Invented) born on Christmas
Nad, Nadelyne

Nadia
(Slavic) hopeful
Nada, Nadea, Nadi, Nadie, Nady, Nadya

Nadine
(Russian, French) dancer
Nadeen, Nadene, Nadie, Nadyne, Naidyne

Nadya
(Russian) optimistic; life's beginnings

Naeemah
(African) breathtaking

Nahtanha
(African) warm

Nai
(Japanese) intelligent
Nayah

Naida
(Greek) nymph-like
Naya

Nailah
(African) successful
Naila

Naimah
(Arabic) happy
Naima

Najet
(African)
Naajet

Nakesha
(African-American) combo of Na and Kesha
Naka, Nakeisha, Nakie, Nakisha

Nakia
(Arabic) purest girl
Nakea

Nakita
(Russian) precocious
Nakeeta, Nakeita, Nakya, Naquita, Nikita

Nala
(African) loved
Nalah, Nalo

Nalani
(Hawaiian) calming
Nalanie, Nalany

Nallely
(Spanish) friend
Nalelee, Naleley, Nallel

Nan
(German, Scottish, English) bold; graceful
Na, Nana, Nannie, Nanny

Nanalie
(American) form of Natalie; graceful; Christmas-born
Nan, Nana, Nanalee

Nance
(American) giving
Nans

Nancy
(English, Irish) generous woman
Nan, Nancee, Nanci, Nancie, Nansee, Nonie

Nanette
(French) giving and gracious
Nanet

Nani
(Greek) charming beauty
Nan, Nannie

Nanice
(American) open-hearted
Nan, Naneece, Naneese, Naniece

Nanna
(Scandinavian) brave
Nana

Nanon
(French) slow to anger
Nan, Nanen

Naomi
(Hebrew) beautiful woman
Naomie, Naomy, Naynay, Nene, Noma, Nomah, Nomi

Nara
(Greek, Japanese) happy; dreamy
Narah, Nera

Narcissa
(Greek) narcissistic
Narcisse, Nars

Narcissie
(Greek) conceited; daffodil
Narci, Narcis, Narcissa, Narcisse, Narcissey, Narsee, Narsey, Narsis

Nastasia
(Greek, Russian)
gorgeous girl
Nas, Nastasha, Natasie

Natalia
(Russian, Latin) born on
Christmas; beauty
*Nat, Nata, Natala,
Natalea, Natalee,
Natalie, Natalya, Nati,
Nattie, Nattlee, Natty*

Natarsha
(American) splendid
Natarsh, Natarshah

Natasha
(Latin, Russian)
glorious; born on
Christmas
*Natacha, Natashah,
Natashia, Natassia,
Nitasha*

Nathadria
(Hebrew) form of
Nathan; gift of God
*Natania, Nath, Nathe,
Nathed, Nathedrea,
Natty, Thedria*

Nathalie
(French) born on
Christmas
Natalie

Nation
(American) spirited;
patriotic
Nashon, Nayshun

Natosha
(African-American) form
of Natasha; born on
Christmas
*Nat, Natosh, Natoshe,
Natty*

Naveen
(Spanish) snowing

Navita
(Hispanic) original
Nava, Navite

Nayeli
(African) of beginnings

Nazly
(American) idealistic
Nazlee, Nazli, Nazlie

Neal
(Irish) spirited
Neale, Neel, Neil

Neala
(Irish) spirited
*Neal, Neeli, Neelie,
Neely, Neila*

Necie
(Hungarian) intense
Neci

Neda
(Slavic) Sunday baby

Nedda
(English) born to money
Ned, Neddy

Nedra
(English) secretive
Ned, Nedre

Neely
(Irish) sparkling smile
*Nealy, Neelee, Neilie,
Nelie*

Nefris
(Spanish) glamorous
*Nef, Neff, Neffy, Nefras,
Nefres*

Neia
(African) promising

Neith
(Egyptian) feminine
Neithe

Nekeisha
(African-American) bold
spirit
*Nek, Nekeishah,
Nekesha, Nekisha,
Nekkie*

Nelda
(American) friend
*Neldah, Nell, Nellda,
Nellie*

Nelia
(Spanish) short for
Cornelia; yellow-haired
*Neelia, Neely, Nela,
Nelie, Nene*

Nell
(English) sweet charmer
Nelle, Nellie

Nellie
(English) short for
Cornelia and Eleanor
Nel, Nela, Nell, Nelle,
Nelli, Nelly

Nelliene
(American) form of
Nellie; charming
Nell, Nelli, Nellienne

Nelvia
(Greek) brash
Nell, Nelvea

Nemoria
(American) crafty
Nemorea

Nereida
(Spanish) sea nymph
Nere, Nereide, Nereyda,
Neri, Nireida

Neressa
(Greek) coming from the
sea
Narissa, Nene, Nerissa,
Nerisse

Nerys
(Welsh) ladylike
Neris, Neriss, Nerisse

Nessa
(Irish) devout
Nessah

Nessie
(Greek) short for
Vanessa
Nese, Nesi, Ness

Nestora
(Spanish) she is leaving
Nesto, Nestor

Neta
(Hebrew) growing and
flourishing

Netira
(Spanish) flourishing

Netra
(American) maturing
well
Net, Netrah, Netrya,
Nettie

Netta
(Scottish) champion
Nett, Nettie

Nettie
(French) gentle
Net, Netti, Netty

Nettiemae
(American) combo of
Nettie and Mae;
small-town girl
Mae, Netimay,
Nettemae, Nettie,
Nettiemay

Neva
(Russian, English) the
newest; snow
Neeva, Neve, Niv

Nevada
(Spanish) place name;
girl who loves snow
Nev, Nevadah

Neve
(Irish) promising
princess

Nevina
(Irish) she worships God
Nev, Niv, Nivena, Nivina

Newlin
(Last name as first
name) healing
Newlinn, Newlinne,
Newlyn, Newlynn

Neyda
(Spanish) pure
Ney

Nia
(Greek) priceless
Niah

Niamh
(Irish) promising

Niandrea
(Invented) form of
Diandrea; pretty
Andrea, Nia, Niand,
Niandre

Nicelda
(American) industrious
Niceld, Nicelde, Nicey

Nichele
(American) combo of
Nicole and Michele;
dark-skinned
Nichel, Nichelle, Nishele

Nichole
(French) light and lively
Nichol

Nichols
(Last name as first name) smart
Nick, Nickee, Nickels, Nickey, Nicki, Nickie, Nicky, Nikels

Nick
(American) short for Nicole
Nik

Nicki
(French) short for Nicole
Nick, Nickey, Nicky, Niki

Nicks
(American) fashionable
Nickee, Nickie, Nicksie, Nicky, Nix

Nico
(Italian) victorious
Nicco, Nicko, Nikko, Niko

Nicola
(Italian) lovely singer
Nekola, Nick, Nikkie, Nikola

Nicolasa
(Spanish) spontaneous; winning
Nico, Nicole

Nicole
(French) winning
Nacole, Nichole, Nick, Nickie, Nikki, Nikol, Nikole

Nicolette
(French) a tiny Nicole; little beauty
Nettie, Nick, Nickie, Nicoline, Nikkolette, Nikolet

Nicolie
(French) sweet
Nichollie, Nikolie

Nidia
(Latin) home-loving
Nidie, Nidya

Niesha
(African-American) virginal
Neisha, Nesha, Nesia, Nessie

Nieves
(Spanish) snows
Neaves, Ni, Nievez, Nievis

Nike
(Greek) goddess of victory; fleet of foot; a winner

Niki
(American) short for Nicole and Nikita
Nick, Nicki, Nicky, Nik, Nikki, Nikky

Niki-Lynn
(American) combo of Niki and Lynn
Nicki-Lynn, Nicky-Lynn, Nikilinn, Nikilyn

Nikita
(Russian) daring
Nakeeta, Niki, Nikki, Niquitta

Nikithia
(African-American) winning; frank
Kithi, Kithia, Nikethia, Niki

Nikole
(Greek) winning
Nik, Niki

Nima
(Arabic) blessed
Nimah

Nina
(Russian, Hebrew, Spanish) bold girl
Neena, Nena, Ninah

Nina-Lina
(Spanish) combo of Nina and Lina; lovely
Nina Lina, Ninalena, Ninalina

Nirvana
(Hindi) completion; oneness with God
Nirvahna, Nirvanah

Nissa
(Hebrew) symbolic
Niss, Nissah, Nissie

Nissie
(Scandinavian) pretty; elf
Nisse, Nissee

Nita
(Hebrew) short for
Juanita
Neeta, Nite, Nittie

Niu
(Chinese) girlish;
confident

Nixi
(German) mystical
Nixee, Nixie

Niy
(American) lively
Nye

Noa
(Hebrew) chosen
Noah

Noel
(Latin) born on
Christmas
*Noela, Noelle, Noellie,
Noli*

Nohelia
(Hispanic) kind
Nohelya

Nola
(Latin) sensual
Nolah, Nole, Nolie

Nomble
(African) beautiful
Nombi

Nona
(Latin) ninth; knowing
*Nonah, Nonie, Nonn,
Nonna*

Nora
(Greek, Scandinavian,
Scottish) light; bright;
from the north
Norah, Noreh

Noranna
(Irish) combo of Nora
and Anna; honorable
*Anna, Nora, Norana,
Norannah, Noranne,
Noreena*

Noreen
(Latin) acknowledging
others
*Noire, Norin, Norine,
Norinne, Nureen*

Norika
(Japanese) athletic
Nori, Norike

Norma
(Latin) gold standard
*Noey, Nomah, Norm,
Normah, Normie*

Norris
(English) serious
Nore, Norrus

Nota
(American) negative
Na, Nada, Not

Nova
(Latin) energetic; new
*Noova, Novah, Novella,
Novie*

Novak
(Last name as first
name) emphatic
Novac

Novia
(Spanish) sweetheart
Nov, Novie, Nuvia

Nu
(Vietnamese) confident
Niu

Nueva
(Spanish) new; fresh
Nue, Nuey

Numa
(Spanish) delightful
Num

Numa-Noe
(Spanish) combo of
Numa and Noe; delight
Numanoe

Nunibelle
(American) combo of
Nuni and Belle; pretty
Nunibell, Nunnibelle

Nunu
(Vietnamese) friendly

Nura
(Aramaic) light-footed
Noora, Noura, Nurrie

Nuria
(Arabic) light
Noor, Noura, Nur

Nurlene
(American) boisterous
Nerlene, Nurleen

Nuvia
(American) new
Nuvea
Nydia
(Latin) nest-loving;
home and hearth
woman
Ny, Nydie, Nydya
Nylene
(American) shy
*Nyle, Nylean, Nyleen,
Nyles, Nyline*
Nysa
(Greek) life-starting
*Nisa, Nissa, Nissie,
Nysa, Nyssa*
Nyx
(Greek) lively
Nix

Obede
(English) obedient
Obead
Obedience
(American) obedient
Obey
Obey
(American) obedient
Oceana
(Greek) ocean-loving;
name given to those
with astrological signs
that have to do with
water
Oceonne, Ocie, Oh
Octavia
(Latin) eighth child; born
on eighth day of the
month; musical
Octivia, Octtavia
Odalis
(Spanish) humorous
*Odales, Odallis,
Odalous, Odalus*

Odele
(Hebrew, Greek)
melodious
Odela, Odelle, Odie
Odelia
(Hebrew, Greek) singer
of spiritual songs
*Odele, Odelle, Odie,
Odila*
Odelita
(Spanish) vocalist
Odelite
Odessa
(Place name) traveler on
an odyssey
Odessah, Odie, Odissa
Odette
(French) good girl
Oddette, Odetta
Odile
(French) sensuous
Odyll
Odilia
(Spanish) wealthy
*Eudalia, Odalia, Odella,
Odylia, Othilia*
Ohara
(Japanese) meditative
Oh
Oksana
(Russian) praise to God
Oksanah, Oksie
Ola
(Scandinavian) bold
Olah

Olaide
(American) lovely; thoughtful
Olai, Olay, Olayde

Olga
(Russian) holy woman
Ola, Olgah, Ollie

Olidie
(Spanish) light
Oli, Olidee, Olydie

Olino
(Spanish) scented
Olina, Oline

Olive
(Latin) subtle
Olyve

Olivia
(English) flourishing
Olive, Olivea, Oliveah, Ollie

Olwen
(Welsh) magical; white
Olwynn

Olya
(Latin) perfect
Olyah

Olympia
(Greek) heavenly woman
Olimpia, Ollie

Olynda
(Invented) form of Lynda; fragrant; pretty
Lyn, Lynda, Olin, Olinda, Olynde

Oma
(German) grandmother; (Hebrew) pious
Omah

Omanie
(Origin unknown) exuberant
Omanee

Omayra
(Latin) fragrant (Spanish) beloved
Oma, Omyra

Omesha
(African-American) splendid
Omesh, Omie, Omisha

Omie
(Italian) homebody
Omee

Omorose
(African) lovely

Ondina
(Latin) water spirit
Ondi, Ondine, Onyda

Oneida
(Native American) anticipated
Ona, Oneeda, Onida, Onie, Onyda

Oni
(African) desired child

Onie
(Latin) flamboyant
Oh, Oona, Oonie, Una

Opal
(Hindi) the opal; precious
Opale, Opalle, Opie

Ophelia
(Greek) helpful woman; character from Shakespeare's Hamlet
Ofelia, Ophela, Phelie

Oprah
(Hebrew) one who soars; excellent
Ophie, Ophrie, Opra, Oprie, Orpah

Ora
(Greek) glowing
Orah, Orie

Oraleyda
(Spanish) light of dawn
Ora, Oraleydea, Oralida

Oralie
(Hebrew) light of dawn
Oralee, Orla

Orbelina
(American) excited, dawn
Lina, Orbe, Orbee, Orbeline, Orbey, Orbi, Orby

Orene
(French) nurturing
Orane, Orynne

Orfelinda
(Spanish) pretty dawn
Orfelinde, Orfelynda

Orianna
(Latin) sunny; dawn
Oriana, Oriannah, Orie
Orin
(Irish) dark-haired
Oren, Orinn
Oriole
(Latin) golden light
Oreole, Oriel, Oriol
Orlanda
(German) famed
Orly
(French) busy
Orlee
Ormanda
(Latin) noble
Ormie
Orna
(Irish) dark-haired
Ornah
Ottolee
(English) combo of Otto
and Lee; appealing
Ottalie, Ottilie
Otylia
(Polish) rich
Oteelya
Ovalia
(Spanish) helpful
Ova, Ove, Ovelia
Owena
(Welsh) feisty
Oweina, Owina, Owinne

Ozara
(Hebrew) treasured
Ozarah

Pabiola
(Spanish) small girl
Pabby, Pabi, Pabiole
Pace
(Last name as first
name) charismatic
Pase
Pacifica
(Spanish) peaceful
Pacifika
Padgett
(French) growing and
learning; lovely-haired
Padge, Padget, Paget
Page
(French) sharp; eager
*Pagie, Paige, Paje,
Payge*
Pageant
(American) theatrical
*Padg, Padge, Padgeant,
Padgent, Pagent*
Paisley
(Scottish) patterned
Paislee, Pazley

Pal
(American) friend; buddy
Palemon
(Spanish) kind
Palem, Palemond
Paley
(Last name as first name) wise
Palee, Palie
Pallas
(Greek) wise woman
Palace, Palas
Palma
(Latin) successful
Palmah, Palmeda, Palmedah
Paloma
(Spanish) dove
Peloma
Pam
(Greek) sweet as honey
Pama, Pamela, Pammie, Pammy
Pamela
(Greek) sweet as honey
Pam, Pamala, Pamalla, Pamee, Pamelinn, Pamelyn, Pammee, Pammi, Pammie, Pammy, Pamyla, Pamylla
Pandora
(Greek) a gift; curious
Pan, Pand, Pandie, Pandorah

Pang
(Chinese) innovative
Pansy
(Greek) fragrant
Pan, Pansey, Pansie, Panze, Panzee, Panzie
Panther
(Greek) wild; all gods
Panthar, Panthea, Panthur, Panth
Paola
(Italian) firebrand
Paolabella
(Italian) lovely firebrand
Paris
(French) capital of France; graceful woman
Pareece, Parie, Parice, Parris
Parker
(English) noticed; in the park
Park, Parke, Parkie
Parminder
(Hindi) attractive
Parnelle
(French) small stone
Parn, Parnel, Parnell, Parney
Parslee
(Botanical) complementary
Pars, Parse, Parsley, Parsli

Parthenia
(Greek) from the Parthenon; virtuous
Parthe, Parthee, Parthene, Parthine, Thenia
Pascale
(French) born on a religious holiday
Pascal, Paschale, Paskel, Paskil
Paschel
(African) spiritual
Paschell
Pash
(French) clever
Pasch
Pasha
(Greek) lady by the sea
Passha
Passion
(American) sensual
Pashun, Pasyun, Pass, Passyun
Pat
(Latin) short for Patricia; tough
Patt, Patty
Patia
(Latin) short for Patricia; hard-minded
Patience
(English) woman of patience
Pacience, Pat, Pattie

Patrice
(French) form of Patricia;
svelte
Pat, Patreas, Patreece,
Pattie, Pattrice, Trece,
Treecc

Patricia
(Latin) woman of
nobility; unbending
Pat, Patrisha, Patsie,
Patsy, Patti, Pattie, Patty

Patrina
(American) noble;
patrician
Patryna, Patrynna,
Tryna, Trynnie

Patsy
(Latin) short for Patricia;
brassy
Pat, Patsey, Patsi,
Patsie, Patti, Patty

Patty
(English) short for
Patricia and Patrice
Pat, Pati, Patti, Pattie

Paula
(Latin) small and
feminine
Paulah, Paulie, Pauly,
Pawlah

Paulette
(French) form of Paula;
little Paula
Paula, Paulett, Paulie,
Paullette

Paulina
(Latin) small;
(Italian) lovely
Paula, Paulena, Paulie

Pauline
(Latin) short for Paula;
precocious
Pauleen, Paulene

Pax
(Latin) peace goddess

Paxton
(Latin) place name;
peaceful
Pax, Paxten, Paxtun

Payton
(Last name as first
name) aggressive
Pay, Paye, Payten,
Paytun, Peyton

Paz
(Spanish, Hebrew)
sparkling; peaceful
Pazia

Paza
(Hebrew) golden child
Paz

Pazzy
(Latin) peaceful
Paz, Pazet

Peace
(English) peaceful
woman
Pea, Peece

Peaches
(American) outrageously
sweet
Peach, Peachy

Pearl
(Latin) jewel from the
sea
Pearlie, Pearly, Perl,
Perla

Pecola
(American) brash
Pekola

Peggy
(Greek) pearl; priceless
Peg, Peggi, Peggie

Pei
(Chinese) place name;
from Tang Pei

Peigi
(Scottish) pearl;
priceless

Pele
(Hawaiian) volcano;
conflicted

Pelham
(English) thoughtful
Pelhim, Pellam, Pellham,
Pellie

Pelia
(Hebrew) marvelous
Peliah, Pelya, Pelyia

Pendant
(French) necklace;
adorned
Pendan, Pendanyt

Penelope
(Greek) patient; weaver
of dreams
*Pen, Penalope, Penni,
Pennie, Penny*

Peninah
(Hebrew) pearl; lovely
Peni, Penny

Penny
(Greek) short for
Penelope; spunky
*Pen, Penee, Penni,
Pennie*

Peony
(Greek) flowering; giving
praise
Pea, Peoni, Peonie

Pepita
(Spanish) high-energy
Peppita

Pepper
(Latin) spicy
Pep, Peppie, Peppyr

Peppy
(American) cheerful
*Pep, Peppey, Peppi,
Peps*

Perfecta
(Spanish) perfection
Perfekta

Perla
(Latin) substantial
Perlah

Peridot
(Arabic) green gem;
treasured
Peri

Perlace
(Spanish) small pearl
*Perl, Perlahse, Perlase,
Perly*

Perlette
(French) pearl; treasured
*Pearl, Pearline, Peraline,
Perl, Perle, Perlett*

Perlie
(Latin) form of Pearl
Perli, Purlie, Perly

Perlina
(American) small pearl
*Pearl, Perl, Perlinna,
Perlyna*

Perouze
(Armenian) turquoise
gemstone
*Perou, Perous, Perouz,
Perry*

Perri
(Greek, Latin) outdoorsy
Peri, Perr, Perrie, Perry

Persephone
(Greek) breath of spring
*Pers, Perse, Persefone,
Persey*

Pesha
(Hebrew) flourishing
Peshah, Peshia

Pershella
(American) philanthropic
*Pershe, Pershel,
Pershelle, Pershey,
Persie, Persy*

Persia
(Place name) colorful
Persha, Perzha

Persis
(Latin) from Persian
Pers, Persus, Perz

Peta
(English) saucy
Pet, Petty

Petra
(Slavic) glamorous;
capable
*Pet, Peti, Petrah, Pett,
Petti, Pietra*

Petronilla
(Greek) form of Peter;
rock; dependable
*Petria, Petrina, Petrine,
Petro, Petrone,
Petronela, Petronella,
Pett*

Petula
(Latin) petulant song
Pet, Petulah, Petulia

Petunia
(American) flower; perky
Pet, Petune

Phaedra
(Greek) bright
Faydra, Faydrah, Padra, Phae, Phedra

Phashestha
(American) decorative
Phashey, Shesta

Phernita
(American) articulate
Ferney, Phern

Phila
(Greek) loving
Phil, Philly

Philadelphia
(Greek) place name;
loving one's fellow man
Fill, Phil, Philly

Philana
(Greek) loving
Filana, Filly, Philly

Philippa
(Greek) horse lover
Feefee, Felipa, Phil, Philippe, Phillie, Phillippah

Philise
(Greek) loving
Felece, Felice, Philese

Philly
(Place name) wild spirit
Filly, Philee, Phillie

Philomena
(Greek) beloved
Filomena, Filomina, Mena, Phil, Phillomenah, Philomen

Phoebe
(Greek) bringing light
Febe, Fee, Feebe, Feebs, Phebee, Phoeb, Phoebey, Phoebie, Phoebs

Phoenix
(Place name) U.S. city;
(Greek) rebirth
Fee, Fenix, Fenny, Phenix, Phoe

Phylicia
(Greek) fortunate girl
Felicia, Phillie, Phyl, Phylecia

Phyllida
(Greek) lovely; leafy
bough
Filida, Phyll, Phyllyda

Phyllis
(Greek) beautiful; leafy
bough; articulate;
smitten
Fillice, Fillis, Phil, Philis, Phillisse, Phyl, Phylis, Phyllys

Pia
(Latin) devout
Peah, Piah

Picabo
(American) place name
Peekaboo

Pier
(Greek) form of Peter;
rock; reliable
Peer

Pierette
(Greek) reliable
Perett, Perette, Piere

Pierina
(Greek) dependable
Peir, Per, Perina, Perine, Pieryna

Pilar
(Spanish) worthwhile;
pillar of strength

Pilvi
(Italian) cheerful
Pilvee

Pink
(American) blushing
Pinkee, Pinkie, Pinky, Pinkye, Pynk

Piper
(English) player of a
pipe; musical

Pippa
(English) ebullient;
horse-lover
Pip, Pipa

Pippi
(English) blushing;
(French) loving horses
Pip, Pippie, Pippy

Pirouette
(French) ballet term
Piro, Pirouet, Pirouetta

Pita
(English) comforting
Peta, Petah

Pitarra
(American) interesting
Pitarr

Pity
(American) sad
Pitee, Pitey, Pitie

Pixie
(American) small; perky
Pixee, Pixey, Pixi

Platinum
(Metal) refined
Plati, Platnum

Pleshette
(American) plush
Plesh

Po
(Italian) effervescent
Poe

Pocahontas
(Native American) joyful
Poca, Poka

Poe
(Animal and river)
peacock; Po River
Po, PoPo

Poetry
(Word as name)
romantic
Poe, Poesy, Poet,

Polina
(Russian) small
Po, Pola, Polya

Polly
(Irish) devout; joyous
Paulie, Pol, Polli, Pollie

Pollyanna
(American, English)
combo of Polly and
Anna; happy-go-lucky
*Polianna, Polliana,
Pollie-anna, Polly*

Pomona
(Latin) apple of my eye
Pomonah

Pompa
(Last name as first
name) pompous
Pompy

Pompey
(Place name) lavish
*Pomp, Pompee, Pompei,
Pompy*

Pony
(American) wild-west girl
Poney, Ponie

Poodle
(American) dog; froufrou
girl
Poo, Pood, Poodly

Poppy
(Latin) flower; bouncy
girl
Pop, Poppi, Poppie

Porsche
(Latin) giving; high-
minded
*Porsh, Porsha, Porshe,
Porshie, Portia*

Portia
(Latin) a giving woman
Porsh, Porsha, Porshuh

Posh
(American) fancy girl
Posha

Posy
(American) sweet
Posee, Posey, Posie

Poupée
(French) French word for
doll
Pou

Powder
(American) gentle; light
*Pow, Powd, Powdy,
Powdyr, PowPow*

Precia
(Latin) important
*Preciah, Presha,
Presheah, Preshuh*

Precious
(English) beloved
*Preshie, Preshuce,
Preshus*

Prema
(Hindi) love

Prescilian
(Hispanic) fashionable
Pres, Priss

Presley
(English) talented
Preslee, Preslie, Presly, Prezlee, Prezley, Prezly
Price
(Welsh) loving
Pri, Prise, Pry, Pryce, Pryse
Prima
(Latin) first; fresh
Primia, Primie, Primma
Primalia
(Spanish) prime; first
Primavera
(Italian) spring child
Primola
(Botanical) flower; from primrose; first
Prim, Prym, Prymola
Primrose
(English) rosy; fragrant
Prim, Primie, Rosie, Rosy
Princess
(English) precious
Prin, Prince, Princie, Prinsess
Prinscella
(American) combo of Princess and Priscilla; princess
Princella, Prins, Prinsce, Prinscilla, Prinsee, Prinsey

Prisciliana
(Spanish) prissy; wise; old
Cissy, Priscili, Priss, Prissy
Priscilla
(Latin) wisdom of the ages
Cilla, Pris, Priscella, Prisilla, Priss, Prissie, Prissy
Prisisima
(Spanish) wise and feminine
Priss, Prissy, Sima
Prissy
(Latin) short for Priscilla; wise; feminine
Prisi, Priss, Prissie
Priti
(Hindi) lovely
Priya
(Hindi) sweetheart
Preeya, Preya, Priyah
Promise
(American) sincere
Promis
Prova
(French) place name; Provence
Pro, Proa, Provah
Pru
(Latin) short for Prudence
Prudie, Prue

Prudence
(Latin) wise; careful
Perd, Pru, Prudie, Prudince, Pruds
Prunella
(Latin) shy
Pru, Prue, Prune, Prunie
Pryor
(Last name as first name) wealthy
Prieyer, Pryar, Prye, Pryer
Psyche
(Greek) soulful
Sye, Sykie
Puma
(Animal) cougar; wild spirit
Poom, Pooma, Poomah, Pumah, Pume
Purity
(English) virginal
Puretee, Puritie
Pyera
(Italian) sturdy; formidable; rock
Pyer, Pyerah
Pyllyon
(English) enthusiastic
Pillion, Pillyon, Pillyun
Pyria
(Origin unknown) cherished
Pyra, Pyrea

Q-Malee
(American) form of
Cumale; open-hearted
*Cue, Q, Quemalee,
Quemali, Quemalie*

Quan
(Chinese) goddess of
compassion

Quanda
(English) queenly
*Kwanda, Kwandah,
Quandah, Qwanda*

Quanella
(African-American)
sparkling
Kwannie, Quanela

Quanesha
(African-American)
singing
*Kwaeesha, Kwannie,
Quaneisha, Quanisha*

Quantina
(American) brave queen
*Kwantina, Kwantynna,
Quantinna, Quantyna,
Tina*

QueAnna
(American) combo of
Que and Anna; genuine
*Keana, KeAnna,
KeeAnna, Queana*

Queen
(English) regal; special

Queenie
(English) queen-like;
royal and dignified
*Kweenie, Quee, Queen,
Queeny*

Queenverlyn
(Invented) combo of
Queen and Verlyn; lady
Queenee, Queenie

Quenby
(Swedish) feminine
*Quenbee, Quenbey,
Quenbi, Quenbie,
Quinbee*

Quenna
(English) feminine
Kwenna

Questa
(French) looking for love
Kesta

Queta
(Spanish) head of the
house
Keta

Quilla
(English) writer
*Kwila, Kwilla, Quila,
Quillah*

Quinby
(Scandinavian) living
like royalty
*Quenby, Quin, Quinbie,
Quinnie*

Quinceanos
(Spanish) fifteenth child
Quin, Quince, Quincy

Quincy
(French) fifth
Quince, Quincie

Quincylla
(American) popular; fifth
child
Cylla, Quince, Quincy

Quinella
(Latin) betting term; a
girl who is as pretty as
two
Quinn

Quinn
(English, Irish) smart
Quin, Quinnie

Quinta
(Latin) fifth day of the
month

Quintana
(Latin) fifth; lovely girl
Quentana, Quinn

Quintessa
(Latin) effervescent
Quinn

Quintilla
(Latin) fifth girl
Quintina

Quintona
(Latin) fifth
Quintwana
(American) fifth girl in the family
Quintuana
Quinyette
(American) likeable; fifth child
Kwenyette, Quiny
Quisha
(African-American) beautiful mind
Keisha, Kesha, Key
Quita
(Latin) peaceful
Keeta, Keetah

Rabbit
(American) lively; energetic
Rabit
Rachael
(Hebrew) peaceful as a lamb
Rach, Rachaele, Rachal, Rachel, Rachie, Raechal, Rasch, Raye
Racheline
(American) combo of Rachel and Line
Rachelene
Rachelle
(French) calm
Rach, Rachell, Rashell, Rashelle, Rochelle
Racquel
(French) friendly
Racquelle, Raquel
Rada
(Polish) glad
Radmilla
(Slavic) glad; hardworking

Rae
(English) raving beauty
Raedie, Raena, Ray, Raye
Raegan
(French) delicate
Reagan, Regan, Regun
Rafaela
(Hebrew) spiritual
Rafayela
Rafferty
(Irish) prospering
Raferty, Raff, Raffarty, Rafty
Rain
(German) actor; tearful
Rainie, Reign
Raina
(German) dramatic
Raine, Rainna, Rayna
Rainbow
(American) hope
Rain, Rainbeau, Rainbo, Rainie
Raine
(Latin) helpful friend
Raina, Rainie, Rane
Rainey
(Last name as first name) giving
Rainee, Rainie, Raney

Rainey-Anne

(American) combo of Rainey and Anne; languid

Rainee, Raineeann, Rainee-Anne, Rainey, Raneyann, Raneyanne

Raisa

(Russian) embraced

Rasa

Raka

(Hindi) royal

Ramona

(Teutonic) beautiful protector

Rae, Ramonah, Ramonna, Raymona

Rana

(Hindi) beauty

Randa

(Latin) admired

Ran, Randah

Randall

(English) protective of her own

Rand, Randal, Randi, Randy

Randelle

(American) wary

Randee, Randele

Randi

(English) audacious

Randee, Randy

Rane

(Scandinavian) queen-like

Rain, Raine, Ranie

Rani

(Hebrew) joyous; (Hindi) queen

Rainie, Ranie

Rania

(Sanskrit) regal

Ranea, Raneah, Raney, Ranie

Raphaela

(Hebrew) helping to heal

Rafaela, Rafe

Raquel

(Spanish) sensual

Racuell, Raquelle, Raqwel

Rasheeda

(Indian) pious

Rashee, Rashida, Rashie, Rashy

Rashel

(Spanish)

Rashell, Rashelle

Rashidah

(Arabic) on the right path

Rashida

Rashinique

(African-American) rash

Rash, Rashy

Raven

(English) blackbird

Ravan, Rave, Ravin

Rawnie

(Slavic) ladylike

Rawani, Rawn, Rawnee

Rayleen

(American) popular

Raylene, Raylie, Rayly

Raynelle

(American) giving hope; combo of Ray and Nelle

Nellie, Rae, Raenel, Raenelle

Raynette

(American) ray of hope; dancer

Raenette, Raynet

Razia

(Hebrew) secretive

Razeah, Raziah

Rea

(Polish) flowing

Raya

Reagan

(Last name as first name) strong

Regan, Reganne, Reggie

Reannah

(English) combo of Rae and Annah; divine

Reana, Reanna, Rennie

Reanne
(American) happy
*Reann, Rennie, Rere,
Rianne*

Reba
(Hebrew) fourth-born
Rebah, Ree, Reeba

Rebecca
(Hebrew) loyal
*Becca, Becki, Beckie,
Becky, Rebeca, Rebeka,
Rebekah*

Rebi
(Hebrew) friend who is
steadfast
Reby, Ree, Ribi

Rebop
(American) zany
Reebop

Reenie
(Greek) peace-loving
*Reena, Reeni, Reeny,
Ren, Rena*

Reese
(American) style-setting
Ree, Reece, Rees, Rere

Reeve
(Last name as first
name)

Regan
(Irish) queenly
Reagan

Regeana
(American) form of
Regina; queen
*Rege, Regeanah,
Regeane*

Regina
(English, Latin)
thoughtful
*Gina, Rege, Regena,
Reggie, Regine*

Regine
(Latin) royal
Regene, Rejean

Rehema
(African) well-grounded
*Rehemah, Rehemma,
Rehima*

Rela
(German) everything
Reila, Rella

Reina
(Spanish) a thinker
Rein, Reinie, Rina

Reith
(American) shy
Ree, Reeth

Remah
(Hebrew) pale beauty
*Rema, Remme, Remmie,
Rima, Ryma*

Remember
(American) memorable
*Remi, Remmi, Remmie,
Remmy*

Remi
(French) woman of
Rheims; jaded
Remee, Remie, Remy

Rena
(Hebrew) joyful singer
Reena, Rinah, Rinne

Renae
(French) form of Renee
Renay, Rennie, Rere

Renard
(French) fox; sly
*Ren, Renarde, Rynard,
Rynn*

Renata
(French) reaching out
*Renie, Renita, Rennie,
Rinata*

Rene
(Greek) hopeful
Reen, Reenie, Reney

Renea
(French) form of Renee;
renewal
Renny

Renee
(French) born again
Rene, Rennie, Rere

Renetta
(French) reborn
Ranetta, Renette

Renita
(Latin) poised
Ren, Renetta, Rennie

Renite
(Latin) stubborn
Reneta, Renita

Renzia
(Greek) form of Renee; peaceful
Renze

Resa
(Greek) productive; laughing
Reesa, Reese, Risa

Reseda
(Spanish) helpful; (Latin) fragrant flower
Res, Reseta

Reshauna
(African-American) combo of Re and Shauna
Reshana, Reshawna, Reshie

Reva
(Hebrew) rainmaker
Ree, Reeva, Rere

Reveca
(Spanish) form of Rebecca; charming
Reba, Rebeca, Reva

Rexanne
(English) combo of Rex and Anne; gracious
Rexan, Rexann, Rexanna

Rexella
(English) combo of Rex and Ella; lighthearted
Rexalla, Rexel, Rexela, Rexell, Rexey, Rexi, Rexy

Rexie
(American) confident
Rex, Rexi, Rexy

Reyna
(English) elegant; (Greek) peaceful woman
Raina, Rayna, Rey

Reynalda
(German) wise
Raynalda, Rey, Reyrey

Reynolds
(Scottish) wispy
Rey, Reye, Reynells, Reynold

Rhea
(Greek) earthy; mother of gods; strong
Ria

Rhianna
(Welsh) pure
Rheanna

Rhiannon
(Welsh) goddess; intuitive
Rhian, Rhiane, Rhianen, Rhiann, Rhianon, Rhyan, Rhye, Riannon

Rhoda
(Greek) rosy
Rhodie, Roda, Rodi, Rodie, Rody, Roe

Rhona
(Scottish) power-wielding
Rona, Ronne

Rhonda
(Welsh) vocal; quintessential
Rhon, Ron, Ronda, Ronnie

Rhondie
(American) perfect
Rond, Rondie, Rondy

Rhonwen
(Welsh) lovely
Rhonwenne, Rhonwin, Ronwen

Ria
(Spanish) water-loving; river
Reah, Riah

Riana
(Irish) frisky
Reana, Rere, Rianna, Rinnie

Riane
(American) attractive
Reann, Reanne

Rica
(Spanish) celestial
Ric, Ricca, Rickie, Rieka, Rika, Ryka

Richelle
(French) strong and artistic
Chelle, Chellie, Rich, Richel, Richele, Richie

Richesse
(French) wealthy
Richess

Ricki
(American) sporty
Rici, Rick, Rickie, Ricky, Rik, Riki, Rikki

Rico
(Italian) sexy
Reko, Ricco

Rida
(Arabic) satisfied
Ridah

Riley
(Irish) courageous; lively
Reilly, Rylee, Ryleigh, Ryley, Rylie

Rima
(Arabic) graceful; antelope
Rema, Remmee, Remmy, Rimmy, Ryma

Rinda
(Scandinavian) loyal
Rindah

Ring
(American) magical
Ringe, Ryng

Riona
(Irish) regal
Rina, Rine, Rionn, Rionna, Rionne

Ripley
(American) unique
Riplee, Ripli, Riplie

Rissa
(Latin) laughing
Resa, Risa, Riss, Rissah, Rissie

Rita
(Greek) precious pearl
Reda, Reita, Rida

Ritalinda
(Spanish) combo of Rita and Linda; treasured
Linda, Retalinda, Retalynde, Rita, Ritalynd, Ritalynda

Ritz
(American) rich
Rits

Riva
(Hebrew) joining; sparkling
Reva, Revi, Revvy

Rivalee
(Hebrew) combo of Riva and Lee; joined
Rivalea, Riva-Lee

River
(Latin) woman by the stream
Riv

Rivers
(American) trendy

Riza
(Greek) dignified
Reza, Rize

Roberta
(English) brilliant mind
Robbie, Robby, Robertah, Robi

Robin
(English) taken by the wind; bird
Robbie, Robby, Robinn, Robinne, Robyn

Robina
(Scottish) birdlike; robin
Robena

Robinetta
(American) combo of Robin and Etta; graceful dancer
Robbie, Robineta, Robinette

Rochelle
(French) small and strong-willed; (Hebrew) dream-like beauty
Roch, Roche, Rochel, Rochi, Rochie, Rochy, Roshelle

Rockella
(Invented) rocker
Rockell, Rockelle

Rocky
(American) tomboy
*Rock, Rockee, Rockey,
Rockie*

Roddy
(German) well-known
*Rod, Roddee, Roddey,
Roddi, Roddie*

Roderica
(German) princess
*Rica, Roda, Roddie,
Rodericka, Rodrika*

Rogertha
(American) form of
Roger; substantial
Rodge

Roksana
(Polish) dawn
Roksanna, Roksona

Rolanda
(German) rich woman
Rolane, Rollande, Rollie

Rolandan
(German) form of
Roland; from a famous
land
*Roland, Rolanden,
Rollie, Rolly*

Roma
(Italian) girl from Rome;
adventurous
Romy

Romaine
(French) daredevil
*Romain, Romane,
Romayne, Romi*

Roman
(Italian) adventurous
*Romi, Romie, Rommie,
Rommye, Romyn*

Romilda
(Latin) striking
*Romelda, Romey, Romie,
Romy*

Romilla
(Latin) from Rome; she
who wanders
*Romella, Romi, Romie,
Romila*

Romilly
(Latin) wanderer
*Romillee, Romillie,
Romily*

Romona
(Spanish) form of
Ramona
*Mona, Rome, Romie,
Romy*

Romy
(French) short for
Romaine; roaming
Roe. Romi, Romie

Rona
(Scandinavian, Scottish)
powerful
Rhona, Ronne, Ronni

Ronda
(Welsh) form of Rhonda;
a standout
Ronni

Ronelle
(English) winner
Ronnie

Roney
(Scandinavian) form of
Rona; lively
Roneye, Roni

Ronneta
(English) go-getter
*Roneda, Ronnete,
Ronnette, Ronnie*

Ronni
(American) energetic
*Ron, Ronee, Roni,
Ronnie, Ronny*

Rori
(Irish) spirited; brilliant
Rory

Rosa
(Italian) rose;
(German) blushing
beauty
Rose, Rossah, Roza

Rosabella
(Italian) combo of Rosa
and Bella; beautiful rose

Rosabelle
(French) combo of Rosa
and Belle; beautiful rose
*Belle, Rosa, Rosabel,
Rosa-Belle*

Rosalba
(Latin) glorious as a rose
Rosalbah, Rosey, Rosi,
Rosie, Rosy

Rosalia
(Italian) hanging roses
Rosa, Rosalea,
Rosaleah, Rosaliah,
Roselia, Rosey, Rosi,
Rosie, Rossalia, Rosy

Rosalie
(English) striking dark
beauty
Leelee, Rosa, Rosalee,
RosaLee, Rosa-Lee,
Rosie, Rossalie, Roz,
Rozalee, Rozalie

Rosalind
(Spanish) lovely rose
Lind, Ros, Rosa,
Rosalyn, Rosalynde,
Rosie, Roslyn, Roslynn

Rosalinda
(Spanish) lovely rose
Rosa-Linda, Rosalynda

Rosalvo
(Spanish) rosy-faced
Rosa, Rosey

Rosamaria
(Italian) combo of Rosa
and Maria; rose; devout
Rosa-Maria

Rosamond
(English) beauty
Rosa, Rosamun,
Rosamund, Rose,
Rosemond, Rosie

Rosanna
(English) lovely
Rosannah

Rosaoralia
(Spanish) combo of
Rosa and Oralia; rosy
Rosa Oralia, Rosa-Oralia,
RoseyO

Rose
(Latin) rose; blushing
beauty
Rosa, Rosey, Rosi, Rosie,
Rosy, Roze, Rozee

Roseanna
(English) combo of Rose
and Anna
Rosana, Rosannah,
Rose, Roseana, Rosie

Roseanne
(English) combo of Rose
and Anne
Rosann, Rosanne, Rose
Ann, Rosie

Rosellen
(English) pretty
Roselinn, Roselyn

Rosemarie
(Latin, Scandinavian)
combo of Rose and
Marie
Rose-Marie, Rosemary

Rosemary
(English) combo of Rose
and Mary; sweetheart
Ro, Rose Mary, Rose,
Rosie

Rosenda
(Spanish) rosy
Rose, Rosend, Rosende,
Rosey, Rosie, Senda

Rosetta
(Italian) longlasting
beauty
Rose, Rosy, Rozetta

Rosette
(Latin) flowering; rosy
Rosett, Rosetta

Roshall
(African-American) form
of Rochelle; dreamy
Rochalle, Roshalle

Roshawna
(African-American)
combo of Rose and
Shawna
Rosh, Roshanna, Roshie,
Roshona, Shawn

Roshell
(French) form of Rochelle; small and strong-willed
Rochelle, Roshelle

Roshumba
(African-American) gorgeous
Rosh, Roshumbah

Roshunda
(African-American) flamboyant
Rosey, Roshun, Roshund, Rosie, Roz

Rosie
(English) bright-cheeked
Rose, Rosi, Rosy

Rosita
(Spanish) pretty
Roseta, Rosey, Rosie, Rositta

Rotella
(American) smart
Rotel, Rotela

Roth
(American) studious
Rothe

Rotnei
(American) bright
Rotnay

Rowena
(Scottish) blissful; beloved friend
Roe, Roenna, Rowina

Roxanna
(Persian) bright
Roxana, Roxie

Roxanne
(Persian) lovely as the sun
Roxane, Roxann, Roxie, Roxy

Roxy
(American) sunny
Rox, Roxi, Roxie

Royetta
(American) combo of Roy and Etta; cowgirl
Etta, Roy, Roye, Royett, Royette

Roynale
(American) motivated
Roy, Royna, Roynal

Roz
(French) short for Rosalind
Ros, Rozz, Rozzie

Rozena
(American) form of Rosena; pretty
Roze, Rozenna

Rozonda
(American) pretty
Rosonde, Rozon, Rozond

Rubena
(Hebrew) sassy
Rubyn, Rubyna, Rueben

Rubianney
(American) combo of Rubi and Anney; shining
Rubi, Rubianey, Rubianne, Rubi-Anney, Rubyann

Rubilee
(American) combo of Ruby and Lee; shining
Ruby Lee, Rubylee

Rubina
(Pakistani) gem
Rubi

Rubra
(French) from Ruby; jewel
Rube, Rue

Ruby
(French) precious jewel
Rubi, Rubie, Rue

Ruby-Jewel
(American) combo of Ruby and Jewel; sassy
Rubijewel, Rubyjewel, Ruby-Jule

Ruchi
(German) brash

Rudy
(German) sly
Rudee, Rudell, Rudie

Rue
(English, German) looking back
Ru

Ruelynn
(American) combo of
Rue and Lynn; smart and
famous
*Rue Lynn, Ruelin,
Ruelinn, Rue-Lynn,
Rulynn*

Rufaro
(African) happy

Rula
(American) wild-spirited
Rue, Rulah, Rewela

Rumer
(English) unique
Ru, Rumor

Ruri
(Japanese) emerald
Rure, Rurrie, RuRu

Rusbel
(Spanish) beautiful girl
with reddish hair
Rusbell, Rusbella

Russo
(American) happy
Russoh

Rusty
(English) red-haired girl
Rustee, Rusti

Ruta
(Lithuanian) practical
Rue, Rudah, Rutah

Ruth
(Hebrew) loyal friend
Rue, Ruthie, Ruthy

Ruthanne
(American) combo of
Ruth and Anne
Ruthann

Ruthemma
(American) combo of
Ruth and Emma
Routhemma, Ruthema

Ruthie
(Hebrew) friendly and
young
*Ruth, Ruthey, Ruthi,
Ruthy*

Ryan
(Irish) royal; assertive
*Ryann, Ryen, Ryunn,
Rian*

Ryanna
(Irish) leader
*Rianna, Rianne, Ryana,
Ryanne, Rynn*

Ryba
(Hebrew) traditional
Reba, Ree, Riba, Ribah

Rylee
(Irish) brave
*Rilee, Rili, Ryelee, Ryley,
Ryli, Ryly*

Ryn
(American) form of Wren
Ren, Rynn

Ryne
(Irish) form of Ryan;
divine; special
Rynea, Ryni, Rynie

Rynie
(American) woods-loving
Rinnie, Ryn

Rynn
(American) outdoorsy
woman
*Rin, Rynna, Rynnie,
Wren*

Rynnea
(American) sun-lover
Rynnee, Rynni, Rynnia

S

Saba
(Arabic) morning star
Sabah

Sabella
(English) spiritual
*Bella, Belle, Sabela,
Sabell, Sabelle, Sebelle*

Sabina
(Latin) desirable
*Sabeena, Sabine,
Sabinna, Say*

Sable
(English) chic
Sabelle, Sabie

Sablette
(American) luxurious
Sable, Sablet

Sabra
(Hebrew) substantial
Sabe, Sabera, Sabrah

Sabrina
(Latin) place name;
passionate
*Breena, Brina, Brinna,
Sabe, Sabreena,
Sabrinna*

Sacha
(Greek) helpful girl
Sachie, Sachy

Sachi
(Japanese) girl
Sachie, Sashi, Shashie

Sadie
(Hebrew) charmer;
princess
*Sade, Sadee, Sady,
Sadye, Shaday*

Saffron
(Indian) spice
Saffrone, Safron

Saga
(Scandinavian) sensual
Sagah

Sagal
(American)
action-oriented
Sagall, Segalle

Sage
(Latin) wise
Saige

Sahare
(American) loner

Sahri
(Arabic) giving

Saida
(Hebrew) happy girl
Sada, Sadie

Sailor
(American) outdoorsy
Sail, Saile, Sailer, Saylor

Sajah
(Hindi) meritorious
Sajie, Sayah

Salama
(African) safe

Salena
(Latin) needed; basic
Salene, Sally

Salima
(Arabic) healthy
Salma

Salina
(French) quiet and deep
Sale, Salena

Sally
(Hebrew) princess
Sal, Salli, Sallie

Salma
(Hebrew) peaceful;
(Spanish) ingenious
Sal, Sally, Salmah

Salma
(Hindi) safe
Sal, Salwah

Salome
(Hebrew) sensual;
peaceful
*Sal, Salohme, Salomey,
Salomi*

Salowmee
(Invented) form of
Salome; peaceful
Sal, Salomee, Salomie,
Salomy, Slowmee

Salvadora
(Spanish) saved
Sal, Salvadorah

Samantha
(Hebrew) good listener
Sam, Samath, Sammi,
Sammie

Samara
(Hebrew) God-led;
watchful
Sam, Samora

Sami
(Hebrew) insightful
Sam, Sammie, Sammy

Samia
(Hindi) joyful
Sameah, Samee,
Sameea, Samina,
Sammy

Samuela
(Hebrew) selected
Samm, Sammi, Sammy,
Samula

Samyrah
(African-American)
music-loving
Samirah, Samyra

Sandi
(Greek) defends others
Sand, Sanda, Sandee,
Sandie, Sandy

Sandra
(Greek) helpful;
protective
Sandrah, Sandy

Sandrea
(Greek) selfless
Sandreea, Sandie,
Sanndria

Sandreen
(American) great
Sandrene, Sandrin,
Sandrine

Sanila
(Indian) full of praise
Sanilla

Sanjuana
(Spanish) from San Juan;
God-loving
Sanwanna

Sanjuanita
(Spanish) from San Juan;
combo of San Juan and
Juanita; believer
Juanita, Sanjuan

Sanna
(Scandinavian) truthful
Sana

Santana
(Spanish) saintly
San, Santanne, Santie,
Santina

Santeene
(Spanish) passionate
Santeena, Santene,
Santie, Santina, Santine,
Satana

Santia
(African) lovable
Santea

Santonina
(Spanish) ardent

Sapphire
(Greek) precious gem
Safire, Saphire, Sapphie,
Sapphyre

Sara
(Hebrew) God's princess
Sae, Sarah, Saree, Sarrie

Sarah-Jessica
(American) charismatic
Sarah Jessica, Sara-Jess,
Sarajessee, Sarajessica

Sarai
(Hebrew) contentious
Sari

Sarajane
(American) combo of
Sara and Jane
Sarahjane

Saralee
(American) combo of
Sara and Lee

Saramay
(American) combo of
Sara and May
Sarah-May, Saramae

Saree
(Hebrew) woman of value
Sarie, Sary

Sarilla
(Spanish) princess
Sarella, Sarill, Sarille

Sarina
(Hebrew) strong
Sareena, Sarena, Sarrie

Sarita
(Spanish) regal
Sareeta, Sarie, Saritah

Sasha
(Russian) beautiful courtesan; helpful
Sacha, Sachie, Sascha, Sasheen, Sashy

Saskia
(Dutch) dramatic
Saskiah

Sassy
(Irish) Saxon girl; flirtatious
Sass, Sassi, Sassie

Satchel
(American) unusual
Satchal

Satin
(French) shiny
Saten

Saturine
(American) form of Saturn
Saturenne, Saturinne, Saturn, Saturyne

Saundra
(Greek) defender
Sandi, Sandra, Sandrah

Savannah
(Spanish) place name; open heart
Sava, Savana, Savanah, Savanna, Seven

Sawyer
(Last name as first name) industrious
Sawya, Sawyar, Sawyhr, Sawyie, Sawyur

Sayde
(American) form of Sadie; charming
Saydey, Saydie

Scally
(Last name as first) introspective
Scalley, Scalli

Scarlett
(English) seductive; unpredictable
Scarlet, Scarletta, Scarlette

Schemika
(African-American) form of Shameka
Schemi, Schemike

Scherry
(American) form of Sherry
Scherri, Scherrie

Schmoopie
(American) baby; sweetie
Schmoopee, Schmoopey, Schmoopy, Shmoopi

Schulyer
(Dutch) form of Skyler; protective
Schulyar, Sky, Skye

Scooter
(American) wild-spirit
Scooder, Scoot

Scotty
(Scottish) girl from Scotland
Scota, Scotti, Scottie

Scout
(French) precocious
Scouts

Scyllaea
(Greek) mythological monster; menace
Cilla, Scylla, Silla

Sea
(American) sea-loving; flowing
Cee, See

Sealy
(Last name as first name) fun-loving
Celie, Seal, Sealie

Seana
(Irish) giving
Seane, Seanna, Suannea

Seandra
(American) form of Deandra; intuitive
Seandre, Seandreah, Seanne

Season
(Latin) special; change
Seas, Seasee, Seasen, Seasie, Seasun, Seazun, Seezun

Sebastiane
(Latin) respected female
Sebastian, Sebbie

Seema
(Hebrew) treasured; softhearted
Seem

Seine
(French) river; flowing
Sane

Sela
(Hebrew) short for Cecilia; substantial
Cela, Celia, Selah, Selia

Selda
(German) sure-footed
Seda, Seldah, Selde, Seldee, Seldey, Seldi, Seldie

Selena
(Greek) like the moon; shapely
Celina, Sela, Seleene, Selene, Selina, Sylena

Selima
(Hebrew) peacemaker
Selema, Selemmah

Selin
(Turkish) calm

Selma
(German) fair-minded female
Selle, Sellma, Selmah, Zele, Zelma

Selona
(Greek) form of Selena; goddess
Celona, Sela, Seli, Selo, Selone

Selsa
(Hispanic) enthusiastic
Sel, Sels

Sema
(Greek) earthy
Semah, Semale, Semele

Semilla
(Spanish) earth mother
Samilla, Sem, Semila, Semillah, Semmie, Semmy, Sumilla

Semone
(American) sentimental
Semonne

Sendy
(American) form of Cindy
Sendee, Sendie

Seneca
(Italian, Native American) leader
Seneka

September
(Latin) serious; month
Seppie, Sept

Septima
(Latin) seventh child
Septimma, Septyma

Sequoia
(Cherokee) giant redwood; formidable
Sekwoya

Serafina
(Hebrew) ardent
Serifina, Seraphina, Seraphine

Seren
(Latin) serene
Ceren, Seran

Serena
(Latin) calm
*Sarina, Sereena,
Serenah, Serina*

Serendipity
(Invented) mercurial;
lucky
*Sere, Seren,
Serendipitee, Serin*

Serenity
(American) serene
*Sera, Serenitee,
Serenitie*

Sesame
(American) inventive
Sesamee, Sezamee

Seth
(Hebrew) set;
appointed; gentle
Sethe

Seymoura
(Invented) form of male
name Seymour; calm
Seymora

Shade
(English) cool
Shadee, Shadi, Shady

Shadow
(English) mysterious
Shado, Shadoh

Shae
(Hebrew) shy
Shay

Shaela
(Irish) pretty
Shae, Shaelie, Shala

Shaelin
(Irish) pretty
*Shae, Shaelyn,
Shaelynn, Shalyn*

Shaeterral
(African-American)
well-shaped
*Shatey, Shatrell,
Shayterral*

Shail
(American) pretty
Shale

Shaine
(Hebrew) pretty girl
Shanie, Shay, Shayne

Shainel
(African-American)
animated
*Shainell, Shainelle,
Shaynel*

Shakira
(Arabic, Spanish) pretty
movement
*Shak, Shakeera,
Shakeerah, Shakeira,
Shakie, Skakarah*

Shakonda
(African-American) lovely

Shalanda
(African-American) vivid
*Shalande, Shally,
Shalunda*

Shaleah
(Hebrew) combo of Sha
and Leah; funny
*Shalea, Shalee,
Shaleeah*

Shaleina
(Turkish) humorist
*Shalina, Shalyna,
Shalyne*

Shalonda
(African-American)
enthusiastic
*Shalie, Shalondah,
Shalonna, Shelonda*

Shamara
(Arabic) assertive
Shamarah, Shemera

Shameena
(Arabic) beautiful
*Shamee, Shameenah,
Shamina, Shaminna*

Shamika
(African-American)
loving
*Shameika, Shameka,
Shamekah, Shamika,
Shemeca*

Shamsa
(Pakistani) adorable

Shana
(Hebrew) pretty girl
*Shaina, Shan, Shanah,
Shane, Shannah,
Shanni, Shannie,
Shanny, Shayna, Shayne*

Shanae
(Irish) generous
Shan, Shanea, Shanee

Shandee
(English) hopeful
Shandi, Shandie,
Shandy

Shandilyn
(American) not forsaken
Shandi, Shandy

Shandra
(American) fun-loving
Chandra, Shan, Shandrie

Shane
(Irish) softspoken
Shanee, Shanie

Shaneka
(African-American)
perky; pretty
Chaneka, Shan,
Shanekah, Shanie,
Shanika

Shanelle
(African-American)
variant of Chanel; stylish
Shanel, Shannel,
Shannell, Shanny

Shania
(African) ambitious;
bright-eyed
Shane, Shaniah, Shanie,
Shaniya, Shanya

Shanice
(African-American)
bright-eyed
Chaniece, Shaneese,
Shani, Shaniece

Shanika
(African-American)
pretty; optimistic
Shan, Shane, Shanee,
Shaneeka, Shaneika,
Shaneikah, Shanequa,
Shaney, Shaneyka

Shaniqua
(African-American)
outgoing
Shane, Shanequa,
Shanie, Shanikwa,
Shaniquah, Shanneequa

Shanique
(African-American)
outgoing

Shanisha
(African-American)
bright
Chaneisha, Chanisha,
Shan, Shanecia,
Shaneisha, Shanie

Shanna
(Irish) lovely
Shanah, Shanea,
Shannah

Shannon
(Irish) smart
Shann, Shanna,
Shannen, Shannyn,
Shanon

Shanny
(Irish) bubbly
Shannee, Shanni,
Shannie

Shanta
(French) singing
Shantah, Shante,
Shantie

Shantara
(French) bright-eyed
Shantay, Shantera,
Shantie

Shantell
(American) bright singer
Chantel, Shantal,
Shantel

Shanti
(Hindi) calm

Shaquan
(American) fine
Shak, Shaq, Shaquanda,
Shaquanna, Shaquie,
Shaquonda

Shaquita
(African-American)
delight
Shaq, Shaqueita,
Shaqueta, Shaquie

Shara
(Hebrew) form of
Sharon; open
Sharah, Sharra, Sherah

Shardae
(Arabic) wanderer
*Chardae, Sade, Shaday,
Sharday, SharDay*

Sharee
(American) dear
Sharie

Shari
(French) beloved girl
*Shar, Sharree, Sher,
Sherri*

Sharice
(French) graceful
*Cherise, Shar, Shareese,
Shares*

Sharif
(Russian) mysterious
*Shar, Shareef, Sharey,
Shari, Sharrey, Shary*

Sharita
(French) charitable
Shar, Shareetah, Shareta

Sharla
(American) friendly
Sharlah

Sharlene
(German) form of
Charlene
*Charleen, Charlene,
Shar, Sharl, Sharleen,
Sharline, Sharlyne*

Sharmeal
(African-American)
exhilarating
*Sharm, Sharma, Sharme,
Sharmele*

Sharna
(Hebrew) broad-minded
Sharn, Sharnah

Sharnea
(American) quiet
*Sharnay, Sharnee,
Sharney*

Sharnelle
(African-American)
spiritual
Sharnel, Sharnie, Sharny

Sharnette
(American) fighter
*Chanet, Charnette,
Shanet, Sharn, Sharnett,
Sharney*

Sharon
(Hebrew) open heart;
desert plain
*Shar, Sharen, Shari,
Sharin, Sharren,
Sharron, Sharry, Sharyn,
Sheron, Sherron*

Sharonda
(African-American) open
Sharondah, Sheronda

Sharrona
(Hebrew) open
*Sharona, Sharonne,
Sherona, Shironah*

Sharterica
(African-American)
beloved
*Sharter, Sharterika,
Shartrica, Sharty*

Shasta
(American)
majestic mind
Shastah

Shatoya
(African-American)
spirited
*Shatoye, Shay,
Shaytoya, Toya*

Shauna
(Hebrewm, Irish)
giving heart
*Shauhna, Shaunie,
Shaunna, Shawna*

Shaune
(American) wide smile
Shaun, Shaunie, Shawn

Shauntee
(Irish) dancing eyes
*Shaun, Shawntey,
Shawntie, Shawnty*

Shavon
(Irish) devout; energetic
*Chavon, Chavonne,
Shavaun, Shavon,
Shavonne*

Shawana
(African-American)
dramatic
Shavaun, Shawahna,
Shawanna, Shawnie

Shawandreka
(African-American) gutsy
Shawan, Shawand,
Shawandrika, Shawann,
Shawuan

Shawn
(American) smiling
Shawne, Shawnee,
Shawnie, Shawny

Shawnda
(Irish) helpful friend
Shaunda, Shaundah,
Shona

Shawneequa
(African-American)
loquacious
Shauneequa,
Shawneekwa

Shawnel
(African-American)
audacious
Shaune, Shaunel,
Shaunelle, Shawn,
Shawnee, Shawnelle,
Shawney, Shawni

Shawnie
(American) playful
Shaunie, Shawni

Shayjuana
(African-American)
combo of Shay and
Juana; cheerful
Shajuana, Shajuanna,
Shay

Shaylie
(Latin) playful
Shaleigh, Shaylea,
Shaylee, Shealee

Shayne
(Hebrew) form of Shane;
pretty
Shaine, Shane, Shay,
Sheyne

Shayonda
(African-American) regal
Shay, Shaya, Shayon,
Shayonde, Sheyonda,
Yona, Yonda

Shea
(Irish) soft beauty
Shae, Shay

Sheba
(Hebrew) short for
Bathsheba; queenly
Chebah, Sheeba,
Sheebah

Sheddreka
(African-American)
dynamo
Shedd, Sheddrik,
Shedreke

Sheela
(Hindi) gentle spirit
Sheelah, Sheeli, Sheila

Sheelyah
(Irish) form of Shelia;
woman
Sheel, Sheil

Sheena
(Hebrew) shining
Sheen, Sheenah, Shena

Sheeneva
(American) combo of
Sheena and Eva; shiny
Shee, Sheen, Sheena,
Sheeny

Sheila
(Irish) vivacious; divine
woman
Shaylah, Sheela, Sheilia,
Sheilya, Shel

Shelby
(English) dignified
Chelby, Shel, Shelbee,
Shelbi, Shelbie

Shelia
(Irish) woman; gorgeous
Shelya, Shelyah, Shillya

Shelita
(Spanish) little girl
Chelita, Shelite, Shelitta

Shelley
(English) outdoorsy;
meadow
Shelee, Shelli, Shelly

Shena
(Irish) shining
Shenae, Shenea, Shenna

Sheneeka
(African-American) easygoing
Shaneeka, Shaneka, Sheneecah, Sheneka

Shepard
(English) vigilant
Shep, Sheperd, Shepherd, Sheppie

Shera
(Hebrew) light-hearted
Sheera, Sheerah, Sherah

Sheray
(French) saucy
Cheray, Sherayah

Sherael
(American) form of Sherry; distinctive
Sheraelle, Sherelle, Sherryelle

Sheree
(French) dearest girl
Sheeree, Sher, Shere

Sherele
(French) bouncy
Sher, Sherell, Sherrie

Sheresa
(American) dancer
Sher, Sherisa, Sherissa, Sherri

Sheretta
(American) sparkling
Shere, Sherette

Sheri
(French) sparkling eyes
Sher, Sherri, Sherrie

Sherice
(French) artistic
Cherise, Sher, Shereece, Sherisse

Sheridan
(Irish) free spirit; outstanding
Cheridan, Cheridyn, Sheridyn, Sherridan

Sherilyn
(American) combo of Sheri and Lyn
Sharilyn, Sheralyn, Sheri-Lyn, Sheri-Lynn, Sherry-Lynn

Sherita
(French) stylish
Cherita, Sheretta

Sherleen
(American) easygoing
Sherl, Sherlene, Sherline, Sherlyn, Shirline

Sherlitha
(Spanish) feminine
Sherl, Sherli

Sherolynna
(American) lovely
Cherolina, Sher, Sheralina, Sherrilina

Sherrill
(English) bright
Cheril, Cherrill, Sherelle, Sheril, Sherrell, Sheryl

Sherrunda
(African-American) free spirit
Sharun, Sharunda, Sherr, Sherrunde, Sherunda

Sherry
(French) outgoing
Sher, Sheri, Sherreye, Sherri, Sherrie, Sherye

Sherrylynn
(American) combo of Sherry and Lynn
Sharolyn, Sher, Sherilyn, Sherry, Sherylynn

Sheryl
(French) beloved woman
Cheryl, Sharal, Sher, Sheral, Sheril, Sherill

Shevonne
(Gaelic) ambitious
Shavon, Shevaune, Shevon

Sheyenne
(Native American) form
of Cheyenne; audacious
*Shey, Shianne, Shyann,
Shyanne, Shyenne*

Sheyn
(Hebrew) beauty

Shifra
(Hebrew) beautiful
woman
Sheefra, Shifrah

Shikendra
(African-American)
spirited
Shiki, Shikie, Skikend

Shiloh
(Hebrew) gifted by God
Shilo, Shy

Shine
(American) shining
example
Shena, Shina

Shiney
(American) glowing
Shine, Shiny

Shinikee
(African-American)
glorious
*Shinakee, Shinikey,
Shynikee*

Shira
(Hebrew) song; singer
Shirah, Shiree

Shireen
(English) charmer
*Shareen, Shiree,
Shireene, Shirene, Shiri,
Shiry, Shoreen, Shureen,
Shurene*

Shirleen
(American) nature-loving
Shirlene, Shirline

Shirley
(English) bright
meadow; cheerful girl
*Sherlee, Sherley, Sherly,
Shir, Shirl, Shirly*

Shlonda
(African-American)
bright
Londa, Schlonda, Shodie

Shola
(Hebrew) spirited
Sholah

Shona
(Irish) open-hearted
Shonah, Shonie

Shonda
(Irish) runner
*Shondah, Shonday,
Shondie, Shounda,
Shoundah*

Shonta
(Irish) fearless
*Shauntah, Shawnta,
Shon, Shontie*

Shony
(Irish) shining
*Shona, Shonee, Shoni,
Shonie*

Shoshana
(Hebrew) beautiful; lily
*Shoshanna,
Shoshannah, Shoshauna*

Shulondia
(African-American)
dynamic
*Shulee, Shuley, Shuli,
Shulonde, Shulondea,
Shulondiah*

Shuntay
(African-American)
Shuntae

Shura
(Greek) protective

Shyanne
(Native American) form
of Cheyanne
Shy

Shyla
(English) creative
Shila, Shy, Shylah

Shyne
(American) standout
Shine

Sia
(Welsh) calm; believer
Cia, Seea

Sian
(Welsh) believer

Siana
(Welsh) ebullient
Sian, Siane

Sibley
(Anglo-Saxon) related
Siblee, Sibly

Sibyl
(Greek) intuitive
*Cibyl, Cyb, Cybil, Cybill,
Cybyl, Sib, Sibbi, Sibbie,
Sibby, Sibella, Sibylla,
Sybela, Sybil, Sybyl*

Sidonia
(French) spiritual
Sid, Sidoneah, Sydonya

Sidonie
(French) appealing
Sidonee, Sidony, Sydoni

Sidra
(Latin) star
*Cidra, Siddey, Siddie,
Siddy, Sidi, Sidrie, Sydra*

Sienna
(Place name) delicate;
reddish-brown
Siena, Siene

Sierra
(Place name) peaks;
outdoorsy
*Cierra, Searah, Searrah,
Siera, Sierrah, Sierre*

Sigfrid
(German) peacemaker
*Sig, Sigfred, Sigfreid,
Siggy*

Signe
(Latin) symbol
Sig, Signie, Signy

Sigourney
(English) leader who
conquers
*Sig, Siggie, Signe, Signy,
Sygourny*

Sigrid
(Scandinavian) lovely
*Segred, Sig, Siggy,
Sigrede*

Sigrun
(Scandinavian) winning
Cigrun, Segrun

Sikita
(American) active
Sikite

Silvanna
(Spanish) nature-lover
*Sil, Silva, Silvana,
Silvane, Silvanne, Silver*

Silver
(Anglo-Saxon) light-
haired
Silva, Silvar, Sylver

Silvia
(Latin) deep; woods-
loving
Sill, Silvy, Siviah, Sylvia

Simi
(Lebanese)
Sim

Simica
(American)
Sim, Simika, Simmy

Simona
(American) form of
Simon; wise
Sim, Simon, Sims

Simona
(Hebrew) svelte
*Simonah, Symmie,
Symona, Syms*

Simone
(French) wise and
thoughtful
Sim, Simonie, Symone

Sinai
(Place name)
Mt. Sinai

Sinclair
(French) person from
St. Clair; admired;
(Last name as first
name) dynamic
*Cinclair, Sinclare,
Synclair, Synclare*

Sinead
(Irish) singer; believer in
a gracious God
Shanade

Siobhan
(Irish) believer; lovely
*Chevon, Chevonne,
Chivon, Shavonne,
Shevon*

Siphronia
(Greek) sensible
*Ciphronia, Sifronea,
Sifronia, Syfronia*

Siren
(Greek) enchantress
Syren

Sirena
(Greek) enchantress
*Sireena, Sirenah, Sirine,
Sisi, Sissy, Syrena*

Sissy
(Latin) short for Cecilia
or little sister; immature;
ingenue
*Cissee, Cissey, Cissy, Sis,
Sissi, Sissie*

Sistene
(Italian) spiritual
Sisteen, Sisteene

Skye
(Scottish) place name;
high-minded; head in
the clouds

Skyler
(Dutch) protective;
sheltering
*Schuyler, Skieler, Skilar,
Skiler, Skye, Skyla,
Skylar, Skylie, Skylor*

Slane
(Irish) form of Sloane;
striking
Slaine

Sloane
(Irish) strong
Sloan, Slone

Smiley
(American) radiant
*Smile, Smilee, Smiles,
Smili, Smily*

Snooks
(American) sweetie
Snookee, Snookie

Snow
(American) quiet
Sno, Snowdrop, Snowy

Socorro
(Spanish) helpful
Socoro

Sofya
(Russian) wise
Sofi, Sofie, Sofiya

Solana
(Spanish) sunny
Solanah, Soley, Solie

Solange
(French) sophisticated
Solie

Soledad
(Spanish) solitary
woman
*Saleda, Solada, Solay,
Sole, Solee, Solie, Solita*

Soleil
(French) sun

Soline
(French) solemn
Solen, Solenne, Souline

Sommer
(English) warm
*Sommie, Summer,
Summi*

Sonay
(Asian) bright-eyed
Sonnae

Song
(Chinese) independent

Sonia
(Slavic) effervescent
*Soni, Sonnie, Sonny,
Sonya*

Sonja
(Scandinavian) bright
woman

Sonnet
(American) poetic
Sonnett, Sonni, Sonny

Sonoma
(Place name) wine-
loving
Sonomah

Sonora
(Place name) easygoing
Sonorah

Sonseria
(American) giving
Seria, Sonsere, Sonsey

Sonya
(Greek) wise
Sonia, Sonje

Soo
(Korean) gentle spirit

Soon-Yi
(Chinese) delightful;
assertive
Soozi
(American) form of Suzy;
friendly
Soos, Sooz, Souz,
Souze, Souzi
Sophia
(Greek) wise one
Sofeea, Sofi, Sofia,
Sofie, Sophea, Sophie,
Sophy
Sorangel
(Spanish) heavenly
Sorange
Soraya
(Persian) royal
Sorcha
(Irish) bright
Shorshi, Sorsha, Sorshie
Sorrel
(English) delicate
Sorel, Sorell, Sorie,
Sorree, Sorrell, Sorri,
Sorrie
Sozos
(Hindi) clingy
Sosos
Spencer
(English) sophisticate
Spence, Spenser

Spirit
(American) lively;
spirited
Spirite, Spyrit
Sprague
(American) respected
Sprage
Spring
(English) springtime;
fresh
Spryng
Stacey
(Greek) hopeful and
spiritual
Stace, Staci, Stacie,
Stacy, Staycee
Stacia
(English) short for
Anastasia; devout
Stace, Stacie, Stasia,
Stayshah
Stanise
(American) darling
Stanee, Staneese, Stani,
Stanice, Staniece
Starla
(American) shining
Starlah, Starlie
Starlite
(American) extraordinary
Starlight, Starr
Starr
(English) shining star
Star

Stasia
(Greek, Russian)
Stacie, Stasie, Stasya
Stefanie
(Greek) regal; (German)
crowned
Stafanie, Stefannye,
Stefany, Steff, Steffany,
Steffie, Stephanie
Steffi
(Greek) short for
Stephanie; crowned;
athletic
Steffie, Steffy, Stefi
Stefnee
(American) form of
Stephanie/Stefanie;
regal
Stef, Steffy
Stella
(Latin) bright star
Stele, Stelie
Stephanie
(Greek) regal
Stefanie, Steff, Steffie,
Stephenie, Stephney
Stephene
(French, Greek) dignified
Steph, Stephie, Stephine
Stephney
(Greek) crowned
Stef, Steph, Stephie,
Stephnie

Sterla
(American) quality
Sterl, Sterlie, Stirla

Stevie
(Greek, American) jovial
Steve, Stevee, Stevey, Stevi

Stockard
(English) stockyard; sturdy
Stockerd, Stockyrd

Storelle
(Invented) legend
Storee, Storell, Storey, Stori

Stormy
(American) impulsive
Storm, Stormi, Stormie

Story
(American) creative
Stori, Storie, Storee, Storey

Sue
(Hebrew) flower-like; lily
Susy, Suze, Suzy

Suellen
(American) combo of Sue and Ellen
SueEllen, Sue-Ellen

Sugar
(American) sweet
Shug

Sugy
(Spanish) short for the name Sugar; sweet
Sug, Sugey, Sugie

Suki
(Japanese) beloved
Suke, Sukie, Suky

Sula
(Greek) sea-going
Soola, Sue, Suze

Sullivan
(Last name as first name) brave-hearted
Sulli, Sullie, Sullivin, Sully

Summer
(English) summery; fresh
Somer, Sommer, Sum, Summie

Sun
(Korean) obedient girl
Suna, Suni, Sunnie

Sundancer
(American) easygoing
Sunndance

Sunday
(Latin) day of the week; sunny
Sun, Sundae, Sundaye, Sundee, Sunney, Sunni, Sunnie, Sunny, Sunnye

Sunna
(American) sunny
Sun, Suna

Sunny
(English) bright attitude
Sonny, Sun, Sunni, Sunnye

Sunshine
(American) sunny

Suprina
(American) supreme
Suprinna

Surrender
(Word as name) dramatic
Surren

Susan
(Hebrew) lily; pretty flower
Soozan, Sue, Susahn, Susanne, Susehn, Susie, Suzan

Susannah
(Hebrew) gentle
Sue, Susah, Susanna, Susie, Suzannah

Susie
(American) short for Susan
Susey, Susi, Susy, Suze, Suzi, Suzie, Suzy

Suz
(American) short for Susan; lily; pretty flower
Suze

Suzanne
(English) fragrant
*Susanne, Suzan,
Suzane, Suzann, Suze*

Suzette
(French) pretty little one
Sue, Susette, Suze

Svea
(Swedish) patriotic
Svay

Svetlana
(Russian) star bright
Sveta, Svete

Swanhildda
(Teutonic) swan-like;
graceful
*Swan, Swanhild, Swann,
Swanney, Swanni,
Swannie, Swanny*

Sweeney
(Irish) young and
rambunctious
Sweenee, Sweeny

Sweetpea
(American) sweet
Sweet-Pea, Sweetie

Swell
(Invented) good
Swelle

Swift
(Last name as first
name) bold
Swiftie, Swifty

Swoosie
(American) unique
Swoose, Swoozie

Sybil
(Greek) future-gazing
*Sibel, Sibyl, Syb, Sybill,
Sybille, Sybyl*

Sydlyn
(American) quiet
Sidlyn, Sydlin, Sydlinne

Sydney
(French) enthusiastic
*Sidney, Syd, Sydnee,
Sydnie*

Syl
(Latin) woods-loving
Sill

Sylvana
(Latin) forest; natural
woman
Silvanna, Syl, Sylvie

Sylvia
(Latin) sylvan; girl of the
forest
Syl, Sylvea

Sylvie
(Latin) sylvan;
peacefulness
*Sil, Silvie, Silvy, Syl,
Sylvey, Sylvi, Sylvy*

Sylwia
(Polish) serene; in the
woods
Silwia

Symira
(American) enthusiastic
*Sym, Symra, Syms,
Symyra*

Symone
(Hebrew) good listener
Sym

Symphony
(American) musical
*Simphony, Symfonie,
Symfony, Symphonee,
Symphonie*

Synora
(American) languid
*Cinora, Sinora, Synee,
Syni, Synor, Synore*

Synpha
(American) capable
Sinfa, Sinpha, Synfa

Syreta
(American)
Sireta

Tabia

(African) talented girl

Tabitha

(Greek) graceful; gazelle

Tabatha, Tabbatha, Tabbi, Tabytha

Tacha

(American) form of Tasha (from Natalie); born on Christmas

Tach

Tacho

(American) form of Tasha (from Natalie); born on Christmas

Tacie

(American) healthy

Tace, Taci, Tacy

Taesha

(American) sterling character

Tahisha, Taisha, Taisha, Tisha

Taffeta

(American) shiny material

Tafeta, Taffetah, Taffi, Taffy

Taffy

(Welsh) sweet and beloved

Taffee, Taffey, Taffi

Tai

(American) fond

Tie, Tye

Tajudeen

(Spanish) clingy

Taj, Tajjy, Taju

Takara

(Japanese) beloved gem

Taka, Taki

Takeya

(African-American) knowing

Takeyah

Takia

(Arabic) spiritual

Taki, Tikia, Tykia

Takira

(American) combo of Ta and Kira; prayerful

Kira, Takera, Tikiri

Takisha

(African-American) combo of Ta and Kisha; joyful

Takeisha, Takish, Tekisha, Tykisha

Talent

(American) self-assured

Talynt

Talesha

(African-American) friendly

Tal, Taleesh, Taleisha, Talisha, Tallie, Telesha

Tali

(Hebrew) confident

Talia

(Greek) golden; dew from heaven

Tahlia, Tali, Tallie, Tally, Talya, Talyah

Talibah

(African) intellectual

Tali, Talib, Taliba

Talitha

(African-American) inventive

Taleta, Taletha, Talith, Tally

Tallulah

(Native American) leaping water; sparkling girl

Talie, Talley, Tallula, Talula, Talulah

Talluse

(American) bold

Talloose, Tallu, Taluce

Talou
(American) saucy
Talli, Tallou, Tally

Tam
(Japanese) decorative

Tamaka
(Japanese) bracelet;
adorned female

Tamala
(American) kind
*Tam, Tama, Tamela,
Tammie, Tammy*

Tamar
(Hebrew) palm; breezy
Tama, Tamarr

Tamara
(Hebrew) royal female
*Tamera, Tammy, Tamora,
Tamra*

Tamay
(American) form of
Tammy; soft
Tamae, Tamaye

Tambara
(American) high-energy
*Tam, Tamb, Tambra,
Tamby, Tammy*

Tamber
(American) combo of T
and Amber; energetic
*Amber, Tam, Tambey,
Tambur*

Tambusi
(African) frank
Tam, Tambussey, Tammy

Tame
(American) calm

Tamefa
(African-American) form
of Tameka
Tamefah, Tamifa

Tamesha
(African-American) open
face
*Tamesh, Tamisha,
Tammie, Tammy*

Tamesis
(Spanish) name for the
Thames River
Tam, Tamey

Tamika
(African-American) lively
*Tameca, Tameeka,
Tameka, Tamieka,
Tamikah, Tammi,
Tammie, Tammy, Temeka*

Tamiko
(Japanese) the people's
child
Tami, Tamico, Tamika

Tamirisa
(Indian) night; dark
*Risa, Tami, Tamirysa,
Tamrisa, Tamyrisa*

Tammi
(American) sweetheart
*Tam, Tammie, Tammy,
Tammye*

Tamra
(Hebrew) sweet girl
Tammie, Tamora, Tamrah

Tamsin
(English) benevolent
*Tam, Tami, Tammee,
Tammey, Tammy,
Tammye, Tamsa,
Tamsan, Tamsen*

Tamyrah
(African-American)
vocalist
Tamirah

Tana
(Slavic) petite princess
Taina, Tan, Tanah, Tanie

Tandy
(English) team player
Tanda, Tandi, Tandie

Tane
(Polynesian) fertile

Tanesha
(African) strong
*Tanish, Tanisha,
Tannesha, Tannie*

Tangela
(American) combo of Tan
and Angela
T'Angela

Tangelia
(Greek) angel
Gelia, Tange, Tangey

Tangenika
(American) form of
former country
Tanganyika
Tange, Tangi, Tangy

Tangi
(American)
Tangee

Tango
(Spanish) dance
Tangoh

Tangyla
(Invented) form of
Tangela; special
Tange, Tangy

Tani
(Slavic) glorious
Tahnie, Tanee, Tanie

Tania
(Russian, Slavic)
queenly
Tannie, Tanny, Tanya

Tanina
(American) bold
*Tan, Tana, Tanena,
Taninah, Tanney, Tanni,
Tannie, Tanny, Tanye,
Tanyna*

Tanise
(American) unique
Tanes, Tanis

Tanish
(Greek) eternal
Tan, Tanesh, Tanny

Tanisha
(African-American)
talkative
*Taniesha, Tannie,
Tenisha, Tinishah*

Tansy
(Latin) pretty
Tan, Tancy, Tansee, Tanzi

Tanuneka
(African-American)
gracious
Nuneka, Tanueka, Tanun

Tanya
(Russian) queenly
bearing
*Tahnya, Tan, Tanyie,
Tawnyah, Tonya*

Tanyanika
(African-American)
combo of Tayna and
Nika; wild spirit
*Nike, Tanya, Tanyani,
Yanika*

Tanyav
(Slavic) regal
Tanyev

Tanyette
(Italian) talkative
Tanye, Tanyee, Tanyett

Tanze
(Greek) form of Tansy;
eternal
*Tans, Tansee, Tanz,
Tanzee, Tanzey, Tanzi*

Tapa
(Spanish) little snack
Tapas

Tapice
(Spanish) covered
*Tapeece, Tapeese,
Tapese, Tapiece, Tapp,
Tappy*

Taquanna
(African-American) noisy
*Takki, Takwana,
Taquana, Taque, Taquie*

Taquesha
(African-American) joyful
Takie, Takwesha

Taquilla
(Spanish) form of
tequila, the liquor; lively
*Takela, Takelah, Taque,
Taquella, Taqui, Taquile,
Taquille*

Tara
(Gaelic) towering
Tarah, Tari, Tarra

Taro
(Card name) farsighted
Taroh

Tarsha
(American) combo of
Tasha and Tara
Tarsh, Tay

Taryn
(American) combo of
Tara and Karyn;
exuberant; (Irish) bright;
combo of Tara and Erin
*Taran, Taren, Tarran,
Tarrin, Tarron*

Tasha
(Russian) Christmas-
born baby
*Tacha, Tahshah, Tash,
Tashie, Tasia, Tasie, Tasy,
Tasya*

Tashanah
(African-American)
spunky
Tash, Tashana

Tashanee
(African-American) lively
Tashaunie

Tashawndra
(African-American)
bright smiling
*Tasha, Tashaundra,
Tashie*

Tashel
(African-American)
studious
*Tasha, Tashelle, Tashelle,
Tochelle*

Tashza
(African-American) form
of Tasha; bright
Tashi, Tashy, Tashzah

Tassi
(Slavic) bold
Tassee, Tassey, Tassy

Tate
(English) short

Tateeahna
(Invented) form of
Tatiana; snow queen

Tatiana
(Russian) snow queen
*Tanya, Tatania, Tatia,
Tatianna, Tatiannia,
Tatie, Tattianna, Tatyana,
Tatyanna*

Tatum
(English) cheery; high-
spirited
Tata, Tate, Tatie, Tayte

Tavia
(Latin) short for Octavia;
light
Tava, Taveah, Tavi

Tawannah
(African-American)
talkative
*Tawana, Tawanda,
Tawanna, Tawona*

Tawanner
(American) loquacious
Tawanne, Twanner

Tawanta
(African-American) smart
Tawan, Tawante

Tawny
(American) tan-skinned
*Tawn, Tawnee, Tawni,
Tawnie*

Tawnya
(American) form of
Tonya; tan
*Tawnie, Tawnyah, Tonya,
Tonyah*

Tawyn
(American) reliable; tan
*Tawenne, Tawin,
Tawynne*

Tayla
(American) doll-like
Taila, Taylah

Taylor
(English) tailor by trade;
style-setter
*Tailor, Talor, Tay, Taye,
Taylar, Tayler*

Teagan
(Irish) worldly; creative
Teague, Teegan, Tegan

Teague
(Irish) creative
Tee, Teegue, Tegue

Teah
(Greek) goddess
Tea

Teale
(English) blue-green;
bird
Teal, Teala

Teamikka
(African-American) form
of Tamika; lively
Teamika

Teana
(American) form of Tina;
high-energy
Teanah, Teane

Tecoa
(American) precocious
Tekoa

Teddi
(Greek) cuddly
Ted, Teddie, Teddy

Tedra
(Greek) outgoing
Teddra, Tedrah

Tejuana
(Mexican) place name
T'Juana, Tijuana

Tekira
(American) legendary
Tekera, Teki

Tekla
(Greek) legend; divine
glory
*Tekk, Teklah, Thekla,
Tikla, Tiklah*

Telina
(American) storyteller
*Teline, Telyna, Telyne,
Tilina*

Telsa
(American) form of
Tessa; successful
Telly

Temetris
(African-American)
respected
*Teme, Temi, Temitris,
Temmy*

Tempest
(French) tempestuous;
stormy
*Tempeste, Tempie,
Tempyst*

Templa
(Latin) spiritual;
moderate
Temp, Templah

Tenesha
(African-American)
clever
*Tenesia, Tenicha,
Tenisha, Tennie*

Tennille
(American) innovative
*Tanielle, Tanile, Ten,
Teneal, Tenile, Tenneal,
Tennelle, Tennie*

Teo
(Spanish) from Spanish
male name Teodoro;
God's gift
Teeo, Teoh

Teodora
(Scandinavian) God's gift
Teo, Teodore

Tequila
(Spanish) alcoholic
beverage
*Tequela, Tequilla, Tiki,
Tiquilia*

Teresa
(Greek) gardener
*Taresa, Terese, Terhesa,
Teri, Terre, Tess, Tessie,
Treece, Tressa, Tressae*

Terese
(Greek) nurturing
Tarese, Therese, Treece

Tereso
(Spanish) reaper
Tere, Terese

Teri
(Greek) reaper
Terre, Terri, Terrie

Terilyn
(American) combo of Teri
and Lynn
*Terelyn, Terrelynn,
Terrilynn, Terri-Lynn*

Terolyn
(American) combo of
Tere and Carolyn;
harvesting; flirtatious
*Tarolyn, Tero, Terolinn,
Terolinne*

Terra
(Latin) earthy; name for someone born under an astrological earth sign
Tera, Terrie

Terrell
(Greek) hardy
Ter, Teral, Terell, Terrelle, Terrie, Teryl

Terrena
(Latin) smooth-talking
Terina, Terrina, Terry

Terry
(Greek) short for Theresa
Teri, Terre, Terrey, Terri, Tery

Tertia
(Latin) third
Ters, Tersh, Tersha, Tersia

Tess
(Greek) harvesting life
Tesse

Tessa
(Greek) reaping a harvest
Tesa, Tessie, Teza

Tessica
(American) form of Jessica; friendly
Tesica, Tess, Tessa, Tessie, Tessika

Tessie
(Greek) form of Theresa; wonderful
Tessey, Tessi, Tezi

Thada
(Greek) appreciative
Thadda, Thaddeah

Thadyne
(Hebrew) worthy of praise
Thadee, Thadine, Thady

Thalassa
(Greek) sensitive
Talassa, Thalassah, Thalasse

Thalia
(Greek) joyful; fun
Thalya

Tharamel
(Invented) form of the word caramel; dedicated
Thara

Thea
(Greek) goddess
Teah, Teeah, Theah, Theeah, Theo, Tiah

Theda
(American) confident
Thada, Thedah

Thelma
(Greek) giver
Thel

Theodora
(Greek) sweetheart; God's gift
Dora, Teddi, Teddie, Teddy, Tedi, Tedra, Tedrah, Theda, Theo, Theodorah, Theodrah

Theola
(Greek) excellent
Theo, Theolah, Thie

Theone
(Greek) serene
Theonne

Theresa
(Greek) reaping a harvest
Reza, Teresa, Terri, Terrie, Terry

Therese
(Greek) reaping a harvest
Tereece, Terese, Terise, Terry

Theta
(Greek) letter in Greek alphabet; substantial
Thayta, Thetah

Thim
(Thai) ice cream; sweet

Thirzah
(Hebrew) pleasant
Thirza, Thursa, Thurza

Thomasina
(Hebrew) twin
Tom, Toma, Tomasa, Tomasina, Tomina, Tommie, Toto

Thora
(Scandinavian) thunder-like
Thorah

Thyra
(Scandinavian) loud
Thira

Tia
(Greek) princess; (Spanish) aunt
Teah, Tee, Teia, Tiah

Tian
(Greek) lovely
Ti, Tiane, Tiann, Tianne, Tyan, Tyann, Tyanne, Tye

Tiana
(Greek) highest beauty
Tana, Teeana, Tiane, Tiona

Tianth
(American) pretty and impetuous
Teanth, Tia, Tian, Tianeth

Tiara
(Latin) crowned goddess
Teara, Tearra, Tee, Teearah, Tierah, Tira

Tibby
(American) frisky
Tib, Tibb, Tybbee

Tibisay
(American) uniter
Tibi, Tibisae

Tichanda
(African-American) stylish
Tichaunda, Tishanda

Tiena
(Spanish) earthy
Teena

Tierah
(Latin) jeweled; ornament
Tia, Tiarra, Tiera

Tierney
(Irish) wealthy
Teern, Teerney, Teerny, Tiern

Tifaya
(Greek) form of Tiffany
Tifaya, Tifayane, Tiff, Tiffy

Tiffany
(Greek) lasting love
Tifanie, Tiff, Tiffanie, Tiffenie, Tiffi, Tiffie, Tiffy, Tiphanie, Tyfannie

Tigress
(Latin) wild
Tigris, Tye, Tygris

Tiki
(Place name) kinetic energy
Tekee

Tilda
(German) short for Matilda; powerful
Telda, Tildie, Till, Tylda

Tilla
(German) industrious
Tila

Tilly
(German) cute; strong
Till, Tillee, Tillie

Timmie
(Greek) short for Timothie; honorable
Tim, Timi, Timmy

Timothie
(Greek) honorable
Tim, Timmie, Timothea, Timothy

Tina
(Latin, Spanish) little and lively
Teena, Teenie, Tena, Tiny

Tionne
(American) hopeful
Tionn

Tipper
(Irish) pourer of water; nurturing
Tip, Tippy, Typper

Tippett
(American) giving

Tippie
(American) generous
Tippi, Tippy

Tirrza
(Hebrew) sweet;
precious
*Thirza, Thirzah, Tirza,
Tirzah*

Tisa
(African) ninth child
Tesa, Tesah, Tisah

Tish
(Latin) happy
Tysh

Tisha
(Latin) joyful
*Tesha, Ticia, Tishah,
Tishie*

Tishunette
(African-American)
happy girl
Tish, Tisunette

Tobago
(Place name) West
Indies island; islander
Bago, ToTo

Tobi
(Hebrew) good
Tobie, Toby

Toffey
(American) spirited
*Toff, Toffee, Toffi, Toffie,
Toffy*

Toinette
(Latin) wonderful
*Toin, Toinett, Toney,
Tony, Toynet*

Tollie
(Hebrew) confident
*Toll, Tollee, Tolli, Tolly,
Tollye*

Toma
(Latin) short for
Tomasina
*Tomas, Tomgirl, Tommi,
Tommie, Tommy*

Tomeka
(African-American) form
of Tamika
Tomeke

Tomiko
(Japanese) wealthy
Miko, Tamiko, Tomi

Tomitria
(African-American) form
of Tommy
Tomi

Tommie
(Hebrew) sassy
Tom, Tomi, Tommy

Tonaya
(American) valuable
Tona, Tone

Tonia
(Latin) a wonder
*Toneah, Tonya, Tonyah,
Toyiah*

Tonietta
(American) combo of
Toni and Etta; valuable
Toni, Toniett, Toniette

Tonisha
(African-American) lively
*Nisha, Tona, Toneisha,
Tonesha, Tonie, Tonish*

Toni
(Latin) meritorious
Tone, Tonee, Tonie, Tony

Tonia
(Latin) daring
*Tonni, Tonnie, Tony,
Tonya*

Topaz
(Latin) gemstone;
sparkling
Tophaz

Topekia
(American) form of
Topeka
*Topeka, Topeke,
Topekea*

Topsy
(English) topnotch
Toppie, Topsi, Topsie

Tora
(Scandinavian) thunder

Tori
(Scottish) rich and
winning
*Toree, Torri, Torrie, Torry,
Tory*

Torill
(Scandinavian) loud
Toril, Torille

Torrance
(Place name) confident
Torr, Torri

Tosha
(American) form of Tasha
Tosh

Tosha
(Slavic) priceless
Tosh, Toshia

Tova
(Hebrew) good woman
Tovah

Toy
(American) playful
Toia, Toya, Toye

Tracey
(Gaelic) aggressive
*Trace, Tracee, Traci,
Tracie, Tracy*

Tracilyn
(American) combo of
Tracy and Lynn;
combative
*Trace, Tracelynn,
Tracilynne, Tracy-Lynn*

Tranell
(American) confident
*Tranel, Tranelle, Traney,
Trani*

Traniqua
(African-American)
hopeful
*Tranaqua, Tranekwa,
Tranequa, Trani,
Tranikwa, Tranney,
Tranniqua, Tranny*

Trazanna
(African-American)
talented
Traz, Trazannah, Traze

Tree
(American) sturdy

Treece
(American) short for
Terese
Treese, Trice

Treena
(American) form of Trina
Treen

Tremira
(African-American)
anxious
Tremera, Tremmi

Treneth
(American) smiling
Trenith, Trenny

Trenica
(African-American)
smiling
Trenika, Trinika

Trenise
(African-American)
songbird
*Tranese, Tranise,
Trannise, Treenie,
Treneese, Treni,
Trenniece, Trenny*

Trenyce
(American) smiling
Trienyse, Trinyce

Tressa
(Greek) reaping life's
harvest
*Tresa, Tresah, Tress,
Trisa*

Tressie
(American) successful
*Tress, Tressa, Tressee,
Tressey, Tressi, Tressy*

Tricia
(Latin) humorous
*Tresha, Trich, Tricha,
Trish, Trisha*

Trina
(Greek) perfect;
scintillating
Tina, Treena, Trine, Trinie

Trinidad
(Place name) spiritual
person
Trini, Trinny

Trinlee
(American) genuine
Trinley, Trinli, Trinly

Trinity
(Latin) triad
Trin, Trini, Trinie,
Trinitee, Triniti

Trish
(American) short for
Patricia; funny
Trysh

Trisha
(American) short for
Patricia: funny
Tricia

Trishelle
(African-American)
humorous girl
Trichelle, Trichillem,
Trish, Trishel, Trishie

Trissy
(American) tall
Triss, Trissi, Trissie

Trista
(Latin) pensive;
sparkling love
Tresta, Trist, Tristie,
Trysta

Tristen
(Latin) bold
Tristan, Tristie, Tristin,
Trysten

Tristica
(Spanish) form of Trista;
pretty
Trist, Tristi, Tristika

Trixie
(Latin) personable
Trix, Trixi, Trixy

Trixiebelle
(American) combo of
Trixie and Belle; sweet
personality
Belle, Trix, Trixeebel,
Trixiebell, Trixybell

Trudy
(German) hopeful
Trude, Trudi, Trudie

True
(American) truthful
Truee, Truie, Truth

Truette
(American) truthful
Tru, True, Truett

Truffle
(Food name)
Truff, Truffy

Trulencia
(Spanish) honest
Lencia, Tru, Trulence,
Trulens, Trulense

Truly
(American) honest
True, Trulee, Truley

Trusteen
(American) trusting
Trustean, Trustee,
Trustine, Trusty, Trusyne

Truth
(American) honest
Truthe

Try
(American) earnest
Tri, Trie

Tryna
(Greek) form of Trina
Trine, Tryne, Trynna

Tsonka
(American) capricious
Sonky, Tesonka,
Tisonka, Tsonk

Tuenchit
(Thai)

Tuesday
(English) weekday

Tulia
(Spanish) glorious
Tuli, Tuliana, Tulie,
Tuliea, Tuly

Tully
(Irish) powerful; dark
spirit
Tull, Tulle, Tulli, Tullie

Turin
(American) creative
Turan, Turen, Turrin,
Turun

Turquoise
(French) blue-green
Turkoise, Turquie,
Turrkoise

Tursha
(Slavic) warm
Tersha

Tweetie
(American) vivacious
Tweetee, Tweetey, Tweeti

Twiggy
(English) slim
*Twiggie, Twiggee,
Twiggey*

Twyla
(English) creative
Twila, Twilia

Twynceola
(African-American) bold
Twin, Twyn, Twynce

Tye
(American) talented

Tyeoka
(African-American)
rhythmic
Tioka, Tyeo, Tyeoke

Tyesha
(African-American)
duplicitous
*Tesha, Tisha, Tyeisha,
Tyiesha, Tyisha*

Tyisha
(African-American)
sweet
*Isha, Tisha, Ty, Tyeisha,
Tyish*

Tyler
(American) stylish;
tailor
Tielyr, Tye

Tymitha
(African-American) kind
*Timitha, Tymi, Tymie,
Tymith, Tymy, Tymytha*

Tyne
(American) dramatic;
(Old English) sylvan
Tie, Tine, Tye

Tyneil
(African-American)
combo of Ty and Neil;
helpful
Tyne, Tyneal, Tyniel

Tynisha
(African-American)
fertile
Tinisha, Tynesha, Tynie

Tyra
(Scandinavian) assertive
woman
Tye, Tyrah, Tyre, Tyrie

Tyrea
(African-American) form
of Thora; thunder
Tyree, Tyria

Tyrina
(American) ball-of-fire
*Tierinna, Tye, Tyreena,
Tyrinah*

Tyronna
(African-American)
combo of Tyronne and
Anna; special
*Tierona, Tye, Tyrona,
Tyronnah*

Tyson
(French) son of Ty
Ty, Tysen

Tyzna
(American) ingenious,
assertive
Tyze, Tyzie

Udavine
(American) thriving
Uda

Udele
(English) prospering
woman
Uda, Udell

Ula
(Celtic) jewel-like beauty
Ule

Ulanda
(American) confident
Uland, Ulandah, Ulande

Ulani
(Hawaiian) happy;
(Polynesian) happy
Ulanee

Ulrika
(Teutonic) leader
*Ulree, Ulric, Ulrica, Ulrie,
Ulry, Urik*

Ulyssia
(Invented) from Ulysses;
wanderer
*Lyss, Lyssia, Uls, Ulsy,
Ulsyia*

Uma
(Hebrew) nation;
worldview
Umah

Una
(Latin) unique
Unah

Undine
(Latin) from the ocean
Undene, Undyne

Undra
(American) one; long-
suffering

Unique
(Latin) singular
Uneek

Unity
(English) unity of spirit
Unitee

Unn
(Scandinavian) loving
Un

Ural
(Place name) Ural
Mountains
Ura, Uralle, Urine, Uris

Urania
(Greek) universal beauty
Uraine, Uraneah

Urith
(Hebrew) bright
Urit

Ursa
(Greek, Latin) star; bear-
like
Urs, Ursah, Ursie

Ursula
(Latin) little female bear
Ursa, Urse, Ursela, Ursila

Usha
(Indian) dawn;
awakening

Usher
(Word as name) helpful
Ush, Ushar, Ushur

Utopia
(American) idealistic
Uta, Utopiah

Uzbek
(Place name) for
Uzbekistan
Usbek

Uzetta
(American) serious
Uzette

Uzma
(Spanish) capable
Usma, Uz, Uzmah

Vada
(German) form of Valda;
winner
Vaida, Vay

Val
(Latin) short for Valerie;
strong

Valarie
(Latin) strong
Val, Valerie

Valda
(German) high spirits
Val, Valdah

Vale
(English) valley; natural
Vail, Vaylie

Valeda
(Latin) strong woman
Val, Valayda, Valedah

Valencia
(Spanish) place name;
strong-willed
Val, Valensha, Valincia

Valentina
(Latin) romantic
*Val, Vala, Valentin,
Valentine*

Valeny
(American) hard
Val, Valenie

Valeria
(Spanish) having valor
Valeri, Valerie, Valery

Valerie
(Latin) robust
Val, Valarie, Valery, Vallie

Valerta
(Invented) form of
Valerie; courageous
Valer, Valert

Valeska
(Polish) joyous leader
Valeske

Valetta
(Italian) feminine
Valettah, Valita, Valitta

Valkie
(Scandinavian) from
Valkyrie; fantastic
*Val, Valkee, Valki, Valkry,
Valky*

Vallie
(Latin) natural
Val, Valli, Vally

Vallie-Mae
(Latin) from Valentina
and Mae; romantic
*Valliemae, Vallimae,
Vallimay*

Valora
(Latin) intimidating
Val, Valorah, Valorie

Valore
(Latin) courageous
Val, Valour

Valoria
(Spanish) brave
Vallee, Valora, Valore

Value
(Word as name) valued
Valu, Valyou

Valyn
(American) perky
Valind, Valinn, Valynn

Vamia
(Hispanic) energetic
Vamee, Vamie

Vanda
(German) smiling beauty
Vandah, Vandi

Vanessa
(Greek) flighty
*Nessa, Van, Vanesah,
Vanessah, Vanna,
Vannie, Venesa*

Vania
(Hebrew) gifted
Vaneah, Vanya

Vanille
(American) from vanilla;
simplistic
*Vana, Vani, Vanila,
Vanile, Vanna*

Vanity
(English) vain girl
Vaniti

Vanna
(Greek) golden girl
Van, Vana, Vannah

Vanya
(American) form of
Vanna; self-assured
*Vani, Vanja, Vanni,
Vanyuh*

Vara
(Greek) strange
Varah, Vare

Varda
(Hebrew) rosy
Vardah

Varaina
(Invented) form of
Loraine

Vasteen
(American) capable
*Vas, Vastene, Vastine,
Vasty*

Vaughan
(Last name as first
name) smooth talker
Vaughn, Vawn, Vawne

Veata
(Cambodian) smart;
organized
Veatah

Veda
(Sanskrit) wise woman
Vedah, Veida, Vida

Vedette
(French) watchful
Veda, Vedett

Vega
(Scandinavian) star
*Vay, Vayga, Vegah,
Veguh*

Veleda
(German) intelligent
Vel, Veladah, Velayda

Velinda
(American) form of
Melinda; practical
*Vel, Velin, Velind, Vell,
Velly, Velynda*

Vell
(American) short for
Velma; practical
Vel, Velly, Vels

Velma
(German) hardworking
Vel, Velmah

Velvet
(French) luxurious
Vel, Vell, Velvete, Velvett

Veneradah
(Spanish) honored;
venerable
Ven, Venera, Venerada

Venice
(Place name) coming of
age
*Vanice, Vaniece,
Veneece, Veneese*

Venitia
(Italian) forgiving
*Esha, Venesha, Venn,
Venney, Venni, Vennie,
Venny*

Vennita
(Italian) from Venice,
Italy; having arrived
*Nita, Vanecia, Ven,
Venesha, Venetia,
Venita, Vennie, Vinetia*

Venus
(Latin) loving; goddess
of love
Venise, Vennie

Vera
(Russian) faithful friend
Verah, Verie

Verda
(Latin) breath of spring
Ver, Vera, Verdah, Verde

Verdad
(Spanish) verdant;
honest
*Verda, Verdade, Verdie,
Verdine, Verdite*

Verdie
(Latin) fresh as
springtime
*Verd, Verda, Verdee,
Verdi, Verdy*

Verena
(English) honest
*Veren, Verenah, Verene,
Virena*

Verenase
(Swiss) flourishing;
truthful
*Ver, Verenese,
Verennase, Vy, Vyrenase,
Vyrennace*

Verity
(French) truthful
*Verety, Veritee, Veriti,
Veritie*

Verlene
(Latin) vivacious
Verleen, Verlie, Verlynne

Vermekia
(African-American)
natural
*Meki, Mekia, Verme,
Vermekea, Vermy,
Vermye*

Verna
(Latin) springlike
Vernah, Verne

Vernice
(American) natural
Verna, Vernie, Verniece

Vernicia
(Spanish) form of
Vernice; springtime
Vern, Verni, Vernisia

Veronica
(Latin) real
*Nica, Ronica, Varonica,
Veron, Veronika,
Veronnica, Von*

Veronique
(French) realistic
woman; form of Veronica
*Veroneek, Veroneese,
Veroniece*

Versperah
(Latin) evening star
Vesp, Vespa, Vespera

Vertrelle
(African-American)
organized
*Vertey, Verti, Vertrel,
Vetrell*

Vesela
(Origin unknown) open
Vess

Vesta
(Latin) home-loving;
goddess of the home
Vess, Vessie, Vestah

Vevay
(Latin) form of Vivian;
lively
*Vevah, Vi, Viv, Vivay, Vivi,
Vivie*

Vi
(Latin) short for Viola;
kind
Vy

Vianey
(Spanish) form of Vivian;
alive
*Via, Viana, Viane, Viani,
Vianne, Vianney, Viany*

Vianne
(French) striking
Vi, Viane, Viann

Vicky
(Latin) short for Victoria
*Vic, Vick, Vickee, Vicki,
Vickie, Vikki*

Victoria
(Latin) winner
*Vic, Vicki, Victoriah,
Vikki, Viktoria*

Victory
(Latin) a winning woman
Vic, Viktorie

Vida
(Hebrew) short for
Davida
Veeda

Vidella
(Spanish) life
*Veda, Vida, Videline,
Vydell*

Vidette
(Hebrew) loved
*Viddey, Viddi, Viddie,
Vidett, Videy*

Vienna
(Latin) place name
Viena, Viennah, Vienne

Viennese
(Place name) from
Vienna
Vee, Viena, Vienne

Viet
(Place name) form of
Viet Nam
Vee, Viette

Vilma
(Spanish) form of Velma;
industrious
Vi, Vil

Vina
(Hindi) musical
instrument
Vin, Vinah, Vinnie, Vinny

Vinah
(American)
up-and-coming
Vi, Vyna

Vincentia
(Latin) winner
Vin, Vinnie

Vincia
(Spanish) forthright;
winning
Vincenta, Vincey, Vinci

Viola
(Latin) violet; lovely lady
Vi, Violah

Violanth
(Latin) from the purple
flower violet
*Vi, Viol, Viola, Violanta,
Violante*

Violet
(English, French) purple
flower
*Vi, Viole, Violette,
Vylolet*

Violyne
(Latin) from the purple
flower violet
*Vi, Vio, Viola, Violene,
Violine*

Virgilee
(American) combo of
Virgi and Lee; pure girl
*Virge, Virgee, Virgi,
Virgilea, Virgileigh,
Virgy, Virgylee*

Virginia
(Latin) pure female
*Giniah, Verginia, Virgie,
Virginya, Virgy*

Viridiana
(Spanish) combo of Viri
and Diana; ostentatious
*Di, Diana, Diane, Viri,
Viridi, Viridiane*

Virtue
(Latin) strong; pure

Vita
(Latin) animated; lively;
life
Veda, Veeta, Veta, Vete

Viv
(Latin) short for Vivian;
vital

Viva
(Latin) alive; lively
Veeva

Vivecca
(Scandinavian) lively;
energetic
*Viv, Viveca, Viveka,
Vivica, Vivie*

Vivi
(Hindi) vital
Viv

Vivian
(Latin) bubbling with life
*Viv, Vive, Vivi, Viviana,
Vivien, Vivienne, Vivyan*

Vivianna
(American) inventive
Viviannah, Vivianne

Vivilyn
(American) vital
Viv, Vivi

Vix
(American) short for
Vixen
Vixa, Vixie, Vyx

Vixen
(American) flirt
Vix, Vixee, Vixie

Voila
(French) attention; seen
Vwala

Voletta
(French) mysterious
Volette, Volettie

Vonda
(Czech) loving
Vondah, Vondi

Vondrah
(Czech) loving
Vond, Vondie, Vondra

Vonese
(American) form of
Vanessa; pretty
*Vonesa, Vonise, Vonne,
Vonnesa, Vonny*

Voni
(Slavic) affectionate
Vonee, Vonie

Vonna
(French) graceful
*Vona, Vonah, Vonne,
Vonni, Vonnie*

Vonnala
(American) sweet
*Von, Vonala, Vonnalah,
Vonnie*

Vonshae
(American) combo of
Von and Shae; confident
Von, Vonshay

Voyage
(Word as name) trip;
wanderer
Voy

Wade
(American) campy

Wafa
(Arabic) loyal

Wakeen
(American) spunky
*Wakeene, Wakey,
Wakine*

Wakeishah
(African-American)
happy
*Wake, Wakeisha,
Wakesha*

Walda
(German) powerful
woman
Waldah, Wally

Waleria
(Polish) sweet

Waleska
(Last name as first
name) effervescent
Wal, Walesk, Wally

Walker
(English) active; mover

Wallis
(English) from Wales;
openminded
*Walis, Wallace, Wallie,
Wally*

Wanda
(Polish) wild; wandering
*Wandah, Wandie,
Wonda*

Warma
(American) warmth-filled
Warm

Warner
(German) outgoing;
fighter
Warna, Warnar, Warnir

Wenda
(German) adventurer
Wend, Wendah, Wendy

Wendy
(English) friendly;
childlike
*Wenda, Wende, Wendee,
Wendi, Wendie, Wendye*

Weslie
(English) woman in the
meadow
Wes, Weslee, Wesli

Wheeler
(English) inventive
Wheelah, Wheelar

Whitley
(English) outdoorsy
Whitlee, Whitly, Witlee

Whitman
(English) white-haired man
Whit, Wittman

Whitney
(English) white; fresh
Whit, Whitne, Whitnee, Whitnie, Whytnie

Whitson
(Last name as first) white
Whits, Whitty, Witte, Witty

Whittier
(Literature) distinguished
Whitt

Whoopi
(English) excitable
Whoopee, Whoopie, Whoopy

Whynesha
(African-American) kind-hearted
Whynesa, Wynes, Wynesa, Wynesha

Wiktoria
(Polish) victor
Wikta

Wilda
(English) wild-haired girl
Willie, Wyle

Wile
(American) coy; wily
Wiles, Wyle

Wilhelmina
(German) able protector
Willa, Willhelmena, Willie, Wilma

Willa
(English) desirable
Will, Willah

Willette
(American) open
Wilet, Wilett, Will, Willett

Willine
(American) form of Will; willowy
Will, Willene, Willy, Willyne

Willis
(American) sparkling
Wilice, Will, Willice

Willow
(American) free spirit; willow tree
Willo

Wilona
(English) desirable
Wilo, Wiloh, Wilonah, Wylona

Wilma
(German) sturdy
Wilmah, Wylm

Win
(German) flirty
Winnie, Wyn, Wynne

Wind
(American) breezy
Winde, Windee, Windey, Windi, Windy, Wynd

Winetta
(American) peaceful; country girl
Winette, Winietta, Wyna, Wynette

Winifred
(German) peaceful woman
Win, Windy, Winefred, Winnie, Winniefred, Winnifreed

Winkie
(American) vital
Winkee, Winky

Winner
(American) outstanding

Winnie
(English) winning
Wini, Winny, Wynnie

Winnielle
(African) victorious female
Winielle, Winniele, Wynnielle

Winona
(Native American) firstborn girl
Winonah, Wye, Wynona, Wynonah, Wynonna

Winter
(English) child born in winter
Wynter

Wonder
(American) filled with wonder
Wander, Wonda, Wondee, Wondy, Wunder

Wonila
(African-American) swaying
Waunila, Wonilla, Wonny

Wood
(American) smooth talker
Woode, Woodee, Woodie, Woody, Woodye

Wova
(American) brassy
Whova, Wovah

Wren
(English) flighty girl; bird
Renn, Wrin, Wryn, Wrynne

Wyanda
(American) form of Wanda; gregarious
Wyan

Wyetta
(French) feisty

Wylie
(American) wily
Wylee, Wyley, Wyli

Wymette
(American) vocalist
Wimet, Wimette, Wymet, Wynette

Wynne
(Welsh) fair-haired
Win, Winwin, Wynee, Wynn, Wynnie

Wyomie
(Native American) horse-rider on the plains
Why, Wyome, Wyomee, Wyomeh

Wyss
(Welsh) spontaneous; fair
Whyse

Xanadu
(Place name) *Kubla Khan*'s Xanadu is an idyllic, exotic place
Zanadu

Xandra
(Greek) protective
Xandrae, Zan, Zandie, Zandra

Xanthe
(Greek) beautiful blonde; yellow
X, Xanth, X-Anth, Xantha, Xanthie, Xes, Zane, Zanthie

Xaviera
(French) smart
Zavey, Zavie, Zaviera, Zavierah, Zavy

Xena
(Greek) girl from afar
Zen, Zena, Zennie

Xeniah
(Greek) gracious entertainer
Xen, Xenia, Zenia, Zeniah

Xiomara
(Spanish) congenial
Xylene
(Greek) outdoorsy
Leen, Lene, Xyleen, Xyline, Zylee, Zyleen, Zylie
Xylia
(Greek) woods-loving
Zylea, Zylia

Yadira
(Hindi) dearest
Yaffa
(Hebrew) beautiful girl
Yafa, Yafah
Yahaira
(Hebrew) precious
Yajaira
Yahnnie
(Greek) giving
Yahn, Yanni, Yannie, Yannis
Yaki
(Japanese) tenacious
Yakee
Yamileth
(Spanish) girl of grace
Yami
Yana
(Slavic) lovely
Yanah, Yanni, Yannie, Yanny
Yannette
(American) combo of J and Annette; melodic
Yanett, Yannett, Yanny

Yaquelin
(Spanish) form of Jaqueline
Yackie, Yacque, Yacquelyn, Yaki, Yakie, Yaque, Yaquelinn, Yaquelinne
Yara
(Spanish) expansive; princess
Yarah, Yare, Yarey
Yarine
(Russian) peaceful
Yari, Yarina
Yarita
(Hispanic) flashy
Yasmine
(Arabic) pretty
Yasmeen, Yasmen, Yasmin
Yaura
(American) desirous
Yara, Yaur, YaYa
Yazmin
(Persian) pretty flower
Yazmen
Yebenette
(American) little
Yebe, Yebey, Yebi
Yelena
(Russian) friendly
Yemaya
(African) smart; quirky
Yemye

Yenny
(American) combo of Y
and Jenny; happy
Yen, Yeni, Yenney, Yenni

Yessenia
(Spanish) devout
Jesenia, Yesenia

Yeva
(Russian) lively; loving
Yevka

Yina
(Spanish) winning
Yena

Yodelle
(American) old-
fashioned
*Yode, Yodell, Yodelly,
Yodette, Yodey*

Yoko
(Japanese) good;
striving
Yokoh

Yola
(Spanish) form of
Yolanda; violet
Yolanda, Yoli

Yolanda
(Greek) pretty as a violet
flower
*Yola, Yolana, Yolandah,
Yolie, Yoyly*

Yolie
(Greek) violet; flower
Yolee, Yoli

Yonaide
(American)
Yonade, Yonaid

York
(English) forthright
Yorkie, Yorkke

Young
(Korean) forever

Ysanne
(English) graceful
*Esan, Esanne, Essan,
Ysan, Ysann*

Yu
(Asian) jade; a gem

Yue
(Asian) happy

Yuette
(American) capable
Yue, Yuete, Yuetta

Yuliana
(Invented) combo of
Y and Juliana
*Ana, Yuli, Yuliann,
Yulianne*

Yuna
(African) gorgeous
Yunah

Yurianna
(Invented) combo of Yuri
and Anna; royal
Yuri, Yuriann, Yurianne

Yuta
(American) dramatic
Uta

Yvette
(French) lively archer
Yavet, Yevette, Yvete

Yvonne
(French) athletic
*Vonne, Vonnie, Yavonne,
Yvone, Yvonna*

Zachah
(Hebrew) Lord remembered; brave-hearted
Zach, Zacha, Zachie, Zachrie

Zahavah
(Hebrew) golden girl
Zahava, Zeheva, Zev

Zahra
(African) blossoming
Zara, Zarah

Zaida
(Spanish) peacemaker
Zada, Zai

Zainab
(Arabic) brave

Zaira
(Arabic) flower
Zara

Zaire
(Place name)
Zai, Zay, Zayaire

Zambee
(Place name) from Zambia
Zambi, Zambie, Zamby, Zamby

Zan
(Greek) supportive; (Chinese) praiseworthy
Zander, Zann

Zana
(Greek) defender; energetic
Zanah

Zandra
(Greek) shy; helpful
Zan, Zondra

Zane
(Scandinavian) bold girl
Zain

Zanita
(American) gifted
Zaneta, Zanetta, Zanette, Zanitt, Zeneta

Zanth
(Greek) leader
Zanthe, Zanthi, Zanthie, Zanthy

Zara
(Hebrew) dawn; glorious
Zahra, Zarah, Zaree

Zarmina
(Origin unknown) bright
Zar, Zarmynna

Zaylee
(English) heavenly
Zay, Zayle, Zayley, Zayli, Zaylie

Zayna
(Arabic) wonderful
Zayne

Zazalesha
(African-American) zany
Lesha, Zaza, Zazalese, Zazalesh

Zazula
(Polish) outstanding

Zeb
(Hebrew) Jehovah's gift

Zef
(Polish) moves with the wind
Zeff

Zela
(Greek) blessed; smiling

Zelda
(German) practical
Zell, Zellie

Zelia
(Latin) sensual
Zeleah

Zenae
(Greek) helpful
Zen, Zenah, Zennie

Zenia
(Greek) open
Zeniah, Zenney, Zenni, Zennie, Zenny, Zenya

Zephyr
(Greek) the west wind;
wandering girl
*Zefir, Zeph, Zephie,
Zephir*

Zesta
(American) zestful
Zestah, Zestie, Zesty

Zeta
(English) rose; Greek
letter
Zetah

Zett
(Hebrew) olive;
flourishing
Zeta, Zetta

Zhenia
(Latin) bright
Zennia, Zhen, Zhenie

Zhi
(Chinese) of high
character; ethical

Zhong
(Chinese) honorable

Zhuo
(Chinese) smart;
wonderful
Zuo

Zi
(Chinese) flourishing;
giving

Zia
(Latin) textured
Zea, Ziah

Zila
(Hebrew) shadowy
Zilah, Zilla

Zimbab
(Place name) from
Zimbabwe
Zimbob

Zina
(Greek) hospitable
woman
Zinah, Zine, Zinnie

Zinnia
(Botanical) flower
Zenia, Zinia, Zinny, Zinya

Zipporah
(Hebrew) bird in flight
*Ziporah, Zippi, Zippie,
Zippy*

Zita
(Spanish) rose; (Arabic)
mistress
Zeeta, Zitah

Zoann
(American) combo of Zo
and Ann; alive
Zoan, Zoanne, Zoayn

Zoe
(Greek) lively; vibrant
Zoee, Zoey, Zoie, Zooey

Zofia
(Polish) skilled

Zola
(French) earthy
Zolah

Zolema
(American) confessor
Zolem

Zona
(Latin) funny; brash
Zonah, Zonia, Zonna

Zoom
(American) energetic
*Zoomi, Zoomy,
Zoom-Zoom*

Zora
(Slavic) beauty of dawn
*Zorah, Zorrah, Zorre,
Zorrie*

Zoralle
(Slavic) ethereal
*Zoral, Zoralye, Zorre,
Zorrie*

Zorianna
(American) combo of
Zori and Ann; practical
*Zoree, Zori, Zoriannah,
Zory*

Zorka
(Slavic) dawn
Zorke, Zorky

ZsaZsa
(Hungarian) wild-spirited
Zsa, Zsaey

Zulah
(African) country-loving
Zoola, Zoolah, Zula

Zuleyka
(Arabic) sparkling
Zelekha, Zue, Zuleika,
Zuley

Zulma
(Arabic) vibrant
Zul, Zule, Zulmah

Zuni
(Native American)
creative
Zu

Zuwena
(African) good

Zuzanna
(Polish) misunderstood
Zu, Zue, Zuzan

Bibliography

"America's 40 Richest Under 40." *Fortune* Online. 16 Sept. 2002
   <http://www.fortune.com>.

"The American States." Collin, P.H., ed. *Webster's Concise Desk Dictionary*. New York:
   Barnes & Noble Books, 2001.

"The Animal Kingdom." Collin, P.H., ed. *Webster's Concise Desk Dictionary*. New York:
   Barnes & Noble Books, 2001.

Baby Center Baby Name Finder Page. 1 Dec. 2002
   <http://www.babycenter.com/babyname>.

Baby Chatter Page. 1 Dec. 2002 <http://www.babychatter.com>.

Baby Names/Birth Announcements Page. 1 Oct. 2002
   <http://www.princessprints.com>.

Baby Names Page. 1 Dec. 2002 <http://www.yourbabysname.com>.

Baby Names Page. 1 Nov. 2002 <http://www.babynames.com>.

Baby Names Page. 1 Oct. 2002 <http://www.babyshere.com>.

Baby Names World Page. 15 Jan. 2003 <http://www.babynameworld.com>.

Baby Zone Page. "Around-the-World Names." 15 Jan. 2003
   <http://www.babyzone.com/babynames>.

"Biographical Names." Collin, P.H. ed. *Webster's Concise Desk Dictionary*. New York:
   Barnes & Noble Books, 2001.

"Biographical Names." *The Merriam-Webster Dictionary*. Springfield, Mass: Merriam
   Webster, Inc., 1998.

"Books of the Bible." Collin, P.H., ed. *Webster's Concise Desk Dictionary*. New York:
   Barnes & Noble Books, 2001.

Celebrity Names Page. 1 Nov. 2002 <http://www.celebnames.8m.com>.

"Common English Given Names." *The Merriam-Webster Dictionary*. Springfield, Mass:
Merriam Webster, Inc., 1998.

Death Penalty Info Page. 1 Feb. 2003 "Current Female Death Row Inmates."
<http://www.deathpenaltyinfo.org/womencases.html>.

Dunkling, Leslie. *The Guinness Book of Names*. Enfield, UK: Guinness Publishing,
1993.

eBusinessRevolution Page. 1 Nov. 2002
<http://www.ebusinessrevolution.com/babynames/a.html>.

ePregnancy Page. 1 Dec. 2002 <http://www.Epregnancy.com/directory/Baby_Names>.

"Fifty Important Stars." Gove, Philip Babcock, ed. *Webster's Third New International
Dictionary of the English Language Unabridged*. Springfield, Mass: Merriam-Webster,
Inc., 1981.

"Gambino Capos Held in 1989 Mob Hit." Jerry Capeci. This Week in Gangland, The
Online Column Page. 1 Aug. 2002
<http://www.ganglandnews.com/column289.htm>.

Hanks, Patrick, and Flavia Hodges. *A Dictionary of First Names*. Oxford:
Oxford University Press, 1992.

Harrison, G.B. ed. *Major British Writers*. New York: Harcourt, Brace &World, Inc.,
1959.

HypoBirthing Page. "Baby Names." 1 Oct. 2002 <http://www.hypobirthing.com>.

Indian Baby Names Page. 1 Nov. 2002
<http:// www.indiaexpress.com/specials/babynames>.

Irish Names Page. 15 Jan. 2003 <http://www.hylit.com/info>.

Jewish Baby Names Page. 15 Jan. 2003 <http://www.jewishbabynames.net>.

Kaplan, Justin, and Anne Bernays. *The Language of Names: What We Call Ourselves and Why It Matters*. New York: Simon & Schuster, 1997.

"Months of the Principal Calendars." Gove, Philip Babcock, ed. *Webster's Third New International Dictionary of the English Language Unabridged*. Springfield, Mass: Merriam-Webster Inc., 1981.

"Most Popular Names of the 1990s." Social Security Administration Online. 1 Nov. 2002 <http://www.ssa.gov/OACT/babynames>.

"Most Popular Names of the 1980s." Social Security Administration Online. 1 Nov. 2002 <http://www.ssa.gov/OACT/babynames>.

"Most Popular Names of the 1970s." Social Security Administration Online. 1 Nov. 2002 <http://www.ssa.gov/OACT/babynames>.

"Most Popular Names of the 1960s." Social Security Administration Online. 1 Nov. 2002 <http://www.ssa.gov/OACT/babynames>.

"Most Popular Names of the 1950s." Social Security Administration Online. 1 Nov. 2002 <http://www.ssa.gov/OACT/babynames>.

"Most Popular Names of 2001." Social Security Administration Online. 1 Nov. 2002 <http://www.ssa.gov/OACT/babynames>.

"Most Powerful Women in Business." *Fortune* Online. 14 Oct. 2002 <http://www.fortune.com>.

"Movie-Star Names." Internet Movie Database online. 1 Nov. 2002 <http://www.imdb.com>.

Origins/Meanings of Baby Names from Around the World Page. 1 Nov. 2002 <http:// www.BabyNamesOrigins.com>.

Oxygen Page. "Baby Names." 1 Nov. 2002 <http://www.oxygen.com/babynamer>.

Parenthood Page. 1 Nov. 2002
   <http:// www.parenthood.com/parent_cfmfiles/babynames.cfm>.

"The Plant Kingdom." Collin, P.H., ed. *Webster's Concise Desk Dictionary*. New York:
   Barnes & Noble Books, 2001.

Popular Baby Names Page. 1 Nov. 2002 <http://www.popularbabynames.com>.

"Presidents of the United States." Collin, P.H. ed. *Webster's Concise Desk Dictionary*.
   New York: Barnes & Noble Books, 2001.

"Prime Ministers of the U.K." Collin, P.H. ed. *Webster's Concise Desk Dictionary*.
   New York: Barnes & Noble Books, 2001.

Racketeering and Fraud Investigations Page. 4 Feb. 2003
   <http://www.oig.dol.gov/public/media/oi/mainz01.htm>.

Rick Porelli's AmericanMafia.com Page. 21 June 2002
   <http://www.americanmafia.com/news/6-21-02_Feds_Bust.html>.

Rosenkrantz, Linda, and Pamela Redmond Satran. *Baby Names Now*. New York: St.
   Martin's Press, 2002.

Rosenkrantz, Linda, and Pamela Redmond Satran. *Beyond Charles and Diana: An
   Anglophile's Guide to Baby Naming*. New York: St. Martin's Press, 1992.

Rosenkrantz, Linda, and Pamela Redmond Satran. *Beyond Jennifer and Jason*. New
   York: St. Martin's Press, 1994.

Schwegel, Janet. *The Baby Name Countdown*. New York: Marlowe & Company
   (Avalon), 2001.

"Signs of the Zodiac." Gove, Philip Babcock, ed. *Webster's Third New International
   Dictionary of the English Language Unabridged*. Springfield, Mass: Merriam-Webster
   Inc. Publishers, 1981.

Television-show credits. 1 Oct. 2002–25 Feb. 2003.

Texas Department of Criminal Justice Page. "Offenders on Death Row." 1 Feb. 2003 <http://www.tdcj.state.tx.us/stat/offendersondrow.htm>.

Trantino, Charlee. *Beautiful Baby Names from Your Favorite Soap Operas*. New York: Pinnacle Books, 1996.

20,000+ Names Page. "20,000+ Names from Around the World." 1 Nov. 2002 <http:// www.20000-names.com>.

United Kingdom Baby Name Page. 15 Jan. 2003 <http://www.baby-names.co.uk>.

Wallace, Carol McD. *The Greatest Baby Name Book Ever*, New York: Avon, 1998.

About the Author

With daughter Jennifer Shoquist, M.D., Diane Stafford co-authored *Potty Training for Dummies*, *No More Panic Attacks*, *Migraines for Dummies*, and *The Encyclopedia of Sexually Transmitted Diseases*.

Stafford has been Editor-in-Chief of *Health & Fitness Magazine*, *Texas Woman Magazine*, *Houston Home & Garden Magazine*, *Dallas-Fort Worth Home & Garden Magazine*, *Philanthropy in Texas*, and *Latin Music Magazine*. Stafford also co-owned *Health & Fitness* and *Texas Woman*, and helped with startups of *Health & Fitness* in New Orleans, Philadelphia, and Miami. Today, she writes and edits books and does volunteer work for Houston's Emergency Aid Coalition Clothing Center. She has written hundreds of magazine articles.

Notes

Notes

Look for these titles from Sourcebooks

101 Things Every Kid
Should Do Growing Up
$12.95 U.S./$19.95 CAN
hardcover • 1-57071-861-X
$9.95 U.S./$15.95 CAN
paper • 1-57071-862-8
288 pages • 5¾ x 6½

301 Bright Ideas
for Busy Kids
$12.95 U.S./$19.95 CAN
paper • 1-4022-0050-1
384 pages • 4¼ x 9

The New Mom's
Companion
$13.95 U.S./$21.95 CAN
paper • 1-4022-0014-5
320 pages • 6½ x 8

On the Go with Baby
$14.95 U.S./$23.50 CAN
paper • 1-57071-952-7
336 pages • 4¼ x 9

The Parenting Bible
$14.95 U.S./$23.50 CAN
paper • 1-57071-907-1
464 pages • 7 x 9

Preschool for Parents
$12.95 U.S./$19.95 CAN
paper • 1-57071-172-0
192 pages • 6 x 9

The Secret Language
of Children
$21.95 U.S./$34.95 CAN
hardcover • 1-57071-932-2
368 pages • 6 x 9

What Every Parent Needs
to Know about 1st, 2nd &
3rd Grades
$12.95 U.S./$19.95 CAN
paper • 1-57071-156-9
184 pages • 6 x 9

Look for the 365 Series from Sourcebooks

365 Games Babies Play
$12.95 U.S./$19.95 CAN
paper • 1-4022-0108-7
408 pages • 5¼ x 8

365 Games Toddlers Play
$12.95 U.S./ $19.95 CAN
paper • 1-4022-0176-1
408 pages • 5¼ x 8

365 Afterschool Activities
$12.95 U.S./$19.95 CAN
paper • 1-57071-080-5
416 pages • 5¼ x 8

365 Days of Creative Play
$12.95 U.S./$19.95 CAN
paper • 1-57071-029-5
384 pages • 5¼ x 8

365 Foods Kids Love to Eat
$12.95 U.S./$19.95 CAN
paper • 1-57071-030-9
416 pages • 5¼ x 8

365 Ways to
Raise Great Kids
$12.95 U.S./$19.95 CAN
paper • 1-57071-398-7
416 pages • 5¼ x 8